BEYOND CORPORATE GOVERNANCE

BEYOND

CORPORATE GOVERNANCE

Understand & Manage the
THREE HIDDEN KEY DRIVERS
to Help Prevent
Derailment in Business

ISABELLE NÜSSLI

LEVERAGE YOURSELF AG

COPYRIGHT © 2021 ISABELLE NÜSSLI

BEYOND CORPORATE GOVERNANCE
Understand & Manage the Three Hidden Key Drivers
To Help Prevent Derailment in Business

ISBN   978-1-5445-0993-8 *Hardcover*
        978-1-5445-0995-2 *Paperback*
        978-1-5445-0994-5 *Ebook*

To true leadership: reflective, emotionally intelligent, authentic, courageous, agile, visionary, inspirational, and effective!

CONTENTS

APPENDICES

ABBREVIATIONS

ACFE	Association of Certified Fraud Examiners
ADR	American Depositary Receipt
AI	Artificial Intelligence
BJR	Business Judgment Rule
BOD	Board of Directors
CAGR	Compound Annual Growth Rate
CC	Swiss Civil Code
CCCC	Chairperson CEO Collaboration Contract
CEO	Chief Executive Officer
CFO	Chief Financial Officer
CHF	Swiss Franc
CO	Swiss Code of Obligations
CQ	Global Intelligence
D&O	Director and Officer (Insurance)
EQ	Emotional Intelligence
EQ-I	Emotional Quotient Inventory
EU	European Union

FBI	Federal Bureau of Investigation
FF	Following Pages
FFM	Five Factor Model
FINMA	Financial Market Supervision
GA	General Assembly
HDS	Hogan Development Survey
HP	Hewlett-Packard
HS	Hubris Syndrome
IPO	Initial Public Offering
IQ	Intelligence Quotient
IRS	Internal Revenue Service
LAQ	Leadership Archetype Questionnaire
MAOA	Monoamine Oxidase A
MHS	Multi-Health Systems
NYSE	New York Stock Exchange
OECD	The Organization for Economic Cooperation and Development
ORA	Organizational Role Analysis
ROA	Return on Assets
SDT	Self-Development Theory
SME	Small- and Medium-Sized Enterprises
SOB	Seductive Operational Bully
US	United States

INTRODUCTION

Let us fast-forward from 513 BC when Heraclitus declared, "There is nothing permanent except change" to the sixteenth century when Niccolò Machiavelli wrote, "There is nothing more difficult to take in hand, more perilous to conduct, or more uncertain in its success, than to take the lead in the introduction of a new order of things."[1] Clearly, change is here to stay. And today, even the nature of change is changing!

In the early 1990s,[2] in a graduate school for future generals (the US Army War College), the term VUCA was coined. The goal was to anticipate and describe the world after the Cold War. VUCA means:[3]

V: Volatility. Speed and magnitude of change.

U: Uncertainty. Lack of predictability of past incidents to predict future outcomes.

---

1   Sattar Bawany, "Leading Change in Today's VUCA World: Leadership Excellence Essentials," HR.com, February 2016, 31.

2   Bob Johansen and James Euchner, "Navigating the VUCA World," *Research Technology Management* 56, no. 1 (2013): 10–15.

3   S. Chadra, "VUCA World: Provoking the Future," *Human Capital* 20, no. 8 (2017): 14–18, 14f.

C: Complexity. Several challenging factors involved in an issue.

A: Ambiguity. More than one interpretation; lack of clarity.

Each of these elements is already quite challenging to understand and deal with. But in a VUCA world, the elements do not operate in isolation. They are networked. This very interrelation triggers an erratic, unforeseeable confluence.

VUCA also describes today's fast-changing, turbulent business environment. As this book will show, rational planning processes often fall short or even fail. The solution is agility. This calls for strategic vision, multifaceted risk management, and true change leadership.[4]

CHANGE IN A VUCA WORLD

Because change involves human beings and can trigger emotions, uncertainties, and contradictions, it is not enough just to manage change. True change leadership recognizes and anticipates the human factor, which is even more challenging in a VUCA world with its increased, multilayered complexity and speed.

The VUCA leadership mindset needs to embrace new opportunities and not be threatened by changes such as rapid technological advances, a globalized economy, and the dramatic rise of both e-commerce and the virtual workplace.[5] Modern, agile talent recruiting and management processes—emphasizing leadership assessment and development, employee engagement and growth, stretching people, risk-taking, and open discussions about change—are major factors in achieving targeted business performance.[6]

In the past, when a civilization went through a disruptive technical rev-

---

4   Ibid., 14.

5   Chadra, "VUCA World: Provoking the Future."

6   Ibid.

olution, the subsequent change in the world was profound but slower moving. For example, the invention of the printing press by Gutenberg, the mass production of books, the printing of the Gutenberg Bible and the wide spread of Luther's theses arguably triggered the Reformation; two centuries of religious wars, including the Thirty Years' War; and the separation of Europe into Protestant and Catholic sectors.[7]

Today's changes are different, with their speed and breadth—and pervasive media influences—having an intense impact on more people at once than ever before.[8] Successful change leaders and recruiters know that people matter—a lot. It is tempting to dive into rational plans and processes rather than face the more challenging yet critical human issues. But as this book will show, mastering the "soft" side of change management needn't be a mystery.[9]

This book brings together theory and findings from the fields of law, business, and psychology and applies them to the phenomenon of organizational derailment—such as fraud, corruption, and corporate scandal—in an effort to determine the causes of such negative outcomes. In doing so, it supplies novel insights of use to business leaders, recruiters, stakeholders, and practitioners.

Specifically, the book is concerned with making sense of why, despite organizations' investment in legal support, corporate governance, and leadership selection, there remains much conflict, especially within the "magic triangle" of owner, board of directors, and management that leads to excesses, fraud, and scandals. Moreover, this book assesses how change as a trigger, the human factor as a root cause, and leadership as an accelerator serve as hidden key drivers for such derailment, and it examines what can be done about it.

---

7   Nicholas Davis, "Learning from Luther about Technological Disruption," *Finanz und Wirtschaft*, November 6, 2017, https://www.fuw.ch/article/learning-from-luther-about-technological-disruption/; Christopher McFadden, "The Invention and History of the Printing Press," *Interesting Engineering*, September 12, 2018, https://interestingengineering.com/the-invention-and-history-of-the-printing-press.

8   Chadra, "VUCA World: Provoking the Future."

9   Bawany, "Leading Change in Today's VUCA World," 32.

Since this book focuses on derailment within organizations, it is necessary to understand the term. *Derailment* is an obstruction that diverts the organization from its intended course. Examples are severe conflict, excesses, fraud, and scandal. What goes off the rails is the mission and performance of the business. Figuring out what triggers the derailment—and how to prevent it—is the focus of this book. (The significant types of derailment are explained in appendix 1.)

CORPORATE GOVERNANCE IS NOT ENOUGH

In the 1990s and 2000s, infamous scandals and tales of excess surrounded international firms such as Enron and Tyco (US), the Royal Bank of Scotland (UK), ABB (Switzerland), Shell (Netherlands), HIH Insurance (Australia), Parmalat (Italy), and many more. What has been learned? How much has corporate governance, which was put on the map after these scandals grew in number and became public, contributed to improvement? The emergence of subsequent scandals—involving Lehman Brothers and AIG (US), Volkswagen (Germany), Petrobras (Brazil), Toshiba (Japan), FIFA (Switzerland), Barclays and Tesco (UK), the Abraaj Group (Dubai), Luckin Coffee (China/US) and others—suggests that corporate governance has not helped very much.

Corporate governance defines mechanisms, processes, and relations by which corporations are led and controlled. Berle and Means (1932) described a conflict of interest between owners and managers that called for control mechanisms (called the "principal agent" theory).[10] This marked the start of corporate governance as a tool to separate and balance control and management to prevent or decrease conflicts between principals (owners) and their agents (management).

In subsequent years, cumulative conflicts and scandals triggered an adjustment of hard law (corporate law) and soft law (corporate governance) around the world. However, derailment persists, often with its

---

10   Adolf A. Berle and Gardiner C. Means, *The Modern Corporation and Private Property* (New York: Macmillan, 1932).

roots in conflict within the magic triangle of owner, board of directors (BoD), and management (e.g., CEOs).

The widespread acceptance of corporate governance standards demonstrates its importance. Yet, as the long list of examples throughout this book will show, corporate governance has not contributed nearly enough to the reduction of severe conflict in business. This holds true for all types of organizations: public, private, nonprofit, national or international, successful, or crisis ridden. As stakeholders find new and creative ways to leverage new laws, regulations, and guidelines for personal gain, this even adds new layers of complexity.

In many countries, increasingly strict legal frameworks have provoked a rising number of lawsuits against directors and officers, and these have amplified the need for insurance against liabilities. This adds another level of pressure in an already turbulent, fast-changing environment— in a culture of media scrutiny that plays an increasingly greater part.

It is time to stop, pause, and reflect on why stricter legal frameworks have not reduced conflicts of interest as intended. There must be other reasons and causes that are unaccounted for in legal frameworks that distort organizational dynamics.

This book will shed light on the three key drivers for negative outcomes that cannot be minimized or eliminated with a stiffer legal framework. In particular, the role human beings play, especially in leadership positions and during change, will be considered and discussed.

This book will demonstrate that there is a certain type of person that tends to derail. It will uncover elements that drive such persons and propose ways in which they might develop and improve. Derailments involve human aspects and can, to a large extent, be avoided or proactively managed through appropriate leadership and recruiting.

This book digs deep into human nature to understand how derailment arises and how it can be prevented or resolved. It works on the assumption that behavior can reveal why and how people engage in conflict. Discussion of relevant theory and evidence will shed light on how observation of behavior patterns induced by a person's interests can help us discover and predict dysfunctionalities and provide valuable information on that person's potential for development. An increased awareness of this can lead to better leadership.

Since opposing opinions, beliefs, principles, and/or values and interests are frequent among the magic triangle of owners, BoD, and managers, these people play a crucial role. They can either be the originators of bad conflicts or the skilled leaders who resolve and/or avoid them. What will differentiate any organization from others is the way conflicts are managed and derailment minimized.

WE DON'T NEED SUPERHEROES

Understanding past and current leadership selection and development can help owners and BoDs define the types of future leaders required to deal with the increased pressures of the VUCA environment. There is a lot that organizations can do to reduce the potential for derailment and maximize performance by improving leadership and organizational culture despite or because of change. With these points in mind, valuable advice and checklists will be supplied to owners, board members, CEOs, management teams, aspiring leaders, executive search firms, investors, lawmakers, and judges.

Often, leaders are viewed as superheroes, and even more worrisome, they try to behave as such. They are seen as invincible, having all the answers. This could be because leadership is considered rational. Both classic law and economics assume that leadership is a rational task carried out by rational leaders. The persistence of this assumption may be linked to a belief that leaders should not show their human side, including their weaknesses and shadows, because rational, pragmatic, and objective thinking is superior to feeling.

But only superheroes are superhuman, and relationships within the magic triangle of shareholders, BoD, and management often do not work very well. Severe conflict, excesses, fraud, and even scandal are frequent, sometimes with dramatic consequences (such as lawsuits, jail time, or financial ruin) for the individuals concerned, their organizations, employees, and society at large.

Linked to this, much has been written about company law (which governs the rights, regulations, relations, and conduct of persons, companies, and organizations) and about corporate governance (which defines mechanisms, processes, and relations by which organizations are controlled and directed). Most companies[11] have a well-thought-out corporate governance system in place. This has gained importance after major scandals in the 1990s and 2000s: think of Enron, Tyco, and a number of players during the global financial crisis. It is designed to serve as a "magic tool" that solves all potential compliance-, power-, or role-related issues.

But organizations are systems with their own dynamics, of which only a minor part is conscious and rational because they involve the complexity of both the business and the human element. If unable to express their human side, leaders can become susceptible to harmful practices, such as power games and risky and overpriced takeovers. Therefore, behavior cannot easily be predicted by just looking at organizations and their rules.

One would think that the extraordinary demands of our changing world would force leaders to focus on what really matters: clients, markets, products, employees. However, organizational politics, severe conflicts, excesses, and fraud do not seem to have decreased as societal change has increased. When power is involved, human beings are not entirely rational. British historian Lord Acton said, "Power corrupts, and absolute power corrupts absolutely."[12]

---

11   In this book, the terms *company*, *organization*, and *businesses* will be used interchangeably.

12   Acton Institute, Lord Acton Quote Archive, accessed May 1, 2019, http://www.acton.org/research/lord-acton.

But not all leaders act in harmful ways when faced with power and turbulent environments. Why might some people be more prone than others to such behavior? Drawing upon a psychodynamic perspective, this book will demonstrate that this is linked with deep-rooted personalities and behavioral patterns.

Very often, changes made within a company affect the power balance within that company. The ways in which people react when their positions are threatened, together with their worldviews and how they assume roles and handle power, are often shaped by how they grew up.

Change triggers, emotions, and uncertainties. Too many well-thought-out and well-meant plans go off the rails in business because of unconscious factors that influence behavior. The techniques applied by leaders to implement these plans and/or lead change often assume the rational side of behavior—their own, their colleagues', and that of key stakeholders. The emotional side is neglected. But as this book will show, mastering the soft side of change management—in combination with the harder side that includes plans, processes, and governance—can reduce or avoid harmful outcomes and improve performance.

WHO SHOULD READ THIS BOOK?

First, this book addresses owners and shareholders who select their board members and senior management. It also targets boards of directors who recruit CEOs and bear the ultimate responsibility and liability for their actions. By raising their awareness of the main drivers of conflict, this book will enable business owners and BoDs to spot people who might derail, either develop or exit them, and thus improve business performance and agility. Better understanding the psychodynamics of leadership in a changing environment will also enable readers to assess what types of future leaders are needed to meet the demands of a fast-changing business world.

The book is also a must-read for CEOs and management teams (potential CEOs). Awareness of the human drivers of conflict will permit them to lead change by anticipating its impact on people and power balances within a solid legal framework. It will also facilitate self-awareness, which is crucial for better management of self and others. Being proactive in learning about their own behavioral patterns and how they play out under pressure will allow leaders to stay ahead of and better deal with potential, severe conflict.

Moreover, discoveries from business and psychology, such as irrationality in decision-making and judgment, can and should be incorporated into the world of law. Since perceptions are based on personal experiences, it is impossible for judges to make interpretations without using personal lenses shaped by their own pasts. They are at least unconsciously biased. Like leaders, judges are well advised to start with themselves. If they become aware of their own emotions, perceptions, and patterns—and their origins—they will be able to increase their decision-making abilities in two ways: discovering when and how their own personalities influence their decision-making, and better understanding other people's motives and drivers.

And finally, since this book sheds light on important elements of the assessment and installment of top leaders, it will also be of interest to executive recruiters and search firms. Furthermore, it will provide insights of value to anybody interested in understanding the different drivers of conflict, e.g., business consultants and practitioners seeking to reduce derailment and improve performance.

PART 1

INSUFFICIENT SYSTEMS

CHAPTER 1

TRADITIONAL FRAMEWORKS

As stated, one of the main questions this book aims to address is why the implementation of the legal frameworks described above have not resulted in a significant decrease in negative outcomes for organizations. One could argue that perhaps there would have been an even greater number of conflicts had the focus on corporate governance not been set. Nevertheless, more could still be done to improve matters.

In this chapter, consideration will be given to existing frameworks of corporate law and corporate governance. Then, to assess what is working and what is not—and why that might be—analyses of specific cases of scandals will be presented. These examples span the period before and after corporate governance was seriously considered, in order to draw comparisons and to discuss how best to measure the success of corporate governance.

CORPORATE LAW AND CORPORATE GOVERNANCE

Discussion of derailment in business (e.g., severe conflicts, excesses, and scandals) centers around corporate law (hard law) and corporate governance (soft law):

- Corporate law addresses conflicts between shareholders and managers, among shareholders, and between shareholders and other stakeholders.
- Corporate governance cements principles that are defined by corporate law. Unlike the former, this can be customized by each company.

In order to assess how corporate governance deals with the prevention and handling of negative outcomes and analyze its effectiveness, it is important to start with an overview of legal frameworks of both hard law and soft law, which vary from country to country. (Extended information on the legal framework, including detailed references, can be found in appendix 2.)

Hard law and soft law complement each other in a fair, flexible way that ensures market viability.[13] Governments face significant challenges in defining the ideal balance between regulation and freedom.[14]

HARD LAW (CORPORATE LAW)

Corporate law serves as a framework for corporate governance. Corporate law facilitates the coordination between people involved in organizations and reduces opportunism.

Corporate law around the globe has evolved with a cross-country convergence followed by an increased divergence. The initial set of rules was simple and imitated existing charters of corporations. But it did not predict or reflect innovations that led to industrialization, isolated socioeconomic changes within individual countries, or weaknesses uncovered in the structure of corporate law.

---

13 Christoph B. Bühler, "Corporate Governance *Und Ihre Regulierung in Der Schweiz*," *ZGR Zeitschrift für Unternehmens und Gesellschaftsrecht* 41, nos. 2–3 (2012): 228.

14 Ibid., 229.

Pistor, Keinan, Kleinheisterkamp, and West[15] provide a comprehensive analysis of the evolution of corporate law and its international roots. Their analysis of corporate law's evolution starts in the early nineteenth century. It includes the jurisdictions of France, Germany, UK, and the US—origin countries—and Chile, Colombia, Israel, Japan, Malaysia, and Spain—"transplant countries" that adopted their corporate laws from the four origin countries, directly or indirectly.

The most common legal systems that countries follow are either common law or civil law. In brief:[16]

- *Common law:* In general, common law is not codified, meaning that there is no comprehensive collection of legal statutes and rules. It largely abides by precedents (judicial decisions made in similar previous cases).
- *Civil law:* In contrast, civil law (often called European Continental Law) is codified. This means that nations that apply civil law systems have comprehensive legal codes that are continually updated.

SOFT LAW (CORPORATE GOVERNANCE)

Although the widespread belief is that corporate governance was first described by Berle and Means[17] in 1932 before the term was coined by Jensen and Meckling in 1976, business regulation of the Swiss Kreditanstalt (now Credit Suisse) goes back as far as 1859.[18]

Corporate governance evolved around what economists call "agency problems." Berle and Means discovered that the interests of sharehold-

---

15 Katharina Pistor et al., "Evolution of Corporate Law: A Cross-Country Comparison," *University of Pennsylvania Journal of International Law* 23, no. 4 (2002): 791–871.

16 "The Common Law and Civil Law Traditions," The Robbins Collection: School of Law (Boalt Hall), University of California at Berkeley, https://www.law.berkeley.edu/library/robbins/CommonLawCivilLawTraditions.html; S. B., "What Is the Difference between Common and Civil Law?" The Economist, July 17, 2013, https://www.economist.com/blogs/economist-explains/2013/07/economist-explains-10.

17 Berle and Means, *The Modern Corporation and Private Property*.

18 Joseph Jung, "Alfred Escher (1819–1882): Aufstieg, Macht, Tragik," in *Nzz Libro* (Zurich: Verlag Neue Zürcher Zeitung, 2014), 242.

ers (principals) and executives (agents) diverge when ownership and control are separated, which often leads to conflict.[19] Both parties are driven by their self-interest. Following the scandals of the 1990s and 2000s, corporate governance experienced an upswing and has been widely discussed since.

There are almost countless definitions of corporate governance, such as:

- Organization for Economic Co-operation and Development (OECD): "Procedures and processes according to which an organization is directed and controlled [...] specifies the distribution of rights and responsibilities among the different participants in the organization [...] and lays down the rules and procedures for decision-making."[20]
- Cadbury: "The system by which business corporations are directed and controlled."[21]

In contrast to laws and statutes, corporate governance regulations are not strictly binding and thus cannot be enforced. This is why they are called soft law.[22]

Corporate governance is built on the understanding of self-regulation and presents corporate bodies with recommendations on how they should design their legal margins for maneuver. Good corporate governance can be considered as well-understood corporate law.[23]

The Cadbury Report published in the UK in 1992 is considered a

---

19   Maria Mahler and Thomas Andersson, *Corporate Governance: Effects on Firm Performance and Economic Growth* (Paris: OECD, 1999), 6.

20   OECD, *Glossary of Statistical Terms*, s.v. "Corporate Governance," accessed June 14, 2016, https://stats.oecd.org/glossary/detail.asp?ID=6778.

21   Stephen Bloomfield, *Theory and Practice of Corporate Governance: An Integrated Approach* (Cambridge: Cambridge University Press, 2013).

22   Kevin Jackson, "Global Corporate Governance: Soft Law and Reputational Accountability," *Brooklyn Journal of International Law* 35, no. 1 (2010): 44.

23   Bühler, "Corporate Governance," 237.

breakthrough in corporate governance. Many other countries followed and launched their own governance codes.[24]

The question remains whether convergence or divergence of corporate governance will prevail. Arguments in favor of convergence are reflected in common international standards and regulations. Arguments in favor of divergence are related to hindering factors, such as culture, resistance, ownership structures, economic progress, politics, and religion.[25]

Why is there still so much bad conflict despite corporate governance systems? It is crucial to learn how bad conflicts originate; to understand why they often cannot be resolved with traditional strategies, methods, and systems; and to establish how they can be prevented and/or managed.

As the following chapter will show, derailment can lead to severe and long-lasting consequences for the companies, the parties involved, shareholders, and other stakeholders.

SCANDALS BEFORE AND AFTER THE CORPORATE GOVERNANCE DEBATE

Corporate governance is widely introduced and often considered to serve as the "magic tool" to prevent or solve all potential compliance-, power-, or role-related issues.

However, this chapter will show that corporate governance has not been able to thwart the kind of derailment it set out to thwart. The nature of the scandals and the functions of the key persons involved have remained pretty much the same.

---

24   European Corporate Governance Institute (ECGI), "Index of Codes," http://www.ecgi.org/codes/all_codes.php.

25   Adrian Davies, *The Globalisation of Corporate Governance: The Challenge of Clashing Cultures* (New York: Routledge, 2011), 49; Mehrani Sasan, Mohammad Moradi, and Hoda Eskandar, "Corporate Governance: Convergence vs. Divergence," *British Journal of Economics* 9, no. 1 (2014): 24ff.

There is a long list of international business cases in the 1990s and 2000s involving scandals (mostly involving excess and fraud) that put corporate governance on the map globally. The following cases are just a few examples. (The full list can be found in appendix 3.)

ENRON

In 2001, Enron (a US-based commodities, energy, and services corporation) ran into a corporate corruption and accounting fraud scandal which ended in the largest American bankruptcy at the time. Huge debts were kept off the balance sheet, earnings were overstated by several hundred million dollars, shareholders lost $74 billion, thousands of employees lost their jobs, and thousands of employees and investors lost their savings. The key players were the CEO, the CFO, and the former CEO.[26]

ABB

Or take ABB, a Swedish-Swiss multinational conglomerate and one of the world's largest engineering companies. In 2002, despite the company's loss of Swiss Franc (CHF) 691 and CHF 4 billion of debt, the chairperson and the CEO awarded themselves CHF 233 in pension and retirement benefits. The publication of these payments caused an uproar in corporate Switzerland and beyond, shocked investors around the world, and entailed tougher disclosure rules.[27]

The responsibility for these scandals is linked to the "magic triangle" of CEOs, top executives, BoDs, founders/owners, plus gatekeepers (auditors). Almost all of these corporate scandals feature a similar dynamic: overstatement of financial results or redirection of company

---

26 Stephen Bloomfield, *Theory and Practice of Corporate Governance: An Integrated Approach* (Cambridge: Cambridge University Press, 2013), 5ff; "The 10 Worst Corporate Accounting Scandals of All Time," *Accounting Degree Review*, http://www.accounting-degree.org/scandals/; Syed Balkhi, "25 Biggest Corporate Scandals Ever," *List 25*, October 29, 2018, http://list25.com/25-biggest-corporate-scandals-ever/; Sean Farrell, "The World's Biggest Accounting Scandals," *The Guardian*, July 21, 2015, https://www.theguardian.com/business/2015/jul/21/the-worlds-biggest-accounting-scandals-toshiba-enron-olympus; Michael W. Peregrine, "Enron Still Matters, 15 Years after Its Collapse," *The New York Times*, December 1, 2016, https://www.nytimes.com/2016/12/01/business/dealbook/enron-still-matters-15-years-after-its-collapse.html.

27 "About ABB," www.abb.com; "Barnevik's Bounty: Scandal and Poor Performance Have Forced ABB to Open Up," *The Economist*, February 28, 2002, http://www.economist.com/node/1011457.

means to personal use by executives. In each case, the BoD seems to have been "absent."

Considering the objectives of corporate law and corporate governance, how could this happen? And what may have been the reasons for such behaviors by the magic triangle?

- **Executives:** Were they driven by excessive narcissism, hubris, inflated ego, and greed to pursue their own interests—money, power, status—instead of performing their fiduciary duties to uphold the interests of the company and other stakeholders?
- **BoDs:** Were they ignorant of what was going on, or did they prefer not to harm their relationships with other board colleagues? Did their concern about protecting reputations rank higher than their duty to execute their responsibilities to all stakeholders? Did they worry about reelection?
- **Owners:** Shareholders also have responsibilities that they must be aware of and hold in high regard. Could it be that they remained too passive and blamed the executives and the BoDs instead of bearing their own responsibility? In some cases, they were involved in fraudulent behavior.

Narcissism: "Selfishness, involving a sense of entitlement, a lack of empathy, and a need for admiration, as characterizing a personality type." Although narcissism is a natural part of infantile development, excessive narcissism can derail. (See chapter 5, "Key Driver Three: Leadership as an Accelerator," in the subsection "The Dark Side of Leadership.")

Hubris: "Excessive pride or self-confidence." (See chapter 5, "Key Driver Three: Leadership as an Accelerator" (in the subsection "The Dark Side of Leadership.")

Ego: "A person's sense of self-esteem or self-importance." Although ego is important and serves survival, inflated ego increases the risk of derailment (similar to excessive narcissism).

In the cases listed above, all responsible parties seem to have been driven by their own motives and interests. As the focus on corporate governance has dramatically increased since these scandals became public, one might expect fewer derailments of such scale to occur due to better control mechanisms.

What has been learned? How much has corporate governance, which was put on the map *after* these scandals grew in number and became public, contributed to improvement?

The following text looks at the time period after corporate governance had been widely introduced, which led to a widespread adjustment of codes of conduct. It assesses the nature of the scandals and the involved parties and compares them to those in the cases described above.

LEHMAN BROTHERS

Lehman Brothers, a US-based global financial services company, belongs to a long list of examples. In 2008, *Fortune* magazine ranked the company as the number one most admired securities firm. That same year, it became public that over $50 billion in loans were hidden and disguised as sales, and toxic assets had been sold to Cayman Island banks (to be bought back eventually). The company made us believe that it had $50 billion more cash and $50 billion less in toxic assets than in reality. Key players were the CEO and further executives.[28]

VOLKSWAGEN

In 2016, a scandal around the major German car maker Volkswagen was made public and, with it, the falsification of emissions data on nearly 600,000 diesel cars, pretending they were more environmentally friendly. In addition, software was installed into car computers

---

28   Farrell, "The World's Biggest Accounting Scandals"; "The 10 Worst Corporate Accounting Scandals of All Time"; "World's 8 Biggest Corporate Scandals of All Time," *Your Finance Book*, January 15, 2016, http://yourfinancebook. com/biggest-corporate-scandals/.

(called a "defeat device") that detected when the car was being checked. Key players were the former CEO and senior executives.[29]

Before analyzing and comparing the above examples, negative outcomes pertaining to conflict will be described in relation to three further companies. Because more comprehensive information is available on these companies, they serve as illustrative examples for further analysis. All three companies have international operations and all three depict bad conflicts. The companies are: Sika (conflicts 2014–2018); CALIDA (2015–2016); a third company referred to here as "Otherco" for reasons relating to confidentiality (2011–2015).

SIKA GROUP (SIKA)—SWISS-BASED, PUBLIC, SPECIALTY CHEMICALS FOR CONSTRUCTION

Members of the founding family, successors of Sika's founder, announced in December 2014 that they were going to sell their 16 percent shares, with 52 percent voting control of the company, to the French company Saint-Gobain (multinational corporation, producer of construction and high-performance materials) for CHF 2.75 billion. The majority of the BoD and the management of Sika strongly opposed the family's intentions. The BoD therefore restricted the voting rights of the registered shares held by the family's holding for particular decisions at the General Assembly (GA) to 5 percent. The opposing fronts consisted on one side of a highly successful management team that had increased the stock price tenfold between 2003 and 2016, from CHF 1 to 10 billion, and on the other side of the family, which held 16 percent of the share capital but controlled 52 percent of the voting power via registered voting shares.[30]

29   Melissa Burden, "VW to Pay $2.8B Fine, Gets 3 Years Probation," *The Detroit News*, April 21, 2017, http://www.detroitnews.com/story/business/autos/foreign/2017/04/21/volkswagen-emissions-scandal/100736014/; Nicholas Iovino, "VW Can't Dodge 2nd Securities Action over Emissions Scandal," *Courthouse News Service*, July 19, 2017, https://www.courthousenews.com/vw-cant-dodge-2nd-securities-action-emissions-scandal/.

30   Daniel Hug and Franziska Pfister, "Der Kampf wird immer kostspieliger," *NZZ Neue Zürcher Zeitung*, accessed July 1, 2016, http://www.nzz.ch/nzzas/nzz-am-sonntag/uebernahmeschlacht-um-sika-der-kampf-wird-immer-kostspieliger-ld.14399; Thomas Schürpf, "Völlig verhärtete Fronten," *NZZ Neue Zürcher Zeitung*, accessed May 7, 2018, http://www.nzz.ch/wirtschaft/unternehmen/fall-sika-jetzt-haben-wieder-die-aktionaere-das-wort-ld.13274.

The GA of April 12, 2016, showed how hardened the fronts were. They used the GA and the media in the run-up to the assembly to cement their positions. At the GA, Sika's chairperson used his powerful position to decide on the time slots allocated to each speaker (depending on the side) and to make comprehensive statements himself.[31] There was no less tension in the air one year later at the GA on April 11, 2017.[32]

The Sika case describes a conflict between two groups: the shareholding family, and BoD and management. Both sides submitted multiple claims against each other and the company. Before the case was settled to everyone's surprise in 2018 (there were pending claims on both sides, and important decisions were about to be made by the courts), the case seemed to have come down to a purely legal dispute that looked like it was going to take years to get resolved because the ultimate decision lay with the Swiss Federal Court.

Outcome of the Sika Case

The fifth general assembly in a row of April 12, 2018, served as a platform for fights. The BoD again restricted the family's voting right and prevented a change of control.[33]

On May 11, 2018, Sika AG and its founding family reached a complex deal to end an over three-year hostile legal dispute. The parties terminated all legal proceedings, putting an end to the legal standoff. The family sold their stake of 17 percent for CHF 3.22 billion to Saint-Gobain. The latter gave up the special voting rights, which had formed the heart of the conflict with further Sika shareholders, the BoD, and management. Furthermore, Saint-Gobain sold 6.97 percent of the shares to Sika for CHF 2.08 billion and remained the largest

---

31   Hug and Pfister, "Der Kampf wird immer kostspieliger"; Schürpf, "Völlig verhärtete Fronten."

32   Ernst Meier, "BAAR: Sika-Streithähne bleiben stur," *Luzerner Zeitung*, accessed September 9, 2018, https://www.luzernerzeitung.ch/wirtschaft/baar-sika-streithaehne-bleiben-stur-ld.85797.

33   Ernst Meier and Caroline Freigang, "So dreckig war die Schlammschlacht um Sika, " *Basler Zeitung*, accessed June 10, 2018, https://bazonline.ch/wirtschaft/unternehmen-und-konjunktur/so-dreckig-war-die-schlammschlacht-um-sika/story/25817052.

shareholder, owning 10.75 percent but not taking over the control. Sika introduced a single share class.[34] The BoD was restructured. All three BoD representatives of the founding family stepped down, and a representative of the Bill & Melinda Gates Foundation took a seat. The six independent directors remained on the BoD.[35]

This was considered a win-win-win because Saint-Gobain's profit accounted for EUR 600 million, the family received CHF 500 million more than agreed in the sales contract, and the company Sika remained independent. On the same day, the share price rose by 8.6 percent, valuing the company at 21 billion CHF, almost triple what it was before the announcement of the original deal. Also, Saint-Gobain's share price rose by 3 percent.[36]

To provide some perspective on the company's written policies versus the actual events, Sika's website says the company is committed to openness and transparency.[37] It also has a corporate governance system in place that describes the following elements: group structure and shareholders, capital structure, BoD, board committees, group management, shareholders participation rights, delineation of powers of authorization, change in corporate control and defense measures, auditor, information policy.[38]

Despite all these commitments, elements, measures, and mechanisms, bad conflicts still arose.

What were the consequences of Sika's adjustments on the BoD and

34 Jan Dahinten and Andrew Marc Noel, "Sika, Saint-Gobain Sign Deal to End Bitter Takeover Battle," *Bloomberg*, May 11, 2018, https://www.bloomberg.com/news/articles/2018-05-11/saint-gobain-sika-reach-deal-ending-three-year-legal-standoff?in_source=video_page.

35 "Sika zieht Schlussstrich unter Streit mit der Eignerfamilie," *Moneycab*, May 17, 2018, https://www.moneycab.com/2018/05/17/sika-zieht-den-schlussstrich-unter-den-streit-mit-der-eignerfamilie/.

36 Dahinten and Noel, "Sika, Saint-Gobain Sign Deal."

37 "Corporate Governance: Bekenntnis zu Offenheit und Transparenz," SIKA, accessed June 4, 2016, http://www.sika.com/de/group/investors/corporate-governance.html.

38 "Sika AG, Sika Geschäftsjahr 2016: Corporate Governance, 2016"; "SIKA AG, Sika Geschäftsjahr 2015: Corporate Governance, 2015," 59–61.

management levels in 2012 and of the family's planned change in ownership in 2014? Changes made at strategic (BoD) and operational (management) or ownership levels impact a company's power balance, the strategy formulation process, and the corporate governance system. (More on this topic in chapter 3, "Key Driver One: Change as a Triggering Element.")

Although the outcome is described as a win for all three parties, a bitter aftertaste remains. The question is whether all three supposed winners are true winners? How much harm has this tug-of-war and these power games caused—especially when so much time, public exposure, and money were invested in the fights?

In some ways, the Sika case is a typical one, in others not. Although the company and its stakeholders experienced an acrimonious battle over a period of three years, the business itself got more and more profitable during this time period. This might also be the reason why a sudden agreement was reached in the end. Two parties made a lot more money than initially expected, and a third party (BoD) was reimbursed for its time and effort, remained in charge, and was titled as the winners of the winners.

The Swiss business newspaper, *NZZ* described that the chairperson and CEO "appeared to have acted highly self-confident, occasionally even with a triumphant undertone during the press conference, at which neither representatives of Saint-Gobain nor of the family were present."[39]

Why would such an undertone be necessary if one was a real winner? And what about the small shareholders? It seems that those will need to foot the bill.

The consequences of the deal led to a reduction of the equity financing

---

39 Dominik Feldges, "Sika muss sich die neu gewonnene Freiheit teuer erkaufen," *NZZ Neue Zürcher Zeitung*, accessed June 10, 2018, https://www.nzz.ch/wirtschaft/sika-muss-sich-die-neu-gewonnene-freiheit-teuer-erkaufen-ld.1385114.

by half to a level of 25 percent and resulted in a net debt of twice the operational cashflow (EBITDA).[40]

CALIDA GROUP (CALIDA)—SWISS-BASED, MANUFACTURING AND SALE OF LINGERIE

Conflict among the long-standing CALIDA CEO, the founding and majority shareholding family (holding 35 percent of the shares), and the BoD emerged around the strategy development process in 2015. Unlike the BoD and the family who intended to focus on organic growth, the CEO preferred continued acquisitions to conquer challenging market conditions in Europe.[41]

Although the CEO stepped down from his operational role in March 2016, he ran for reelection to the BoD in May of that year. The difference of opinions regarding a future strategy was not the only reason why the BoD and the family wanted to eject him from the BoD. The chairperson spoke of a "break of trust" that happened when the CEO publicly announced confidential information that the company was looking for a new CEO. The second largest shareholder, a group of investors, wanted to keep the CEO as a director for another year to maintain continuity, but the CEO was ultimately not reelected at the 2016 GA.[42]

The CALIDA case shows another example of conflicts within the magic triangle, although the distribution of power differed from the one at Sika: the CEO formed one party, and the BoD and owner/shareholder the other. CALIDA has a twelve-page corporate governance report in place that has many similarities to Sika's.[43]

---

40 Ibid.

41 Christoph G. Schmutz, "Calida will eine neue Ära einläuten," *NZZ Neue Zürcher Zeitung*, accessed May 7, 2018, http://www.nzz.ch/wirtschaft/calida-will-eine-neue-aera-einlaeuten-1.18717501.

42 Ibid.

43 CALIDA Holding AG, *Corporate Governance Report 2015* (Sursee, Switzerland: CALIDA Group, 2016), 69ff.

OTHERCO—US-BASED SHIPPING COMPANY

Otherco's shareholder structure was established in the late 1990s. The majority of the shares remained with the founding family, who had sold a large minority to employees, including members of the management team. The minority pool was an independent legal entity.

Part of the management team's strategy was to focus on acquisitions to leverage the share price. This was not in the long-term interests of the BoD and the family. In 2008, the company was facing a market crisis, a lack of required operational leadership skills, and a management team that was not used to a strong BoD, due to the BoD having been adjusted shortly beforehand.

The CEO, who was a large minority shareholder, was replaced by a new CEO who engaged in company politics early on. The former CEO remained with the company. Disputes and politics intensified when the new CEO became a shareholder, which, among other reasons, forced the BoD to terminate his contract.

Comments made in the public domain stated that he was let go because of insufficient performance.

The CEO started a new company and hired away key employees but left his former colleague and head of communications to initiate and lead the subsequent press campaign. Clients were fed incorrect information. The poached employees, while fulfilling their employment contracts with Otherco, were told to lay down their tools on strategically important projects. The remaining management team and branch heads were encouraged to break away and become independent in order to weaken the company.

Together with a crisis manager, the BoD stabilized and normalized the situation, applied a forward strategy, and acquired a major competitor.

In this case again, although the shareholder structure, products, and markets differ from the previous two cases, conflicts arose between part of the management team—mainly the CEO—as one party, and the BoD and the family as the other party. As this book will show, a change in ownership and management in the late 1990s marked the start of the conflicts of interest, and it escalated with further and concurrent changes of ownership, management, and strategy in 2008.

Similar to Sika and CALIDA, Otherco had a corporate governance system in place. Although it was not defined in writing, it was based in the shareholder agreement, the organizational regulations, and the functional chart.

WHAT HAPPENED?

The cases described show no evidence that enhanced corporate governance has reduced scandals. There are hardly any differences among the cases before and after the corporate governance debate, including their root causes and triggers for derailment.

It is time to stop, pause, and reflect on how and why so many bad conflicts and scandals could happen despite corporate governance. What are the underlying conditions that drive this derailment? There must be other reasons and causes unaccounted for in legal frameworks that distort organizational dynamics. Ultimately, this book will take a deep dive into human behavior and shed light on why people behave a certain way when they are about to lose power and/or recognition.

MEASURING SUCCESS OF CORPORATE GOVERNANCE

The first group of companies (before the corporate governance debate) experienced a misuse of power, mainly by the CEO and executives, sometimes the chairperson and other directors, and on occasion, the founder/owner. The root causes of derailment appear to be self-interest, diverging interests among parties, power, and greed. Triggering events seem to involve changes in strategy, management, or ownership that led to strategy differences as well as a lack of accountability, transparency, responsibility, and control ("absence" of the BoD). The cases also involved a key driver that accelerates or intensifies conflict: leadership.

A close look at the second group of companies (after the corporate governance debate) again shows conflicts of interest within the magic triangle that played out publicly. Again, the root causes appear to be diverging interests among different parties, greed, and power games, while triggering events seem to be changes in strategy, management, or ownership. And again, the discussions circle around leaders and therefore leadership as derailment's accelerator or intensifier. The BoD seemed to be slightly more active than before the corporate governance debate.

When these root causes, triggering events, and intensifiers of conflicts are present and strong, a platform to play out power can always be found. Although size, ownership structure, industries, and geographies differed in the cases, it appears the derailment emerged because of certain individuals' appetite for (and fear of losing) power, which became prevalent when changes stretched the parties' different interests.

Root causes and triggering events as elements of the three key driving forces for derailment are more closely examined in this book, also with reference to these cases.

The cases from the previous section lend weight to the suggestion that corporate governance has done little to minimize derailment and prevent scandals. Before further analyzing the triggering events, root causes, and accelerators of conflict, the following questions need to be addressed:

- Has corporate governance at least had a positive impact on transparency, accountability, control, and performance?
- If so, how?
- How can the efficacy of corporate governance be measured?

Considering the many different customized models that exist, corporate governance seems difficult to measure. This is partly because it is a multidimensional concept that manifests in varied domains, and thus, it is hard to establish standard measurement criteria. At present, there is no general method that a reliable comparative analysis can be built on. Several mutually reinforcing components define corporate governance.[44] Some of these indicators that are used to measure corporate governance are seen in the Sika and CALIDA cases, such as capital structure, BoD, executive management, compensation, shareholdings and loans, shareholders' participation, changes of control, auditing body, and information policy.

In terms of performance, the majority of studies reveal that corporate governance has had a positive impact, but not for the same reasons. According to a 2008 research report published by the Association of British Insurers (ABI), companies with good corporate governance achieve 18 percent higher returns than companies with poor corporate governance. In turn, a breach of governance best practice can harm a company's (industry-adjusted) Return on Assets (ROA) by approximately 1 percent per year.[45]

One approach suggests focusing on the ownership structure relative to a company's performance. In a comprehensive survey, it is argued that ownership structure has an impact on performance in the sense that owner-controlled firms significantly outperform manager-controlled firms because large shareholders are more active monitors. It refers to another study that found higher management turnover when large shareholders are present because of increased monitoring.[46]

Another approach looks at a company's maturity related to performance and finds that increasing maturity leads to a higher dilution

---

44 Roberto García-Castro et al., "A Cross-National Study of Corporate Governance and Employment Contracts," *Business Ethics: A European Review* 17 (2008): 260.

45 "ABI Research Corporate Governance Pays for Shareholders and Company Performance," ABI Association of British Insurers, February 2, 2008, https://www.abi.org.uk/News/News-releases/2008/02/ABI-Research-Corporate-governance-pays-for-shareholders-and-company-perfomance.

46 Klaus Gugler, *Corporate Governance and Economic Performance* (Oxford: Oxford University Press, 2001), 14ff.

of ownership, a decrease in the monitoring of management, and consequently, the opportunity for selfish behavior. Therefore, corporate governance can become more effective in ensuring company performance as companies mature.[47]

There are also opposing views on the impact of corporate governance on performance. Sumantra Ghoshal, founding Dean of the Indian School of Business in Hyderabad, for example, believes that the consequences of an applied "agency theory"[48] are not predictable. He sees little difference if the number and influence of independent board members are increased to control management, or if a dual leadership structure (separation of chairperson and CEO roles) is put in place to reduce CEO power, or if managers are paid in stock options to ensure their support of shareholders' interests.[49]

In the presented cases, it appears that neither ownership structure nor the company's maturity was directly related to performance or to the emergence of conflict. Sika has even further increased its profitability during the dispute while CALIDA maintained its results, and Otherco was facing a crisis in performance before and during the outbreak of its conflict. Profits can hardly be impacted by just one cause.

Regarding ownership structure, Otherco is a midsized, private company; Sika and CALIDA are both larger, publicly traded companies. As described, all three had a corporate governance system in place.

Even 80 percent of the board members of Enron were high-profile, independent, and chaired a large part of the committees. They had a dual leadership structure, the senior executives were compensated

---

47   Maria Maher and Thomas Andersson, *Corporate Governance: Effects on Firm Performance and Economic Growth* (Paris: Organisation for Economic Co-operation and Development, 1999), 33.

48   The agency theory tries to explain the relationship between two parties (a principal and an agent). In this relationship, the principal delegates work to the agent, and the agent carries out that work under a contract. Matti Kurvinen, Ilkka Töyrylä, and D. N. Prabhakar Murthy, *Warranty Fraud Management: Reducing Fraud and Other Excess Costs in Warranty and Service Operations* (Chichester, UK: Wiley, 2016), 344.

49   Sumantra Ghoshal, "Bad Management Theories Are Destroying Good Management Practices," *Advanced Institute of Management Research (AIM)* 4, no. 1 (2005): 80.

with generous stock options, and the company was active in one of the most advanced markets for corporate control.[50]

IN SUM

Essentially, corporate governance is a broadly discussed topic and its components aim at increasing the health of companies. Corporate governance has a high degree of market acceptance. It appears that it has helped improve the reporting system and raise awareness of stakeholder approaches and activism as well as the responsibilities and liabilities of boards and management. But lawsuits have increased too.

Many of the described companies that ran into a scandal had a corporate governance system in place. An example is Volkswagen, known for Germany's well-praised two-tier system. Another is Toshiba, known for its efforts in corporate governance as one of a few listed Japanese companies that replaced traditional governance structures with an "American-style" system of executive officers and BoD committees with independent directors.[51]

Since opinions strongly differ and all viewpoints offer valid arguments, it is evident that the impact of corporate governance on a company and its performance is difficult to establish. However, the cases described do not show evidence that enhanced corporate governance has reduced greed and power games and, ultimately, derailment and scandals.

Root causes and triggering events are strong factors for the inability of corporate governance to contribute to conflict reduction. Are there any other reasons? What is missing? Could it be that the perspective of corporate governance discussions needs to be adapted or even fundamentally changed? Upcoming chapters will address these topics.

---

50   Ibid., 81.

51   Bruse Aronson, "The Toshiba Corporate Governance Scandal: How Can Japanese Corporate Governance Be Fixed?" *JURIST*, August 10, 2015, http://www.jurist.org/forum/2015/08/bruce-aronson-toshiba-scandal.php.

What about the legal framework itself? Does it contain weaknesses that contribute to the underlying causes of conflict? The following chapter looks at possible flaws of the legal framework itself, which is necessary before a solution can be approached.

CHAPTER 2

FLAWS OF TRADITIONAL FRAMEWORKS

Corporate law provides a legal backbone of business law and it leaves companies with freedom to maneuver, for example, in the definition of their corporate governance systems. However, revisions usually take years or even decades. Corporate governance is more flexible and can be adapted more easily and frequently. It aims to ensure that information, reporting, and control structures are in place, an adequate BoD is set up, and conflicts are minimized.

Regardless of these laws, guidelines, and recommendations, the legal framework appears to have flaws. Is the framework just incomplete? Or is it a matter of perspective? The most prevalent flaws can be summarized as follows.

THE FRAMEWORKS ARE REACTIVE

Can conflicts among human beings best be addressed by determining who is right and who is wrong after the damage has been done?

Both corporate law and corporate governance have a reactive dynamic.

Lawsuits often lead to more lawsuits and eventually resolve a dispute publicly and often at great cost in money and reputations. Corporate governance models are based on best practices created as a consequence of negative outcomes.

Corporate governance models might positively impact transparency, accountability, and control of a company. However, their adaptation to changing circumstances often lags behind. Most companies adjust their models irregularly, despite the flexibility of soft law.

Such static circumstances, in combination with a focus on the legal framework only, can lead to negative outcomes. Therefore, it is important to change perspective, and the key word is proactiveness. What if defining an adequate corporate governance strategy no longer focused on past scandals but on proactive adaptations toward a company's predicted future events?

How can conflicts proactively be prevented? What types of situations provide fertile soil for conflicts to grow, and who tends to plant the seed? And if there is fertile ground for conflict, how might leaders misuse their power to manage the terrain? What type of person would be predisposed to misuse power? Can hiring processes be improved to avoid conflict outbreaks, and if so, how? Chapter 5, "Key Driver Three: Leadership as an Accelerator," will address these questions and provide recommendations and advice on possible solutions.

THE PRINCIPAL-AGENT MODEL IS TOO SIMPLE

The principal-agent model is foundational to many corporate governance models. It assumes that shareholders/owners act as principals and managers as agents who tend to be self-centered and use company resources to satisfy their own interests. Using stereotypes as it does, the principal-agent model is arguably not sufficiently nuanced to account for complex governance challenges, which can be economic, cultural, social, political, or moral in nature. Yet many companies make use of the theory in such situations and in doing so influence millions of people, either directly via their employees or indirectly.[52]

The theory assumes that the interests of all groups of principals (owners) and of all groups of agents (managers) are the same. It is argued here that a more differentiated perspective is appropriate, emphasizing the unique circumstances of diverging interests impacting companies' strategy formulation processes. These would include different interests among owners (e.g., owner families vs. institutional investors) and managers (e.g., entrepreneurial CEOs vs. business mercenaries).

As chapter 3, "Key Driver One: Change as the Triggering Element," will elaborate, the roles of the principal and the agent have evolved over past decades. It will describe the interrelation and interaction between ownership and management and how it impacts a company's strategy and corporate governance. It will further explain why shareholders' interests in their rights have increased after the scandals of the 1990s and 2000s, and why D&O (Directors & Officers) liability insurance is ballooning.[53]

ACTORS TWIST RULES TO SUIT THEIR AGENDAS

Looking at the numerous old and new case examples that led to conflicts, excesses, and scandals, it appears that more and stricter laws and regulations lead to another effect: the opportunity to use them to support one's own story.

For example, when the CEO of Volkswagen AG during the emission scandal gave a radio interview, he initially tried to play down the scandal as an undertaking that went wrong. He stated, "We didn't lie [...] we just misinterpreted American law." When he realized his error in judgment after the conversation, he pleaded with the reporters to

---

52 Ghoshal, "Bad Management Theories," 80.

53 Harry Korine and Pierre-Yves Gomez, *Strong Managers, Strong Owners: Corporate Governance and Strategy* (New York: Cambridge University Press, 2014), ix.

broadcast the interview at a later time. When part of the interview was published, he asked to rerun the conversation. Shortly before meeting the former administrator of the American Environmental Protection Agency (EPA), the CEO publicly apologized using statements such as "it was noisy around me," "there were too many reporters around that kept calling me," etc. He then confessed that Volkswagen would certainly have accepted US law to the fullest extent.[54]

Whether the law was deliberately or unintentionally misunderstood, the principle *ignorantia legis non excusat* (Latin for "ignorance of the law does not excuse"[55]) would apply.

Further, common corporate governance principles such as the principal-agent theory discussed above are sometimes manipulated to cement positions. This was demonstrated at the Sika GA in 2016. In their statements, each party referred to principal-agent theory. The representative of the founding family drew upon Berle and Means's original concept and positioned the family/majority owner in the role of principal and management in the role of the agent. Conversely, representatives of the BoD and management turned principal-agent upside down and cast themselves as principal and the family as agent.[56]

At the same Sika GA 2016, a similar phenomenon could be observed regarding articles in the Swiss civil law ("Good Faith"—Article 2(1) CC) and the BoD's fiduciary duty described in the Swiss corporation law ("Duty of Care and Loyalty"—Article 717(1) CO). A representative of the Sika family stated that the family has always acted in good faith. An external speaker and supporter of the family's opposing party emphasized that the BoD and management had acted in good faith. The BoD itself claimed it had complied with the "Duty of Care

---

54 SSU/nvs, "VW-Chef Müller blamiert sich beim," *Spiegel*, January 12, 2016, http://m.spiegel.de/wirtschaft/unternehmen/a-1071573.html.

55 Oxford Reference, "ignorantia juris non excusat," Oxford University Press, accessed July 25, 2017, http://www.oxfordreference.com/view/10.1093/oi/authority.20110803095957244.

56 SIKA General Assembly, April 12, 2016.

and Loyalty" article and therefore acted solely in the best interests of the company.[57]

According to "Acting in Good Faith," each person is requested to act in good faith when executing individual rights and fulfilling individual duties. This principle is anchored in the Swiss civil law and holds true for the entire area of private law. It is grounded in a valid preexisting legal relationship, but it protects only justified and objectively legitimized confidence—not just subjective confidence.[58]

According to the "Duty of Care and Loyalty," members of the BoD are required to carry out their duties with all due diligence and protect the interests of the company in good faith. Included here is an obligation of secrecy and, if needed, an obligation to abstain from any matters benefiting their personal interests and harming those of the company.[59]

Both articles are behavioral maxims that—falling under the discretion of the judge—can be applied to specific cases. These two articles do not coincide regarding their potential addressees: Acting in "Good Faith" addresses anybody who is involved in a legal relationship. It requires loyal behavior when rights and duties are exercised. "The BoD's Duty of Care and Loyalty" is more narrowly defined because it addresses board members and third parties who are charged with the management of the company.

However, with reference to content, "The BoD's Duty of Care and Loyalty" goes further than acting in "Good Faith" because it also protects third-party interests (those of the company). Acting in "Good

---

57 Ibid.

58 Christa Sommer, "Die Treuepflicht des Verwaltungsrats, Art. 717 Abs. 1 OR," *Schweizer Schriften zum Handels und Wirtschaftsrecht* 298 (2010): 24f, https://www.dike.ch/download/sample/Sommer_Treuepflicht.pdf.

59 Stefanicki Katrin, "Clarification on the Rights and Duties of the Board of Directors in a Recent Court Judgement—A General Overview," *Deloitte*, May 14, 2018, https://blogs.deloitte.ch/tax/2018/05/clarification-on-the-rights-and-duties-of-the-board-of-directors-in-a-recent-court-judgement-a-gener.html.

Faith" requires loyal behavior "only" in the exercise of an individual's rights and duties.[60]

So how is it possible that the parties can use the same article (Good Faith) to make opposite points? And why can they use both articles to convey a similar message?

First, the area of discussion (Good Faith and Duty of Care and Loyalty) triggers emotions, and hence affects the public opinion because it addresses ethics and morality and leaves enough leeway to be used to one's own benefit. Second, as chapter 5, "Key Driver Three: Leadership as an Accelerator" (in the subsection "Influence of Upbringing on Leadership and Implications for Leadership Selection") will describe in more detail, these articles are based on the assumption that human beings are rational. But very often, they are not, and what is considered rational by one person might be considered irrational by others.

The duty of corporate bodies under "The BoD's Duty of Care and Loyalty" led to the creation of the business judgment rule (BJR).[61] The rule presumes that, "in making a business decision the directors act on an informed basis in good faith and in the honest belief that the action was in the best interests of the company."[62] Hence, even apparent judgment mistakes do not necessarily lead to a director's personal liability. The BJR is corporate law that focuses on procedures and not on results. Originating in the US, the rule is recognized in other countries such as Germany, Austria, Liechtenstein, and Switzerland.[63] In Switzerland for example, the rule has become widely known and applied since a decision of the Federal Supreme Court in

---

60 Sommer, "Die Treuepflicht des Verwaltungsrats," 24f.

61 Alessandro Bernasconi and Melanie Koller, "Aspekte der aktienrechtlichen Verantwortlichkeit nach OR 754," University of Zurich, April 24, 2013: 1.

62 Supreme Court of Delaware, *Aronson v. Lewis*, 473 A.2d 805, 812; overruled by Supreme Court of Delaware, *Brehm v. Eisner*, 746 A.2d 244, February 9, 2000, in Lori McMillan, "The Business Judgment Rule as an Immunity Doctrine," *William & Mary Business Law Review* 4 (2013): 527.

63 Carl Baudenbacher, "Uniform Liability Standards for the Private and the Public Sector—Lessons from the Hypo Alpe Adria Debacle," EMBL-HSG, University of St. Gallen (2016), 4.

June 2012 in which it was acknowledged as a major principle of Swiss corporation law.[64]

The BoD of Sika called for the application of the BJR to foster approval for its arguments to oppose the sale of the majority shares to Saint-Gobain. The BoD claimed that an analysis of the situation led to their decision that a sale would not be in the best interests of the company.[65]

According to Swiss corporation law, it is not at the discretion of the BoD to decide whether the sale of an owner's shares is good for the company or not. This is particularly relevant with Sika because it was the 100 percent of family-owned shares of Schenker-Winkler Holding (shareholder of Sika shares) that changed hands when the sale took place and not the direct shares of Sika. Furthermore, regarding the owners' voting rights, which the BoD tried to restrict, had the parties not agreed on ending the legal dispute in 2018, it would only have been at the court's discretion to decide whether shareholders' interests had been harmed.

Therefore, it does not appear that the BJR could have been applied in this case. The chances of it being applicable would have been higher if the BoD itself, for example, had decided to carry out an acquisition. And even assuming that the BJR had been applied in the Sika case, it might have been difficult for the BoD to prove it had thoroughly analyzed this complex and far-reaching endeavor and its consequences in only two days, including a Sunday.

Although the case has been settled, questions remain such as why the BoD did not get back to the family with the response, "We have received the information regarding the selling intention, and we will thoroughly review the consequences for Sika." Why was such time

---

64 Hans-Ueli Vogt and Michael Bänziger, "Das Bundesgericht anerkennt die Business Judgment Rule als Grundsatz des schweizerischen Aktienrechts, GesKR, 2016, 609"; judgment code 4A_74/2012, E. 5.2, with reference to BGE court ruling 132 III 564 E. 5.1, p. 572f.

65 Adrian Blum, "Sika-VRP Hälg: 'Wir haben fair analysiert,'" *Finanz und Wirtschaft*, August 12, 2014, http://www.fuw.ch/article/sika-vrp-halg-wir-haben-fair-und-unvoreingenommen-analysiert/.

pressure imposed by BoD members if they were seriously interested in analyzing the situation in the best interests of the company?

LAWSUITS ARE INCREASING

Liability claims in business have grown substantially. A 2014 study by Allianz Global Corporate & Specialty showed that this trend is related to an increased awareness of people's rights as well as governments' increased need to protect weaker groups and offer them better access to justice. A growing number of laws has led to a growing number of claims, including collective claims, even outside the US (renowned for its class action lawsuits). This trend has led to an internationalization of law firms.[66]

Allianz Global Corporate & Specialty 2017 reported three years later, in 2017, that never before have corporate leaders been under such scrutiny over alleged wrongdoing than now. "There is a growing trend towards seeking punitive and personal legal action against officers for failure to follow regulations and standards. Claims severity is rising due to higher legal costs, increasing complexity, expanding regulatory investigations and cross-border actions." This holds true for Asia, Latin America, the US, and Europe.[67]

This section sheds light on the legal side of the previously described cases that were embroiled in a scandal and elaborates on the related lawsuits and their outcomes.[68] The extract of cases shows the involvement of the parties within the magic triangle. Again, the list is just the tip of the iceberg. (An extended yet by far not exhausted list can be found in appendix 4.)

---

66   Stuart Collins, "Global Claims Review 2014: Loss Trends and Emerging Risks for Global Businesses," *Global Risk Dialogue Magazine*, 2014, 29ff, https://www.agcs.allianz.com/content/dam/onemarketing/agcs/agcs/reports/AGCS-Global-Claims-Review-2014.pdf.

67   "Allianz Global Corporate & Specialty, Global Claims Review: Liability in Focus," Allianz, 2017: 5.

68   Bloomfield, *Theory and Practice of Corporate Governance*, 5ff; "The 10 Worst Corporate Accounting Scandals of All Time"; Balkhi, "25 Biggest Corporate Scandals Ever"; Farrell, "The World's Biggest Accounting Scandals."

ENRON

Enron's former chairperson/CEO died during the process, the former vice-chairperson committed suicide, the CEO was sentenced to jail for twenty-four years, and the CFO for four years—charged with fraud, money laundering, and conspiracy. The company filed for bankruptcy. Accounting company, Arthur Andersen, taken down by the scandal, was found guilty of fudging Enron's accounts and for obstructing justice by shredding audit documents.[69]

VOLKSWAGEN

After Volkswagen pleaded guilty to criminal charges for its ten-year conspiracy, a $2.8 billion fine and three years of probation were issued. Civil penalties of $1.5 billion were imposed. Volkswagen also agreed to pay $11.2 billion to buy back or repair diesel vehicles in the US and to contribute $4.7 billion to federal pollution reduction. In the US, six current and former Volkswagen executives (including the former CEO) were accused in criminal cases; five of them were charged with serious fraud in Germany.[70]

D&O INSURANCE IS BALLOONING (AND NOT HELPING)

As a result of cases such as those listed above, top executives and directors are realizing that the risk of becoming personally liable is closely linked with taking up leadership roles. Therefore, they are increasingly seeking to secure protection through indemnification agreements and D&O liability insurance. All large, publicly listed companies have D&O insurance, and demand among small- and medium-sized enterprises (SMEs) has significantly increased. However, indemnification agreements determine that the organization will pay for costs caused by fiduciary duty cases *if* the director acted

---

69   Bloomfield, *Theory and Practice of Corporate Governance*, 5ff; "The 10 Worst Corporate Accounting Scandals of All Time;" Balkhi "25 Biggest Corporate Scandals Ever"; Farrell, "The World's Biggest Accounting Scandals."

70   Burden, "VW to Pay $2.8B Fine."

in good faith.[71] This entails that liability based upon any intentionally dishonest or fraudulent act are excluded.

MEDIA CAN MANIPULATE

It is the media's job to uncover, shake up, and make information public—for the good. The media have a crucial accountability function. But the line is thin: inaccurate reporting through biased coverage can contradict the fundamental principles of independent journalistic ethics and guidelines, such as the Press Council's code of conduct.

Scandals affecting companies or disputes within the magic triangle are a field day for the media. This is often why conflicts worsen and are prolonged—as seen with ABB, Sika, CALIDA, and Otherco.

In the Sika case, for instance, the media were used as a dispute platform on which opposing parties used public relations agencies to showcase their stories to increase public pressure. This, in turn, worsens the conflict. The creation of idols and the glorification of CEOs by the media leads stakeholders to believe what they read. "Star status" helps increase the margin for maneuver, but glory can be short-lived.[72]

Often, the media help create stars and later use their status against them if there are signs or evidence that they are about to fail or lose their jobs and, with them, their power. It is common for the media to become the author of a leader's biography—a dangerous undertaking.

The power of the media and its inherent responsibility is a sensitive issue, as seen in the case of Otherco. To encourage headhunted employees to ultimately leave the company, the former CEO used the media

---

71 Max Haller, "Organhaftung und Versicherung. Die aktienrechtliche Verantwortlichkeit und ihre Versicherbarkeit unter besonderer Berücksichtigung der D&O-Versicherung," 2008, 249; David F. Larcker and Brian Tayan, "Seven Myths of Boards of Directors," Stanford Closer Look Series at Stanford Graduate School of Business (September 30, 2015): 3, https://www.gsb.stanford.edu/sites/default/files/publication-pdf/cgri-closer-look-51-seven-myths-board-directors.pdf.

72 Mathew Hayward, Violina Rindova, and Timothy Pollock, "Believing One's Own Press: The Causes and Consequences of CEO Celebrity," *Strategic Management Journal* 25, no. 7 (2004): 637–53, 641ff, https://doi.org/10.1002/smj.405.

to spread false information about the BoD and the majority-owning family. Together with the company's head of communications—a former colleague and friend—and a journalist from a business magazine, he launched a fabricated story. This one journalist started the story and drew it out through consecutive editions without speaking with the BoD or the family to hear their views or to collect evidence.

Other journalists copied the story without questioning it or doing further research. This false public information almost destroyed the company—employees and clients initially believed what they read. The family decided not to try to prove the truth but to ride the storm, not only because it was a priority to calm the customers but also because they were told by another journalist that "the truth should not get in the way of a good story." Conflicts sell.

Here's another example. Swissair, Switzerland's former national airline, was founded in 1931 and became one of the world's leading international airlines.[73] In 2001, the airline was grounded due to the major and risky expansion strategy ("Hunter strategy") and intentional false increase of depreciation time length for fixed assets on the balance sheets. In April 2001, it faced an annual loss of CHF 2.6 billion because of the cleanup of the Hunter strategy.[74]

The Swissair case showed how far the power of the media can go. According to Knorr and Arndt, all Swiss journalists were granted a 50 percent discount for all flights within Europe and 25 percent on all intercontinental travel, whether the trip was business or private. These discounts were obtained until the mid-1990s and created strong incentives to choose Swissair as the preferred carrier. As a result, media reports on the strategy pursued by its parent, SAirGroup, were rather favorable compared to the coverage of airlines of other countries. This dynamic might have led to ignorance regarding other

---

73 Andreas Knorr and Andreas Arndt, "Swissair's Collapse—An Economic Analysis," Institute for World Economics and International Management at Universität Bremen (2003): 15.

74 Jürgen Dunsch, "Swissair-Pleite: Luftnummer," *Frankfurter Allgemeine Zeitung*, January 16, 2007, https://www.faz.net/aktuell/wirtschaft/swissair-pleite-luftnummer-1411598.html.

airlines' quality, which further improved the image of Swissair. The incorrect belief that Swissair was unparalleled, as it had been for a long time, meant increasing threats from competitors were underestimated or disregarded.[75]

To conclude, it needs to be addressed that although the media has an important role as watchdog, it needs to be aware of the fine line between uncovering and making public on one side and staying accurate, honest, ethical, and fair in its reporting on the other side. Otherwise, too much harm is caused.

IN SUM

The challenge of answering the main question of this book—why derailment continues despite corporate governance—does not primarily lie in the strengths and weaknesses of individual corporate governance models and systems but on the elaboration of the underlying conditions. As demonstrated in the previous chapters, the legal framework has flaws when it comes to avoidance of negative outcomes and solution providence. The framework's reactive character, the tendency to oversimplify and the possibility to freestyle get in the way. There are also other underlying conditions—key drivers—that cause and increase conflicts. These will be discussed next.

---

75 Knorr and Arndt, "Swissair's Collapse."

PART 2

THE MISSING PIECES

CHAPTER 3

KEY DRIVER ONE

CHANGE AS A TRIGGERING ELEMENT

Chapter 1, "Traditional Frameworks," showed that conflicts have triggering elements, root causes, and accelerators or intensifiers. Each of these three serves as a function of a related key driver. This chapter will focus on the first of three drivers: change as a triggering element. The volume and magnitude of change boosted by globalization has never been experienced before. Due to breakthrough technologies, demographic shifts, and political transformations, the world has become more fast-paced and interconnected than ever—VUCA. The socioeconomic consequences are immeasurable.

According to Harry Korine (adjunct professor of strategy at INSEAD and lecturer at the London Business School and the University of St. Gallen) and Pierre-Yves Gomez (professor of strategy and director of the French Corporate Governance Institute), in organizations, a change at the ownership or management level can affect the strategy and vice versa; any change in strategy can impact ownership or management.[76] Under these circumstances, corporate governance

---

76   Korine and Gomez, *Strong Managers, Strong Owners*, 4f.

is supposed to ensure decision-makers' control and accountability. Strategy, ownership, and management are integral parts of a company's governance system. Therefore, a change of any of these three elements will have an impact on corporate governance. For example, a revision of the organizational strategy can increase a company's risk, and this requires its corporate governance to be adjusted to keep control and accountability.

As the cases in chapter 1 demonstrated, chances for shareholders/ owners, BoDs, and management to get into a dispute are very high, as they all have different interests. And even within the same category, interests differ. A change in strategy is just one possible occasion when these interests collide.

Defining a company's strategy is most often a political process. There is no such thing as "the best strategy" because strategy is not neutral, but the outcome of the collision of different interests. Consequently, decisions related to strategy and governance will be primarily defined by the group that has the power, that imposes its view following its own values and methods, and that apparently wins the debate. In order to increase power, some shareholders or directors form alliances with management. To understand the mechanisms of strategic decision-making, it is crucial to know the drivers of coalitions between ownership and management. For the purpose of minimizing conflicts and power games, it is easier to understand different interests and expectations than to pursue convergence.[77]

Hence, ownership, management, and strategy are closely linked and therefore cannot be treated in isolation. Surprisingly, this is not reflected in academia, where strategy and ownership are looked at as two separate topics. One of them concerns shareholders' roles and rights and is handled by the fields of law and finance. The field of economics covers the second topic: strategy formulation and market competition. In practice, this separation is reflected in the field of

---

77   Ibid., ixff.

professional services—ownership is treated by investment banks and law firms, whereas strategy formulation processes are covered by management consultants.[78]

The beginning of formal corporate governance, rooted in the separation between ownership and management, was marked by the development of the principal-agent theory. As discussed in chapter 1, this theory implies that a conflict exists between principals and agents and suggests that their conflicting interests are aligned with their incentives.

This chapter does not challenge whether that separation is still valid. It analyzes, based on Korine and Gomez's insights, why—in contrast to the simplified principal-agent theory—interests differ among and within groups of shareholders and management and how this is played out. For this, it is important to understand the groups' differing values and methods and how those impact the strategy formulation process.[79]

CHANGE WITHIN THE ORGANIZATION

An illustrative example of consequences of changes in ownership involves the German company TUI, Europe's largest travel group. In 1959, the company—at that time a coal and steel producer called "Preußische Bergwerks-und Hütten AG"—became the first German state-owned firm to be privatized. Since then, it has experienced numerous, dramatic changes in—and disputes over—both ownership and strategy. In short:[80]

- Ownership changes included: privatization, two dominant shareholders, dispersed shareholdings, industrial shareholders, reduction of government holding, new shareholders, activists.
- Strategy changes included: departure from state control, diversifi-

---

78   Ibid., 2f.

79   Ibid., 2f.

80   Ibid., 14ff.

cation, refocus on core business, international expansion, further diversification, further internationalization, divestments, radical change, acquisition, renaming, growth of and departure from specific division.

CHANGE IN OWNERSHIP

Against common perception, shareholders cannot be seen and treated as a homogenous group. Differences are manifold, for example, in regard to the horizon of investment (long-term vs. short-term), objectives (economic vs. social), degree of activity (active vs. passive), portfolio concentration, and size. Hence, shareholders' values and methods differ.[81]

Shareholders who have a business relationship focus on return, liquidity, and risk. On the contrary, institutional shareholders concentrate on employment stability, business objectives, value systems, and the company's future. There is a distinction between owners with *external values* (competitors and performance of equity market) and those with *internal values* (commitment to and continuity of the company). Shareholders with internal values do not plan to exit the company in the foreseeable future.[82]

Another differentiating factor is the method with which shareholders try to exert influence on the company. There are *vocal methods* (decision-making, elaboration of plans, recruitment of directors and managers) and *silent methods* (threaten to sell shares, review holdings, or announce expectations). The combination of values and methods produces four categories and types: rebel, entrepreneur, broker, and sleeper.[83]

---

81 Anne Beyer, David Larcker, and Brian Tayan, "Does the Composition of a Company's Shareholder Base Really Matter?" Stanford Closer Look Series at Stanford University, July 31, 2014, 1, https://www.gsb.stanford.edu/sites/default/files/publication-pdf/cgri-closer-look-42-shareholder-composition.pdf.

82 Korine and Gomez, *Strong Managers, Strong Owners*, 22.

83 Ibid., 23f.

TABLE 1: VALUES AND METHODS OF SHAREHOLDING

| | | METHODS | |
		VOCAL	SILENT
VALUES	EXTERNAL	**Activist** (e.g., Icahn fund)	**Trader** (e.g., investment fund)
	INTERNAL	**Entrepreneur** (e.g., familly in family enterprise)	**Sleeper** (e.g., industrial shareholder)

Source: Korine and Gomez, *Strong Managers, Strong Owners*, 24.

Any given category can transform into another. For example, an Activist can become an Entrepreneur and take a public company private. In turn, an Entrepreneur or Sleeper can become an activist or trader by starting to focus on maximizing the value of his or her investment.[84]

Or if a family starts to lose either influence or interest in its business, it moves from the category of Entrepreneur to that of Sleeper. For example, Mr. Otherco, who had just sold a large minority of his shares to management and shifted from a dual leadership structure to the role of chairperson, left for another continent for a few years. He changed his ownership category from Entrepreneur to Sleeper. When he returned from abroad, he moved back into the category of Entrepreneur. The other directors had remained passive. Management had gotten used to the silent method and did not want Mr. Otherco to vocalize change.

The change that involves the highest potential for conflict is the one from Sleeper to Activist.[85] This can happen when a family business is passed on from one generation to the next, and the family successors no longer want to be entrepreneurs (vocal, internal). After a period of being Sleepers, they adopt external values, become Activists and look for an exit. This is what happened at Sika. The founding family had one representative on the BoD. After changes in management and the BoD in 2012, the power balance shifted, which intensified conflicts of inter-

---

84 Ibid., 25ff.

85 Ibid., 25ff.

ests. Different shareholder groups had different interests, although they were Activists as well (like the family). The family had the feeling that it was no longer heard, and it lost interest in the continuation of the long-held tradition of entrepreneurial shareholding. It decided to sell the company to a strategic buyer. These different changes impacted the strategy formulation process, which magnified subsequent conflicts.

Another example is when management is invested and suddenly starts to become active, vocal, and external. This was the case with Otherco and quite a few publicly listed companies such as Deutsche Bank and UBS. A change in one shareholder category can affect the direction and even the influence of another shareholder category.

The key is in the distribution of power. In family enterprises and business partnerships, a change of ownership identity can strongly impact the history of the business, depending on the values and methods of the new generation. The process of attracting new shareholders needs to be carefully prepared and executed in privately held companies, e.g., insider vs. outsider shareholders. In publicly held companies, shareholder change is common, although interests amongst Activists—risk vs. growth vs. value—may vary even more strongly.[86]

It is important for any company to pay close attention to shifts of either categories or identities of owners to avoid disagreement with, or even blockage of, necessary changes, as this can negatively influence the strategy formation process. As such shifts can have an incremental character, they are not always easily observed.

CHANGE IN MANAGEMENT

Management is in charge of operations. If there is a change in management, either due to succession or disagreement over strategy, the first question is whether an insider or outsider should be selected as successor. The perception is that insiders tend to follow the current

---

86 Ibid., 25ff.

path; outsiders tend to change direction. But this is not the right lens through which to view the situation for two reasons. First, the company's situation may have been misdiagnosed, e.g., there being a crisis on the horizon. Second, there might be a false sense of security in expecting people to be that predictable; insiders could favor a new direction and outsiders a current path.[87]

The first step should be to focus not on insiders vs. outsiders but on the company's context and the required values and methods of the potential successor.

Executives tend to have different methods and values in the way they approach change.[88]

Management methods are summarized as "disruptive"—change oriented, bring in new approaches, plans, strategy, people—and "continuative"—focus on continuation of a path, process improvements, best practices.

There is a differentiation between the internal and external values of executive succession as described in the previous section. The following category types—in regard to their name—are modified from the ones used by Korine and Gomez: disrupter, change agent, functionalist, preserver.

TABLE 2: VALUES AND METHODS OF EXECUTIVE SUCCESSION

		METHODS	
		DISRUPTIVE	CONTINUATIVE
VALUES	EXTERNAL	Disrupter	Functionalist
	INTERNAL	Change Agent	Preserver

Source: Isabelle Nüssli, based on Korine and Gomez, *Strong Managers, Strong Owners*, 45.

---

87   Ibid., 43.

88   Ibid., 44f.

Functionalists tend to prefer continuity, disruptors seek rupture, but both subscribe to external values. Change agents also tend to seek rupture, preservers are inclined toward continuity, but both subscribe to internal values. Good examples of change agents are Jack Welch (GE) and Steve Jobs (Apple). Disruptors would be Jean-Marie Messier (Vivendi Universal) and Jürgen Schremp (DaimlerChrysler).[89]

Conflicts within a management team often emerge because the team members fall into different categories and thus have different, even opposing, values and methods that impact strategy.

Situations get even more complex when executives assume new roles with new employers who have different shareholder structures from those to which they are accustomed, e.g., switching from a public to a private company. This is what happened at Otherco. The new CEO came from a large public company where he had led a division, then joined privately held SME Otherco. He was expected to change from disruptor to functionalist, but he did not. It must be realized by both parties, by the BoD, and by the executive that executives do not easily adjust to new ownership forms. Not only must they be coached in their new roles and governance, but they must also be wise enough to accept them.

Management candidates' values, methods, and roles are indicators of their future behavior.[90] Therefore, their performance track record contributes only part of the story, a topic that this book will treat in greater detail in chapter 5, "Key Drivers Three: Leadership as an Accelerator."

If the new CEO starts to form alliances, special attention is required. The new CEO, together with fellow managers, can enter a relationship with a group of shareholders and/or a shareholder group can try to exert influence on the CEO. This is what happened at Otherco. The new CEO formed an alliance with one board member.

---

89   Korine and Gomez, *Strong Managers, Strong Owners*, 45ff.

90   Ibid., 51.

Another example is Sika. To gain bargaining power in opposing the family's interests, the CEO formed an alliance with the chairperson and five directors, and with other shareholder groups that had similar interests. In turn, the family's alliance consisted of three directors who served as its representatives and representatives of other shareholders. The interests were in line within the alliances.

CHANGE IN THE ORGANIZATION OR ORGANIZATIONAL STRUCTURE

Organizational changes happen frequently, but the multilayered impact that change can have is often underestimated and approached reactively instead of proactively. In addition to change that happens on the level of management and ownership, changes to legal form (e.g., an IPO or de/centralization) and the organization structure (org chart) can cause the power balance to shift in unexpected ways, leading to negative outcomes that could have been avoided.

Organizational structures experience frequent changes that almost always lead to power shifts. These shifts impact the direction of a company. Owners and BoDs should be aware of the embedded risks: these power shifts leave winners and losers, and this can lead to conflicts within the management team.[91]

At Otherco, a change in the organizational structure in response to the new strategy intensified diverging interests within the management team. Preservers were resistant to the organizational change, Functionalists wanted to comply with standards and processes, and Disruptors focused on the market.

The restructuring of Otherco led to a higher degree of independence between its business units. The new CEO was given more power to enhance the information flow and decision-making. Diverging interests in regard to strategy within the management team and between

---

91   Ibid., 87ff.

management and the BoD made it easier for the CEO to cut a group of key employees out of that division and found a new company behind the backs of the BoD and the family.

Answers to emerging questions, such as what drives a person to act that way and why would subordinates follow their boss almost blindly will be illuminated in appendix 6, in the "Followership and Leader-Follower Interactions and Theories" section.

CHANGE IN LEGAL FORM

Let us revisit some scandals of the 1990s and 2000s in the context of changes in legal form. Until the early 1970s, the investment banking industry in the US was dominated by the following six partnerships: Merrill Lynch, Salomon Brothers, Goldman Sachs, Bear Stearns, Morgan Stanley, and Lehman Brothers. After the prohibition of an initial public offering (IPO) by the New York Stock Exchange ended in 1970,[92] all six partnerships went public between 1971 and 1999. They started to establish profit centers and increased their risk appetite. Their ownership identities changed from majority to minority ownership by partners. An increased requirement for capital drove the desire to go public, which increased the amount of money executives could borrow to leverage their bets. Corporate governance was not able to keep up with these changes, even less so when the economic climate declined. Apart from other context-related variables, it was the ownership change that led to a change in strategy because of diverging interests, e.g., risk appetite and expectations of return on equity.[93]

The interests of the different parties get accentuated with an IPO, which changes the dynamic of each group involved. It is important to thoroughly assess the reason for going public: Is it capital, liquidity or a strategic choice? Furthermore, the time needed to prepare for an

---

92   Alan Morrison and William Wilhelm, "The Demise of Investment-Banking Partnerships: Theory and Evidence," Oxford Financial Research Centre Working Paper, AFA 2006 Boston Meetings Paper, 18, https://ssrn.com/abstract=569109 or http://dx.doi.org/10.2139/ssrn.569109.

93   Korine and Gomez, *Strong Managers, Strong Owners*, 65ff.

IPO can be used to change the strategy so that the company looks more attractive to investors. The surprise arises when the investors realize, for example, that the strategy was changed to show only excessive growth, driven by the self-interest of existing owners. This is what happened to the shareholders of Indian-based SKS Microfinance, the first microfinance provider in Asia that went public in the years leading up to the IPO of 2009.[94]

The time period after an IPO has its own dynamic. In order to prevent unwanted changes after an IPO, a dual share structure can be implemented, as done by the Sika family formerly owning 16 percent of the capital and 52 percent of the voting shares. However, despite dual share classes, power shifted to a group of directors who restricted the family's voting power at the GAs from 2015 to 2017. Since the parties reached a deal while many claims were pending before the courts, the latter never had to decide whether or not this was legal. It is left to opposing opinions by the parties, various legal experts, and the media.

Further examples are Google, Facebook, Groupon, and Rupert Murdoch's Twenty-First Century Fox, Inc., who all issued dual-class shares. This was the subject of great media attention.[95] A dual share structure can either help prevent a power shift or aggravate conflicts and power games, depending on the circumstances and the people involved.

CHANGE IN STRATEGY

A major change in strategy very often leads to further changes, such as the need for capital, requirements for management skills, or new ways of processing information. Such changes can have a strong impact on ownership, management and corporate governance. For example, a newly acquired company brings in new people, new processes, and

---

94 Ibid., 72.

95 Matt Orsagh, "Dual-Class Shares: From Google to Alibaba, Is It a Troubling Trend for Investors?" *Market Integrity Insights* (blog), CFA Institute, April 1, 2014, https://blogs.cfainstitute.org/marketintegrity/2014/04/01/dual-class-shares-from-google-to-alibaba-is-it-a-troubling-trend-for-investors/; Mark Sweney, "Murdoch Family Defeat Shareholder Revolt over News Corp Voting Structure," *The Guardian*, November 18, 2014, https://www.theguardian.com/media/2014/nov/18/murdoch-family-news-corp-shareholder-revolt.

probably new risks, which all impact elements of corporate governance, such as accountability, reporting, and accounting mechanisms.[96]

As discussed in chapter 2, "Flaws of Traditional Frameworks," corporate governance is rarely adjusted, and if it is, adjustments are usually made reactively after an incident has occurred. This process is risky.

Conversely, Hilti,[97] a foundation-owned, large construction equipment company, provides a good example. It has a culture of future mindset orientation, recruiting new board members based on qualifications that the company will (or might) need over the next five years. This is the time when discussion around the adaptation of the corporate governance system can be included in the recruitment process.[98]

Change in strategy can be considered as a test that reveals who has decision-making power within a company. At CALIDA, for example, it was the CEO's plan to continue the expansion strategy and acquire new companies, whereas the BoD and the family decided to focus on sustainable, organic growth. The CEO's run for reelection to the BoD failed, and the power game led to a CEO change.

At Otherco, the crisis evolved due to rapid growth and the CEO's acquisition and expansion plans. The BoD's proposal to adjust the strategy in accordance with its long-term orientation, sustainable, organic growth and reduction of risky projects opposed the CEO's interest in short-term orientation, large projects and acquisitions to raise the share price. Globalization and growth can strengthen a CEO's position and power, which can be good or bad for a company, depending on the CEO's ability to execute the growth strategy and the way he or she assumes and handles power.

---

96   Sweney, "Murdoch Family Defeat Shareholder Revolt."

97   With over 23,000 employees in over 120 countries, Hilti is one of the international leaders in offering technology-leading products, systems, and services to the international construction industry, Hilti, "About Us," accessed November 2, 2017, https://www.hilti.com/content/hilti/W1/US/en/company/about-hilti/company-profile/about-us.html.

98   Korine and Gomez, *Strong Managers, Strong Owners*, 109.

IN SUM: CONSEQUENCES OF CHANGE FOR CORPORATE GOVERNANCE

Korine's and Gomez's extensive research, supported by the Sika, CALIDA, and Otherco cases, but unlike those postulated in principal-agent theory, shows that interest among shareholders and managers and between these two groups can differ strongly. It also shows that the impact changes in ownership and management have on strategy and corporate governance is defined by stakeholders' methods and values and by shifts in these. A change in legal form that acquires new types of shareholders or a change in organizational structure can have an impact on management, strategy or risk and consequently corporate governance.[99] The impact that all of these types of change can have on a company's corporate governance system varies.

A change of management can help detect corporate governance failures. It matters which persons are hired, especially in family businesses, where continuity with the founder's intentions might be at risk.

New management with a new strategy can lead to new risks and call for different control mechanisms. Corporate governance, as a system that focuses on structure, processes, procedures, and accountability, should be adapted when changes occur. A good example is Jeffrey Peek, former Merrill Lynch investment banker: When he first joined the American bank CIT as CEO, he exposed the company to high-risk lending groups as a result of his aggressive expansion plans. Control and reporting mechanisms imbedded in corporate governance could not keep up.[100] The bank was eventually rescued due in large part to the help of US federal regulators.[101]

A new executive can accumulate power and therefore dominate the decision-making process, which is likely to impact the roles of the BoD and the shareholders. This can happen in both publicly and pri-

99   Ibid., 90.

100   Ibid., 55.

101   Tomoeh Murakami Tse, "CIT's Bankruptcy Raises New Questions about Bailout," *The Washington Post*, November 15, 2009, http://www.washingtonpost.com/wp-dyn/content/article/2009/11/15/AR2009111502280.html.

vately held companies, but more often in mature companies. Again, it can be positive or negative if a new CEO accumulates power.

When a new executive is hired, it is rather unusual for the BoD and shareholders to (proactively) think about the consequences of such change on different elements. This does not mean that harsher measures must be imposed on the new executive but rather that the BoD and shareholders should be aware of the potential shift of power and its impact on strategy and corporate governance. Hence, the selection process of a new executive is not only about the job itself. The BoD needs to consider potential changes of strategy, their possible impact on corporate governance, and the way the new executive might handle newly assumed power—from the outset and over time.

Underlying all of these factors is the human element as another hidden key driver of negative outcomes. The next chapter will address the human element and thereby further address the main question of this book: Why do conflicts continue despite corporate governance?

CHAPTER 4

KEY DRIVER TWO

THE HUMAN ELEMENT AS A ROOT CAUSE

The various elements of a corporate governance system need to be regularly reviewed and proactively modified in case there is a perceived or initiated change that could trigger conflict. The more diverse the BoD, owners, and managers are, the more complex the interaction becomes between these groups and the more complex the impact on corporate governance.

However, even the most accurate and comprehensive system is of little help if the person in charge misuses power and authority. As the many cases described earlier demonstrate, derailment of executives seems to happen quite often, and when it happens, it almost always causes serious harm to people and organizations.

This raises questions about human nature. Why do people have different behavioral patterns, and where does this behavior originate? Why do people handle power differently? The human element involves the following considerations:

- The meaning of power for different people.
- The reasons people behave certain ways, e.g., initiating or getting involved in politics or misusing power.
- What makes people want to stay in power at any price.
- The types of person at risk of derailment and the range for them to improve.
- How different executives handle rising uncertainty and unpredictability triggered by an increasingly hyper-turbo world.
- Whether and how conflict-causing behavior can be predicted to prevent conflicts.
- What can be done by those who select people to fill key roles.

In order to prevent and manage organizational conflict, these considerations need to be put on center stage. Thus, the following sections will dig deep into the origins and development of human behavior. Theory and evidence relating to biological and environmental influences, personality development, and cultural differences will be discussed in the context of organizational dynamics.

NATURE (GENETICS) VS. NURTURE (ENVIRONMENT)

The debate over whether human behavior is inherited (nature) or learned (nurture) goes back at least as far as 350 BC. Philosophers such as Plato (428–347 BC) and his student Aristotle (384–322 BC) theorized about the drivers of human behavior. Plato was convinced that innate factors drive both behavior and knowledge, while Aristotle proposed that behavior and thoughts are the product of experience.[102]

Other famous philosophers such as Locke, Hobbes, and Rousseau (see sidebar) also debated on the topic and focused on the fundamental philosophical question of whether human nature is inherently good or bad.

---

102 Diana Sutherland, "Are Dichotomies like Nature vs. Nurture Useful for Understanding the History and Philosophy of Development?" 2013, 2, https://www.academia.edu/9371530/Are_dichotomies_like_Nature_versus_Nurture_useful_for_understanding_the_history_and_philosophy_of_development; Saul McLeod, "Nature vs. Nurture in Psychology," *SimplyPsychology*, accessed May 7, 2017, https://www.simplypsychology.org/naturevsnurture.html.

LOCKE, HOBBES, AND ROUSSEAU

"To understand political power aright, and derive it from its original, we must consider what estate all men are naturally in."

—JOHN LOCKE[103]

A fundamental philosophical question concerns whether human nature is inherently good or bad. Opinions vary.

English philosopher Thomas Hobbes (1588–1679) understood the human state of nature as a war of everybody against everybody: *homo homini lupus est,* which means that "a man is a wolf to another man." Thus, humans by their very nature cannot live in peace and so must submit themselves to absolute power or autocracy. War in this analogy is not understood as actual fighting but as the willingness to fight. In such a state, life and property are not secure, which leads to a state of constant fear.[104]

Contrary to this, the English philosopher John Locke (1632–1704) viewed the state that humans inhabit not as one of fighting but as one of perfect freedom of action. Thus, individuals are not dependent on anybody else's will. This state is one of equality, meaning that no person has more power than another (with all power and jurisdiction being reciprocal).[105]

Similar to Locke, Franco-Genevan philosopher and writer, Jean-Jacques Rousseau (1712–1778) also had a positive conception of humankind. He believed that humans are born free and good by

103 John Locke, *Second Treatise of Government* (New York, 1690), 3.

104 Thomas Hobbes, *The Elements of Law, Natural and Politic: Part I, Human Nature, Part II, De Corpore Politico; with Three Lives,* ed. J. C. Gaskin (Oxford: Oxford University Press, 1999), xiii; Franz Hespe, "Homo homini lupus— Naturzustand und Kriegszustand bei Thomas Hobbes," in *Handbuch Kriegstheorien,* ed. Thomas Jäger and Rasmus Beckmann (Wiesbaden, Germany: VS Verlag für Sozialwissenschaften, 2011), 178f; Gregory S. Kavka, "Hobbes's War of All against All," in *The Social Contract Theorists: Critical Essays on Hobbes, Locke, and Rousseau,* ed. Christopher W. Morris (Oxford: Rowman and Littlefield, 1999), 2.

105 Locke, *Second Treatise of Government,* 3; H. W. Kent, *Bibliographical Notes on One Hundred Books Famous in English Literature* (New York: Grolier Club, 1903), 86.

nature. But, unlike Locke, Rousseau believed that humans get corrupted in society, within which malleable passions and skills are shaped by human interaction. In contrast to Hobbes's view, however, he believed that they do not fight each other.[106]

Two extreme theories on nature versus nurture can be distinguished: nativism and environmentalism.

Nativists believe that humans' characteristics stem from evolution (nature). They believe that human behavior and knowledge are innate. Differences among people are defined by a genetic code, they argue. The earlier such characteristics are present, the more they are influenced by genetic factors. In contrast, aspects that are not present at birth are the product of maturation, which, for example, steers babies' attachments, the learning of languages, and the development of cognitive abilities.[107]

Environmentalists believe that humans are born with a blank slate and that experiences gradually fill this slate. Consequently, behavioral differences and psychological characteristics emerge through learning. Upbringing (nurturing) determines crucial aspects of a child's development. A child's attachment style, for example, is the result of received affection and attention. Language is learned through imitation of others, and cognitive development stems from stimulation in the environment.[108]

Today, such extreme positions are rare because the existence of evidence supporting both arguments has led to more nuanced views.

Social constructivists, for example, believe that knowledge has less emerged from interactions with the nonsocial environment than

106 J. T. Scott, *Jean-Jacques Rousseau: Human Nature and History* (London: Routledge, 2006), 1f; Christopher Bertram, "Jean Jacques Rousseau," *Stanford Encyclopedia of Philosophy*, accessed October 17, 2017, https://plato.stanford.edu/entries/rousseau/.

107 Sutherland, "Are Dichotomies like Nature vs. Nurture Useful," 2; McLeod, "Nature vs. Nurture in Psychology."

108 Ibid.

among people in a community.[109] Understandings of the world therefore result from active and cooperative relations among people rather than being automatically driven by the forces of nature.

Within more mainstream perspectives, prevalent questions today concern the extent to which human behavior is influenced by both heredity *and* environment, and how these factors interact.[110] The following text will shed light on the influence of genes (nature) and environment (nurture) and draw on research in the field of behavioral genetics that deals with the interplay between genetics and behavior.

(Further information on representatives of either position can be found in appendix 5.)

GENETICS

Opinions on linking a specific gene with a particular behavior vary. Twin studies play a crucial role in establishing the influence of genes on particular behaviors, but they are often correlational in design and, in these cases, cannot establish cause-and-effect relationships between variables. The increasing availability of DNA analyses will, however, allow the testing of hypotheses about specific genes and their effects.[111] And some researchers do claim to have linked particular genes to specific behaviors, e.g., the SLC18A (psychological disorder gene), SLC6A4 (stress gene), FKBP5 (trauma gene), ADRA2B (pessimist gene), OPRM1 (resilience gene), and RS4950 (leadership gene).[112]

---

109 Bryan Roche and Dermot Barnes-Holmes, "Behavior Analysis and Social Constructivism: Some Points of Contact and Departure," *Behavior Analyst* 26, no. 2 (2003): 218.

110 McLeod, "Nature vs. Nurture in Psychology."

111 Jan-Emmanuel De Neve and James H. Fowler, "Credit Card Borrowing and the Monoamine Oxidase A (MAOA) Gene," *Journal of Economic Behavior & Organization*107, pt. B (2014): 429.

112 Karsten Drath, *Resilienz in der Unternehmensführung: Was Manager und ihre Teams stark macht* (Freiburg, Germany: Haufe-Lexware, 2014), 284.

THE WARRIOR GENE

Scientists have been reporting a connection between violent aggression and antisocial behavior and a particular gene on the X chromosome. This gene, called MAOA or monoamine oxidase A, provides instructions for making the enzyme that is also called monoamine oxidase A. This enzyme affects the function of neurotransmitters such as dopamine, serotonin, and epinephrine (adrenaline) in areas of the brain that regulate impulsiveness and cognitive ability. The MAOA gene has been studied for three decades and is often called the "warrior gene." More recently, MAOA has even been related to borrowing behavior.[113]

The correlation was first put on the map by studies of a large Dutch family, where all male members were extremely violent. As Brunner found ten years later, this implied that a defective version (mutation) of the MAOA gene might account for their violent behavior.[114]

In 2002, British researchers found a link between violent aggression and a common allele of the MAOA gene. It is called MAOA-L and produces low levels of the MAOA enzyme. This (less efficient) allele has been linked with impulsive and addictive behavior and a lack of conscientiousness. The correlation with negative attributes appears to be substantially stronger in persons who carry the allele and have experienced some sort of trauma or abuse in childhood.[115]

Using a discovery and replication sample of twelve thousand individuals from a representative data set, De Neve and Fowler assumed that credit card debt (an expensive form of debt) would be experienced more often by people who look for immediate gratification, typically fail to consider future consequences, and show reduced information processing. They therefore hypothesized that people with less efficient variants of the MAOA gene run a higher risk of accruing credit card

113 John Horgan, *The End of War* (San Francisco: McSweeney's, 2012); De Neve and Fowler, "Credit Card Borrowing," 429.

114 Rosie Mestel, "Does the 'Aggressive Gene' Lurk in a Dutch Family?" *New Scientist*, October 30, 1993, https://www.newscientist.com/article/mg14018970-600-does-the-aggressive-gene-lurk-in-a-dutch-family/.

115 De Neve and Fowler, "Credit Card Borrowing," 429; Horgan, *The End of War*.

debt. The result of their association studies, involving relatively large samples based on self-reports, indicated a link between the MAOA gene and credit card debt. Nevertheless, such studies call for follow-up studies that adhere to an experimental design.[116]

So, is there a warrior gene? Since some MAOA follow-up studies have failed to replicate original findings, time will tell whether the warrior gene claims can eventually be verified.[117]

If there is indeed a warrior gene, how might it relate to leaders' behavior? Are aggression, antisocial behavior, impulsive behavior, and lack of conscientiousness associated with the MAOA gene prevalent among leaders? If so, how do they play out in powerful leadership positions?

The fact that certain negative behaviors seem to be substantially stronger in MAOA carriers who have experienced some sort of trauma or abuse in childhood indicates that the environment also plays a part in aggressive behavior. Thus, leaders exhibiting these sorts of behavior may be influenced by both genetic and environmental factors.[118]

Complex behavioral traits and disorders seem to be caused by different genes interacting with numerous environmental factors. It is therefore important to consider how behavior is influenced by the environment (e.g., one's childhood, upbringing, or life-changing experiences) and how this behavior can be improved.

GENETICS PLUS ENVIRONMENT/UPBRINGING

For a better understanding of the role genetics and environment play in shaping our behavior, the terms *temperament*, *character*, and *personality* need to be explored.

---

116 De Neve and Fowler, "Credit Card Borrowing," 429, 434.

117 Horgan, *The End of War*; De Neve and Fowler, "Credit Card Borrowing," 429.

118 Floor E. A. Verhoeven et al., "The Effects of Maoa Genotype, Childhood Trauma, and Sex on Trait and State-Dependent Aggression," *Brain and Behavior* 2, no. 6 (2012): 806–13.

Temperament and personality: Temperament describes the biologically defined style that is present at birth—a natural instinct that is not learned. But it can be nurtured as a person grows; caregivers play a crucial role. The personality of an individual is acquired on top of temperament and is influenced by factors such as education, socialization, and sources of pressure.[119]

Character and personality: The word *character* stems from Greek and means "engraving." Character differentiates one person from another. It is an imprint by nature *and* nurture that defines who a person really is. Scholars who distinguish character from personality describe character as something that "encompasses the deep underlying structures that make a person distinctive." By contrast, personality "involves only visible, superficial behavior." In addition, unlike character, personality might not have a moral connotation (a good vs. bad character).[120]

Personality can be described as the outcome of the interaction between genetic predispositions (biological aspects) and environment or context (family, culture, social roles, etc.). It defines motivation and ambition; shapes values, beliefs, abilities, and patterns; and defines the way individuals interact with their internal and external worlds. It also strongly influences a person's ethical and moral principles. Constant and sustainable characteristics of a person's way of functioning are called personality traits. They become more prominent with the years and—together with behavior—are so intrinsic to the personality that they are not visible to the person.[121]

PERSONALITY DEVELOPMENT

Today, it is assumed that 50 percent of the variance in personality

---

119 S. Prabhat, "Difference between Temperament and Personality," Differencebetween.net, accessed February 24, 2018, http://www.differencebetween.net/language/words-language/difference-between-temperament-and-personality/.

120 Manfred Kets de Vries, *The Leader on the Couch: A Clinical Approach to Changing People and Organisations* (San Francisco: Jossey-Bass, 2006), 52–54.

121 Ibid., 52–54; Manfred Kets de Vries, INSEAD, *The Personality Audit: Participant Guide* (Fontainebleau, France: INSEAD Global Leadership Centre and M. F. R. Kets de Vries, 2005), 6.

characteristics is genetic and 50 percent is unique (nonshared) environmental influences. Family (shared) environmental influences seem to have a minor impact.[122]

Human beings are a product of nature (gene) and nurture (environment), but what does this mean for this book? As this section will show, certain environmental influences are important with regard to the assessment and selection of future leaders.

This book is chiefly concerned with the last of these perspectives. Specifically, there are fundamental building blocks of personality that serve as stabilizers, but personality continues to develop throughout a person's life.

Consideration will now be given to stages of development throughout the lifetime, drawing upon Erikson's eight-stage theory of psychosocial development.

STAGES OF DEVELOPMENT

Researchers from different fields share the opinion that individuals are products of both nature and nurture. This has resulted in the emergence of several stage theories of development within which preparedness for levels of maturation are understood as biologically determined and thus core to each person. However, within these models, interaction between caregivers and children (even later as adults) is also thought to be crucial regarding the interpretation and integration of experiences.

Behavioral patterns—"a recurrent way of acting by an individual or group toward a given object or in a given situation"[123]—are the outcome of these developments, which are based in the interplay between nature and nurture.

---

122 Wiebke Bleidorn, Christian Kandler, and Avshalom Caspi, "The Behavioural Genetics of Personality Development in Adulthood—Classic, Contemporary, and Future Trends," *European Journal of Personality* 28 (2014): 244f.

123 Dictionary.com, "Behavior Pattern," accessed May 7, 2017m http://www.dictionary.com/browse/behavior-pattern.

This book, however, emphasizes the work of Erik Erikson,[124] as his theory of eight stages of psychosocial development is often cited as a milestone in elucidating human development, by explaining the proposed link between predispositions and the environment. Affirming the nature-nurture linking, his work describes the stages that everyone should pass through from infancy to adulthood.

Although the stages exist from birth, they only unfold based on the "natural plan" and the influence of the environment. Each stage builds on the previous one, and during it, the person experiences challenges (called "psychosocial crises") that can have a positive or negative outcome for the person's development. Crises that are not successfully mastered may turn into problems later.

Thus, each stage should be successfully completed in order to have a healthy development. Accordingly, in earlier stages, the behavior and responses of caregivers strongly contribute to the health of the development process.

The following eight stages are divided into five stages of early development, up to the age of eighteen years, and three stages that range into adulthood.[125]

Stage 1: Hope
Basic Trust vs. Basic Mistrust
(Infancy, 0–18 Months)
Key Question: Can I trust the world?

Erikson's first stage focuses on the crisis between trust and mistrust

---

124 Erik H. Erikson (1902–1994) was a German-born American developmental psychologist and psychoanalyst known for his theory on psychosocial development of human beings. His works were strongly influenced by Sigmund Freud's theory of "Structural and Topographical Models of Personality." "Erik H. Erikson," Erikson Institute, accessed July 28, 2017, https://www.erikson.edu/about/history/erik-erikson/; Saul McLeod, "Erik Erikson," *SimplyPsychology*, accessed November 2, 2017, http://www.simplypsychology.org/Erik-Erikson.html.

125 Erik H. Erikson, *Identity, Youth and Crisis* (New York: Norton, 1968), 91–141; Erik Erikson, *The Life Cycle Completed: A Review* (New York: Norton, 1981), 269–83; Erik Erikson, *Childhood and Society* (New York: Norton, 1993), 247–74; Alexander Stone Macnow, ed., *MCAT Behavioral Science Review: Created for MCAT2015* (New York: Kaplan, 2014), 220; M. R. Leming and G. E. Dickinson, *Understanding Dying, Death, and Bereavement* (Stamford, CT: Cengage Learning), 95.

as a result of the interaction with caregivers, especially the mother. Erikson defines trust as "an essential truthfulness of others as well as a fundamental sense of one's own trustworthiness."

The infant is uncertain about the world as a safe place. To soothe this feeling and meet its basic needs, it looks to caregivers for stability, consistency, and comfort.

The child's understanding of the world and society come from the caregivers and their interaction with the child.

The mastery of stage 1 leads to the virtue of hope. An infant who experiences trust will have a source of hope when facing the next stage. In turn, if the caregiver fails to provide an environment of affection, security, and stability, e.g., by being rough or unpredictable, the infant will develop a sense of mistrust. Mistrust can lead to anxiety, frustration, suspicion, and insecurity.

Stage 2: Willpower
Autonomy vs. Shame and Doubt
(Early Childhood, 18 Months to 3 Years)
Key Question: Is it okay to be me?

As children experience physical development and learn to control their motor abilities, they start to assert their independence, explore the environment, and discover the effects of certain behaviors. Caregivers play an important role in allowing children to explore, experiment, or seek assistance in order for their will to be asserted.

As they gain increased muscular coordination and mobility, toddlers become capable of satisfying some of their own needs. They begin to feed themselves, wash and dress themselves, and use the bathroom.

There is a sensitive line within encouragement, support, independence, and criticism over control and lack of assortment. The latter can lead to shame, doubt, lack of confidence, self-esteem, and dependence on others. The mastery of this stage leads to the virtue of willpower.

Stage 3: Purpose
Initiative vs. Guilt
(Preschool, 3–5 Years)
Key Question: Is it okay for me to do, move, and act?

Children at this age become more mobile and explorative of time and space. They take more action and initiative while interacting with other children in school. The opportunity to become more assertive and decisive leads to a feeling of freedom. They set goals and test leadership. In turn, if they experience too much control or criticism, they develop a feeling of guilt and become followers, or if they do not reach their goals, they might develop aggression and harshness.

The mastery of stage 3 leads to the virtue of a sense of purpose. The dilemma lies between initiative and guilt. Some guilt is good, as it helps children control themselves and feel conscious about their behavior, but too much and too frequent guilt can harm creativity and interaction with others. A caregiver's support of initiative (e.g., by helping the child make adequate decisions and by setting boundaries) is important. Parents are also influential in the way the child deals with new feelings of sexual interest.

Stage 4: Competence
Industry vs. Inferiority
(Latency, School Age, 6–12 Years)
Key Question: Can I make it in the world of people and things?

At this stage, teachers and peers play a more important role. If children do not develop a sense of trust, self-esteem, and assertiveness during this stage, they will experience doubt in their abilities and capabilities, which in turn boosts insecurity, guilt, shame, and feelings of inferiority about their skills. In turn, if they are encouraged and become assertive, they develop a feeling of industriousness and are self-confident in reaching their goals. This leads to the formation of moral values. This is the stage of the challenge between industry vs. inferiority, where a balance between modesty and competence needs to be found. The mastery of this stage leads to the virtue of competence.

Stage 5: Fidelity
Identity vs. Role Confusion
(Adolescence, 12–18 Years)
Key Question: Who am I and what can I be?

This stage is crucial for the transition from childhood to adulthood and the formation of identity. As adolescents search for their sense of self, they are concerned with how they are perceived by others.

Changes to the body and perceptions of one's roles lead to a reexamination of previous identification and identity. It is not only about "Who am I?" but also about "What can I be?" which includes identities relating to career, gender, relationships, beliefs, values, religion, etc.

The mastery of stage 5 leads to the virtue of fidelity, which is characterized by self-confidence and self-esteem—both of which are necessary for free association with people and ideas. The foundation for fidelity is laid by others' values, loyalty, and integrity.

Failure to master this stage can lead to a confusion of identity and role, a fragile self-esteem, and questionable choices in terms of job, education, and involvement in politics. If people feel that they are forced into identities, it can lead to negative senses of identity and foster rebellion and unhappiness.

Erikson defined the term "identity crisis," which is something that needs to be mastered in stage 5. This includes the reconciliation between the person *I am today* and the person *I'm expected to be(come) by others*. It probably is the most impactful crossroad on the human development journey.

A sense of identity is crucial for everyone. Answers to questions such as, "What is my role in this world?" and "What are my abilities, values, and beliefs?" need to be found. Despite the presence of biological factors, identity is a social construct that continues to evolve over a person's life.

Stage 6: Love
Intimacy vs. Isolation
(Early Adulthood, 18–35 Years)
Key Question: Can I love?

Young adults can be tempted to follow trends or group pressure and mix their identities with those of others in order to belong. If they managed to stabilize an identity, they now start establishing relationships that include intimacy.

Success in completing stage 6 means that commitment to another person outside the immediate family can be established. This includes learning how to make compromises and sacrifices, triggering feelings of happiness, safety, support, and care within a relationship.

The mastery of this stage leads to the virtue of love.

If a young adult is not able to establish commitment and avoids intimacy and relationships, a sense of isolation, fear, loneliness, and in severe cases, even depression can occur.

Stage 7: Care
Generativity vs. Stagnation
(Adulthood, 35–65 Years)
Key Question: Can I make my life count?

Stage 7 is called "middle adulthood" or "middle age" and centers around the settlement of careers and relationships. While being productive and contributing to society, the individual develops a sense of being a part of a bigger picture.

Generativity is related to the next generation. Raising children, having socially valued work, and giving back provide a sense of productivity and accomplishment, a sense of generativity.

Success of stage 7 leads to the virtue of care.

Failure to master this stage will lead to a feeling of unproductivity, stagnation, and dissatisfaction for reasons of self-centeredness or lack of will to give back to society.

Stage 8: Wisdom
Ego Integrity vs. Despair
(Maturity, 65 to Death)
Key Question: Is it okay to have been me?

A general result of growing older is a slowing down of productivity. Retirement is a new phase that is explored.

In this stage, people reflect upon their accomplishments through retrospection. If one can establish a feeling of integrity, it is possible to see that life so far has been meaningful, successful, and worth living.

If feelings of stagnation, unproductivity, and failure to reach set goals prevail, one becomes unhappy, unsatisfied, and full of despair, which often leads to depression.

The mastery of stage 8 leads to the virtue of wisdom. Wisdom helps people look back at their lives and feel a sense of completeness and closure, and its achievement depends on the degree to which earlier stages have been resolved positively.

As stated above, each stage builds on the previous one. If any stage is not mastered during the appropriate phase of life, the delay will affect future personality development. It is like an echo that is heard in stages to follow. An unresolved crisis will be more difficult to solve at a later stage.

ASSESSMENTS OF ERIKSON'S STAGES OF DEVELOPMENT

Many theorists and scientists acknowledge the strengths of Erikson's theory. Its focus on the entire life span sets it apart from earlier theories. The idea that one's ego and sense of identity are shaped over the life span was a big leap in Freudian thought.[126] It offers adults the chance to recognize the impact of—and therefore set out to compensate for—deprivations in their childhoods. And Erikson's influence has reached far beyond psychoanalysis, affecting the fields of child development and life-span studies, education, medicine, law, and the humanities.[127]

But Erikson has also attracted some criticism.[128]

To begin with, Erikson does not elaborate on the underlying reasons for a crisis occurring in a development phase. What actions and experiences make a person master or fail a phase? How can the level of success be measured?

It is also unclear what happens if people master stages early, or if they accomplish stage goals, but then something happens that undoes their work (divorce, redundancy, etc.). In the case of the latter, do people regress and have to complete the stage again?

In addition, Erikson's model does not apply across geographical and historical contexts. He includes cultural and societal influences on a person's development, such as employment, marriage, and family, yet he does not consider how such influences vary across geographies. The applicability of his model to non-Western cultures is therefore somewhat limited.

Nevertheless, Erikson's theory of psychosocial development under-

---

126 "Erik Erikson, 91, Psychoanalyst Who Reshaped Views of Human Growth, Dies," *The New York Times*, May 13, 1994, http://www.nytimes.com/books/99/08/22/specials/erikson-obit.html.

127 Ibid.

128 Ibid.

lines the strong impact that external factors, e.g., caregivers, can have on a person's development from childhood through adulthood. It suggests that a person's behavioral patterns are not set in stone. There are crucial building blocks that serve as stabilizers, but the development of personality continues throughout a person's life span. Later in the book, Erikson's theory will help us understand more about the origin of harmful behavior patterns such as hubris, lack of self-esteem, shame, or arrogance.

INFLUENCE OF CULTURE AND IMPLICATIONS FOR ORGANIZATIONS

Entrepreneur and author of *Winning Practices of a Free, Fit, and Prosperous People*, Mark Bitz states that culture has a different meaning to different people. He uses the metaphor of culture as a human software that serves as a secondary operating system that is layered onto the one based on instinct.[129]

Researchers[130] have found cross-cultural variations in the exact meanings and nature of emotions (see sidebar) such as shame, anger, and happiness. As analyzed by Niiya, Ellsworth, and Yamaguchi, there are even emotions that are unique to certain cultures, such as *amae* in Japan, *fago* in Ifaluk, and *lajya* in India.[131]

---

129 Mark Bitz, *Winning Practices of a Free, Fit, and Prosperous People* (Naples, FL: Flourish Books, 2019), 95.

130 Shinobu Kitayama, Hazel R. Markus, and Masaru Kurokawa, "Culture, Emotions, and Well-Being: Good Feelings in Japan and the United States," *Cognition and Emotion* 14, no. 1 (2000): 93–124; M. Boiger, E. Ceulemans, J. De Leersnyder, Y. Uchida, V. Norasakkunkit, and B. Mesquita, "Beyond Essentialism: Cultural Differences in Emotions Revisited," *Emotion* 18, no. 8 (2018): 1142–62; Hillary Anger Elfenbein, Manas K. Mandal, Nalini Ambady, Susumu Harizuka, and Surender Kumar, "Cross-Cultural Patterns in Emotion Recognition: Highlighting Design and Analytical Techniques," *Emotion* 2, no. 1 (2002): 79f.

131 Yu Niiya, Phoebe C. Ellsworth, and Susumu Yamaguchi, "Amae in Japan and the United States: An Exploration of a 'Culturally Unique' Emotion," *Emotion* 6, no. 2 (2006): 279, 291.

EMOTIONS VS. FEELINGS

Emotions and feelings are not interchangeable, although they share similar elements. Feelings are a conscious experience. Emotions, in contrast, manifest either consciously or subconsciously.[132]

For example, conflicting feelings can accompany an emotion (e.g., love can be both uplifting and painful), or feelings can be induced apart from the emotions (e.g., a drink can temporarily elevate the mood even though the person is sad). Also, the same feeling (e.g., rising blood pressure) can be related to different underlying emotions, such as joy or anger.[133]

Culture therefore can shape emotions and feelings that drive our actions, which can lead to misunderstandings between cross-cultural people or groups. The perception of oneself as independent or interdependent, for example, determines judgments and behavior. This is perhaps best illustrated in the notion of the Western "I-self" vs. the non-Western "We-self." The difference for the "I-self" and the "We-self" can be explained as follows:[134]

> In the West we conceptualize the self as an "I-self," an autonomous entity, the source of decisions, thoughts and actions. This self is separate from other selves [individuals]. In this society it is important to become independent, to assert the self, and to contend against other selves if necessary.[135]

> In Japan, and many other non-Western cultures [...] many commentators have described the self as a "We-self," deriving from connections

---

132 Neel Burton, "What's the Difference between a Feeling and an Emotion?" *Psychology Today*, December 19, 2014, https://www.psychologytoday.com/us/blog/hide-and-seek/201412/whats-the-difference-between-feeling-and-emotion.

133 Harold Anthony Lloyd, "Law and the Cognitive Nature of Emotion: A Brief Introduction," *Wake Forest Law Review* 54, no. 4 (2019).

134 Michael Lewis, "The Self in Self-Conscious Emotions," *Monographs of the Society for Research in Child Development* 57 (1992): 85–95. Kitayama, Markus, and Kurokawa, *Culture, Emotions and Well-Being*.

135 Keith Oatley and Jennifer M. Jenkins, *Understanding Emotions* (n.p.: Wiley, 1996), 42f.

to the family, colleagues, and the social group. It is important to fit in with other people and live in harmony with them.[136]

The former centers around autonomy, agency, assertiveness, competitiveness, and personal achievement; the latter, connectedness, cohesion, and collective gain. These contrasting ways of being are rooted in distinct social structures, e.g., individualist vs. collectivist.

Another axis of difference relates to "tight" social norms, which are inflexible and intolerant of deviance, vs. "loose" norms, which are more flexible and tolerant of diversity. There are also low-context vs. high-context behavioral norms (see the following section "Cultural Map"), which carry different expectations.[137]

In East Asia, for instance, behaviors are reportedly influenced by situations more so than in the US, where they tend to be influenced to a greater degree by emotions. Japanese culture is described as collectivist, tight, and nonverbal. Thus, psychoanalysis is not widely accepted there because it is perceived as immature to show emotions and feelings and even more so to talk about them. Society expects reserved and composed behavior.[138]

Kitayama, Markus, and Kurokawa conclude that assumptions that people are independent and motivated by personal interests, such as those inherent in principal-agent theory, often draw upon Western cultural perspectives. Thus, the cultural specificity of thoughts, feelings, and emotions needs to be considered in theories of not only social and individual psychology but also in theories of leadership, particularly in the cross-cultural context of an increasingly globalized world. Hence, in order to understand organizational conflict in

---

136 Ibid., 43.

137 David Livermore, *Customs of the World: Using Cultural Intelligence to Adapt, Wherever You Are* (Chantilly, VA: The Teaching Company, 2013): 74–80.

138 Shigeru Iwakabe, "Psychotherapy Integration in Japan," *Journal of Psychotherapy Integration* 18, no. 1 (2008): 103. Nangyeon Lim, "Cultural Differences in Emotion: Differences in Emotional Arousal Level between the East and the West," *Integrative Medicine Research* 5, no. 2 (2016): 107.

international businesses, it is important to examine the subjective experiences of people from different cultures and acknowledge their perspectives and the impact these have on their values and beliefs.[139]

For example, when talking about personality, identity, and leadership in a globalized world, it is difficult to define what is meant by a 'developed and mature personality.'

Developmental models such as Erikson's may not fully apply in non-Western contexts. This has implications for leadership training. When developing Japanese employees in the US, for example, should the coach encourage them to adapt to US culture, or should the coach take their own culture into account to benefit from its unique strengths and perhaps avoid dissonance amongst employees?

Bitz brings it to the point: "While many things are necessary to flourish, the overarching one is culture, one of the most potent and poorly understood forces on the planet. Like the air we breathe, its effects remain unnoticed until it fails."[140]

CULTURAL MAP

Erin Meyer[141] developed a cultural map consisting of eight scales that represent the behavior of executives where culture gaps are most prevalent:

1. **Communicating.** Ranging from *high-context* (sophisticated, nuanced, layered) to *low-context* (precise, simple, explicit).
2. **Evaluating.** Ranging from *direct negative feedback* (frank) to *indirect negative feedback* (political, diplomatic, tactful).
3. **Persuading.** Ranging from *principle first* (specific thinking, deductive argument, less focus on "how" and more on "why," conclusions

---

139 Kitayama, Markus, and Kurokawa, *Culture, Emotions and Well-Being.*

140 Bitz, Winning Practices of a Free, Fit, and Prosperous People, 95.

141 Erin Meyer, "Navigating the Cultural Minefield," *Harvard Business Review* 92, no. 5 (2014): 119–23.

based on facts, preferred by southern Europeans, French, Germans, Russians) to *application first* (holistic thinking, inductive argument, more focus on "how," conclusions based on observations, preferred by British and Americans).

4. **Leading.** Measures degree of respect for authority figures, ranging from *egalitarian* to *hierarchical*; based on Hofstede's concept of power distance.

5. **Deciding.** Measures level of consensus-mindedness, ranging from *consensual* to *top-down*. Against common presumptions, the most egalitarian cultures are not necessarily the most democratic, and the hierarchical cultures may seek agreement first.

6. **Trusting.** Ranging from *task-based* (from the head: trust built through work, cognitive) to *relationship-based* (from the heart: trust as a consequence of affective connection).

7. **Disagreeing.** Assesses the level of tolerance and productivity of open disagreement, ranging from *confrontational* to *avoids confrontation*.

8. **Scheduling.** Measures value placed in a structured vs. flexible way, ranging from *linear time* (adherence to schedule) to *flexible time* (schedule as suggestion).

The scales do not measure behavior in absolute terms but patterns between different groups respective to one another. For example, in American and French cultures, both tend to be high-context, but the French culture produces more direct feedback givers. Mexican and Spanish cultures are on the same context level, but the Mexican culture produces more indirect (less frank) feedback givers. It is important for leaders to manage across the map.

Even with the help of the cultural map, it can be quite challenging to bridge the cultural gap. This is why Meyer herself adds four rules to follow:

1. Challenges should not be underestimated—leadership styles have been developed over a longtime period and are difficult to change.

2. Application of multiple perspectives is key—look through different cultural lenses on a specific culture and manage across the map.

3. Positive elements can be found in other approaches—a new environment can foster discomfort, confusion, and inefficiency, but these differences could become a team's or company's biggest asset.
4. Globalization leads to more diverse and dispersed teams which requires adaptability. Leaders need to adjust and readjust their own style to widen their comfort zone and move more swiftly back and forth along all eight dimensions.

The theory described here relates to the "good conflicts" discussed in chapter 7, "Crucial Leadership Skills (and How to Develop Them)." Leading across the culture map and breaking through stereotypes can trigger good conflicts that encourage fresh thinking, new questions, open-mindedness and flexibility. This leads to better leadership/staff development and a work culture of inclusion, teamwork, creativity, and innovation that opens a variety of new pathways to ultimately improve business performance.

CHAPTER 5

KEY DRIVER THREE

LEADERSHIP AS AN ACCELERATOR

To summarize the key drivers of negative outcomes, the first is change, which involves the impacts of change (of ownership/management, organizational, or legal structure) on ownership, management, strategy, and/or corporate governance, and the associated shifts in power balance. The second key driver is the "human element" which relates to the origins and development of our personalities and how they shape values, thoughts, feelings, actions, and interactions with others.

Leadership, and (or because of) the power that comes with it, is the third key driver that can contribute to conflict emergence, even serving as an accelerator to it.

This chapter sheds light on different aspects that play key roles within leadership in further explaining reasons for derailment in business. Firstly, it highlights the commonalities, flaws, and challenges among different leadership theories, definitions, and styles, and describes the complexity involved in the selection, development, and performance measure of leaders. Secondly, it shows how precondition and upbringing influence how people strive for and deal with power and the potential loss of it. In Kets de Vries' words: "Leadership is the exercise of power, and the quality of leadership—good, ineffective, or destructive—depends on an individual's ability to execute power."[142] This speaks to the prevalent irrational side of the supposedly rational business world.

Thirdly, because dysfunction of disposition can override valuable skills, this chapter discusses in greater detail the so-called dark side of leadership, which sheds light on the consequences of increased pressure on leaders. It speaks to the irrational and unproductive behavior triggered by fear, guilt, and compassion that can lead to overdrive and excesses. Statistics show that the estimated percentage of senior executives showing at least one shadow-side trait, the number of managers rated as bad by their employees and the embedded risk of high-potential for derailment, are all astonishingly high. The chapter also touches on common pathologies and extreme types such as narcissism, hubris, sociopathy, and psychopathy.

COMMONALITIES OF LEADERSHIP THEORIES

Early leadership concepts such as Great Man Theory and Trait Theory focused mainly on leaders' presumably innate characteristics and behaviors. Approaches such as situational leadership and servant leadership focused on what leaders do instead of on the traits they possess.[143]

In 1978, a pivotal leadership study by Burns shed light from a different angle. He combined different concepts from the fields of political science and personality theory and therefore reached a more holistic view of leadership. His study served as a catalyst for other researchers in

---

142 Manfred F. R. Kets de Vries, *Leaders, Fools and Impostors*, rev. ed. (Lincoln, NE: iUniverse, 2003), 20.

143 Tanya Robertson, "Leadership Theory vs. Leadership Style," *Houston Chronicle*, accessed November 15, 2017, http://smallbusiness.chron.com/leadership-theory-vs-leadership-style-32967.html.

bringing the leader back into the leadership study. A newly awakened interest in watching the leader in action emerged.[144]

(For an overview of the history of leadership and leadership theories, definitions and styles, and of followership and leader-follower interactions and theories, see appendix 6.)

Comparing and contrasting the many different leadership approaches and various attempts by different researchers to classify and/or synthesize them, Kilburg and Donohue came up with some generalizations on the concept of leadership and the state of leadership theory:[145]

- Leadership is complex: due to the complexity of the human element, individual and group behavior cannot easily be predicted when assessing and developing organizations.
- Leadership can be expressed by anyone who participates in the system. Leadership is strongly dependent on leaders', followers', and other stakeholders' personal characteristics and capabilities. But traits and characteristics are not the only element that counts toward the success of a leader. Most theories, particularly the more recent ones, see leadership as being influenced by a combination of thoughts, feelings, behaviors, personal knowledge, skills, abilities, attitudes, values, ethics, beliefs, virtues, vices, history, and capabilities.
- The external environment is viewed by most as having an impact on performance, whether it results in success or failure.

Typologies of leadership can be useful for forming concepts and structuring prevalent trends in leadership research and for creating comparison criteria for different cases. However, they generalize and therefore limit the focus on individual in-depth analysis. Hence, discussion of leadership behavior and actions, and attempts to capture

---

144 Manfred F. R. Kets de Vries, "The Organizational Fool: Balancing a Leader's Hubris," *Human Relations* 43, no. 8 (1990): 755.

145 Richard R. Kilburg and Marc D. Donohue, "Toward a 'Grand Unifying Theory' of Leadership: Implications for Consulting Psychology," *Consulting Psychology Journal* 63, no. 1 (2011): 14.

their complexity, should contemplate how traits and characteristics of leaders are reflected in familiar behavior patterns and how the consequences of associated dysfunctions impact organizations.

It is very challenging to translate research outcomes into leadership models in order for them to be effective and easily understood. Historic models could not anticipate the effects of the fast-changing world and evolving interactions between leaders and followers.[146]

Over the past century, leadership studies have tended to utilize quantitative methodologies. Recently, this focus seems to have shifted toward qualitative and mixed-method approaches. Such approaches have enabled deeper exploration of the complex phenomena at play. Mysteries currently being unraveled include whether leaders are born or made, how relationships between leaders and their teams affect the former's performance, where the fine line is between the success and failure of charismatic leaders, how performance of individuals and groups is impacted by leading through technology.[147]

The following points can be summarized on leadership in organizations: the topic is highly complex and dynamic; the development of leadership research shows a strong tendency toward a more holistic approach; increasingly positive aspects have found their way into literature; the facts that (a) leadership is increasingly shared and (b) subordinates and other stakeholders belong to the complex systems that have become widely acknowledged.

FLAWS, CHALLENGES AND WARNING SIGNS OF LEADERSHIP APPROACHES

Many leadership approaches and theories have limited their focus to processes, procedures, rules, and abstract models, or on traits, skills,

---

146 Ibid., 13.

147 Bruce Avolio, Fred O. Walumbwa, and Todd J. Weber, "Leadership: Current Theories, Research, and Future Directions," *Annual Review of Psychology* 60 (2009): 442.

and outcomes. Thus, they have not (or have only superficially) discussed questions around the following:

Flaws, a holistic and unifying framework, today's challenges and new requirements, and with them the comprehensiveness that informs the dynamic context in which leaders are selected and measured, a clear and concise definition of leadership and of "the right/real" leader. Hence, attempts will now be made to elaborate on and discuss these aspects.

NO HOLISTIC, UNIFYING MODEL

Millions of books and articles have been published on the topic of leadership, and in May 2020, Google showed 4.7 billion web pages for the word "leadership." It is challenging to find a clear, precise, and rigorous definition that manages to grasp the essence of the concept.

In his studies on leadership from 1900 onward, Rost found that interdisciplinary approaches on leadership did not evolve until the 1980s. Earlier works focused on leadership of/in education, the military, and business. As a result, the vast body of literature on the topic is somewhat disconnected. For example, various terms and models stemming from different disciplines appear to describe and account for the same phenomena. Rost describes the following three main issues that limit or prevent the further development of leadership theories, approaches, and models:[148]

1. Most literature focuses on traits, skills, and outcomes but foregoes the definition and purpose of leadership. In addition, existing literature emphasizes the content rather than the process of leadership or dynamic relationships among stakeholders.
2. As a result of the lack of a clear and precise definition of leadership, many different views and opinions exist, yet there are no criteria on how to compare and contrast them.

---

148 Erik De Haan, "The Leadership Shadow: How to Recognise and Avoid Derailment, Hubris and Overdrive," *Leadership* (2015): 3.

3. Consequently, an integrated domain or profession of leadership is missing.

Each model that has been developed, regardless of the discipline from which it emerged, strongly contributes to the overall understanding of leadership. The development of a holistic scheme that could hold all the bits together would require a long list of elements, such as the unexpected macroscopic behavior of the model, complexity of the human system, or diverse characteristics of members of organizational systems.[149]

The various models and theories of leadership are undoubtedly helpful in starting a discourse on leadership beliefs, values, and practices. Some, however, argue that much of the knowledge on leadership is overly reductionist, having been generated using a scientific approach, hence the turn to qualitative and mixed-method approaches in recent years. This change in approach might facilitate the development of a more holistic and unifying framework.[150]

According to Kilburg and Donohue, a model that would account for a more integrated and integrative approach could be phrased as:

> Leadership is a complex, multidimensional, emergent process in which the leader(s), follower(s), and other formal and informal stakeholders in a human enterprise use their characteristics, capabilities, thoughts, feelings, and behaviors to create mutually influencing relationships that enable them to co-evolve strategies, tactics, structures, processes, directions, and other methods of building and managing human enterprises with the goal of producing adaptive success in their chosen niche(s) in the competitive, evaluative, and evolving global ecology of organizations."[151]

---

149 Kilburg and Donohue, "Toward a 'Grand Unifying Theory' of Leadership," 13f.

150 Ibid., 14.

151 Ibid., 15.

This definition spans a wide range of aspects such as the external environment, situations, personal traits, characteristics, abilities, capabilities, emotions, feelings, thoughts, and behaviors of all parties involved; relationships; the complex organization system including structures, procedures, processes, contents, and structures; and performance.[152] Because leadership is vital to people and organizations, it is important to develop a grand unifying leadership theory.[153]

NO DISTINCT MEASURE OF THE LEADER'S INFLUENCE ON ORGANIZATIONAL PERFORMANCE

It is common that leaders are looked at to explain the performance of organizations, since they are the ones in charge and responsible, holding the power and authority that come with the title. At the same time, just as it is difficult to attribute success or failure in a sporting match to the team's leader alone, in business, it would seem unreasonable to claim that the price of a traded stock can be solely attributed to the present leadership. Many other stakeholders will have played their parts, as well as structural and environmental factors. Regardless, it is all too easy to draw a direct conclusion and celebrate or blame the leader at the top company level, despite the impossibility of tracing a pure, causal chain from the leader's behavior to the specific outcome.[154] (See also chapter 8, "Detecting and Avoiding Danger," in the subsection "Assess Current and Future Leaders More Thoroughly.")

Challenges and Warning Signs for Traditional Leadership Selection Criteria and Methods

The selection of the right leaders is one of the most important tasks of the shareholders (with respect to new board members via the GA) and of the BoD (with respect to the CEO). Since the CEO selection

---

152 Ibid., 15.

153 Ghoshal, "Bad Management Theories," 87; Kilburg and Donohue, "Toward a 'Grand Unifying Theory' of Leadership," 6–26.

154 Kilburg and Donohue, "Toward a 'Grand Unifying Theory' of Leadership," 17.

process is led by the BoD, it is rather straightforward although challenging. Selecting directors, however, is more differentiated.

The control over the director selection process can lie either with the shareholders (in cases where ownership is concentrated so that the shareholder or a group of shareholders control the GA) or with the BoD, which presents new candidates to the GA for election in cases of a more widely dispersed ownership. A CEO's impact on a company can be significant as they hold the most power due to their control of information and operations. In any case, the recruiting process of both directors and CEOs is key and it needs to be thorough, rigorous, well-planned, well-executed, and defensible.[155]

As mentioned, the goal is to select the right leader, but it is difficult to distinguish between a "right" leader and a "wrong" one. A real leader can be described as someone who has integrity, who generates meaning and builds trust, and who lives and communicates values. Such leaders energize their subordinates and move the human heart. This raises a number of challenges.[156] A lot of businesspeople are ill at ease when discussions turn to social skills such as moving hearts. Moreover, how can such skills be measured?

Not seldom, in practice, BoDs are not adept at evaluating the current CEO or at selecting a potential successor and can shy away from this difficult task. A study conducted in 2013 by Larcker, Miles, and Tayan, from the Miles Group and the Rock Center for Corporate Governance, discovered that evaluations of CEOs' performance tend to focus on financial performance, such as operating and stock price results and accounting. Nonfinancial metrics such as customer service, employee satisfaction, innovation, or talent discovery and development play a rather minor role in comparison to financial evaluation criteria,

---

155 Jay W. Lorsch and Rakesh Khurana, "Changing Leaders: The Board's Role in CEO Succession," *Harvard Business Review* 77 (1999): 2.

156 Warren Bennis and James O'Toole, "Don't Hire the Wrong CEO," *Harvard Business Review* 78 (2000): 171.

although their positive correlation with the long-term success of organizations have been proven.[157]

Larcker et al. further state that more than 20 percent of directors admit that they only moderately or marginally understand the strengths and weaknesses of their current CEO. In addition, BoDs generally lack the skills required to evaluate potential candidates for the CEO role. With an external candidate, the focus lies on the financial track record and perceived leadership qualities and much less on how the candidate's prior company and the current company might differ in operating conditions, or how the candidate's leadership style can take root in a new environment. Along the same lines, it might be even more difficult to evaluate an internal candidate who is untested or unproven as a CEO.

Consequently, the BoD tends to take a rearview-mirror approach and look for easily measurable elements—facts and figures such as past financial performance, stock price increases, or cost cutting,[158] along with education and technical or functional proficiencies.

Skills that are rather easy to measure are important but not comprehensive in a selection process. Presumably, many leaders pass measurable skills tests (e.g., psychometric tests; see sidebar), yet many if not most fail to become "real" leaders once they are in power. Structural factors relating to industry issues or the financial landscape may well play a part, but this does not explain why other leaders succeed in such climates. Hard-to-measure social skills (although widely used but often only to feel good about showing a focus on the human element without needing to go into detail), for example, are fundamental. But also, context matters. A company's context needs to be thoroughly and critically analyzed. Special challenges/circumstances (e.g., turnaround situations, product development, cost cutting) call for different weightings of necessary skills.

---

157 David Larcker, Stephen Miles, and Brian Tayan, "Seven Myths of CEO Succession," *Stanford Closer Look Series*, 2014, 3.

158 Ibid., 3f.

One way to better understand what makes people behave in unpredictable or negative ways once they assume leadership, and with it power, is to analyze and understand different personalities, their recurring patterns, and their origins. Thus, although it has gained importance and momentum in the recent past, a further flaw of even current leadership models still is a lack of or insufficient acknowledgment of the influence of nurture such as upbringing.

PSYCHOMETRIC TESTS

Origins of testing for proficiency go back to 2200 BC, when the Chinese emperor used tests to assess government officials' fitness for office.[159] Psychometrics as a science started in Cambridge between 1886 and 1889. The first laboratory dedicated to the subject was set up by James McKeen Cattell. He saw synergies between psychophysics of Wilhelm Wundt (who's first assistant he was) and Sir Francis Galton's mathematical approach to the examination of individual differences and their distribution.[160]

Many researchers have further developed and helped raise psychometric tests since.

WHAT IS A PSYCHOMETRIC TEST?

Psychometric tests are a standard and scientific method that is applied to measure the mental capabilities and behavioral style of human beings. These tests are designed to determine whether a candidate is suitable for a specific role based on the requested personality characteristics and cognitive abilities (aptitude). Psychometric tests identify the extent to which a candidate's personality

---

159 C. Eugene Walker, *Clinical Psychology: Historical and Research Foundations* (New York: Springer, 2013).

160 John Rust, "Psychometrics 1889," Cambridge Judge Business School at the University of Cambridge, https://www. psychometrics.cam.ac.uk/about-us/our-history/first-psychometric-laboratory.

and aptitude are in line with those required for the role.[161] Their goal is to understand a candidate's unique personality style and how he or she will behave and influence others within a context (e.g., in a company and with others).

There's a lot of diverse, also opposing, literature, research, and data on psychometric tests, and it is not easy to get a clear overview. There is no such thing as "the" or "a" psychometric test.

There are intelligence tests (assess intelligence), aptitude tests (assess capability), achievement tests (assess degree of accomplishment), creativity tests (assess capacity for novelty), personality tests (assess traits), interest inventories (assess preferences for activities), behavioral tests (measure behaviors and their consequences), neuropsychological tests (measure cognitive, sensory, perceptual, or motor functions). Five Factor Model and Dark Triad (discussed earlier in this chapter in the, in the subsection "The Dark Side of Leadership") also fall into the category of psychometric tests.[162]

Psychometric tests are predominantly applied by large companies. Data suggests that over three-quarters of *The Times* Best Companies to Work For and 80 percent of Fortune 500 firms use psychometric tests.[163]

Are they the right means to identify leadership and derailment potential? This question arises because although these tests have existed for almost 150 years and have been continuously developed, there still are many leadership-related scandals and excesses caused by derailment of individuals. A closer look to the advantages and disadvantages of psychometric tests helps the analysis.

---

161 "What Are Psychometric Tests?" Institute of Psychometric Coaching, https://www.psychometricinstitute.com.au/psychometric-guide/introduction_to_psychometric_tests.html.

162 Adrian Furnham, "Current Development in Psychometric Tests," *European Business Review*, September 20, 2019, https://www.europeanbusinessreview.com/current-development-in-psychometric-tests/.

163 Katie Jacobs, "Is Psychometric Testing Still Fit for Purpose?" People Management, February 22, 2018, https://www.peoplemanagement.co.uk/long-reads/articles/psychometric-testing-fit-purpose.

Advantages:

- Tests provide quantitative data on temperament and ability which helps compare and contrast candidates with regard to the same criteria.
- They are scientific instruments and are based on theoretical foundations.
- They are comprehensive and are embracing the basic features of ability and personality that lay the foundation for variety in behavioral patterns.
- They don't allow for corruption, favoritism, and bias.
- The data is in the system and can be reexamined in the future (accuracy of predictability).
- They mitigate biases.
- They draw on a large amount of information in a short period of time.
- They increase objectivity.
- They are a supporting tool to help detect and/or prevent derailment.

Disadvantages:

- Candidate's potential lack of self-awareness and therefore inability to give an answer won't best reflect the candidate's true feelings.
- Irrationality of behavior during the test: a candidate's bad mood or condition of test anxiety can harm their performance in an unexpected way.
- The test questions may not be read or understood correctly, which harms the quality and accuracy of the answer.
- Some candidates know how to intentionally sabotage the process itself (giving unrelated or meaningless answers) or the outcome (creating a false impression). This is true for personality tests, not for intelligence or aptitude tests.
- The outcome of the tests may leave room for misinterpretations by (although trained) third parties.

- It might be too expensive to conduct the test, even more so when often and widely applied.
- Overreliance on such tests.
- Temptation to oversimplify since human beings are complex.

Aside from a list of researchers that don't believe in the benefit of psychometric tests, there is a long list of researchers who see advantages of such tests but add that they are not sufficient in isolation.[164] The author of this book shares this opinion.

If a company intends to use psychometric tests to determine and measure a candidate's leadership potential, it should combine these tests with a series of interviews, assessments, role-play exercises, meetings with owners and/or BoD, and reference checks after having looked at the candidate's background and track record, all of which will help provide a more comprehensive picture of a person's competencies, values, personality traits, and intelligence and help answer questions related to forward-thinking, teamwork, and inspiration. But the key to testing, identifying, and evaluating candidates is a constant communication stream between the recruiters and the candidates. In addition, what's called "chemistry" is something that can't be measured with any test, including transference and countertransferences.

Hence, psychometric tests are helpful, but their results should be interpreted with caution and in context, and they should certainly not serve as a replacement for personal judgment. The recruiter (owner, BoD, even CEO) will always first need to critically analyze the candidate's role in question, the business context, and the working environment, and then identify the ideal candidate's skills and personality traits. In doing so, it is key that they keep practicing, which means leveraging their own experience and skills and learning to trust their intuition so that they can spot, develop, or exit people

---

164 Eugene F. McKenna, *Business Psychology and Organisational Behaviour: A Student's Handbook* (Philadelphia: Psychology Press, 2000), 45–47.

who might derail early and develop those with great potential, all of which improve business performance and agility.

This is why such recruiting and selection processes need time and resources, not least because the directors (especially the chairperson) need to spend time with the CEO (candidate). The process should not be sped up just because a candidate scored remarkably well in a test. Trust and trust building matter at the very beginning of a relationship.

As the previous chapters have shown, there is no formula for the attributes of a leader and leadership. Developing leadership and leaders is a journey. Human beings are rational and the world is in a flux. The approach of psychometric testing toward human behavior is rather absolute and rational.

Looking forward, the advancement in technology (AI, gamification) will make psychometric tests more sophisticated and accurate. This should never let owners and BoDs stop using their intuition (which gets better with practice) or not get to know a candidate in person to build trust. Psychometric tests need to be context-dependent and be used to inform decision-making, not to make a decision.

In the words of Fiona Knight, senior leadership specialist at Russell Reynolds, "Psychometrics is not an exact science, it's a social one [...] gives you evidence, but you have to look at other areas too. It can pull you back to your objectivity and strengthen your decision, but it can't make the decision for you."[165]

ROLE OF POWER IN LEADERSHIP

An important aspect of leadership and one that brings out the good, the bad, and the ugly in people is power. This section draws on Man-

---

165 Jacobs, "Is Psychometric Testing Still Fit for Purpose?"

fred Kets de Vries's description of the influence of power,[166] which strongly overlaps with numerous researchers. Kets de Vries is a professor of leadership and organizational change at INSEAD, a management scholar, a psychoanalyst, and a multiple bestselling author.

Power often triggers contradictory, uneasy, and suspicious feelings with regard to how it is received or executed, which touches on human beings' basic dilemma: strong or weak, leading or following, controlling or submissive. Humans use or abuse power from the moment they are born. Survival instincts and the way a sense of self can grow and develop are related to the experience and perception of power by others (e.g., parents, and by ourselves, toward others).

A childhood experience of imbalance between nurturing and helplessness may trigger a feeling of psychological injury. Excessive frustration experienced from the environment (a way of coping with discipline) increases the child's natural sense of impotence. Common reactions can be rage, vengeance, desire for personal power, and imaginary ideas of omnipotence. This is a lifelong pattern unless it is resolved when the person is growing up. Otherwise, it might have a fatal impact if the person assumes a leadership position and learns to play and enjoy the power game.

Such leaders who have suffered psychological injury in childhood are convinced that general codes of conduct do not apply to them. They believe they are selected for good reason and legitimately have privileges. These beliefs of omnipotence stem from covering their helplessness.

Power is a drug whose stimulating and life-sustaining effects can lead to addiction. Since leaders with power have worked hard and long to get into a powerful position, they are often unwilling to release it.

The scope of power can range from positive to catastrophic. This

---

166 Ibid., 15–30.

makes power an ambivalent and impactful variable in the area of human aspirations.

Letting go of power is difficult. Powerful positions trigger good feelings that come with public admiration and recognition. This is one reason why many leaders who have reached the top do not let go of power, despite feelings of dissatisfaction with their performance, loneliness, isolation, emptiness, and lack of purpose. They also may not know what to do, to reach for next, and may lack a clear direction or goal. Kets de Vries calls this state "the CEO blues," which occur as a result of having executed and enjoyed power for too long. There is an advantage for people who take on leadership positions later in life as their timeline is somewhat limited, which decreases the chances of experiencing these feelings.

Most often, letting go of power is difficult due to a sense of loss: loss of vitality, work, status, recognition, admiration, prestige, influence, health, sense, or contact. The loneliness, emptiness, and depression that leaders fear as a result of loss of power is often intensified by the isolation of their powerful positions. The potential feeling of turning from hero to nobody from one day to the next triggers a tremendous degree of anxiety. These fears are closely related to the losses already experienced on the way to the top. They have already made huge sacrifices to obtain power, relating to family, friends, spouses, health, and self-interests. Hanging on to power helps prevent or prolong such painful realities.

Psychological and emotional factors play a much bigger role than just financial or social ones. Why? Because of the timing of aging. Aging starts to be felt in the phase of life at which a person reaches a powerful leadership position. Realizing that time is finite triggers fear of death.

Leaders need to look the truth in the eye and overcome the unconscious illusion of immortality. At top leadership levels, the increased presence of narcissism and hubris—combining predisposition with power—entails a bigger psychological reaction to decline than at other levels of the hierarchy.

"The key to immortality is first living a life worth remembering."

—BRUCE LEE

INFLUENCE OF UPBRINGING ON LEADERSHIP AND IMPLICATIONS FOR LEADERSHIP SELECTION

What are the qualities and skills beyond the common, measurable ones that play a fundamental role in the way power is used? These qualities may seem to be difficult if not impossible to assess/predict.[167]

Therefore, it is important to look further back at the life of the candidate. Although human beings strive for happiness and fulfillment (Diener and Tay's revised Maslow model intends to find a balance between the striving for happiness as the end goal and the fulfillment of both personal and social goals to reach it),[168] they sometimes behave in very odd ways resulting from the impact of their upbringing on how they deal with authority and power.

The recruiting party (e.g., BoD or owner), must learn how to identify the leader's strengths and weaknesses that go beyond the basic analysis. It is crucial to first critically analyze the position in question, the context and the working environment, and then to identify the ideal candidate's skills and personality traits in order to spot the candidates who possess them.

Organizational outcomes and leadership performance are impacted by the characteristics and patterns of people's behaviors. It is expected that good leaders understand the needs, desires, hopes, and abilities of their subordinates. Further, they need to convince them to buy into their vision for the organization. Leaders must take action, communicate their expectations, and bear responsibility for those.

---

167 Lorsch and Khurana, "Changing Leaders," 5ff.

168 Hans Villarica, "Maslow 2.0: A New and Improved Recipe for Happiness," *The Atlantic*, August 17, 2011, https://www.theatlantic.com/health/archive/2011/08/maslow-20-a-new-and-improved-recipe-for-happiness/243486/#.TkvKIRv8USE.facebook.

Bad leadership is more than a lack of common skills, such as technical, cognitive, and strategic ones. The dysfunction of disposition can override these valuable skills. A leader's dysfunctionality, for instance, a lack of sensitivity and empathy or a tendency to micromanage, creates substantial harm to people and companies. As many as 65–75 percent of managers are rated as "bad" by their employees. On top of that, almost 30 percent of "high potentials" have an embedded risk for derailment.[169] This statistic is quite alarming.

It is a myth that the only thing that matters is what is known or what can be seen (the conscious). But this view is held up by the collective unconscious of the business world, despite its proven insufficiency to resolve complex issues that occur in organizations. Most businesspeople do not like to regard people in organizations as being subject to both conscious and unconscious wishes, fantasies, fears, anxieties, and conflicts. Instead, they prefer to understand them as conscious beings with simple drivers.[170]

People often find it hard to accept or appreciate the value of concepts applied to business that result from fields like psychology. Such explanations of humanity ask for different means of verification compared to empirical science, and this can be a challenging concept for people accustomed to relying on facts and figures. Paradoxically, people tend to consciously deny the presence of unconscious processes but constantly live out such processes via their behaviors and actions.

THE CLINICAL PARADIGM AND PSYCHODYNAMIC VIEW

The connecting piece between the apparent certainties of hard science and ambiguities of the unconscious mind is a conceptual framework created by Kets de Vries, called the "clinical paradigm."[171] This framework not only acknowledges but focuses on the human element.

---

169 Eric Nelson and Robert Hogan, "Coaching on the Dark Side," *International Coaching Psychology Review* 4, no. 1 (2009): 7.

170 Kets de Vries, *The Leader on the Couch*, 2f.

171 Ibid., 2–6.

Recognition of the value of work within this paradigm is crucial because organizations and social processes are made up of and influenced by human beings. Even in large groups, people behave according to laws that cannot be tested experimentally. In addition, abnormal behavior is more normal than most people think or want to admit.

Do executives truly behave logically? Is management a rational task carried out by rational individuals with a focus on organizational goals? Past and present conflicts and scandals resulting from destructive behaviors by leaders in business and politics around the world suggest not. It is therefore crucial to understand the underlying mental activity and behavior of such people.

Everybody, even the most successful business leader, is capable of behavior that is highly irrational. Too many well-thought-out and well-meant plans go off the rails in business because of unconscious factors that influence behavior. Yet, in order to change this, the techniques applied often focus on the rational side of behavior. The emotional side gets neglected.

The field of psychoanalysis has been frequently and successfully applied in exploring the meaning of human events. Its methods of investigation involve taking people's pasts into account. Hence, the psychodynamic approach provides a feasible way of analyzing the hidden dynamics of organizations by attempting to make sense of executives' deeper wishes and fantasies, and to demonstrate how these influence behaviors at work. Central to this approach is the concept of the *unconscious*.

(Although the notion has existed for thousands of years, both of the terms "subconscious" and "unconscious mind" are linked with Freud and psychoanalysis.)[172]

---

172   Michael C. Miller, "Unconscious or Subconscious?" *Harvard Health Blog*, Harvard Health Publications, August 1, 2010, http://www.health.harvard.edu/blog/unconscious-or-subconscious-20100801255.

Sigmund Freud (1856–1939), an Austrian neurologist, depth psychologist, and cultural theorist, invented psychoanalysis, a method that helps analysts cure patients by making (repressed) unconscious thoughts, motivations, and conflicts that are based on dreams and fantasies conscious.[173]

Freud was the first to describe unconscious functioning in a systematic way. His focus lay with the process of oppression, which describes distressed and unwanted thoughts and emotions that are intentionally forgotten or forbidden to get access to the consciousness. Yet they are not forgotten because they continue to influence the person without him/her being aware of it. For psychoanalysts, the conscious forms only the tip of the iceberg of the mind. Freud knew that the unconscious was more than just a storehouse for the unwanted thoughts and the associated emotions and thus contains inherited tendencies and ego processes.[174]

Carl Gustav Jung (1875–1961), a Swiss psychiatrist and founder of analytical psychology, called the unconscious the "second psychic system." Each individual shares the same collective, universal, and impersonal nature. This so-called collective unconscious is inherited and can therefore not be developed individually. It only becomes conscious secondarily.[175]

Freud's theories were influenced by others and range from the Oedipus complex to the importance of dreams to psychic energy. His theories were widely admired and accepted but also fiercely criticized. Whether one agrees with him or not, his influence on the discipline of psychology has been undeniably significant.[176]

---

173 Ibid.

174 Susan Long and Maurita Harney, "Socioanalytic Interviewing," in *Socioanalytic Methods: Discovering the Hidden in Organisations and Social Systems* (London: Karnac Books, 2013), 5.

175 Ibid., 9.

176 Saul McLeod, "Psychoanalysis," *SimplyPsychology*, accessed February 27, 2017, http://www.simplypsychology.org/psychoanalysis.html.

It was Freud's goal to describe the origins of mental disorders and find ways to treat them. He was convinced that the hidden (unconscious) contents of people's minds caused these disorders. Freud used the terms *subconscious* and *unconscious* interchangeably but used the term *unconscious* more often. Other literature that speaks about the mind and its functioning (e.g., neuroscience, psychiatry, and psychology) also prefers the term *unconscious*.[177]

In contrast to psychoanalysts, neuroscientists have trouble dealing with the unconscious as a place (as it implies). There is no such place in anatomy. Freud was a neurologist and was thinking in the context of neurobiology. Apparently, he did not have the machines and tools that are available today in order to locate and analyze the complex functioning of cells in the brain region.[178]

Today, when psychoanalysts and therapists use the term *unconscious*, they associate it with a complex but well-known psychological phenomenon. Neuroscientists accept the use of this term because they agree that the understanding of mental content must go further than just thoughts and emotions.[179]

This book uses the term *unconscious* as described above. It assumes that a lot that goes on within people is beyond their control. Increased awareness of this, it is argued, will enhance self-control, self-management, effective leadership, and well-being.

The sophistication of psychoanalytic theory has increased. Today, it includes discoveries from fields such as anthropology, neurophysiology, cognitive psychology, family systems theory, dynamic psychiatry, developmental psychology, and individual and group psychotherapy. Although some elements of Freud's theories no longer hold true in regard to new information about the functioning of the mind, core

---

177 Miller, "Unconscious or Subconscious?"

178 Ibid.

179 Ibid.

aspects of psychoanalytic theory have been scientifically and empirically tested and verified. To consider today's psychoanalytic theory as overtaken is like attacking modern physics because Newton did not know of and hence did not understand Einstein's theory of relativity.[180]

It is important that leaders detect their own and their subordinates' cognitive and affective distortions to recognize how unconscious fantasies and behaviors that are outside of awareness influence decision-making and management processes. Although Freud did not directly observe how his theories and ideas could be applied to business, some of his followers such as Klein, Bion, and Winnicott did.

A psychodynamic view can help shed light on the hidden organizational dynamics linked to individual motivation, leadership, collusions, social defenses, "neurotic" organizations (marked by particular neurosis of top-level executives), or toxic cultures, as well as the degree to which people and organizations can become prisoners of their own past.[181]

Proponents of the clinical paradigm acknowledge the limitations of rationality and dismiss a purely economic, behaviorist view of the business world. Management scholars might want to recognize that organizations are systems that have their own conscious, unconscious, rational, and irrational lives. The clinical paradigm described below plays a crucial role in shedding light on the underlying sources of the behavior and actions of leaders and followers. Since the first step toward psychological well-being is psychological awareness, organizations cannot function well and be successful if the irrationality of leaders' and followers' inner theatres is not considered by those at the top.[182]

---

180 Kets de Vries, *The Leader on the Couch*, 6.

181 Ibid., 7.

182 Ibid., 8.

The underpinnings of the clinical paradigm are based on four premises:[183]

1. All behavior has an explanation, which means there is a rationale behind every (rational and irrational) human behavior and action. To put meaning behind apparently irrational behavior calls for not only detective work but also a high degree of emotional intelligence.
2. A large part of the mental world (thoughts, emotions, feelings, motives) is out of awareness. Very often, people do not realize what they do and—even less so—why they do it. Since people's conscious realities are influenced by their unconscious thinking, people who are not aware of their dysfunctions cannot assume responsibility for them.
3. The way people regulate their emotions determines who they are. Emotions and cognition define behavior. Patterns of emotions, thoughts, and behavior shape personality. The way infants emotionally react is mainly biological and linked with the fundamental human need systems (see the following section, "The Inner Theatre"). However, socialization starts early on through the reactions of primary caregivers. As mentioned in chapter 4, "Key Driver Two: The Human Element as a Root Cause," each individual is born with a certain temperament. This temperament, however, offers only a predisposition to certain emotions. The regulation of emotions becomes integral to each person once they reach adulthood. When people are able to become aware of their emotions, they intensify contact with themselves. Daily life shows that some people are more able to show emotions appropriately and comfortably than others who have difficulty finding words for them.
4. The human development process occurs at an interpersonal and intrapersonal level. Each individual is a product of his or her past, and forever influenced by the developmental experiences provided by caregivers. This is why experiences during childhood are crucial for the development of the personality, especially how people

183 Ibid., 9–11.

form and handle relationships. These experiences lead to preferred response patterns that tend to become repetitive.

THE INNER THEATRE

"Man stands in his own shadow and wonders why it's dark."

—ZEN PROVERB

Each person has an "inner theatre," a program that is incorporated from both nature and nurture. Although everybody has an inner theatre, the focus here is on the inner world of executives in particular. The inner theatre is a product of genetic inheritance and childhood experience. The interplay between the two leads to highly complex motivational need systems that define a person's unique inner theatre. And the interface of these needs with external factors (caregivers, siblings, teachers, and other significant persons) determines a person's uniqueness. Each individual carries these mental schemas (a product of the mentioned interplay) throughout life.[184]

There are three influencing and regulating factors that determine how important each need system is for an individual: inborn and learned response patterns, the role of primary caregivers, and the degree to which someone tries to recall and adopt positive emotional states experienced during childhood. The most basic need system is the one that deals with an individual's physiological needs, such as food, drink, sleep, and breathing. Another system regulates a person's need for sensual enjoyment, and another handles the need to respond to situations through antagonism and withdrawal.[185]

In the context of organizational life, two more high-level systems are relevant: the attachment/affiliation need system and the exploration/assertion need system.[186]

---

184 Ibid., 12.

185 Ibid.

186 Ibid., 13f.

- *The need for attachment and affiliation:* A crucial basic need of human beings is seeking relationships with others. Interacting and sharing seems to be a universal need. According to Jung, the level of this need defines whether a person is more extraverted or introverted. The balance between attachment and affiliation determines the level of self-worth and sense of self-esteem.
- *The need for exploration and assertion:* Exploration is developed early, and its success leads to a satisfaction that continues into adulthood. Of the same importance is the need to decide on one's own action and self-assertion.

The way people related to and interacted with primary caregivers or other significant figures during their first years impacts the way they relate to others as an adult (particular to authority figures). Basic wishes such as to be understood or loved, or hindered or hurt, fill the script of life. This script influences relationships with others and leads to consistent patterns that define how people expect others to respond to them and how they react to others. These basic wishes are projected onto others. For example, leaders' dominant leadership styles (e.g., conflict avoidance or initiation of tyrannical behavior, micromanagement or politics-playing) derive from their inner scripts. Very often, the scripts that are created in childhood become unproductive in adulthood and can lead to a self-destructive cycle of repetitive patterns.[187]

Although a behavior is acquired in childhood and carried into adulthood, it does not mean that it cannot be changed. The key lies in recognizing the degree to which the present (personal lens) is shaped by the past. Otherwise, mistakes get repeated.

The business world is full of people who have not managed to detect such repetitive behavior and thus have become dysfunctional. The above described clinical paradigm can help such individuals to detect strengths and weaknesses and understand why they resist change and

---

187 Ibid., 15f.

how they can increase productivity and efficacy. Such awareness can help read and rewrite necessary elements of the script of the inner theatre.

In the context of the magic triangle, owners must learn to assess and understand what drives a chairperson's or director's personality, and directors need to understand what drives a CEO's personality.

The following statements found in business journals illustrate the insights described above.

"I've seen talented executives who are very effective in their current jobs but who don't handle real authority well. It's hard to measure that capacity [...] yet when the guy assumed the top job, he didn't know how to handle the authority. He turned out to be overly autocratic, and we hadn't been able to foresee that."

—G. G. MICHELSON[188]

"What's most difficult to gauge is how an individual will act once he [...] is at the very top of the organization. As people rise through the ranks, it's fairly easy to track their accomplishments, to see how well they've worked with other people [...], but those kinds of measures tell you little about how someone will respond to being in charge."

—ALFRED ZEIEN[189]

"There's a mystery component that is difficult to evaluate. All of a sudden, you've got [...] temptations to let power go to your head. Whether or not a person will be sturdy enough to stand up to the temptations is a tremendous challenge for the board to judge. The better you know the person's sense of ethics and ability to put up with pressure, the better

---

188 Lorsch and Khurana, "Changing Leaders," 5ff.

189 Ibid.

you can judge whether he is going to be swayed by the power of the CEO office."

—GEORGE KENNEDY[190]

The above statements show how important it is to look beyond the common criteria for selecting candidates (e.g., education and professional track records). Studies increasingly provide powerful insights into the behavior of people in power and the origins of that behavior in their childhood experiences.

Garrard and Robinson state that there is a fast-growing desire to learn and understand more about the link between leadership and childhood.[191]

VIGNETTES

The following portraits (the first two are adopted from Shayne Hughes,[192] and the third one is a common type brought up by this book's author) show that human beings have a personal survival system that operates automatically and seamlessly.

- John is a risk-averse CFO who only feels comfortable making decisions if he has all the information at hand.
- Mike comes across as a sarcastic CEO, and thus his subordinates prefer not to show any weakness when he is present.
- Bonny is an entrepreneur with a tendency to micromanage. Everything went well at her company while it was in the startup phase. But once it began to develop and grow, she still preferred not to delegate.

Very often, people criticize and label others without knowing about their current life, their background, or their upbringing. We don't

---

190 Ibid.

191 Peter Garrard and Graham Robinson, *The Intoxication of Power* (London: Palgrave Macmillan), 203.

192 Shayne Hughes, "What Does My Childhood Have to Do with My Leadership?" *HuffPost*, August 1, 2013, http://www.huffingtonpost.com/shayne-hughes/what-does-my-childhood-ha_b_3678394.html.

know that John's father lost everything betting, even the family business. John was deeply marked by the quick change from being affluent to becoming poor. Mike grew up in a large family in which competition among his siblings was high. Hence, the development of a thick skin and harsh responses helped him survive. And Bonny's mother was highly controlling. Her relationship with her father was not good.

John, Mike, and Bonny were not aware of these negative behavioral patterns as a primitive set of behavioral options that triggered responses to life. Thus, they could only take responsibility for them and start to change them once they were brought into consciousness, probably with external help such as that of a coach.

It was crucial for them to detect and analyze the unconscious filters that were influencing their worldviews and interpretations of events and judgments of others. In order to learn about their own restrictive leadership behaviors, they realized it was not enough to just know that a different behavior was needed. They had to rewire their drivers (what originally set this behavior into motion) in order to be able to make significant adjustments to their standard leadership styles. They found the clues in their childhoods.

There is a close link between the leader's personality, leadership style, and the corporate culture. This link is even stronger in organizations with centralized power, for example, when the chairperson and CEO positions are combined into one role (nondual or single leadership; see chapter 9, "Checks and Balances," in the subsection "Implement Good (Corporate) Governance").

It is common for executives to compensate for the harm caused to their self-esteem by caregivers in childhood. These caregivers were either too distant or overpampering, neither of which helped them establish a healthy sense of personality.[193]

---

193 Kets de Vries, "Putting Leaders on the Couch," *Harvard Business Review* 82 (2004): 4.

Very often, such narcissistic wounds strongly contribute to an increase of appetite for fame and recognition by third parties. According to Kets de Vries, one example regards Larry Ellison. His stepfather constantly reminded him that he would never be able to achieve anything. This injury is the root cause for his present-day leadership style. His organization Oracle shows aggressive traits.[194]

Travis Kalanick, founder and former CEO of Uber is another example. His pattern to push limits hard seems to be deeply ingrained and was formed in childhood. In middle school, he was a wiry but smart student who scored high grades, which made him an easy target for older kids. He experienced severe bullying, and this traumatic childhood experience made him swear to himself never to be bullied again in life. And so, he turned the tables on his torturers, switched sides, and became an aggressor himself. This pattern was formed over years and was shown in his risk-taking attitude in two technology startups and further crystallized in his positions at Uber.[195]

Kalanick's reputation as highly aggressive and having a strong will to win at all costs led to a "Hobbesian culture" that became the focus of allegations, such as widespread sexual harassment and unprofessional conduct. Aside from Kalanick's personality, his leadership style seems to align with his life motto "to win at any price." He is reported to be a strong micromanager who likes to get involved in minor details. His accumulation of power caused a law firm that reviewed Uber's cultural reform to urge the company to redistribute some of it.[196]

The risk to the reputation of both person and company is massive. Stories about companies with an aggressive corporate culture have found their way into social media. Oracle and Uber are two examples,

194 Ibid.

195 Mike Isaac, "Uber's C.E.O. Plays with Fire," *The New York Times*, April 23, 2017, https://www.nytimes.com/2017/04/23/technology/travis-kalanick-pushes-uber-and-himself-to-the-precipice.html.

196 Jena McGregor, "Travis Kalanick May Have Resigned as Uber's CEO—but He Isn't Going Away, *Washington Post*, June 22, 2017, https://www.washingtonpost.com/news/on-leadership/wp/2017/06/22/travis-kalanick-may-have-resigned-as-ubers-ceo-but-he-isnt-going-away/?utm_term=.e18ad923836c.

but Wells Fargo had also built a toxic sales environment boosted by high pressure and sales targets, which led to a fake accounts scandal. Amazon is apparently known for its hard-charging corporate culture.[197]

Analysts increasingly focus on culture as they realized that companies that better understood how their employees were doing were more successful navigating uncharted waters. They have learned to understand that they better avoid investing in companies with aggressive cultures because such cultures often lead to scandal.

The percentage of companies that have made reference to organizational culture in earnings calls has increased by 20 percent between 2010 and 2016, rising from 19 percent to 39 percent.[198]

It is likely that the majority of executives who are overly focused on power, work, and money experienced some sort of deprivation in their childhood. They feel the need to have large compensation packages, as it increases their control and independence in an environment they learned to believe (early on) is not controllable. The critical phase starts when their successful track record will not let them pause. Work turns into their life's purpose, often impairing personal relationships. At some point, they start to realize the deterioration that gives them the feeling of being stuck. Depression appears, but they consider it a weakness to talk about their discomfort.

VALVES

There are various valves that help ease the above described pressure. For example, in search of excitement and purpose, executives may make an acquisition (most of which are risky, aggressive, and over-

---

197 Jena McGregor, "Why a Toxic Workplace Is Now a Much Bigger Liability for Companies," *Washington Post*, February 24, 2017, https://www.washingtonpost.com/news/on-leadership/wp/2017/02/24/why-a-toxic-workplace-is-now-a-much-bigger-liability-for-companies/?tid=a_inl&utm_term=.96cb71d7cc44.

198 Ibid.

priced),[199] throw extravagant parties, or become involved in excessive and/or extreme sports.

But eventually, these people need to slow down, especially when they face retirement. At this point, depression arrives if it has not already. The constant pressure and challenges of leadership, entailing responsibility for people, performance, and change-affected uncertainties, can be not only very stressful but also highly seductive.

Valves can lead to deceitful actions. The Association of Certified Fraud Examiners (ACFE) found that fraud offenders tend to show red flags when engaged in fraudulent behavior. The most frequent warning signs are living above one's means, disproportional control issues, a "wheeler-dealer" attitude combined with a lack of scruples, and recent issues in the family or divorce. In almost 80 percent of the cases, at least one of these warning signs manifested during the fraud.[200]

The most tragic option to escape job pressure/loss, however, is suicide. Switzerland, for example, has seen several cases in recent years in which well-known and successful leaders committed suicide, such as the CEOs of Julius Baer, Swisscom, Ricola, and Zurich Insurance Group, and the CFO of the latter. The suicide of Martin Senn, then CEO of Zurich Insurance Group, occurred after he was separated from the company. He had lost his sister and father as a teenager. He assumed responsibility for his mother and two sisters, and in this (father) role, he was "not allowed" to fail. These events and the role he assumed profoundly marked him and shaped his life strategy of "battle through."[201] It is critical for executives who are about to lose their jobs to be supported through the departure process and afterwards.

The tragic death of Carsten Schloter, former CEO of Swisscom—a major telecommunications provider in Switzerland—is another exam-

---

199 Garrard and Robinson, *Intoxication of Power*, 45ff.

200 Association of Certified Fraud Examiners (ACFE), *Report to the Nations on Occupational Fraud and Abuse: 2016 Global Fraud Study* (Austin, TX: ACFE), 5.

201 Stefan Barmettler and Ohanian Mathias, „Der stille Schaffer," *Handelszeitung*, June 2, 2016, 6.

ple. He said in an interview with *Die Schweiz am Sonntag*, "I had great difficulties in my childhood to accept authority and I was not able to be led by anybody."[202] Changes in the chairperson position of Swisscom seem to have had an impact on the power balance. In addition, Schloter seems to have been less and less able to cope with increased pressure from a changing world. In an interview with Sonntag, he stated, "I was facing greater difficulties to come and needed to rest and to reduce the pace."[203]

The Swiss executive suicide rate can be compared to those of other European countries.[204]

Studies show that there are cultural differences regarding the social acceptability of failure.

In the US, for example, failure is likely to be seen as an intrinsic factor of the business system and a risk-taking mindset can lead to great reward. There are many accomplished people today—even celebrated as heroes—who are proud of their past "failures," which they consider as indicators of their resilience.[205]

By contrast, failure in Japan is seen as shameful, and this has an impact on risk-taking. A former Japanese government that was in power for more than half a century tried to encourage greater tolerance for failure, hoping it would boost the stagnant economy. But shortly after, the Japanese voters dismissed the ruling party that had initiated change in how tolerance of failure is seen.[206]

---

202 Marc Kowalsky, „Carsten Schloter: Tod eines CEO," BILANZ, last visited March 26, 2017, http://www.bilanz.ch/unternehmen/carsten-schloter-tod-eines-ceo; Marc Kowalsky, „Was den deutschen Topmanager in den Tod trieb," Die Welt, https://www.welt.de/wirtschaft/article119750051/Was-den-deutschen-Topmanager-in-den-Tod-trieb.html (last visited March 28, 2017).

203 Kowalsky, „Was den deutschen Topmanager."

204 Ralph Atkins, "Suicide Highlights Swiss Executive Stress," SWI swissinfo.ch, June 1, 2016, (last visited June 20, 2016), http://www.swissinfo.ch/eng/zurich-insurance_suicide-highlights-swiss-executive-stress/42194504.

205 Peter S. Goodman, "Failure Offers Lessons Japan Would Rather Forget," New York Times, September 6, 2009, http://www.nytimes.com/2009/09/06/weekinreview/06goodman.html?_r=2.

206 Ibid.

Each person has a different survival behavior that was developed during childhood and works unconsciously and therefore automatically. It is the power of the unconscious. Such behavioral patterns serve as defense mechanisms that help overcome fear or prevent unfavorable situations.

As the previous section has revealed, different experiences and factors that are rooted early in life define leadership abilities. It is invaluable to become aware of and familiar with one's childhood to learn about one's leadership style.

There is a wide range of research that provides evidence that successful leaders grew up in families with strong, supportive mothers. Often, fathers were not present. Jack Welch's (former chairperson and CEO of General Electric) autobiography talks about this. Another example is Richard Branson (founder of the Virgin Group), whose mother told him that he could achieve anything he wanted.[207]

Perceptions of power, authority, hierarchy, status, and control vary from country to country, and hence, some leadership styles might work in one country and/or one corporate culture while being dysfunctional in another. All these differences find their origins in different upbringings—a discovery that is not comfortable for leaders who prefer to believe that they are in control of their own behavior. With no exception, each person has blind spots and particular behavioral aspects that are unconscious.[208]

In an interview,[209] Kets de Vries explains that people's childhood experiences can be approximately divided into three different groups. Roughly 20 percent had a happy childhood. Roughly 20 percent had a rather difficult childhood and experienced some sort of suffering because they experienced negligence or overpampering as a child.

---

207 Kets de Vries, "Putting Leaders on the Couch," 2.

208 Ibid., 3.

209 Art Kleiner, "The Thought Leader Interview: Manfred F.R. Kets De Vries." *strategy+business*, no. 59 (2010), 4f.

They forever thirst for admiration and recognition because the development of their sense of self-esteem has not kept up with their age. This is why they feel the constant need to prove themselves to others and might even acquire destructive personality traits.

The third group accounts for approximately 60 percent of people. People of this group, together with the 20 percent in the second group, see life as a struggle, and so they need to make sure that they get what they can. Some push themselves to break through and search for a different approach to life or even help the world become better. Examples of great political leaders who managed to rise above are Mandela and Gandhi. Some, however, adapt spiteful and vindictive character traits.

THE DARK SIDE OF LEADERSHIP

As the previous sections demonstrated, today's leaders feel increased pressure relating to different sources: stakeholders' expectations and projections on leaders; the VUCA world; changing, contradictory, or confusing theories and definitions of leadership; emerging conflicts and politics within companies when individuals step into leadership roles. These pressures intensify anxieties, fears (of loss of power, failure, success, envy), doubts, loneliness in command, insecurity, self-doubt, or overconfidence. This causes stress or even depression that might lead to irrational and unproductive behavior.[210]

There is substantial tension that comes with the responsibility for and unpredictability of the outcome of an action or decision. Leaders often feel torn between omnipotence and helplessness. Each person deals with anxieties, but these become stronger with pressure and the responsibility of leadership. This set of themes can form patterns that can either be productive or problematic. Most often, they are both. It is a challenge to deal with these patterns and at the same time

---

210 De Haan, "The Leadership Shadow," 6; T. Kippenberger, "The Dark Side of Leadership: What Drives People to Become Leaders?" *The Antidote*, vol. 2, no. 3 (1997), 11.

encourage, develop, and empower others in order to produce the best outcomes for all parties.[211]

Leaders can ultimately face burnout, physical and psychological challenges, or illness, collapse, or any type of derailment (excesses, fraud, scandal, or personal clashes, which originate in the inability to create and nurture effective working relationships). Derailment is a common, serious issue for executives, with greater susceptibility in higher ranks.[212]

LEADERSHIP SHADOW

In 1963, Jung wrote, "The shadow is that hidden, repressed, for the most part inferior and guilt-laden personality whose ultimate ramifications reach back into the realm of our animal ancestors and so comprise the whole historical aspect of the unconscious."[213]

Jung's understanding of the shadow can be described as the unknown "dark side" of a personality. The word *dark* refers to the primitive, negative, socially debased, unconscious emotions, and impulses of human beings, such as striving for power, greed, envy, selfishness, or rage. The shadow is developed by what people consider evil, inferior, or unacceptable, and denied in themselves. Jung referred to the shadow as the "totality of the unconscious," a notion he adopted from philosopher Nietzsche. But his primary goal was to shed light on the dangers of excessive unconsciousness. Jung realized that human beings' failure to recognize, acknowledge, and handle their shadow side often serves as root cause for problems between individuals and within teams and larger constructs (organizations).[214]

211 De Haan, "The Leadership Shadow," 6.

212 Ibid., 3.

213 C. G. Jung, *Aion: Researches into the Phenomenology of the Self (Collected Works of C.G. Jung Vol. 9 Part 2)*, (Princeton, NJ: Princeton University Press,1968), para. 422, 266.

214 Stephen A. Diamond, "Essential Secrets of Psychotherapy: What Is the 'Shadow'?" *Psychology Today*, April 2012, https://www.psychologytoday.com/blog/evil-deeds/201204/essential-secrets-psychotherapy-what-is-the-shadow.

"That which we do not bring to consciousness appears in our lives as fate."

—CARL JUNG

A list of typical feelings linked to encountering one's shadow includes fear, disgust, remorse, guilt, compassion, grief, and humility. These feelings show the shadow's power and its ability to possess and often overwhelm human beings. Statements such as, "He's not himself today" or "What possessed her to do that?" or "I don't know what came over me" are common indicators of the shadow. The above list of feelings does not contain "shame," a feeling that is common and well known— even in regard to being ashamed of one's own shadow.[215]

De Haan and Kasozi came up with the term *leadership shadow*: "Leadership by nature creates a split between [...] guidance and the ability to follow through [...] a rift between the leader and the team."[216] They also see a possibility to analyze the inner manifestation of the rift as a contrast between a person's positive, sunny, constructive, active side, and his/her negative, needy, anxious, vulnerable, fearful, doubting, and pessimistic side. The pressures that come with leadership help to grow this shadow, which might lead to overdrive, excesses, and hubris. The people who tend to notice such changes are family and direct subordinates. (See chapter 8, "Detecting and Avoiding Danger," in the subsection "Assess Current and Future Leaders More Thoroughly.")[217]

The environment that leaders create spans a wide spectrum, ranging from happy, inspiring, energizing, effective, and motivating to toxic, political, unhappy, or even destructive. How executives use their power is very strongly influenced by their mental health. There are people with personality disorders—pathologies—which, once they

---

215 Christopher Perry, "The Shadow," The Society of Analytical Psychology, (last visited July 28, 2017), https://www. thesap.org.uk/resources/articles-on-jungian-psychology-2/about-analysis-and-therapy/the-shadow/.

216 De Haan, "The Leadership Shadow," 6.

217 Ibid., 6.

are in power, can have a serious negative influence on a company and its people.[218]

Based on Kets de Vries's experiences with and counseling of such leaders, he describes categories of the most common pathologies ("scientific study of diseases, an aspect of somebody's behavior that is extreme and unreasonable and that they cannot control"[219]), adding that, "not everyone falls neatly into one or another of the categories I describe; we are often a bit of this and a bit of that. And most bosses are not mentally ill, but a surprising number of senior executives do have a personality disorder of some kind. Even with executives who are relatively healthy emotionally, you nearly always run across some of the characteristics described here, which need to be addressed in similar fashion—though not necessarily accompanied by medication and formal therapy."[220]

The categories are as follows:[221]

- **Pathological narcissism:** Despite their apparent high level of self-confidence, leaders with this disorder have a volatile self-esteem. They do not handle confrontation well, a behavior that goes back to childhood. Pathological narcissists still try to compensate for their perceived inability to please their caregivers (most often parents). A similar impact could also have been caused by a caregiver's unrealistic overstimulation. To build true self-confidence, it can help to place narcissists' delicate sense of self on firm ground and avoid anything that might destroy it. Their need to be recognized must be acknowledged. There is a fine line between avoiding the reinforcement of grandiosity and pointing out their weaknesses. Empathy helps build trust.

---

218 Manfred F. R. Kets de Vries, "Coaching the Toxic Leader," *Harvard Business Review*, vol. 92 (2014), 4ff; Garrard and Robinson, *Intoxication of Power*, 91ff.

219 *Oxford Dictionary*, "pathology," (last visited August 10, 2019), https://www.oxfordlearnersdictionaries.com/definition/english/pathology.

220 Kets de Vries, "Coaching the Toxic Leader," 101.

221 Ibid., 100ff.

- **Manic-depressive:** This leader type is good at drawing people to them. But they are unpredictable, which makes others feel and act like firefighters. They tend to show higher rates of substance abuse and engage in extramarital affairs more often than others. It is important for them to get a reality check because they are not good at sensing how they are perceived by others. It can help to include family and colleagues in the process.
- **Passive-aggressive:** This type of leader has the tendency to repress negative feelings and avoid confrontation. In their childhood, it was not allowed to show direct feelings, so they learned to hide negative emotions or express them indirectly. Examples are that they miss deadlines or are late to meetings. It is important that they learn how to heal their hostility toward others (mainly authorities) and analyze the impact of their childhood on today's behavior and actions. It could be, for example, that they did not dare to oppose a parent. It can help if they are given a boost of self-confidence.
- **Emotionally disconnected:** This type of leader shows great charisma but is not able to describe his or her feelings or interpret other people's feelings. Emotionally disconnected leaders show a rather mechanical behavior, are not good at motivating others, and might, for example, experience stomach or muscle ache during stress. What might help is to directly address current issues and talk them out. Describing discomfort can help such leaders get to know the relationship between pain and their actual feelings.

ORGANIZATIONAL RESEARCH INTO THE DARK SIDE

As a result of the public scandals described in chapter 1, attention within the organizational sciences in regard to negative aspects of organizational life have strongly increased. Adjectives used to describe these aspects are: deviant, aberrant, and toxic. Consequently, organizational researchers have been increasingly interested in the dark side of personality.[222]

The overreliance on the five-factor model or Big Five called for research that went beyond the five factors. The majority of modern research involving dark personality (dark side in contrast to the bright side of the Big Five) have laid focus on the following two approaches that are described in greater detail below:

- *The Dark Triad:* focuses on the three traits: Machiavellianism, narcissism, and psychopathy that focuses on elevating the self and harming others.
- *DSM-IV Axis II Disorder:* focuses on the dark side as negative characteristics that arise when individuals drop their guard.

THE BIG FIVE

The Big Five model is a type of psychometric test, aiming at uncovering the most important dimensions of personality, which are the following five: Openness, Conscientiousness, Extroversion, Agreeableness, Neuroticism—or OCEAN.[223]

Up until the 1980s, there were lots of competing concepts and scales for assessing personality, such as the MBTI (Myers-Briggs Type Indicator) with its four-scale (measuring extroversion, feeling, judging, and intuition), and the twenty-scale CPI (California Psychological Inventory) measuring folk concepts such as the capacity for status and self-control, well-being, tolerance, and achievement via independence. Many personality researchers at that time were hoping to develop a model that would be adopted by the others and transform this fragmented field into one with a common language. What was lacking was

---

222 P. D. Harms, Seth M. Spain, and Sean T. Hannah, "Leader Development and the Dark Side of Personality," *Leadership Quarterly*, vol. 22 (2011): 495.

223 Ibid.

a descriptive model (taxonomy) and with it a definition of overarching domains to simplify a large number of specific instances.[224]

Several independent sets of researchers discovered and defined the five broad traits based on empirical, data-driven research in order for the Big Five to serve as an integrative function and represent the many diverse systems of personality descriptions in a common framework:[225]

- Openness—The extent to which individuals like to learn new things, enjoy new experiences, and are comfortable with the unfamiliar. Those that score high in openness are introspective, insightful, and imaginative and have a large set of interests. On the other hand, a low score in openness indicates close-mindedness, a preference for routines, familiar people, and ideas.
- Conscientiousness—Individuals that score high in this dimension are reliable, prompt, organized, methodic, and thorough. Conscientiousness influences the existence of goal setting and the extent to which goals are kept in the long run. These individuals are likely to be deliberate over choices, behave cautiously, or impulsively, and take obligations toward others seriously. In general, it can be said that this trait is a crucial ingredient for success: very disciplined, high-achieving, and dependable. On the extreme, it can also demonstrate perfectionism, lower spontaneity, flexibility, and higher stubbornness, which all lead to the feeling of stress.
- Extroversion—Unlike introverts that draw their energy from within themselves, extraverts draw energy from interacting with others. Extroverts are likely to be outgoing, energetic, talkative, and assertive. Individuals who score high on extroversion are more likely to feel bored or even anxious because they don't feel comfortable spending too much time with themselves.
- Agreeableness—Agreeable people are friendly, cooperative, and

---

224 Oliver P. John, Laura P. Naumann, and Christopher J. Soto, "Paradigm Shift to the Integrative Big Five Trait Taxonomy: History, Measurement, and Conceptual Issues," in *Handbook of Personality: Theory and Research, 3rd Edition,* ed. O.P John, R.W. Robins, and L.A. Pervin. New York: Guilford Press, January 2008, 114-58.

225 Ibid., 116; Matt Huston, Scott McGreal, Jonathan D. Rasking, and Grant Hilary Brenner, "Big 5 Personality Traits," *Psychology Today,* https://www.psychologytoday.com/us/basics/big-5-personality-traits.

compassionate, kind, affectionate, and sympathetic. Those that score low on this dimension are more likely to be more distant.

- Neuroticism—A synonym sometimes used for neuroticism is emotional stability. It is an indicator of a person's emotional stability and degree of negative emotions. Often, those that score high on neuroticism have a tendency toward emotional instability, anxiety, depression, self-doubt, and negative emotions in general. They are more likely to be moody, tense, experience loneliness, and be hypochondriacs.

Although the Big Five broadly captures the commonalities among most existing systems of personality traits, it still needs to be explained theoretically. However, its advantage is that everybody is able to understand the words that define the different factors.[226]

The results of the Big Five provide an estimate of how high or low an individual scores on each trait in relation to other people. The scores of a large number of test persons address questions such as whether personality differs between groups or how a specific trait tends to correspond with an outcome, such as success in a person's career.

THE DARK TRIAD

The term *Dark Triad* was coined by Paulhus and Williams in 2002.[227]

The Dark Triad is another type of psychometric test and focuses on pathologies that are characterized by motives that aim at elevating the self and causing harm to others.[228] The three traits: Machiavellianism,

---

226 O. P. John, L. P. Naumann, and C. J. Soto, "Paradigm Shift to the Integrative Big Five Trait Taxonomy: History, Measurement, and Conceptual Issues," in *Handbook of Personality: Theory and Research*, ed. O. P. John, R. W. Robins, and L. A. Pervin. New York: Guilford Press, 2008, 147.

227 Daniel N. Jones and Delroy L. Paulhus, "Duplicity among the Dark Triad: Three Faces of Deceit," *Journal of Personality and Social Psychology* 113, no. 2: 329ff; Peter D. Harms, Seth M. Spain, and Sean T. Hannah, "Leader Development and the Dark Side of Personality," *The Leadership Quarterly* 22, no. 3 (June 2011): 495ff.

228 Harms, Spain, and Hannah, "Leader Development and the Dark Side," 496.

narcissism, and psychopathy are called the three socially aversive traits. The overlapping constellation is named the Dark Triad.[229]

MACHIAVELLIANISM

Machiavellianism is referred to as a manipulative personality. Individuals were asked how much they agree with statements drawn from the writing of Machiavelli. Those that scored high were called high-Machs. Characteristics are lack of empathy, low affect, having a view on morality that is unconventional, and demonstrating a willingness to manipulate, lie to, and exploit others. They predominantly focus on their own goals and not on those of others. They take pleasure when they manage to deceive others. It seems that Machiavellians favor manipulations of others and enjoy the combative element of negotiations more than other people do.[230]

NARCISSISM

Narcissism is the number one dark-side trait in terms of research attention in the organizational sciences.[231]

A child creates a grandiose, exhibitionistic configuration of him or herself (the grandiose self) and a perfect image of the parents (idealized parent image) in an attempt to keep the perfection and bliss perceived during the first two years of life before the realities of life degrade these images.[232]

Referring to Erikson's eight development phases described in chapter

---

229 Jones and Paulhus, "Duplicity Among the Dark Triad," 4.

230 Seth M. Spain, P. D. Harms, and Dustin Wood, "Stress, Well-Being, and the Dark Side of Leadership," in *The Role of Leadership in Occupational Stress: Research in Occupational Stress and Well-Being* (Bingley, UK: Emerald Group, 2016), 6; Minna Lyons, "Machiavellianism: Introduction to the Dark Triad," *Science Direct*, https://www.sciencedirect.com/topics/psychology/machiavellianism.

231 Spain, Harms, and Wood, "Stress, Well-Being, and the Dark Side."

232 Ibid., 12.

4, "Key Driver Two: The Human Element as a Root Cause," the changes during the first two phases are called narcissistic development.[233]

Narcissism is crucial for the functioning of human beings, as it lays the foundation for a person's self-esteem and identity. However, it is only a well-balanced dose that provides stability in a personality. People who perceive their caregivers as unreliable or disloyal may maintain their feelings of deprivation, emptiness, and anger. A common way to deal with these feelings is by intensifying their narcissistic elements, for example by getting focused on grandiose/idealized notions of power, money, status, authority, glamour, drama, manipulation, or superficial relationships. In this context, many leaders become who they are mainly for negative reasons, either because they have not managed to solve their sense of self or they hold up an unrealistic image of potency.[234]

Narcissism compensates for the feeling of insecurity that many successful leaders have (a reason why most of them are overachievers). Pathological narcissists are successful in making themselves and others believe that they are grandiose. At the same time, however, they feel like a fake, and they worry that the truth will reveal that they are not as great as they pretend to be. This common condition is called impostor syndrome. But these leaders cannot speak about it with anybody. The higher they climb the ladder, the more they experience support by their environment, also because they surround themselves with yea-sayers. It is very difficult to resist such a situation, so the ability to focus only on the company vanishes. Narcissistic leaders are likely to have strong charisma, which causes people around them to project their own fantasies and imagination of grandiosity onto them (transference—see the "Followership and Leader-Follower Interactions and Theories" section in appendix 6).[235]

---

233 Kippenberger, "The Dark Side of Leadership," 12.

234 Manfred F. R. Kets de Vries, *Leaders, Fools and Impostors* (rev. ed., iUniverse, 2003), 20.

235 Kleiner, "The Thought Leader Interview," 5.

Narcissism has a positive and a negative side.[236] Constructive narcissism is a sense of personal equilibrium, healthy self-esteem, ability to reflect and show genuine empathy, survival instinct, and a motivating inner driver. Reactive narcissism is unhealthy self-esteem, self-destruction via egoism, obsessed self-love, loss of reality, heroism, need to pay back, focus on envy, revenge, and victory over others. Similar to unethical leadership, reactive narcissism can even be effective.[237] The line between these two effects is challengingly thin. The goal is to moderate and channel power.

REACTIVE NARCISSISM, HUBRIS, SOBS, AND THE CONSEQUENCES OF DESTRUCTIVE BEHAVIOR

Reactive narcissism (also be called excessive narcissism) and hubris are strongly overlapping, but hubris goes further. As Berglas puts it, "It's not just narcissism; it's much more dangerous than that."[238] When some people get into leadership positions, they show a personality change called Hubris Syndrome (HS).[239] It is the explosive combination of predisposition (narcissism) and function, e.g., CEO or chairperson who can create the dangerous change.[240]

Hubris refers to excessive pride. Persons exhibiting hubris consider themselves godlike. This makes them feel an unlimited pride that is not reduced when they become aware of their weaknesses and failures in their personal aspirations. In ancient Greece, hubris was considered a crime.[241]

Kets de Vries refers to those exhibiting HS as Seductive Operational

---

236 Kets de Vries, "Coaching the Toxic Leader," 4ff; Garrard and Robinson, *Intoxication of Power*, 91ff.

237 Kippenberger, "The Dark Side of Leadership," 12.

238 Steven Berglas, "Rooting Out Hubris, before a Fall," *Harvard Business Review*, April 14, 2014, https://hbr.org/2014/04/rooting-out-hubris-before-a-fall.

239 Garrard and Robinson, *Intoxication of Power*, 17ff.

240 Ibid., 97.

241 Garrard and Robinson, *Intoxication of Power*, 17ff.

Bullies (SOBs). He explains that SOBs' disposition constitutes a mild form of psychopathy.[242] In this book, I will refer to persons exhibiting hubris as SOBs.

Often, the personality trait of hubris was not present before the person reached a powerful leadership position. While hubris is developed during childhood, it is like a dormant seed. Power provides the fertile ground required for its growth. Thus, hubris is acquired, and it is intensified with the tenure of a person's execution of significant power. Those exhibiting hubris consider it normal to break rules or exceed limits that are common for others. HS and power go hand in hand, which means without power, there can be no HS. The syndrome will disappear when SOBs lose power.[243]

Berglas describes hubris as a reactive disorder (either as a consequence of prolonged laudatory or triggered when assuming power) and narcissism as a character disorder (starting early on, defining an individual's entire modus operandi; "a narcissist is pretty much a narcissist all the time").[244]

SOBs are perceived as charming, charismatic, energizing, and convincing. They are decisive, action-oriented, and good at handling superiors, as they tell them what they want to hear. At the same time, however, SOBs are self-centered, have a sense of grandiosity and are both unpredictable and chronic liars (including regarding minor issues). SOBs are true survivors.[245]

HS has predominantly been identified in men (thought to be due to the impact of testosterone) who have previously been highly successful and have grown accustomed to victory.[246] Self-confidence leads to

---

242 Kets de Vries, "The Psycho-Path to Disaster: Coping with SOB Executives," *Organizational Dynamics*, vol. 43, 2014, 18.

243 Garrard and Robinson, *Intoxication of Power*, 17ff.

244 Berglas, "Rooting Out Hubris," 1.

245 Garrard and Robinson, *Intoxication of Power*, 31, 140.

246 Ibid., 31., 140f.

overconfidence. When pride becomes overwhelming so that rational judgment is no longer possible, excessive narcissists start to ignore opposing views. This phenomenon happened to Napoleon in 1812 in his Russian campaign. He dismissed warning signals of forthcoming danger and went with his own assessment, which led to defeat. The pride and arrogance that Napoleon had developed as a result of prior victories made him blind to the danger foreseen by others.[247]

SOBs are dysfunctional and destructive, but they are not aware of their behavior and do not realize that it is different from others' and thus, not normal. It is very important for SOBs to keep their position and power, which reveals destructive behavior such as self-righteousness and arrogance and prevents a healthy exchange of ideas, thoughts, and feelings. Not only do they become inattentive to the needs of their subordinates, but they also lose their loyalty.[248]

In contrast to psychopaths, SOBs manage quite well to channel their energy. ACFE's statistics show that it is not unusual for them to be great actors who know how to disguise their dysfunction. They are found in top executive positions, and for a while, they can be very effective. Estimates suggest that 1 percent of the population and 4 percent of executives have psychopathic traits. The average percentage is highest in the financial industry. It can be said that they live on the trust that people place in them.[249]

Some examples of former hubristic leaders are the CEO and chairperson of Lehman Brothers (Richard S. Fuld Jr.), the CEO of RBS (Fred Goodwin—according to Matt Nixon, his senior executives stated, "Fred was your classic bully," or "I think he had no capacity for compassion. I really mean that."[250]), the CFO of Enron (Andrew Fastow), the CEO of Volvo (Pehr G. Gyllenhammar), and the CEO of

---

247 Ibid., 232ff.

248 Kets de Vries, *Leaders, Fools and Impostors*, 23–24.

249 ACFE, *Report to the Nations*, 5.

250 Matt Nixon, *Pariahs: Hubris, Reputation and Organisational Crises* (Libri Publishing, 2016), 23.

Vivendi (Jean-Marie Messier). They were all known for their charisma, their previous great success, and high recognition by the media and/or government.[251]

SOBs are truly hard to deal with. They play the power game extraordinarily well. They are experts in creating a perception of success attributed to them, while making others look incompetent and without revealing their true interests and motives. They negatively affect people's health. It is their main goal to win so that they can maintain power and control. SOBs are very clever at winning over main decision-makers and undermining opponents. They know very well how to present themselves as self-sacrificing. The key question is: How can SOBs be spotted and prevented from reaching or abusing power?

It is highly challenging to recognize hubris because it is almost impossible to imagine that there are people with little conscience (little or no guilt or regrets). As they maintain good relationships with their superiors, they often enjoy protection so that claims against them go unheard.

Therefore, other means need to be found to build a case against hubris. It is the leadership selection team's task to develop the ability to detect hubristic characteristics, e.g., young high-potentials who start to change after a promotion to the (very) top despite having previously being perceived as reasonable executives.[252]

PSYCHOPATHY

Although it is difficult to imagine that there might be people who lack a conscience, such people do exist. In the extreme form, they are called psychopaths and sociopaths.

Psychopaths have difficulty becoming emotionally attached to other

---

251 Garrard and Robinson, *Intoxication of Power*, xi, 58, 106, 229.

252 Ibid., 97.

people, and their relationships are rather shallow, artificial, and manipulative. Psychopaths are very rarely able to feel guilty about their own actions, including when they seriously hurt other people. Typical characteristics, such as impulsiveness, aggression, and reckless behavior, as exemplified by serious criminals, have proven to be stable for life and can be measured even before adolescence.[253]

They have a strong genetic component and are often related to damage to the frontal brain and the limbic system. This leads to the assumption that they are not curable, a belief that is backed by the field of neurobiology. Further risk factors for psychopathy are birth trauma, lack of reward for nonaggressive behavior during development, very poor upbringing with a young single caregiver, under- or malnourishment, sexual and physical child abuse, no or low education, boredom, and alcohol or drug abuse. Psychopaths account for 25 percent to 50 percent of all prison inmates. Females are just as likely to be psychopaths as males, but female psychopaths are much less often criminally or physically violent.[254]

By comparison, sociopaths seem to have been mainly influenced by their environment, for example, their childhood and upbringing. Sociopaths also find it difficult to become emotionally attached to others but are more impulsive than psychopaths. Psychopaths are more dangerous because they do not develop guilt as a result of their harmful behavior. Because both groups are good at living a normal life, they are a threat to society.[255]

Neither of these two disorder types is treatable. People with these disorders tell others what they want to hear and pretend that they

---

253 Niels Birbaumer, "Hirnforschung mit Straftätern: Das Böse beginnt im Gehirn," *Frankfurter Allgemeine Zeitung*, June 6, 2015, (last visited May 6, 2018), http://www.faz.net/aktuell/wissen/leben-gene/hirnforschung-mit-straftaetern-das-boese-beginnt-im-gehirn-13649029.html?printPagedArticle=true#pageIndex_2; Harms, Spain, and Hannah, "Leader Development and the Dark Side," 397.

254 Ibid.

255 John M. Grohol, "Differences Between a Psychopath vs Sociopath," Psych Central, (last visited February 26, 2018), https://psychcentral.com/blog/differences-between-a-psychopath-vs-sociopath.

have recognized their mistakes.[256] Only a few become extreme types. All known serial murderers and many dictators show psychopathic behavior, and many were abused or neglected as children, including Stalin, Hitler, Mao, and Saddam Hussein. Although they all seem to meet the criteria for psychopaths from an operations standpoint, only Stalin has been clinically diagnosed as such.[257] The approach of the Dark Triad to subclinical traits strongly influenced the research on normal personality in dysfunctional operation. Dark personality can be considered the middle ground between normal personality and clinical-level pathology.[258]

The related personality inventory developed by Jones and Paulhus is called the Dark Triad Test. It measures the above described three interrelated, socially undesirable traits.[259]

Each individual has elements of these traits in his/her personality, but those with a high level of all three traits are more likely to engage in deviant or counterproductive behavior. Hence, businesses should guard against candidates for leadership positions who may appear the perfect match for the role.

Individuals with Dark Triad traits thrive in interviews in that they come across as convincing, competent, and extroverted. They very well manage to fool the recruiters and charm the executives. See chapter 8, "Detecting and Avoiding Danger" for more information on the Dark Triad Test and the seven steps to protect from these candidates.

DSM-IV AXIS II

Subclinical versions of the DSM-IV Axis II Personality Disorder are often measured with the Hogan Development Survey (HDS), which

256 Kets de Vries, "Coaching the Toxic Leader," 7.

257 James G. Long, "Psychopathy and Politics," *American Thinker*, December 26, 2014, http://www.americanthinker.com/articles/2014/12/psychopathy_and_politics.html.

258 Harms, Spain, and Hannah, "Leader Development and the Dark Side," 497.

259 Jones and Paulhus, "Duplicity Among the Dark Triad," 1ff.

describes the "dark side of personality—qualities that emerge in times of increased strain and can disrupt relationships, damage reputations, and derail peoples' chances of success."[260] HDS identifies eleven interpersonal themes. Each of these dispositions has a positive (bright) and negative (dark) side. If the positive side is not handled well, it flips into the negative or even destructive, which can entail negative consequences for engagement, productivity, staff loyalty, trust, and hence retention rate, and ultimately performance.[261] The main categories are Intimidation (Moving Away), Flirtation and Seduction (Moving Against), and Ingratiation (Moving Toward).[262]

Take "Cautious," for example, one of the five components of the "Intimidation (Moving Away)" category. (For a complete listing of all components of each category, see appendix 7.) The positive side of cautious people is that they are careful. If someone is overly or excessively cautious, the positive aspect can flip into negative aspects such as not accepting criticism, experiencing a feeling of rejection, or being afraid to make mistakes. This disposition originates in childhood. The person learned that unsuccessful experiences are related to a defect that makes them different from others. If the positive side is not handled well, the person does everything to prevent unpredictable situations, including avoiding social interactions and taking decisions.

Another example is the predisposition "Bold," a subset of the "Flirtation and Seduction (Moving Against)" category. The positive side supports confidence and a strong first impression. When flipped into the negative, it can be conceived as arrogance, the person's belief in their own uniqueness and exceptionality, ignoring weaknesses. Such individuals most likely experienced overpampering in their childhood

---

260 Hogan Development Survey: The Dark Side of Personality, Hogan, (last visited June 25, 2018), https://www.hoganassessments.com/assessment/hogan-development-survey/.

261 Harms, Spain, and Hannah, "Leader Development and the Dark Side," 497; Nelson and Hogan, "Coaching on the Dark Side," 504f.

262 Kaiser, Linking Personality and 360 Assessments to Coach and Develop Leader, power point slides for/on 'Symposium at the 28th Annual SIOP Conference', April 2013, Houston TX. Trickey and Hyde, "A Decade of the Dark Side: Fighting our Demons at Work," Psychological Consultancy Limited, 2009, 3f, http://www.psychological-consultancy.com/project/a-decade-of-the-dark-side-fighting-our-demons-at-work/.

and did not learn to accept boundaries and discipline. One negative consequence is that they become insensitive to the effects of their own behavior. They often believe in a two-class system of leaders and subordinates, and assume they belong to the former.

(See appendix 7 for more information on the positive and negative sides of the other nine dispositions.)

By assessing dark-side personality, performance risks can be recognized and mitigated before they become a problem. Each of the described eleven dispositions has a positive and a negative side. The positive side needs to be handled well so that it doesn't flip into the negative side. Improving self-awareness (see chapter 7, "Crucial Leadership Skills (and How to Develop Them)") or asking for feedback (see chapter 8, "Detecting and Avoiding Danger") helps the process and boosts progress.

RELEVANCE TO REAL WORLD CASES

When it comes to the study of dark personality in the workplace, workplace deviance and counterproductive work behaviors seem to be the most popular topic. According to various researchers, there are links between the Dark Triad traits and counterproductive work behaviors. Furthermore, meta-analytic evidence also suggests a relationship between Machiavellianism and unethical, organizational decision-making. Personality plays a key role in the determination of how participants in training programs embrace the learning of new skills that help change behaviors. There was a negative association of dark personality dimensions with change in leadership. It also moderated individual growth curves for leader development, meaning that the development of individuals high in dark-side traits was slower. There is one exception to mention: constructive narcissism was positively associated with change in leadership.[263]

There are quite a few more examples in business and politics that

---

263 Harms, Spain, and Hannah, "Leader Development and the Dark Side," 500ff.

demonstrate how childhood experiences negatively impacted acquired behaviors and worldviews. For example, the former CEO of Otherco once revealed that his birth was highly premature. As a baby, he fought for survival for several months, which, he added, became his life motto: he would do the same for the rest of his life. The fact that he went bankrupt with the business he had taken over from his father who died when he was young left a mark, as he later admitted: the feeling to have failed and the urge to try even harder, (almost) regardless of the costs.

When he was separated from Otherco, he broke into tears, claiming he would never find a job and negotiated a severance package with the BoD. In turn, he promised by handshake and word of honor not to engage in any competitive endeavor.

Shortly after, a newspaper article stated that he was let go because of poor performance. This must have felt like another stab at his self-confidence and reopened old childhood wounds. This was when he began to hire away key employees and build a new, similar company behind Otherco's back and—when the takeover attempt failed—tried to take down Otherco by calling up the country heads, encouraging them to dismiss and become independent so that Otherco would break up. His newly founded company would then take over the remaining bits and reinvite these executives back into the boat. With the exception of one, none of them followed the offer.

Other examples are Sepp Blatter and Gianni Infantino (the former and current presidents of FIFA), who also suffered traumatic experiences as babies. Blatter was born much too early. Infantino almost died as a baby because he needed an urgent blood transfusion, depended on donors from other countries, and struggled for survival until the transfusion was successfully implemented. Both fought for survival, and the fight seems to have carried through.[264]

---

264 APA/dpa, "Fussball: FIFA-Präsident Infantino: Kämpfte als Baby um mein Leben," *Tiroler Tageszeitung*, (last visited June 4, 2016), http://www.tt.com/home/11183804-91/fußball-fifa-präsident-infantino-kämpfte-als-baby-um-mein-leben.csp; David Jones, "From Wedding Singer to FIFA's Godfather: The Hidden Secrets of Sepp Blatter," Daily Mail, June 4, 2011, http://www.dailymail.co.uk/sport/football/article-1394109/Sepp-Blatter-remarkable-rise.html.

Often, the ways in which these three individuals developed and came to handle power relates to how they were treated by their primary caregivers (e.g., parents) when they were babies, fighting for survival. Such parents are extremely worried for their weak children and thus gave them special treatment, such as overpampering. Therefore, fear of dying, the feeling of being someone special, and a lifelong craving for affection and acknowledgment strongly shape such individuals. The experience of such a trauma is deeply rooted.

Such experiences can also be linked to Erikson's development stages, starting with the first (Hope—Trust vs. Mistrust; Infancy, Zero to Eighteen Months). The key question that defines this stage is "Can I trust the world?" If the infant is uncertain about the world as a safe place, it looks for stability, consistency, and comfort to meet its basic needs. When such severe incidents happen at or right after birth, an environment of affection, security, and stability cannot be provided. The infant develops a sense of mistrust, which can lead to anxiety, frustration, suspicion, and insecurity.

The second phase might have a minor influence, depending on the development of the infant. In stage 2 (Will—Autonomy vs. Shame and Doubt; Eighteen Months to Three Years), the key question is "Is it okay to be me?" A feeling of lack of self-esteem in this stage can lead to shame, doubt, lack of confidence, and dependence on others.

Because of the immediate risk posed by the estimated 98 percent of senior executives and 25 percent of middle managers showing at least one shadow-side trait, it is crucial for leaders to learn containment (see sidebar). This mechanism helps to maintain aplomb/dignity for leaders and teams while preserving the flow of organizational goal attainment. Containment is a way of compensating for the leader's lack of understanding of their own and others' hidden key drivers in order to focus on their role of maintaining a positive culture and productivity.

CONTAINMENT

Wilfred Bion, a renowned American psychologist and according to Altman, "the second most cited analyst in the contemporary world,"[265] developed the concept of container and contained. It is based on unthinkable experiences to which he was subjected in World War I serving as a tank commander and his work with traumatized soldiers in military hospitals during World War II.[266] Containment builds on Klein's concept of projective identification ("an unconscious fantasy in which aspects of the self or an internal object are split off and attributed to an external object").[267] Thus, it included communication between infant and mother.[268]

The experience of the baby is distress or ill-being, but it cannot grasp the problem. The mother (the container) realizes this but cannot grasp it either. However, her ability to deal with the difficulty (the contained) and find a solution is more pronounced and mature.[269]

Anton Oberholzer states that Bion's model of container/contained has crucial application in organizations. For example, a leader (the container) needs to demonstrate poise and confidence for his employees in the face of challenges or difficulties (the contained) even if he or she cannot grasp the issue. Conversely, a leader who is full of anxiety and not able to take in and metabolize their employees' anxiety but even pours more anxiety into them acts counterproductively. Moreover, a leader's tendency to blame others when things don't go well depends

265 Neil Altman, "Wilfred Bion: From World War I to Contemporary Psychoanalysis," *International Journal of Applied Psychoanalytic Studies*, vol. 13, no. 2 (2016), 163.

266 Chris Mawson, "Wilfred Bion," Melanie Klein Trust, (last visited November 29, 2017), http://www.melanie-klein-trust.org.uk/bion.

267 "Projective Identification," Melanie Klein Trust, (last visited April 23, 2018), http://www.melanie-klein-trust.org.uk/projective-identification.

268 Suzanne Maiello, "Prenatal Experiences of Containment in the Light of Bion's Model of Container/Contained," *Journal of Child Psychology*, vol. 38, no. 3 (2012), 251.

269 Anton Obholzer, "Psychoanalytic Contributions to Authority and Leadership Issues," *Leadership and Organization Development Journal*, vol. 17, no. 6 (1996), 53f.

greatly on the ability to retain a mature attitude versus a defensive stance.[270]

The foundations for these behaviors are early experiences and are subsequently reworked over the course of life. According to Oberholzer, the capacity for containment can be developed, with a focus on the leader's controlled ability to listen (deeply), to take in, and to react.

If leaders lack containment and do not manage to hold back their demons, their organization can very well turn toxic, which—in the best case—entails only high costs to turn around. Thus, the key is to value specific characteristics and patterns while noticing how and when they tilt to shadow side traits. This is absolutely crucial to the success of tackling and managing them. Shadows have a great upside as they offer a valuable and probably highly needed insight into the field of leadership and, with it, the fine line between leaders' driving factors and performance.[271]

IN SUM

Various aspects in this chapter showed why leadership has its place among the top three key drivers for derailment in business and why it has the potential to serve as an accelerator.

Almost countless pieces of research and literature on leadership exists. However, flaws such as the lack of a unified leadership model, a universal leadership definition, and a clear measurement of a leader's influence on performance, as well as the overfocus on traditional leadership criteria, makes the understanding and execution of good leadership challenging.

The chapter has put weight on the strong influence of upbringing on leadership and leadership selection (clinical paradigm, inner the-

---

270 Ibid., 53f.

271 De Haan, "The Leadership Shadow," 8.

atre). Many leaders feel torn between omnipotence and helplessness when they are in power and under pressure and deal with uncertainty. This set of themes can form patterns that can either be productive or problematic or both. As this chapter has shown, leaders' personalities strongly influence their understanding and execution of power. The effects of power can range from positive to disastrous, which makes power an ambivalent and impactful variable in the area of human aspirations and, hence, leadership.

Letting go of power is difficult, as it triggers fear of loss related to the losses already experienced on the way to the top and to power. Hanging on to power helps prevent or prolong such painful realities. Psychological and emotional factors play a disproportionate role because of the sense of losing importance and of aging. Leaders need to learn how their upbringing shaped their behaviors, actions, aspirations, and fears. The Hubris Syndrome increases the reaction to loss and decline.

The definition of and reaction to power gets accentuated in today's VUCA world: an increased change within organizations heightens the pressure on leaders and can uncover their emotional instability.[272] Such situations or circumstances reveal people's shadow sides. If the shadow's traits are not detected and managed, they can trigger valves (suicide, risky mergers, and acquisitions, burnouts) and lead to derailment, which all too often destroys value and harms performance. On the positive side, shadows have a great upside, as they offer a valuable and probably highly needed insight into the field of leadership and, with it, the fine line between leaders' driving factors and performance.[273]

Special attention must be paid to the detection of and handling of persons exhibiting hubris. Because the trauma of deception, exploitation, and manipulation in childhood cannot be quickly repaired, it

---

272 Kippenberger, "The Dark Side of Leadership," 12.

273 De Haan, "The Leadership Shadow," 8.

is not easy at all to cure SOBs. With their inability to develop guilt or regret, SOBs cannot form a healthy and functioning relationship with a coach or therapist. There is hope, however, if the behavior is still (only) narcissistic. If their energy can then be channeled in a positive way, such leaders can be very powerful and energized, which boosts a company's productivity. If not, the price to pay will be high.[274]

Concluding, it can be said that the influence of different aspects of leadership is substantial. In isolation or—even more common—in combination, they can accelerate the likelihood for derailment. It is critical for leaders but also for shareholders and BoD to familiarize themselves with these aspects to help avoid or decrease the chance for costly derailment of individuals or even entire organizations.

ADDENDUM

In an effort to be complete, two more leadership-related aspects are briefly discussed: gender and robots as future leaders.

GENDER

In regard to the derailment of female leaders, it is difficult to draw a conclusion. The much smaller percentage of women in CEO or BoD positions compared to their male counterparts might explain the fewer cases of derailment that include a female leader. In order to underline or oppose this reason, further research and studies are needed.

Also, in relation to the link between women's success and their upbringing, it is difficult to draw generalizations since there are not yet enough female leaders in business. (Further information and research and observation on the gender gap when it comes to women in management and the BoD can be found in appendix 8.)

---

274 Garrard and Robinson, *Intoxication of Power*, 99.

ROBOTS AS FUTURE LEADERS

Since the drivers for negative outcomes in business are change, the human element, and leadership, the question arises whether robots would be better leaders because they might be more rational, predictable, responsible, and consistent when it comes to decision-making. Behavior, patterns, feelings, and emotions that arise from interactions with others, lack of sleep, or any other distracting factors that humans face can harm decision-making. Robots are not bound to biological rhythms but can work day and night, keeping high productivity and quality.[275]

However, although the latter might be likely, robots seem to be prone to replicate and perpetuate biases humans feed into them, which would make assuming they are objective a dangerous thing.[276] Consequently, expectations that intelligent systems will show a higher ethical standard than most human beings are not yet met. It will depend on the algorithms they follow.

However, despite the exponential development of robots and their skills, chapter 7, "Crucial Leadership Skills (and How to Develop Them)" outlines the skillset today's leaders need in order to deal with increasing change and meet stakeholders' rising interests. Leaders not only need to connect information, think beyond algorithms, foster creativity, and perform critical reasoning, but they also need to engage, empower, and inspire their employees and meet and interact with various stakeholders, especially in times of increasing uncertainty and unpredictability.[277]

Spiros Margaris, one of the leading AI (Artificial Intelligence) influ-

---

275 Luis Alvarez, "Could the CEO be Replaced by a Robot," World Economic Forum, January 13, 2017, https://www.weforum.org/agenda/2017/01/could-the-ceo-be-replaced-by-a-robot/.

276 Stephen Buranyi, "Rise of the Racist Robots—How AI Is Learning All Our Worst Impulses," *The Guardian*, August 8, 2017, https://www.theguardian.com/inequality/2017/aug/08/rise-of-the-racist-robots-how-ai-is-learning-all-our-worst-impulses.

277 Alvarez, "Could the CEO be Replaced by a Robot."

encers, argues that it is not about a replication of the human brain but a focus on learning to represent data.[278]

All in all, it is most likely that robots will never fully replace human beings, and not serve as CEOs either, for a simple reason: belonging and attachment are fundamental to humans. To feel related to and accepted by important others is a key basic need.[279] This is because living in a group used to be critical for survival and because relationships matter from birth onward.[280] Recent research revealed a correlation between social isolation and dementia. Older people that were feeling lonely showed a higher likeliness of developing dementia than those that were lacking this feeling.[281]

The words "we know that we don't know"[282] probably best describes the status quo. It is impossible to anticipate the future evolvement of technology and even less so its implications. Until then, the focus lies on human leaders that lead a workforce consisting of human beings.

278 Spiros Margaris, "Machine Learning in Financial Services: Changing the Rules of the Game," SAP, August 2017, 6.

279 Kennon M. Sheldon and Alexander Gunz, "Psychological Needs as Basic Motives, Not Just Experiential Requirements," *Journal of Personality*, vol. 77, no. 5 (2009), 1467f; Matthew Dahlitz, "Basic Psychological Needs," *The Neuropsychotherapist*, (last visited April 18, 2017), http://www.neuropsychotherapist.com/basic-psychological-needs/.

280 Sheldon and Gunz, "Psychological Needs as Basic Motives," 1467f; Dahlitz, "Basic Psychological Needs."

281 Tjalling Jan Holwerda et al., "Feelings of Loneliness, but Not Social Isolation, Predict Dementia Onset: Results from the Amsterdam Study of the Elderly (AMSTEL)," *Journal of Neurology, Neurosurgery, and Psychiatry*, vol. 85 (2014), 135–142.

282 Thomas D. Zweifel, "The Rise of Robots and the Future of Work: Will We All Lose Our Jobs?" LinkedIn, February 26, 2016, https://www.linkedin.com/pulse/rise-robots-future-work-we-all-lose-our-jobs-dr-thomas-d-zweifel/.

CHAPTER 6

INTERRELATION OF THE THREE HIDDEN KEY DRIVERS

This book has now analyzed the legal framework and shown that both hard and soft law have fallen short on reducing negative outcomes. It has further revealed, analyzed, and explained three hidden key drivers for conflicts: change as triggering event, the human element as root cause, and leadership as accelerator/intensifier.

In an ideal world, the legal framework and each of the three hidden key drivers work in isolation and can be looked at and dealt with separately. The real world, however, shows that all of them are closely interrelated, which adds to the complexity, as this chapter will show.

The next chapter will provide an approach to a solution and offer a toolbox to improve the successful interrelation of change and the human element in leadership.

LEADERSHIP DURING CHANGE

There is a wide belief, largely supported by empirical research, that the implementation of organizational change has mainly been unsuccessful. Do change approaches that are leader-centric and see change as linear, sequential, and predictable impede change implementation? In contrast, do approaches that are more facilitatory/engaging and treat change as a complex process enhance change success? It is crucial to assess and understand how change works in practice in the long run.[283]

Innovation is gaining speed in our increasingly globalized world. Moreover, it no longer focuses primarily on initial product sales but more and more on building solutions for and relationships with clients that should be based on trust and understanding.[284]

Many books and articles have been written on how to best manage change. Most of them underestimate an essential aspect: the transition phase and its impact on people (human element), as well as systems. Leaders need to step into the role of a coach and help others navigate through the dynamics of transition.

The perception is still prevalent, however, that successful change is simply a matter of executing a straightforward plan to get from a clearly defined starting point to the targeted objective. Leaders then wonder why their subordinates do not get their tasks accomplished, why deadlines are missed, or why costs get out of hand.[285]

Thus, the challenge does not lie in change itself but in successfully leading people through the transition phase. Change itself focuses on the external (expected new structure, strategy, or principles), but transition focuses on the internal (a psychological realignment or

---

283 Malcolm Higgs and Deborah Rowland, "What Does It Take to Implement Change Successfully? A Study of the Behaviors of Successful Change Leaders," *Journal of Applied Behavioral Science*, vol. 47 (2011), 309f.

284 Ronald Heifetz, Alexander Grashow, and Marty Linsky, *The Theory Behind the Practice: A Brief Introduction to the Adaptive Leadership Framework* (Boston: Harvard Business Press, 2009), 10.

285 William Bridges and Susan Mitchell, "Leading Transition: A New Model for Change," in *Leader to Leader 2: Enduring Insights on Leadership from the Leader to Leader Institute's Award Winning Journal*, ed. Frances Hesselbein and Alan R. Shrader (San Francisco: Jossey-Bass, 2008), 246ff.

adjustment that employees need to undergo before change can be successful).[286]

Transition does not happen automatically. It happens downstream and is slower than change because it embeds three distinct processes, each of which has an uncomfortable character.[287]

The first stage—saying goodbye—asks people to let go of how things were and how they themselves used to be. It feels to them as if they have to give up their identity.

The second stage—neutral zone—requires people to endure the discomfort that comes with change while not rushing into something new or holding on to the old ways. It is during this phase that creativity occurs and transformation happens. However, the longer the neutral zone lasts, the higher the chance for adverse consequences (loss of momentum and hope).

The third phase—moving forward—requires people to embrace the new beginning that often asks for new ways of thinking and behaving.

The process of leading people through the transition is made even more challenging by other organizational trends and technology changes. For example, boundaries within organizations are being broken up or fading away (boundaryless companies will be discussed later in this chapter), and the complexity of systems and networks is increasing. Leaders need to learn how to deal with increasing ambiguity and nonlinearity of data.[288]

ROLE BIOGRAPHY AND ROLE HISTORY

It is not uncommon for companies to experience frequent CEO

---

286 Ibid., 246ff.

287 Ibid., 246ff.

288 Heifetz, Grashow, and Linsky, *The Theory Behind the Practice*, 10.

changes. Why does this happen? Is it governance? Is it the CEO? Is it the CEO's relationship with the BoD?

Yahoo had six CEOs in only one decade (see details in appendix 9).[289]

Hewlett-Packard (HP)[290] experienced a similar revolving door, not only of the CEO but also chairperson and board positions. The company had six CEOs since 2005 and four in only six years. Chairpersonship (or presidency in case of dual leadership) changed even more often (seven in eight years). They had eight new directors from 2010 to 2018. (Further details can be found in appendix 9.)

The accumulated cost of the CEO turnover rose to more than $83 million in severance pay, including a package of more than $25 million to former CEO Léo Apotheker.

To complicate the situation, HP divided into two companies in 2015: HP Incorporated (HP Inc.), which continued to sell personal computers (PCs) and printers, and Hewlett Packard Enterprise (HPE), listed on the New York Stock Exchange as focusing on servers, storage networking, security, and corporate services.

Reasons most often given for changes of CEO or directors relate to the person, e.g., "failed to achieve the performance target," "lacked communication and execution skills." Or, as the story put out to the public, "There was a disagreement over the company's strategy," or "The chairperson and the CEO did not have the same chemistry or

---

289 David F. Larcker and Brian Tayan, "Governance Aches and Pains: Is Bad Governance Chronic?" *Stanford Closer Look Series*, 2016, 2f; Des Luna, "Marissa Mayer out, Thomas Mcinerney in as Yahoo CEO after Verizon Acquisition," *TechTimes*, March 15, 2017, https://www.techtimes.com/articles/201596/20170315/marissa-mayer-out-thomas-mcinerney-in-as-yahoo-ceo-after-verizon-acquisition.htm.

290 David Goldman, "HP CEO Apotheker Fired, Replaced by Meg Whitman," CNN Money, September 22, 2011, http://money.cnn.com/2011/09/22/technology/hp_ceo_fired/index.htm; Max Smolaks, "HP Completes Separation into Two Companies," *Datacenter Dynamics*, November 2, 2015, http://www.datacenterdynamics.com/content-tracks/design-build/hp-completes-separation-into-two-companies/95130.fullarticle; "Meg Whitman Steps Off HP Inc. Board of Directors; Company Appoints Chip Bergh as New Chairman," HP Press Center, July 26, 2017, https://press.ext.hp.com/us/en/press-releases/2017/meg-whitman-steps-off-hp-inc--board-of-directors--company-appoin.html; Traub, "HP CFO Wayman to Retire," CFO, December 11, 2006, http://ww2.cfo.com/human-capital-careers/2006/12/hp-cfo-wayman-to-retire/.

leadership styles." The issue could indeed be traced to the person. But there might be another or an additional reason. The dynamic is more complex.

Governance issues can take many forms, and the main cause might not always be the person in charge. While leaders bring their personalities, capabilities, motivations, expectations, emotions, and personal histories into play, the role itself is part of and influences both system/organization and social context. Therefore, there is a complex interplay between the role and the person filling it.[291]

The leadership role is both psychological (ideas and personal expectations of the person filling it) and sociological (other people's ideas and expectations of the person taking up the role).[292] A role impacts a person's behavior and consequently has an effect on the personality development.

ROLE BIOGRAPHY

Despite the fact that a role is part of a system, it is shaped by the occupier of the role. They will have their own history of roles within different systems, e.g., the family, community, and work. Susan Long calls this history the "role biography."[293]

Each person creates a unique role biography over a lifetime, beginning with childhood, and each role teaches something new. The way a person takes up a role is the sum of each role he or she has had in the past. The shaping goes both ways: the individual shapes the role, and each role shapes the individual.[294]

---

291 Susan Long, "The Transforming Experience Framework," in *Transforming Experience in Organisations: A Framework for Organisational Research and Consultancy*, ed. Susan Long (New York: Routledge, 2018), 10ff.

292 Ibid.

293 Susan Long, "Drawing from Role Biography in Organizational Role Analysis," in *Coaching in Depth: The Organizational Role Analysis Approach*, ed. John Newton, Burkard Sievers, and Susan Long (London: Karnac Books, 2006), 127.

294 Jane Chapman and Susan Long, "Role Contamination: Is the Poison in the Person or in the Bottle," *Socio-Analysis: The Journal of the Australian Institute of Socio-Analysis*, vol. 11 (2009), 53–66.

Contemplating role biographies helps people to find and understand the origins of valences (see sidebar) in roles. A new role is not tackled in isolation. It is important to consider the history of the person taking up the role regarding how he or she has handled roles in the past.[295]

If a manager who is used to screaming and shouting learns that part of his role is also to listen, he can handle the role differently. He does not need to change his personality, but his understanding of the role and how someone in this role should behave. The advantage is that such personal/professional behavior changes can happen rather quickly, as long as the person's perspective doesn't contribute to the inertia. Irving Borwick, managing director of Borwick International Inc., an international management consulting firm, calls this phenomenon "change without change."[296]

VALENCE

The term *valence* was first used in a psychological sense by Kurt Lewin in the 1930s and was adopted by Wilfred Bion: "Valence is the intrinsic attraction (positive valence) or aversion (negative valence) of an event, object, or situation, for a specific individual. It is an unconscious predisposition or tendency for an individual to repeatedly choose to behave in particular ways when placed in provoking contexts."[297]

This refers to the predisposition of an individual to repeat a specific pattern of behavior when experiencing anxiety. If, for example, the individual naturally assumes a mediator role, one would say "he or she has a valence for taking up the role of mediator." Other valences would be to remain quiet or be a challenger to the group.

---

295 Long, "Drawing from Role Biography," 137.

296 Irving Borwick, "Organizational Role Analysis: Managing Strategic Change in Business Settings," in *Coaching in Depth: The Organizational Role Analysis Approach* (London, New York: Karnac Books, 2006), 7–9.

297 Ibid., 17.

Bion speaks of two realities in each group. The first reality is called the work group and is more conscious. The group is busy with the primary task and rational objective of the group. The second reality is called the basic assumption group and is more unconscious. The group is occupied with anxieties and feelings that are founded in maladaptive assumptions about the group. Since the dynamic is unconscious, it disturbs the focus on the primary task.

In consequence, valence is a person's unconscious tendency to either assume a specific role in a group or to make a basic assumption. It is very important to find out the extent to which a group member takes part in the basic assumption mentality.

ROLE HISTORY (AND POISONED ROLES)

Roles in a system each have a history. Thus, they are not neutral. People have hopes and anxieties regarding the contribution of a new leader and the impact this will have on their own roles. In addition to this dynamic, the social or political context and the purpose of the organization will influence the role and its development.

According to Chapman and Long,[298] this history unconsciously impacts the attitudes, feelings, thoughts, and behavior of the people taking up the roles. The researchers focus on the consequences of the interaction between a role, its history, its occupier, and the occupier's role biography.

Consequences can include corruption, perversion, or poisoning of the role. In such cases, the role can contaminate its occupier. Since a role is related to all other roles in a system, these other roles and their tasks can also be contaminated.

The poison is not only in the person but also in the bottle (the system). An example might be the CEO of Enron, a role so poisoned that

---

298 Chapman and Long, "Role Contamination," 53–66.

nobody wanted to assume it. When vacancies cannot be filled for a long time, it is not unusual for administrators or receivers to jump in.

It would be interesting and probably crucial to evaluate whether the CEO roles at Yahoo and HP and the chairperson role at HP were/are contaminated. Their impacts on their occupiers, other roles, and organizations as a whole are very strong. It is recommended that these roles be thoroughly assessed against this background.

Chapter 8, "Detecting and Avoiding Danger," in the subsection "Assess Current and Future Leaders More Thoroughly," demonstrates indicators that can help establish whether an issue lies with the role or with its occupier.

FROM VERTICAL TO HORIZONTAL LEADERSHIP

In the past, it was expected that top management would make the right decisions. Information was transmitted bottom-up; orders came top-down. This is called vertical leadership.[299]

In vertical leadership, people need to believe that leaders are capable. However, the way leadership is executed is different in the vertical model. Leaders need to learn how to persuade, empower, and influence people. The key word is *trust*—mutual trust because of reciprocity (more on trust in chapter 9 "Checks and Balances"). Leaders need to understand social complexity and develop emotional intelligence.[300] (Find more on how to develop emotional intelligence in chapter 7, "Crucial Leadership Skills (and How to Develop Them).")

Depending on the circumstances, situations can arise that require vertical leadership. For example, during the aftermath of 9/11, banks needed to decide quickly whether to buy or sell, and somebody needed to take the lead. It is not easy to quickly switch from the horizontal to

---

299 Charles H. Green, "The New Leadership Is Horizontal, Not Vertical," Trusted Advisor, (last visited May 7, 2018), http://trustedadvisor.com/articles/the-new-leadership-is-horizontal-not-vertical.

300 Ibid.

the vertical model. Leaders need to explain and justify why they are switching, e.g., to speed up decision-making.

In today's VUCA world, the vertical leadership model has major shortcomings. It gives way to the horizontal (or flat) model that is described as networks, relationships, alliances, cultures, cooperation, coaching, and communities. Information comes from everywhere and flows everywhere.[301]

Horizontal leadership calls for the generation of movement around a shared goal. It is about persuading people over whom one has no authority/control to collaborate in a shared purpose.[302] This is how collective intelligence can be created. Even if it appears so, the process is not democratic, it still requires a degree of authority and discipline, and the leader remains responsible for the ultimate decision-making.[303]

As new technologies, fast-changing environments, and increased globalization emerge and evolve, new organizational designs are required. They are more flexible, with horizontal networks replacing vertical hierarchies. This constitutes the creation of organizations without boundaries.

EXAMPLE OF A BOUNDARYLESS COMPANY

A good example of a boundaryless company that has been highly successful is W. L. Gore & Associates (Gore-Tex), with about 10,500 associates around the world and more than $3.7 billion in annual revenues.[304]

Gore-Tex was founded in 1958 in the US by Wilbert Gore and his wife

---

301 Manfred F. R. Kets de Vries, *The Leadership Mystique* (Harlow, UK: Prentice Hall Financial Times, 2006), 55.

302 Green, "The New Leadership Is Horizontal."

303 Kets de Vries, *Leadership Mystique*, 55.

304 N/Aa, "The Gore Story," https://www.gore.com/about/the-gore-story#overview.

Genevieve. Wanting to build a truly innovative company, the Gores decided to abandon any hierarchy and to establish lines of communication that were direct and person to person. Titles such as *boss*, *manager*, and *employee* were replaced by *associate*. Each associate had at least one *sponsor* (no boss), who was another associate. The sponsor's role was to offer support and input for the ongoing development of the respective person, building on his or her strengths. The company has leaders, but even these are called associates. Nobody can give orders or impose commitments on others. They are all self-imposed. Teams are self-organized, and the workforce appoints its CEO based on a group decision.[305]

The original idea of the founders was that the mere peer pressure and the wish to be innovative would serve as glue to hold the company together. Gore-Tex has no rule book or bureaucracy. The company focuses on core values through trust with their associates. The workforce co-owns the company together with the founders.[306] This structure leads to a faster development of products and technologies compared to the competitive landscape.

In sum, the company fosters teamwork, a flat organization, and personal initiatives that all add to the satisfaction and retention of the workforce. Despite—or because of—no titles, no bosses, no formal hierarchy and thus no org chart, Gore-Tex is frequently ranked as one of the best companies to work for. For example, in 2017, for the twentieth consecutive year, W. L. Gore & Associates was among the Fortune 100 Best Companies to Work For—one of just twelve Great Place to Work Legends appearing in every edition of the rankings since the list began in 1998.[307] It was awarded as one of the "Best

---

305 Simon Caulkin, "Gore-Tex Gets Made without Managers," *The Guardian*, November 1, 2008, https://www.theguardian.com/business/2008/nov/02/gore-tex-textiles-terri-kelly.

306 Caulkin, "Gore-Tex Gets Made without Managers"; Amy Calhoun, "Gore Again Named One of the 100 Best Companies to Work For," Gore, March 30, 2016, https://www.gore.com/news-events/press-release/enterprise-press-release-fortune-100-list-2016-us.

307 Calhoun, "Gore Again Named One of the 100 Best Companies."

Workplaces for Diversity" in 2019 and again among the Fortune 100 Best Companies to Work For in 2020.[308]

CRITICS ON BOUNDARYLESS COMPANIES

Hirschhorn and Gilmore assert that it is not possible to create organizations without boundaries. The elimination of hierarchy, function, and geography, they maintain, will be replaced by new and different boundaries that are more psychological than organizational in nature. Since these boundaries are created in people's minds and thus are invisible, they will be harder to manage. It will become essential yet challenging for each person in the system (associate, sponsor, etc.), to recognize these new boundaries and use them to their advantage. Changing and more fluid environments will continue to disrupt traditional business relationships and add to confusion. For example, an engineer and a shop-floor worker with their very different skillsets could face more tension and difficulties in immediately understanding their relationship in a team environment; they may be required to manage their psychological boundaries in a new boundaryless company.[309]

Often, leaders of flexible organizations believe or hope that conflict will decrease if obvious boundaries decrease, as this should automatically foster teamwork. As the example of the engineer and the shop-floor worker shows, the question is how a healthy tension among very different but complementary skillsets can be upheld in a flexible environment.

For leaders, the key lies in managing the new (psychological) boundaries. According to Hirschhorn and Gilmore, these boundaries consist of four dynamic and interrelated types:[310]

---

308 "W. L. Gore & Associates, Inc.," Great Place to Work, https://www.greatplacetowork.com/certified-company/1000289.

309 Hirschhorn and Gilmore, "The New Boundaries of the 'Boundaryless' Company," *Harvard Business Review*, vol. 70, no. 3 (1992), 104–115.

310 Ibid., 104–115.

- Task boundary: People increasingly depend on others and have to establish who does what.
- Political boundary: Groups of people with different interests are prone to political clashes.
- Identity boundary: The identity boundary is about values, whereas the political boundary is about interest.
- Authority boundary: The issuing and following of orders is replaced by increased vulnerability and feedback from below.

There are strategies that help navigate these different types of boundaries.

- Task boundary: Individuals must first define the task and then associate responsibilities and resources.
- Political boundary: It is important for group members to negotiate with each other in healthy ways.
- Identity boundary: Common identity is energizing and motivating. The balance between creating a team spirit (loyalty) and valuing other group members' contributions (respect) is crucial.
- Authority boundary: Most mistakes are related to the authority boundary. Leaders should not fall into the trap of believing that increased collaboration and participation will require them to give up their authority. An authority vacuum can lead to excessive group cohesion and foster passivity. This can lead to political conflicts and identity differences because subordinates cannot see fair decision processes due to the perceived absence of the leader (and his or her authority). Often, the reason for a leader's abdication of authority is self-defense: anxiety of making the right decisions in an increasingly changing and unpredictable business environment that entails risks. A common response made by leaders when they abdicate authority is to adopt mechanistic ways and focus on detailed planning and analysis.[311]

The best way to exercise authority is to replace control with contain-

311 Ibid., 104–115.

ment (see chapter 5, "Key Driver Three: Leadership as an Accelerator," in the subsection "The Dark Side of Leadership") of conflicts, doubts, and anxieties. The best leaders help resolve arising conflicts while being aware of their own and others' feelings—important data and vital signals to understand and manage what is going on in the relationship and at the boundaries.[312]

SPECIFIC BOUNDARYLESS MANAGEMENT SYSTEM: HOLACRACY

Holacracy is a management system in which authority and decision-making processes are distributed throughout the organization.[313] It is seen as an alternative to traditional hierarchies and flat management as a means to bring structure and discipline to a peer-to-peer workplace. Holacracy, a complete system for self-organization, aims at increasing transparency, organizational agility, and accountability while reducing tension and improving operational processes. People are defined by roles and not by titles.[314]

The idea of Holacracy is not new. In 1967, Hungarian author, Arthur Koestler, laid the foundation for the concept in his fictional book *The Ghost in the Machine,* where he coined the term "holon" as something that is simultaneously a whole and a part.[315]

Brian Robertson created the Holacracy brand, adapted his system to today's business world, and launched his company, HolacracyOne, in 2007. He devised basic guidelines that define the structure.

---

312   Ibid., 104–115.

313   Maren Meyer, „Das Ende der Hierarchien: Holacracy schafft den Chef ab," *BILANZ,* December 21, 2016, 68.

314   Meyer, Das Ende der Hierarchien, 68.

315   Joseph Schumpeter, "The Holes in Holacracy: The Latest Big Idea in Management Deserves Some Scepticism," *The Economist,* July 5, 2014, https://www.economist.com/news/business/21606267-latest-big-idea-management-deserves-some-scepticism-holes-holacracy.

Table 3: Holacracy in a Nutshell

TRADITIONAL COMPANIES	HOLACRACY
Job Descriptions	**Roles**
Each person has exactly one job. Job descriptions are imprecise, rarely updated, and often irrelevant.	Roles are defined around the work, not people, and are updated regularly. People fill several roles.
Delegated Authority	**Distributed Authority**
Managers loosely delegate authority. Ultimately, their decision always trumps others.	Authority is truly distributed to teams and roles. Decisions are made locally.
Big Reorgs	**Rapid Iterations**
The org structure is rarely revisited, mandated from the top.	The org structure is regularly updated via small iterations. Every team self-organizes.
Office Politics	**Transparent Rules**
Implicit rules slow down change and favor people "in the know."	Everyone is bound by the same rules, CEO included. Rules are visible to all.

Source: Adapted from http://www.holacracy.org/.

Only about one thousand companies among the countless millions of businesses in the world have reportedly implemented Holacracy throughout the company. These include Zappos, an American online retailer that belongs to Amazon. The CEO, however, is a key element to its success. If the CEO is not willing to give away power, the chances that the new system will work are minimized.[316]

Support and Critics of Holacracy

There exists positive and negative feedback regarding experiences with Holacracy. Some criticize it on the basis that it is easier to separate role and person on paper than in practice. It is important for people to develop, and the human element should not be neglected. Futurist Paul Saffo does not approve of Holacracy because he does not know one company in which Holacracy has worked properly and successfully.[317] In contrast, Peter Gloor, a researcher at MIT, says that an important precondition for implementing Holacracy is that

---

316 Meyer, "Das Ende der Hierarchien," 67; Julian Birkinshaw, "Beware the Next Big Thing," *Harvard Business Review*, vol. 92, no. 5 (2014), 50–57.

317 Ibid., 68.

people enjoy bearing responsibility. He further attests that although Holacracy is difficult to measure, companies such as Apple, Airbnb, and Tesla have only been able to grow extensively and successfully thanks to the "swarm-business" model and engagement of the staff.[318] This opinion is backed by Jeffrey Pfeffer of Stanford University, who notes that it has mainly been young and fast-growing companies that have adopted Holacracy, thanks to its "benign-dictator CEOs" and similar concepts of democratic leadership.[319] In contrast, leaders of long-standing, well-established companies consisting of several hierarchical levels are more prone to oppose Holacracy.[320] Julian Birkinshaw of London Business School writes that, "Nine-tenths of the approximately 100 branded management ideas I've studied lost their popularity within a decade or so. Different attempts in the past to democratize the decision-making process have not shown success.[321]

It remains to be seen if and to what extent Holacracy will bear success in the long term.

Future of Roles in Holacracies

In organizations powered by Holacracy, as people take on different roles concurrently and/or change them more frequently (role biography), the same might apply to role histories. Thus, it can be debated whether the impact of the role biography or the role history has the stronger impact on the person taking up the role. It might even be possible that role biographies in the way described in the previous section "Role Biography and Role History" (role occupiers have their own history of assuming roles) no longer exist.

In any case, according to Schumpeter, it remains essential to overcome the biggest resistance to assuming new roles, which is understanding

---

318 Ibid., 68.

319 Schumpeter, "The Holes in Holacracy."

320 Ibid.

321 Julian Birkinshaw, "Beware the Next Big Thing," *Harvard Business Review*, vol. 92, no. 5 (2014), 50–57.

what actually needs to be done. In Holacracy, this is written in detail in the Constitution.[322]

WHAT WILL WORK LOOK LIKE IN THE FUTURE?

Whether hierarchy, flatter or flat organization, flatarchy or holacracy, the question remains: Is the problem with the organization structure, the leaders, the followers, the roles/role biographies, or all of the above?

What is certain in the VUCA world is that the workplace itself is "volatile, uncertain, complex and ambiguous." Leadership and branded management theories and experiments come and go (mostly, they go).

Two constants remain. One is change. The other is the need to recruit, select, develop, monitor, and retain leaders who anticipate and adapt to rapid global, socioeconomic, and political change and lead through it with the right combination of intelligence, intuition, empathy, and stability.

INFLUENCE OF CULTURE ON ACCEPTANCE OF POWER IN LEADERSHIP

Culture matters. A lot. Business leader and author Jürg Wittwer of *I Am the Monkey* states, "Leading globally is a complex reality, and different cultures anticipate different attitudes for their leadership and constructs for their hierarchies, though management trainings do not yet broadly reflect this."[323]

Differences are manifold. According to Wittwer, some cultures praise ambition while others don't appreciate it. Another example is how charismatic leaders are perceived. They are favored by the Anglo-Saxon countries, such as the UK, US, and Australia. The contrary

---

322 Borwick, "Organizational Role Analysis," 7–9.

323 Jürg Wittwer, *I Am the Monkey: How to Successfully Manage and Live in Foreign Cultures* (Charleston, SC, 2016), 106f.

holds true for the Middle East. Team orientation is appreciated by Latin countries, whereas South Asian and Nordic European countries favor human/individual orientation, compared to Eastern European countries that prefer the autonomous leadership style reflected by strong leaders.[324]

The distribution of equality of power is a critical aspect of leadership. The acceptance of it by leaders and subordinates varies from culture to culture. The Power Distance Index[325]was designed to measure the degree to which unequal distributions of power are expected and accepted by members of institutions and organizations within a country, e.g., how status or social power are perceived within them.

Although power distance suggests inequality, it has to do with the fact that both the followers *and* leaders endorse a society's inequality.

Germany scores 35 out of 100 on the Power Distance Index. Arab countries reach 80 on the scale, which reflects a very high distance compared to Austria's 11. Although Germany and the US are both found somewhere in the middle, there is a difference in regard to the gap between rich and poor people. Since Germany does not have a large gap, as citizens strongly believe in equality, they have the chance to rise in its society. In contrast, the US shows a higher degree of unequal distribution of wealth, and it appears that this gap is getting larger and larger.

Chapter 5, "Key Driver Three: Leadership as an Accelerator," explores how power often triggers contradictory, uneasy, and suspicious feelings in regard to how it is received or executed. The cultural dimension adds another layer of complexity to power and leadership. Although increased globalization and technological change help connect people, leaders need to be aware of their own and their subordinates' cultural

---

324 Ibid., 109.

325 "Power Distance Index," Clearly Cultural, (last visited July 28, 2017), http://www.clearlycultural.com/geert-hofstede-cultural-dimensions/power-distance-index/.

influence and perception in order to improve leadership and decrease the likelihood for negative outcomes.

PART 3

SOLUTIONS
AND TOOLBOX

The three hidden key drivers of derailment have been identified and analyzed both in isolation and in interrelation, in an effort to illustrate and clarify the complexity of derailment and its causes, and thereby to minimize some of the "horror" and uncertainty surrounding derailment.

This chapter provides tools for the successful management of the interrelation of change and the human element in leadership. This begins with putting the "right" leaders into leadership positions—people who put the company's interests first, give and receive trust, create meaning, inspire stakeholders, and make a positive impact on all fronts. Ultimately, the goal is to help prevent or reduce negative outcomes and consequently improve performance. The objective of this section is not to demonstrate which tool can or should be applied in which situation but to present each in an understandable way. The order in which they are presented is not related to any preference or chronology. Each can play a specific role as regards to the individual company, context, and situation. Each company can customize its own toolbox by selecting and filling it with a suitable and unique mix of tools.

CHAPTER 7

CRUCIAL LEADERSHIP SKILLS

(AND HOW TO DEVELOP THEM)

As stated many times in this book, leadership in an ever-changing world is a highly complex field. Therefore, the question of what theory or model to use in a current or new leadership position is a challenging one. The main topic is how leaders, employees, and other stakeholders can create successful organizations in a constantly changing environment. The business world is more diverse than ever, and rapid flux has made markets become highly unpredictable, which requires new leadership approaches.

Leaders are asked to take actions and make decisions even more quickly and be accountable for them. They need to be or become physically and psychologically resilient while meeting the challenges and contradictions that come with complexities. Greater attention and improved communication skills, written and oral, are demanded of leaders. They certainly need to understand the key aspects of the business and are expected to be connected and available 24/7, further increasing an already massive workload. New risks and an increased use of multiple technologies put further challenges on leaders.[326]

All these requirements and many more call for leaders who are not just charismatic but transformational, adaptive to changes from all directions, and connected to stakeholders. Having an open mindset to deal with ambiguities and think in possibilities will help leaders engage not only with others but also with themselves. As this section will show, an understanding of oneself is crucial in order to get to know and lead others.

In addition to these new requirements and changes in the scope and content of leaders' work, organizations have changed. They are more complex and need to meet requirements regarding transparency, connectivity, technology orientation and innovation, decision-making processes, and accountability.

The key question of organizations in a fast-changing environment is to what extent the field of leadership development is still in line with the needs of future leaders. To adapt means to learn and develop constantly. This might call for different/further qualities and a shift in mindset, even more so because leaders bear greater responsibility for the cultivation of other and future leaders.

In order for future leaders to better prepare for and deal with the challenges triggered by the VUCA world, the following skills and qualities and ways to improve them are strongly recommended (the more the merrier).

1. Be emotionally intelligent
    - self-aware
    - self-regulated
    - motivated
    - empathetic

---

326 De Haan, "The Leadership Shadow," 2.

- ○ socially skilled
2. Be agile
  - ○ visionary with a purpose
  - ○ adaptable to change
  - ○ engaged
  - ○ humble
3. Be able to inspire
4. Be authentic (and hold yourself personally accountable)
5. Be courageous to speak the truth
6. Be a good listener
7. Be (self-)reflected

The following sections describe each skill in more detail and discuss how each can be improved. They also show how closely interrelated many of them are.

1. BE EMOTIONALLY INTELLIGENT

Good leaders have high levels of emotional intelligence (EQ). The concept of emotional intelligence is very old, starting with Darwin in 1870 and being further developed by Wechsler, Leeper, Ellis, Gardner, Mayer, Salovy, Caruso, Bar-On, and so on.[327]

In 1995, Goleman's work raised interest in the importance that EQ plays. It is considered to be one of the most crucial components of great leadership. Consequently, a lack of EQ seriously harms leadership quality regardless of the prevalence of technical or analytical skills. EQ not only helps hiring committees identify extraordinary leaders but also positively impacts leaders' performance on the job.[328]

EQ consists of five components: self-awareness, self-regulation (containment), motivation, empathy, and social skills.[329]

---

327 Steven J. Stein and Howard E. Book, *The EQ Edge: Emotional Intelligence and Your Success* (Mississauga, ON: John Wiley & Sons, 2011), 14f.

328 Daniel Goleman, "What Makes a Leader," *Harvard Business Review*, vol. 76, no. 6 (1998), 94.

329 Ibid., 94.

Various studies show the tenure and success rate of CEOs have greatly deteriorated in the past generation. In the past twenty years alone, a third of Fortune 500 CEOs have stayed in position for less than three years. The failure rate of top executives ranges from 30 percent up to 75 percent. Global CEOs' longevity has dropped from 9.5 years in 1995 to 7.6 years today.[330]

Almost 40 percent of CEOs fail to meet performance targets in their first eighteen months.[331] Fernandez-Araoz from Egon Zehnder International discovered that CEOs who failed had been hired based on their IQ, business expertise, and drive but ended up being fired for lack of EQ; this followed the same pattern across the globe.[332]

Two decades ago, Charan and Colvin analyzed Fortune 500 CEO failure and found that the reason for dismissal was typically drastic flaws in execution. Behind this was an inability to put the right people in the right job. Charan and Colvin translated these reasons and found out that the CEOs in question lacked emotional strength in the context of personnel decisions. This implied that the cause of "failure to execute" was bad personnel selection, which was based on missing EQ.[333]

Dotlich and Caior present the eleven most prevalent reasons why CEOs fail: arrogance, melodrama, volatility, excessive caution, habitual distrust, aloofness, mischievousness, eccentricity, passive resistance, perfectionism, and eagerness to please. Most of these reasons can be associated with hubris, ego, and a lack of EQ.[334]

---

330 Ray Williams, "Why Every CEO Needs a Coach," *Psychology Today*, (last visited July 14, 2017), https://www. psychologytoday.com/blog/wired-success/201208/why-every-ceo-needs-coach.

331 Eben Harrell, "Succession Planning: What the Research Says," *Harvard Business Review*, vol. 94, no. 12 (2016), 1.

332 Fernández-Aráoz, *Great People Decisions: Why They Matter So Much, Why They are So Hard, and How You Can Master Them* (Hoboken, NJ: John Wiley & Sons, 2007), 170.

333 Ram Charan and Geoffrey Colvin, "Why CEOs Fail: It's Rarely for Lack of Smarts or Vision. Most Unsuccessful CEOs Stumble Because of One Simple, Fatal Shortcoming," CNN Money, June 21, 1999, https://money.cnn.com/magazines/fortune/fortune_archive/1999/06/21/261696/.

334 D. L. Dotlich and P. C. Cairo, *Why CEOs Fail: The 11 Behaviors That Can Derail Your Climb to the Top - And How to Manage Them* (San Francisco: Jossey-Bass, 2007).

According to Goleman's experience, some argue that a certain degree of EQ is present at birth. It is generally accepted that EQ increases with age and can be learned. But in school, and later in business school, the focus tends to be on fostering rational rather than intuitive thought. And seldom is EQ learned on the job.

EQ is a fundamental leadership ingredient, especially in today's business world, in which cross-cultural interactions, the ability to attract, develop, and retain talent at all levels, teamwork, and increasing pace of change have become the new normal.

But there are EQ development programs that help overcome old habits and patterns and create and nurture new ones. This process is a personal one, which makes practice more time- and cost-intensive. In addition, a person must be willing to learn and develop.

Although the Emotional Quotient has been widely researched and its importance is confirmed, it remained untested or unmeasured until Bar-On introduced a tool called the EQ-i (Emotional Quotient Inventory). The EQ-i is divided into five subthemes consisting of fifteen components (skills and attitudes) in total. The EQ-i 2.0 has been translated into forty-five languages, conducted in sixty-six countries, and reveals links between the EQ and proven success. Concurrently, Stein introduced Multi-Health Systems (MHS) assessments that contain psychological tests. Bar-On's and Stein's work is complementary.[335]

SELF-AWARE

Self-awareness builds the foundation on which the other four building blocks of EQ rest. It is an invaluable tool that can break through narcissism's negative aspects and help one better understand and manage one's shadow side. It focuses on the process of getting to know oneself. Only that which is recognized can be managed. If leaders become more aware of their emotions, feelings, behaviors, and drivers, they

---

335 Stein and Book, *The EQ Edge*, 2–4.

can become more effective. Self-awareness helps prevent the triggering of regressive or destructive behavior in extreme situations.[336]

A developed self-awareness and consciousness help leaders find the presence and behavior needed in a process of change. Leaders get to know their impulses and keep asking themselves repeatedly what other options they could/should have chosen to further increase the chance of progress.[337]

Remember Bonny, John, and Mike (from chapter 5, "Key Driver Three: Leadership as an Accelerator," in the subsection "Influence of Upbringing on Leadership and Implications for Leadership Selection")? John, the risk-averse CFO who feels comfortable making decisions only if he has all the information at hand. Mike, the perceived sarcastic CEO whose subordinates prefer not to show any weakness when he is present. Bonny, the entrepreneur who has a strong tendency to micromanage. None of them were aware of their unconscious negative behavior patterns.

Once they practiced self-awareness in the way described below, they could bring their reactive responses into consciousness and assume responsibility for their actions. It was key for Bonny, John, and Mike to discover and assess the unconscious filters that were influencing how they viewed the world and interpreted events and judgments of third parties.

Finding out with the help of a coach (see chapter 8, "Detecting and Avoiding Danger"), by practicing reflection themselves or applying the methods described below, they were able to increase their self-awareness and learn about their own restrictive leadership behaviors. This was when they realized it was not sufficient to just recognize that they needed to change their behavior. They needed to rewire their drivers that triggered this behavior to be able to make the necessary

---

336 Kleiner, "The Thought Leader Interview," 4.

337 Higgs and Rowland, "What Does It Take to Implement Change Successfully?" 325.

adjustments to their common leadership styles. Not surprisingly, all of them found the clues in their childhoods.

General Awareness

It is helpful to develop general awareness to gain perspective for self-awareness. Because experiences shape people's perceptions and perspectives, any two people can look at the same thing and see it differently. Therefore, one needs to strive for objectivity by getting on a "balcony" to gain some distance. From up there, one can observe oneself and others in the organization in action.

Potential questions to ask oneself: Who is interacting with whom? Who forms alliances with whom? What is the character of the relationships, especially the ones that are not written in the organizational chart? Is there a problem and if so, what does it look like? What are the different opinions, thoughts, and feelings? What do the individual's hidden behavioral patterns look like? Are they a consequence of the company's culture, structure, and processes? Where could there be potential danger regarding values, beliefs, preferences, and loyalties?[338]

It is crucial for leaders to understand the values and beliefs of the people they work with and lead, and especially those they would like to help change and/or adapt to change. Very often, it is not only the lack of logic or facts that makes people stuck but their hearts and stomach—the fear of loss: loss of jobs, status, identity, relevance, or something similar.[339]

Develop Self-Awareness

Developing self-awareness does not happen overnight—it takes time to step back and self-reflect. Hence, self-awareness calls for introspection in order to uncover strengths and weaknesses. It is also important

---

338 Ibid., 20–22.

339 Ibid., 10, 26.

for leaders to ask for feedback on their leadership skills. This helps add new skills, hone existing ones, and make up for any deficiencies.[340] Leaders who know their own limitations—who have an important but rarely well-developed sense of their own abilities and disabilities—are clever enough to recruit and enable others to fill the gaps in their shortcomings with skills complementary to their own.[341] Here are a few recommendations by researchers, authors, and the author of this book. In order to increase the impact of the action plan, the recommendations address the readers directly ("you" form).

1. Ask yourself: What am I doing? Why am I doing it? How is it affecting others?
2. Start a journal to learn about your internal landscape; write down positive and negative emotions and weight them by intensity; describe the situations that have led to the listed feelings; find a pattern of situations that trigger certain (strong) feelings; try to find out what types of people trigger which feelings. What are the links between thoughts and feelings and bodily sensations?[342]

The Johari Window

The Johari Window[343] is a widely known and accepted technique to improve self-awareness. It is a valuable, commonly used coaching or training tool because it is simple and can be applied in different environments and situations. Aside from self-awareness, it also helps understand and improve personal development, communications, interpersonal relationships, team dynamics, and development. It can also be considered as a communication mode that helps with the analysis of interpersonal communication and the way information is

---

340 Nelson and Hogan, "Coaching on the Dark Side," 14.

341 Nixon, *Pariahs*, 105f.

342 Ibid., 63–65.

343 Johari Window, Bloomsbury Business Library—Business & Management Dictionary, http://web.b.ebscohost. com.ezproxy.insead.edu/ehost/detail/detail?vid=11&sid=d985d7c3-0901-4a09-919b-3e6502484002 percent40sessionmgr103&bdata=JnNpdGU9ZWhvc3QtbGl2ZQ percent3d percent3d#AN=26742018&db=bth (last visited July 14, 2017); "Johari Window Model and Free Diagrams," Businessballs, (last visited May 6, 2018), http://www.businessballs.com/johariwindowmodel.htm.

provided and received. The model was invented by Luft and Ingram in 1955 and usually consists of a grid that is divided into four quadrants. Each quadrant stands for a certain type of communication exchange.

Table 4: Johari Window

	KNOWN BY SELF	UNKNOWN BY SELF
KNOWN BY OTHERS	**Open Area**	**Blind Area**
	Awareness of the parts (personality aspects) of myself that I and others perceive, which leads to a minimization of interpersonal conflicts. It can be expanded further through deeper communication, e.g., in the hidden area.	Lack of self-awareness; parts of me that I don't know about that other people do know about. This can lead to ignorance about oneself. Seeking feedback helps reduce the blind area.
UNKNOWN BY OTHERS	**Hidden Area**	**Unknown Area**
	There are parts of myself that I know about that other people don't know about, which leads to defensive behavior and an increased chance of interpersonal conflicts. Disclosing and exposing information and feelings helps reduce the hidden area.	Lack of (self-)awareness; this is the unconscious part of me that neither I nor others recognize. Younger people and people who lack experience or self-belief are expected to have a larger unknown area. Self-discovery, observation by others, or counseling can help reduce this area.

Source: "Johari Window Model and Free Diagrams," Businessballs.

SELF-REGULATED

Self-regulation or psychological containment has also been explored in chapter 5, "Key Driver Three: Leadership as an Accelerator," (in the subsection "The Dark Side of Leadership") with a focus on a person's capacity to listen (deeply), to take in, and to react.

Self-regulation is the capacity to internally manage uncomfortable thoughts, emotions, feelings, and behavior that result from external pressure and stress. Strengthening this ability helps build both self-esteem and self-confidence so that people become more welcoming toward change and comfortable with ambiguity. Within this concept, thinking comes before acting.[344]

It is also the ability to become resilient. The American Psychology Association describes resilience as "the process of adapting well in the face of adversity, trauma, tragedy, threats, and even significant sources of stress—such as family and relationship problems, serious health problems, or workplace and financial stresses. It means 'bouncing back' from difficult experiences."[345]

Impulse control is also included. If leaders manage to regulate themselves, they can refrain from making rash decisions and enacting irresponsible or even destructive behavior.

Develop Self-Regulation

1. **Reflect Before You Act**. Try to think rather than act reflexively, especially if you are prone to being hotheaded and impatient. Pause and create mental space to assess options. Behavior following consideration might have a higher chance of success than shots from the hip. It helps to apply the ABC concept:[346] activating events (what has happened); beliefs (in what different ways the events are interpreted); consequences (what feelings do these different beliefs trigger and how do they affect the options of consequences?). The key is to practice containment while remaining flexible and spontaneous.

2. **Recollect Your Values and Beliefs**. It is important that you know where you do not want to make compromises based on your value system. Construct your own code of ethics so that you can make

---

344 Goleman, "What Makes a Leader," 95–98.

345 "The Road to Resilience: What is Resilience?" American Psychological Association (APA), (last visited November 27, 2017), http://www.apa.org/helpcenter/road-resilience.aspx.

346 R. S. Sharf, *Theories of Psychotherapy and Counseling: Concepts and Cases* (Boston: Cengage Learning, 2015), 351.

swift yet well-considered decisions when moral or ethical issues arise.[347]

3. **Hold Yourself Personally Accountable.** Hold yourself personally accountable for your behavior. If you make a mistake, stand up to it, bear the consequences, and do not blame others. Such behavior gains the respect of others. (More on personal accountability and ways to improve it below.)

4. **Practice Remaining Calm.** Self-regulation improves with practice. Impulse control needs to be learned. It is like building muscles. Try to be aware of your behavior when you are in a conflict or under pressure. Write down all the negative statements you are about to say and then throw away the piece of paper. You will be surprised by how effective this simple exercise is.

MOTIVATED

Being motivated is a mindset that all great leaders demonstrate. It is the passion that drives the answer to the question: "What gets you out of bed in the morning?" Leaders who are motivated show commitment to their organizations, pursue their aims, and have high levels of energy and persistence. Unlike people who are motivated by money, power, ego, and status (all external factors and rewards), real leaders are motivated by a deeply embedded desire to achieve for the sake of achievement.[348] The question remains whether this is always a noble motivation, as achievements should have purposes other than personal validation.

Develop Motivation

There are different ways to improve motivation:[349]

---

347 "Emotional Intelligence in Leadership: Learning How to Be More Aware," Mind Tools, (last visited April 30, 2017), https://www.mindtools.com/pages/article/newLDR_45.htm.

348 Goleman, "What Makes a Leader," 99f.

349 Daniel Goleman, "Emotional Intelligence," (last visited April 30, 2017), http://www.danielgoleman.info/.

1. **Identify the Passion for Your Work.** Step back and reflect on why you accepted your role. If you are unable to figure this out, try to find the root of your lack of motivation. Try to become proud of your accomplishments and to enjoy the privilege of lifelong learning. (As Albert Einstein said, "Once you stop learning, you start dying."[350]) Look for creative challenges and new approaches, and try to energize yourself to get better without becoming dogged. Avoid resting on your laurels and challenge the status quo. As the CEO, ask the BoD to challenge you. Find your purpose (more on finding a purpose, see 2. Agile: Develop a Purpose).

2. **Be Optimistic.** Practice optimism even when things are against you. Containment combined with the motivation for achievement helps conquer the frustration that often follows setbacks. If necessary, try to adjust your mindset and find something good even when problems arise. Practice, practice, practice.

EMPATHETIC

Empathy[351] is the ability to put oneself into others' shoes in order to understand their feelings and behavior and respond accordingly. Empathy helps one develop others, challenge those who behave unfairly, and provide constructive feedback. It is nonjudgmental, whether one agrees or not with someone else. Empathy is a powerful interpersonal tool that can reach its full potential only if the following three misconceptions are overcome:

1. Being empathetic is not the same as being nice or polite. In a (potential) conflict, such an understanding of the other can turn an adversarial relationship into a collaborative one, especially if it is put into words.

2. Empathy often gets confused with sympathy. The latter focuses on the speaker so that statements often start with "I." For example, "I'm sorry to hear about your accident," or "My thoughts are with

---

350 "Albert Einstein: Quotes," Goodreads, (last visited February 26, 2018), https://www.goodreads.com/quotes/7718768-once-you-stop-learning-you-start-dying.

351 Goleman, "What Makes a Leader," 94; Stein and Book, *The EQ Edge*, 134ff.

your family." In contrast, empathetic statements start with "you," as in the example, "You must be sad or happy to hear…"

3. Empathetic comments can positively change a relationship. To be empathetic does not mean to agree but to acknowledge another person's perspective. The validity of another viewpoint is not judged, but its existence is admitted.

4. Interestingly enough, it is most difficult to show empathy during conflicts or under stress, yet this is when it is needed most. In such situations, defense mechanisms arise on both sides that very often lead to unproductive emotional pushes and counterpushes. If leaders practice empathy with their subordinates, they increase the chances that the latter will reciprocate.[352]

Develop Empathy

Here is a handful of ways to improve empathy.

Consider the Subjective Views of Others and Put Yourself in Their Situations

The power of empathetic listening helps prevent projecting your own opinions and feelings, based on your personal past, onto someone else. It is the other person's reality and therefore their truth that counts.[353]

Include Nonverbal Acknowledgment

Your body language reveals a lot, especially if you do not agree with someone's point of view. You might cross your arms, move your feet, or have a tense posture. This signal is immediately conveyed to the other person. It is crucial to pay attention to your body language as well as that of others. Reading others' body language reveals a great deal about how they truly feel about situations regardless of their verbal statements.

---

352 Manfred F. R. Kets de Vries, "Do You Hate Your Boss?" *Harvard Business Review*, vol. 94, no. 2 (2016), 98–102.

353 Stein and Book, *The EQ Edge*, 140–142.

Activate Early Warning Signs

When emotions rise, it might be very helpful to briefly pause and think about potential reactions. Emotions such as anger raise a red flag. It is helpful to find out what bothers someone else and why before reacting prematurely. The challenge is to use self-awareness to take the temperature, practice containment, and be empathetic to understand the other person's viewpoint.[354]

Ask Questions

It is not always possible or easy to determine another person's thoughts and feelings. "Excavating" questions help dig deeper. Such questions are open-ended, such as, "What were you feeling when…" It is important to try to grasp both the other person's feelings and thoughts and the person's expectations and desires. If the feelings are still present, it is helpful to not only acknowledge but also respond to them.[355]

SOCIALLY SKILLED

Social skills are learned in life and come in different phases, ranging from understanding others' thoughts and feelings to being a good teammate, to showing strong negotiation skills. Strong social competencies help one not only to build and maintain relationships and networks but also to manage change.[356]

Leaders need to understand people's key interests so that they can influence them in positive ways. This is important because all internal and external stakeholders need to be aligned with what leaders are trying to achieve in order for it to happen (360-degree influence). As mentioned earlier in this chapter, traditional hierarchies are being replaced by flatter organizational structures, so the interdependence among people in organizations has become more complex. Therefore,

---

354 Ibid., 137f.

355 Ibid., 138–140.

356 Daniel Goleman, "Social Skills," (last visited July 14, 2017), http://www.danielgoleman.info/social-skills-and-eq/.

being able to establish and maintain relationships with a wide range of people is crucial.[357]

Develop Social Skills
Practice and Be Patient

Improving social competence takes time, effort, and stamina.[358] Practice social skills whenever you see an opportunity at work, on the road, or in private life. For example, work to better understand others' thoughts and feelings or to be a good teammate by asking for feedback. As will be described in chapter 8, "Detecting and Avoiding Danger," friends and families might be more capable of providing feedback than complete strangers. Other suggestions are to practice eye contact, practice role-plays, ask for and offer help, or practice negotiation.[359] A measurement for success could be the number and/or quality of one's relationships/network or the way one deals with change.

Have a Role Model

It helps to identify someone who represents the level of social skill you want to attain.[360]

In summary, self-awareness, self-regulation, motivation, empathy, and social skills are the ingredients of emotional intelligence, which can be learned and/or improved. The keyword is practice.

COMBINING EQ WITH "GQ" AND "AQ"

EQ is a subset of "global intelligence" (GQ) that—in addition to the

---

357 Richard Jolly and Randall S. Peterson, "Going Nowhere Fast: Executive Derailment and How to Avoid It," London Business School, March 6, 2017, https://www.london.edu/faculty-and-research/lbsr/going-nowhere-fast#. WSQIUYVOJPY.

358 Goleman, "Emotional Intelligence."

359 Susan H. Spence, "Social Skills Training with Children and Young People: Theory, Evidence and Practice," *Child and Adolescent Mental Health*, vol. 8, no. 2 (2003), 84–96.

360 Goleman, "Emotional Intelligence."

mentioned competencies—also includes worldview (adaptation to the globalized world), cultural curiosity (passion for and interest in different cultures), alignment (including mission, values, beliefs, integrity), collaboration (across cultures including partnerships), integration (from "think global" and "act local" to "think local" and "act global").[361]

2. BE AGILE

Agility has become a highly popular word in business. Although many books, models, and theories have tried to define agility, it is much more challenging to grasp for practitioners because—as Sandhya Johnson puts it—"agility is a complex, multi-dimensional, and context-specific concept that includes the ability to sense unpredictable, environmental change and quickly respond by flexibly marshaling resources, processes, knowledge, and capabilities."[362]

The term *agile* was coined in 2001 in context with a new approach to software development. While searching ways to become more flexible and faster, organizations discovered that the principles of agile software development could not just be applied to this narrow field but much to organizations as a whole.[363]

Agile organizations thrive in an environment that is unpredictable and quickly changing. Such organizations are stable and dynamic, and they not only place focus on clients but also evolve continually to be able to embrace uncertainty and ambiguity. Agile leaders need to be capable of transforming themselves (shift to a mindset of discovery), transforming their teams (build small, diverse, empowered, and connected teams while understanding and addressing their needs),

---

361 Bill George, "Leading a Global Enterprise," Harvard Business School alumni webinar, 2013, 12, https://www.billgeorge.org/wp-content/uploads/2017/04/HBS-Webinar-2-12-13-Leading-Global-Enterprises.pdf.

362 Sandhya Johnson, "Competency Confusers #3: Agility and Adaptability," LinkedIn, (last visited July 23, 2019), https://www.linkedin.com/pulse/competency-confuser-3-agility-adaptability-sandhya-johnson/.

363 Aaron De Smet, Michael Lurie, and Andrew St. George, *Leading Agile Transformation: The New Capabilities Leaders Need to Build 21st-Century Organizations* (McKinsey & Company, 2018), 6.

and transforming their organization (cocreate an agile organizational purpose, design the strategy, operating model and culture):[364]

> Referring to a study from the Global Center for Digital Business Transformation, agile leaders have the following competences: they are *visionary* [and have a purpose], *adaptable* [to change], *engaged*, and *humble*.[365]

These capabilities will now be described in more detail.

VISIONARY AND WITH A PURPOSE

1. **Visionary.** To be visionary as an agile leader means to have a clear sense of the organization's long-term direction, regardless of the short-term uncertainties. To have a clear vision, to communicate it, and make it understood to the stakeholders is especially important in a world that is VUCA. It is more critical for an agile visionary leader to know in which direction the organization needs to head than to have a well-defined idea of how to get there.[366]

2. **With a Purpose.** Purpose is not to be confused with mission. The latter describes what field of business the organization is in (and what not), currently and in the future. It gives focus to management and the workforce. Purpose, in contrast, takes the outward focus further. Purpose defines what the organization is doing for others. It is a way to express the organization's impact on the lives of whoever it is attempting to serve, for example, families, patients, or other organizations. It can also be called the "philosophical heartbeat." To have a purpose is motivational for all stakeholders because the connection does not just occur on the level of the head and intellect but also on the level of the heart.[367]

---

364 Ibid., 6; emphasis added.

365 Michael R. Wade, Andrew Tarling, and Remy Assir, "Agile Leadership in an Age of Digital Disruption," IMD, (last visited July 31, 2019), https://www.imd.org/research-knowledge/articles/agile-leadership-in-an-age-of-digital-disruption/.

366 Ibid.

367 Kenny Graham, "Your Company's Purpose Is Not Its Vision, Mission, or Values," *Harvard Business Review*, vol. 9 (2014), 1.

In order for leaders to take on and bear the reputational and financial risks that come with increased uncertainty and unpredictability, an agile visionary leader must be able to extract a clear, shared, and convincing organizational purpose. But what is the purpose? How much risk is the purpose worth? The answer to these questions lies with each individual's values and beliefs. Conversations with employees across all hierarchies will help distill and define this purpose. It is highly challenging for organizations to determine a shared purpose because to define and live up to one's purpose means to sacrifice other, competing, legitimate purposes. In addition, the chosen purpose will not match the personal purposes and interests of all employees. But sharing a purpose has an upside: it increases guidance, sustenance, and inspiration for the organization as a whole and for its people.[368]

Human beings feel the urge for both desire and yearning, which can be thought of as components of shallow or deeper individual purpose:[369]

1. **Desire:** The impact of conscious and unconscious desires on a person's behavior and experience is powerful. Desire stems from egoistic worries and physical needs. The ego is involved.
2. **Yearning:** Yearning describes the feeling of extensive and deep longing. It is linked to a purpose beyond the self, the ego, and deep desire. It drives a person forward toward meaning and identity.

Develop a Purpose

A good way of determining somebody's purpose is to ask how the person wants to be remembered. This is called the "epitaph question" and helps establish a long-term view on life and focus on what really matters. It forces a person to think about who he or she wants to be and to whom. Lifetimes are finite, and thus probably everybody would

---

368 Heifetz, Grashow, and Linsky, *The Theory Behind the Practice*, 27f; De Smet, Lurie, and St. George, *Leading Agile Transformation*, 6.

369 Long, *Transforming Experience in Organisations: A Framework for Organisational Research and Consultancy*, 7.

agree that to live a life worth remembering is more attractive than wasting time and energy living it meaninglessly.[370]

"One day your life will flash before your eyes. Make sure it's worth watching."

—GERARD WAY

For a leader, it would be counterproductive to put his/her own professional and material gains at risk unless the larger/organizational purpose were in line with the personal one. What could such a personal purpose be? What helps to define whether it is worth taking the risks that come with leadership? By pursuing or achieving a personal purpose, would the company's result be valued by the stakeholders?

Such questions are very challenging, and their answers are based on the leader's personal values, which first need to be clarified. It takes a lot of courage for a leader to find a larger (shared) purpose that suits the organization, that the leader can commit to, and that is in line with the leader's personal values.

There will always be some narrower interests that need to be sacrificed. At the same time, the larger purpose helps adjust the compass in cases of crisis, difficult situations, or challenging decision-making because it helps one maintain focus and offers guidance, sustenance, and inspiration.[371]

As will be described in the next section, self-reflection leads to a higher self-awareness. Consequently, it can be said that this process helps in developing a purpose.

With the bigger picture in mind, leaders must also help others become

---

370 Kets de Vries, "The Epitaph Question," INSEAD Knowledge, September 5, 2016, 1f.

371 Heifetz, Grashow, and Linsky, *The Theory Behind the Practice*, 26–28.

conscious of their own purposes and relevant behaviors, and how those support or harm alignment with organizational purpose.[372]

ADAPTABLE TO CHANGE

A crucial element in the failure of organizations to adapt to changes in the VUCA world is the lack of effective change leadership. Change leaders have a high AQ (Adaptability Quotient)—the ability to anticipate and cope with change and uncertainty.

The fundamental skillset of adaptive leadership includes agility, openness to change, and the ability to handle it.[373]

Since each person has habits and patterns, however, change does not always come easily. Professional development to build resilience is crucial to be able to cope with, adapt to, and thrive in the midst of changing demands.[374]

The word *change* is only one letter different from the word *chance*. Leaders must see "change" as a "chance" for them and the people they lead to grow and develop. For example, engaging in or fostering "good conflict" can help.

Conflict does not necessarily need to be categorically bad. There is also "good/positive/constructive conflict." The positive perspective on conflicts within organizations sees a productive force that opens minds and helps stimulate employees to contribute to overall creativity, innovation, and productivity. For this to occur, the focus cannot be on stiff structure and processes, but instead should be on flexibility and adaptability to the changing environment. Based on this thinking,

---

372 Higgs and Rowland, "What Does It Take to Implement Change Successfully?" 325.

373 Jolly and Peterson, "Going Nowhere Fast."

374 Ibid.

in order for an organization to be successful, it needs good conflicts stemming from diverging perspectives that are discussed.[375]

Advantages of good conflicts can be summarized as follows.[376] They:

1. Encourage new ways of thinking
2. Raise questions
3. Help establish and maintain relationships
4. Increase open-mindedness
5. Prevent stagnation
6. Exercise flexibility and emotional control

Although it might be more comfortable in the short term to agree, conflicts handled in the right way can strengthen relationships between conflicting parties by fostering reciprocal feedback, understanding, and mutual respect. Listening to and taking on broad, diverse opinions opens up new opportunities to create a climate of innovation that enhances creative thinking and ultimately improves performance.

Conflicts can unlock potential that otherwise might not have been generated. Constructive conflict situations raise questions that help create new ideas, insights, and breakthroughs, which in turn help develop both individuals and organizations.

In the absence of conflict, the chances are that everything stays the same. Or, if it is suppressed, the conflict might escalate. Organizations that try to avoid any type of conflict avoid dealing with real problems and needed change. This can be deadly for a company. However, through positive conflicts that are resolved constructively, the organization can drive innovation to meet its customers' needs.

---

375 Robert Bacal, "Organizational Conflict—The Good, the Bad & the Ugly," The World of Work (Work 911), (last visited February 23, 2017), http://work911.com/articles/orgconflict.htm; Leigh Richards, "How Can Conflict Be Good for an Organization?" *Houston Chronicle*, March 6, 2019, http://smallbusiness.chron.com/can-conflict-good-organization-741.html.

376 Richards, "How Can Conflict Be Good for an Organization?"; Sherrie Campbell, "The 10 Benefits of Conflict, *Entrepreneur*, July 28, 2016, https://www.entrepreneur.com/article/279778.

The mindset that every conflict constitutes an opportunity for improvement encourages a positive attitude toward creating and managing conflicts. This helps people learn how conflicts can be managed effectively to boost productivity and change rather than destroy value and hinder organizational improvements.[377]

F. Scott Fitzgerald once stated, "The test of a first-rate intelligence is the ability to hold two opposed ideas in mind at the same time and still retain the ability to function."[378]

Leaders need to stay open and flexible to the possibility that they are wrong in their beliefs. Concurrently, however, they need to believe their actions are the right things to do at the moment they commit to them.[379]

People might become resistant to change and establish defense mechanisms because they fear losses. Leaders need to develop the ability to identify these losses and possible behaviors that come with them. Chapter 8, "Detecting and Avoiding Danger," elaborates on how to overcome immunity to change. Time and persistence are essential to adaptation processes because, although progress is only incremental in time, it is quite radical in the long run.[380]

Demarcation of adaptability to agility: it can be said that agility is a more offensive approach, as it relates to the interface between the organization and the market. In contrast, adaptability takes more of a defensive approach, responding to the pressures of survival.[381]

---

377 Bacal, "Organizational Conflict."

378 "F. Scott Fitzgerald Quotes," BrainyQuote, (last visited March 5, 2018), https://www.brainyquote.com/quotes/f_scott_fitzgerald_100572.

379 Heifetz, Grashow, and Linsky, *The Theory Behind the Practice*, 25.

380 Ibid., 4f.

381 Johnson, "Competency Confusers #3: Agility and Adaptability."

Develop Adaptability to Change

There are many ways to learn how to deal with change in today's VUCA world. Agility, openness, and willingness to change are key ingredients.[382] Because change does not come naturally, and everybody has habits/patterns related to the self or the organization, deliberate action must be taken to build capacity to deal with the many demands that the environment presents, such as:[383]

1. Question everything and embrace the fact that the process of developing resilience might come with painful experiences but also with a clearer understanding of who you are, what you want, and where you are headed.
2. Admit and accept mistakes and make changes to an approach that is no longer productive.
3. Never stop building the capacities of the organization to learn, adjust culture, transform structure, and adapt to new technologies.
4. Stay proactive so that you can better foresee opportunities. Then allocate the resources to seize and exploit those opportunities.
5. Always know what your stakeholders want and need.
6. Be open to new ideas and consider diverging views before you make (or allow others to make) important decisions.
7. Be willing to experiment and to take risks.
8. Subscribe yourself to lifelong learning.
9. Support your team members in their development so that they can recognize and tap their true potential.

Words of wisdom that remain unchanged:

"The future has a way of arriving unannounced."

—GEORGE WILL

---

382 Jolly and Peterson, "Going Nowhere Fast."

383 "Adaptive Leadership Definition," TeamworkDefinition.com, (last visited May 8, 2018), http://teamworkdefinition. com/adaptiveleadership/; Chris Burton, *A Study into Motivation and Engagement—Why We Really Do the Things We Do...* (London: Engage for Success, 2012–2013).

"When you are finished changing, you're finished."

—BENJAMIN FRANKLIN

ENGAGED

Agile leaders are engaged, meaning they are good listeners and communicators (internally and externally), and they are interested in and curious about emerging trends. Their engagement is founded in a desire to explore, discover, learn, share, and discuss ideas and stories. It is both a mindset as well as a defined set of business-oriented activities.[384]

Difference between motivation and engagement: Motivation is the "why" (why do you really do what you do?); engagement is the "what" (what lies at the very core of your motivation to do something?). You can ask what are the things that motivate you to be (dis)engaged.[385]

Develop Engagement

It was found that highly engaged leaders have common denominators. First of all, they have formative stretch experiences at a young age (positive or negative). Second, their sets of beliefs about leading people overlap (importance of personal connection; feeling of responsibility to serve the subordinated, especially during change and crisis). And third, they demonstrate certain behaviors that are supportive in engaging the people around them (to step up, energize, connect, stabilize, serve, grow, and stay grounded.[386]

More specifically, although not all of the above-mentioned points can

---

384 Wade, Tarling, and Assir, "Agile Leadership in an Age of Digital Disruption."

385 Chris Burton, *A Study into Motivation and Engagement—Why We Really Do the Things We Do...*(London: Engage for Success, 2012–2013).

386 Ken Oehler, Lorraine Stomski, and Magdalena Kustra-Olszewska, "What Makes Someone an Engaging Leader?" *Harvard Business Review* (November 7, 2014).

be learned or developed, there is a great number of things leaders can do and/or learn to increase their level of engagement:[387]

1. Learn how to become a good listener
2. Actively share information
3. Find ways to engage that are genuine and authentic
4. Actively ask for and give feedback
5. Communicate transparently and clearly
6. Be empathetic
7. Take a genuine interest in other people's lives
8. Be positive
9. Ask questions
10. Give genuine appreciation

HUMBLE

In today's interconnected and complex world, with its fast-paced changes, leaders can no longer expect to have all the answers. It is crucial for leaders to know their strengths and weaknesses and—with them—their limitations.

Humility is a quality embedded in "servant leadership," a term coined by Greenleaf in an essay published in 1970. Unlike traditional leadership approaches (see appendix 6, "Leadership: History and Development") that feature power at the top exercised by one person, servant leadership focuses on the sharing of power and the needs of others so that they can learn and grow while, at the same time, improving performance.[388]

Based on a study of 1,500 workers conducted in the US, Australia, China, Germany, India, and Mexico, Prime and Salib discovered that

---

387 Charlene Li, "3 Things All Engaged Leaders Have in Common," *FastCompany*, March 20, 2015, https://www.fastcompany.com/3043688/3-things-all-engaged-leaders-have-in-common.

388 Robert K. Greenleaf, "What Is Servant Leadership?" Robert K. Greenleaf Center for Servant Leadership, accessed May 7, 2018, https://www.greenleaf.org/what-is-servant-leadership/.

employees felt a higher degree of belonging and inclusiveness when the following were exhibited by a leader:[389]

1. Acts of humility (learning from feedback and acknowledging mistakes)
2. Empowering others so that they can learn and grow
3. Courage
4. Holding employees responsible for results

Other positive consequences of these leadership behaviors were increased motivation for commitment, collaboration, and innovation. Below the surface of feeling included was uniqueness and belongingness. The latter refers to basic human needs.

Humble leaders know themselves very well. This is how they develop inner strength so that they can show trust and respect to others. By subordinating their egos, they deflate potential hubris and almost certainly prevent derailment.

Develop Humility

Prime and Salib have clear ideas on how humility can be improved:[390]

1. **Talk About Your Own Mistakes:** If leaders show their vulnerability and demonstrate how they have learned from their own mistakes, they become more approachable and legitimize their teaching of subordinates. To demonstrate imperfection is not a sign of weakness but a sign of strength.
2. **Encourage Dialogues and Not Debates:** It is important that leaders do not impose their opinions on others. If employees see that their different viewpoints are included, they feel appreciated and validated. An important aspect of adaptive leadership is being

---

389 Jeanine Prime and Elizabeth Salib, "The Best Leaders Are Humble Leaders," *Harvard Business Review*, vol. 11, no. 5 (2014), 1–5.

390 Prime and Salib, "The Best Leaders Are Humble Leaders," 1–5.

able to look at an issue from different perspectives and hold up concurrent interpretations in one's head.

3. **Welcome Uncertainty and Unpredictability:** Showing humility is when leaders admit that they themselves do not know all the answers and that their team's input and contributions are imperative for finding a solution. It encourages others to display ownership, to step up and pay it forward.

4. **Reverse Role and Practice Followership:** With the increased flattening of organizational hierarchies and the blurring of boundaries, leaders need to encourage and empower others to take up leadership roles. This is how leaders can keep practicing and experiencing what it feels to be a follower. They lead by example.

"During the flames of controversy, opinions, mass disputes, conflict, and world news, sometimes the most precious, refreshing, peaceful words to hear amidst all the chaos are simply and humbly 'I don't know.'"

—CRISS JAMI

Humble leaders are not weak but strong, as they show courage to step back and let others step forward while still maintaining focus and keeping the team motivated. It is crucial for organizations and society at large to acknowledge the strength needed to practice humility.

In summary: agile leaders are visionary (and with a purpose), adaptable (to change), engaged, and humble.

3. BE ABLE TO INSPIRE

The ability to inspire is one of the top leadership skills that employees ask of their leaders. Zenger and Folkman refer not only to the outcome of an IBM study of 1,700 CEOs in 64 countries but also to their own 360-degree feedback data from 50,000 leaders. They proclaim that the ability to inspire leads to the highest degree of employee commitment and engagement.[391]

---

391 Jack Zenger and Joseph Folkman, "What Inspiring Leaders Do," *Harvard Business Review* (June 20, 2013).

Inspiration is drawn from within. It is an influencing process that stimulates others to do something creative or extraordinary. It involves influencing people both mentally and emotionally. It is a pulling and not a driving force that provides a sense of excitement and effortlessness. Especially in situations of change, when a leader wants people to do something different or to change, the desire needs to come from within, as it is one's values, beliefs, experiences, and preferences that increase the good feeling of achieving something (a true and enduring desire to achieve).[392]

Because a large part of the foundation of corporate knowledge and wisdom is based on the gray matter of the employees, talent recruiting, development, and retention provide a competitive advantage. The ability to inspire helps to attract top talent, keeps the workforce motivated, and is therefore a crucial part of leadership development.[393]

DEVELOP ABILITY TO INSPIRE

As Zenger and Folkman wanted to find out how leaders become inspiring, they applied a technique they called the "reverse-engineer exercise." Looking at the leaders with the highest scores (1,000 in total), they discovered things about them that were more or less tangible:[394]

The more tangible ones were that they:

1. Established stretch goals with the team
2. Invested time to develop their subordinates
3. Showed high engagement in collaborating behavior
4. Encouraged innovation

The less tangible ones were that they:

---

392 Surbhi S., "Difference between Motivation and Inspiration," Key Differences, April 8, 2016, http://keydifferences.com/difference-between-motivation-and-inspiration.html.

393 Kets de Vries, The Leader on the Couch, xiv.

394 Zenger and Folkman, "What Inspiring Leaders Do."

1. Showed a higher ability to emotionally connect with their subordinates
2. Had a clearer vision
3. Communicated more effectively and invested time for it
4. Were change champions
5. Served as role models for the workforce

Their research showed that "more is more," meaning the more of the above behavior that could be noticed, the higher the leader scored on "inspiration." And they even took it one step further to try to find out whether a person could learn to be(come) inspirational.

Studying 882 executives from their data set, Zenger and Folkman found that the 310 who chose to improve their ability to inspire were able to move from the forty-second percentile (below average) to the seventieth percentile in three years. With a focus on awareness, good feedback, and a development plan, they were able to improve their ability to inspire.[395]

There are additional activities to improve the ability to inspire.[396] If you are an inspiring leader, you know how to use your unique set of strengths to unlock individuals' and teams' higher performance through empowerment, not command and control. Also, you hold people accountable for results. As an inspiring leader, you:

1. Develop your inner resources (having stress resilience, self-regard, and an optimistic attitude)
2. Connect with others (being vital, humble, and empathetic)
3. Set the right tone (being open, unselfish, and responsible)
4. Show leadership (communicating a vision, staying focused, being a servant)

A well-known example of an inspiring leader is Howard Schultz,

---

395 Ibid.

396 Eric Garton, "How to Be an Inspiring Leader," *Harvard Business Review* (April 25, 2017).

founder of Starbucks. When Schultz returned as CEO after eight years, he noticed that Starbucks's unique customer experience had given way to automation and diversification to strive for throughput and growth. Schultz acted quickly and closed 7,100 US stores for three hours to retrain their baristas in the art of espresso making. In this action, his intentions about what could make Starbucks great again were not doubted.[397]

4. BE AUTHENTIC (AND HOLD YOURSELF PERSONALLY ACCOUNTABLE)
BE AUTHENTIC

Authenticity in the context of leadership means the self-awareness of one's fundamental values, views, and beliefs that, together, form a person's moral compass. Leaders are authentic if they know their moral compasses and align their behavior accordingly.[398]

Although authenticity is often called the "gold standard" of leadership,[399] its interpretation can be controversial.

There are negative aspects of authenticity, e.g., being rude, crude, or an authentic manipulator or jerk (if this is how they define their moral compass). This can do as much harm to an organization and its people as the consequences of the positive aspects of authenticity can do good.[400]

Authenticity, as with beauty, depends on the eye of the beholder. If leaders speak about something with passion, their followers can interpret it as arrogant. If a follower rejects a leader's thoughts and ideas, the leader can interpret this as mindless or thoughtless. Both parties, the leader and the follower, act with authenticity. Therefore, to tell

---

397 Ibid.

398 Stippler et al, *Führung*, 61.

399 Bill George, "The Truth about Authentic Leaders," Harvard Business School Working Knowledge, 2016.

400 Michael Schrage, "When Authenticity Does More Harm than Good," *Harvard Business Review* (October 26, 2015), 1.

someone to work on authenticity could make the interaction deteriorate rather than improve it.[401]

Authenticity is difficult to measure, as it is very personal. Thus, one needs to be true to oneself and hold oneself (and others) personally accountable for individual words and actions.

DEVELOP AUTHENTICITY

Herminia Ibarra's recommendation on how to develop authenticity includes:

1. Try to look at yourself as a "work in progress." Professional identities evolve through trial and error. Develop a personal leadership style that feels right and suits both your and your organization's ever-changing needs.[402]
2. Look at others whose style embodies the type of authenticity that suits you. Take elements and adopt them. Do not look at authenticity as an intrinsic state but as a capability that helps you grow.[403]

Bill George adds tips such as:

1. Be genuine and do not "fake it to make it." The changing environment asks for leadership that adapts to different leadership styles (inspirer, coach, mentor).[404]
2. Be real and share your feelings and address the ones of others. Since people do not connect through their heads but through their hearts, they can relate to you if you are real. But be careful about how and with whom you do it as well as how it might be received. The higher you move in a hierarchy, the more important authenticity becomes, because what is measured is trust. This process

---

401 Ibid.

402 Hermina Ibarra, "The Authenticity Paradox," *Harvard Business Review*, vol. 93, nos. 1–2 (2015), 52–59.

403 Ibid.

404 Bill George, "Becoming a More Authentic Leader," *Harvard Business Review* (December 10, 2015).

is challenging, but you will learn about yourself on the way. The more challenging, the greater the lesson. It is much more difficult to deal with adversity than with success, although success can bring its own set of issues.[405]

HOLD YOURSELF PERSONALLY ACCOUNTABLE

Personal accountability is a crucial step toward the improvement of leadership and lays the foundations for a positive business culture.[406]

There is, however, a distinction between accountability and responsibility. When people bear responsibility, they have a task or a role. They can be responsible for leading companies, but until they fully accept personal accountability for their actions and results, they are not fulfilling their roles (being authentic is not enough). When they are accountable, they stand up for their results, which strongly contributes to an increase in organizational effectiveness. If leaders openly hold themselves accountable, they convey a strong message to their followers, which helps build trust. Very often, organizations in which personal accountability is not lived or promoted show a sudden emergence of accountability when something goes wrong, but this type of accountability is directed at blaming and resenting others.[407]

Leaders must learn to execute and teach personal accountability. Those who do not accept such change (be it leaders or subordinates) must be spotted and coached. If they are not willing or able to embrace it, they must be let go. Otherwise, they will disturb progress, which might lead to conflicts.

---

405 Ibid.

406 Joseph Folkman, "The '8 Great' Accountability Skills for Business Success," *Forbes*, November 14, 2014, https://www.forbes.com/sites/joefolkman/2014/11/14/how-do-you-score-the-8-great-accountability-skills-for-business-success/#345085893c11.

407 Jeff Peevy, "Holding Staff Accountable," *ABRN*, July 2017, 22ff.

DEVELOP PERSONAL ACCOUNTABILITY

Based on a study assessing 40,000 leaders, Joseph Folkman identifies eight behaviors displayed by those who reached high scores on effectiveness for accountability:[408]

1.   **Drive for results.** Clearly define the outcomes that you want to deliver and give employees some control over the way these results are provided.
2.   **Honesty and integrity.** Have the courage to tell the truth. Often, this courage is reinforced because employees see that their boss is open and frank with them.
3.   **Trust.** Give employees the feeling of confidence that their efforts will be rewarded. Never take advantage of subordinates, such as taking credit for their accomplishments or unfairly blaming them. Communicate clear intentions. Create positive relationships, build knowledge, and show consistency. This will help build trust.
4.   **Clear vision and direction.** How can a leader be accountable if he or she does not embrace and convey the company's vision? "Where" we are going and "how" must be clear.
5.   **Problem-solving and technical expertise.** Confusion about how to accomplish one's task hinders the development of accountability. The skills required for the job need to be taught and trained in order for it to be completed successfully.
6.   **Communication.** Effective communication is required to notify others of what they are accountable for.
7.   **Ability to change.** A leader's ability to adapt, to create, and to lead change increases levels of accountability among the workforce. Strong leaders are good at receiving feedback, tackling challenges, being innovative, conveying optimism, demonstrating concern, and setting clear objectives.
8.   **Collaboration and resolving conflict.** Collaborative and cooperative teams are far more successful. And cooperation breeds accountability.

---

408 Folkman, "The '8 Great' Accountability Skills."

5. BE COURAGEOUS TO SPEAK THE TRUTH

It is not unusual for businesspeople to get frustrated and angry, but many of them would not find the courage to disagree openly and directly with someone else. There is a tendency to wrap difficult messages in euphemistic language or find someone else to convey the negative message. The reason behind this behavior is the discomfort in the very moment of telling the truth because it can be shocking to hear the brutal honesty.[409]

Blunt talk can be hurtful. The key is what Rosemary Counter calls "radical candor"[410] and what forms Mindy Mackenzie's nickname: "the velvet hammer."[411]

Truth telling can be dangerous and risky. The message can hurt or upset others, especially one's boss. If leaders share their opinion, they are exposing themselves to others.[412]

However, approaches to directness and disagreement differ from culture to culture. Some cultures prefer more direct negative feedback (clear, frank, efficient; say it as it is and welcome frank criticism) and disagree more openly. Others prefer indirect negative feedback (soft, careful, diplomatic; wrap negative messages with positive ones), show a lower tolerance toward open disagreement, and see it as harmful to relationships.[413]

No matter the culture, criticism that does not include caring makes someone seem like a jerk, and caring that leaves out criticism makes them seem like wimps. The combination of criticism and caring

---

409 Rosemary Counter, "The Case for Telling the Honest Truth," *Canadian Business* (June 2016), 12, https://rosemarycounter.com/the-case-for-telling-the-honest-truth/.

410 Ibid., 12.

411 Mindy Mackenzie, *The Courage Solution: The Power of Truth Telling with Your Boss, Peers, and Team* (Austin: Greenleaf Book Group, 2016), 247.

412 Vladislav Suvák, ed., *Care of the Self: Ancient Problematizations of Life and Contemporary Thought* (Leiden and Boston: Brill-Rodopi, 2018), 79.

413 Meyer, "Navigating the Cultural Minefield," 120–122.

reduces ambiguity and passive-aggressiveness, and it helps improve both relationships and business outcome.[414]

DEVELOP COURAGE TO SPEAK THE TRUTH

Since brutal honesty is better received if it is not revealed as a complete surprise, leaders need to declare their strategies and share openly who they are and what others can expect. Moreover, if they pride themselves on honesty, they need to show it when things go well and when they go wrong. And bluntness should be balanced with genuine compliments and appreciation.[415]

To be truthful to others requires truthfulness to oneself. Increased self-reflection and self-awareness help to spot moments when one is about to be dishonest with oneself.

To tell the truth means to intend to improve oneself (by having courage to get to know oneself) and others (by providing critical feedback).[416]

Being truthful with oneself and others goes hand in hand with being personally accountable for one's actions. A relationship with oneself requires both courage and truth telling. A leader's success is also dependent on authenticity, which requires being honest with oneself.[417]

Sage fools were known for their humor. Humor can play a crucial role in relieving tension.[418] Humor can be considered as "permitted disrespect"—a channel for handling potential conflicts in a socially acceptable way.

---

414 Counter, "The Case for Telling the Honest Truth," 12.

415 Ibid., 12.

416 Suvák, Care of the Self, 79.

417 Mackenzie, The Courage Solution, 9–82.

418 Kets de Vries, "The Organizational Fool," 763.

The person who speaks the truth must know when to speak the whole story or just part of it. There might be a situation when he or she can't say the whole truth because it would cause serious harm to the recipient and/or the organization. The truth holder should never abuse his/her power by hiding important facts for selfish reasons.

6. BE A GOOD LISTENER

It is widely acknowledged and proclaimed that good communication skills are critical for a leader. But in the learning process of becoming a better communicator, the other half of the equation often gets neglected: being a good communicator includes being a good listener.

Listening skills are important in all areas of life. Listening is more than just hearing sounds and words. In Stephen R. Covey's words from his book *The 8th Habit: From Effectiveness to Greatness*, "It is a very, very rare skill. But it is more than a skill. Much more."

Research shows that good listeners tend to make fewer mistakes, get into fewer conflicts, and are more effective thanks to their receiving and being able to use higher-quality information.[419]

Listening means putting time and effort into the activity, moving aside the self, and concentrating on the speaker. Many people have the tendency to do more talking (compelling, influencing, selling) than listening. Good leaders need to deal with both what is said and what is left unsaid.[420]

Most of the time, listening is treated as if there were just one form. The opposite would be not listening. Numerous studies have identified different forms and levels of listening, depending on the depth and,

---

419 Julie Starr, *The Coaching Manual: The Definitive Guide to the Process, Principles and Skills of Personal Coaching*, 2nd ed. (New York: Pearson Education, 2007), 83.

420 Ibid., 84f.

with it, the effort that is directed toward the speaker. The different aspects can be summarized into five levels:[421]

1. **Cosmetic Listening** (not really listening, pretending to be interested). Pretending to listen means that most of the attention and thoughts of the listener are not with the speaker. This may be adequate if listeners feel that speakers are not directing the words to them, that they just enjoy talking.

2. **Conversational Listening** (focusing on what a person is going to say). This level of listening is the most prevalent in daily conversations. It includes listening, talking, listening, talking, etc. The listener's focus is on the speaker, on the speaker's words and on his or her own (future) words. Conversational listening comes naturally and requires little effort.

3. **Selective Listening** (biased listening). The listener selectively filters and summarizes information (maybe while multitasking). The listener is not interested in all the information, maybe because he or she has a different opinion or resists the speaker. People listening selectively tend to interrupt speakers or finish their sentences.

4. **Active Listening** (rephrasing). Active listening requires putting greater effort into understanding the speaker than into responding vocally. Active listening involves staying focused to fully comprehend what the speaker is saying. The listener shows that he or she is listening by making sounds, gestures, or expressions and including clarifying questions. The listener can also summarize what has been heard and provide the speaker with advice, observations, and inferences. Aside from collecting facts, the listener tries to fill in gaps to get a more comprehensive picture.

5. **Deep Listening/Empathic Listening** (uses all senses, third ear, what is not being said). The fifth level goes beyond the normal understanding of the term *listening*. It is characterized by the calm and quiet mind of the listener, the focus and awareness on the speaker, detachment from the self and strong presence in the moment. The listener might want to engage in a dialogue to

---

421 Ibid., 82–96; Coach Gwen, "Levels of Listening," LeaderWhoLeads.com, accessed May 2, 2017, http://www.leaderwholeads.com/levels-of-listening.html.

encourage the speaker's thinking, ask questions, and stay in the conversation. Ongoing deep listening for a long period is almost impossible. It is demanding mental work.

DEVELOP LISTENING

Listening skills can and must be practiced. Leaders can ask themselves the following questions:[422]

1. How often do you not really listen but pretend to listen to someone else?
2. Does your listening depend on the speaker and circumstances?

Ask a friend or colleague to tell you about three situations or issues that he or she wants to change for about thirty minutes. You may ask questions, acknowledge, or clarify what is being said. Afterward, summarize the speaker's point (problem or situation; your own feelings as a listener; what appears to be unsaid). After that, ask for feedback from the speaker (how he or she felt about being listened to, the degree of attention and understanding, and the impact the situations described had on personal feelings). Getting this feedback helps the listener comprehend what behavior triggered a specific result of the speaker's feeling.

Practice, practice, practice.

The penultimate exercise might sound simple, but it helps one become aware of how strongly one is programmed. It shows how much we want to slip something of ourselves into the dialogue.

If ever you get distracted by your own thoughts or something else, you might want to admit it right away. Tell the speaker that you are listening in order to reconfirm your commitment to listening.

---

422 Starr, *The Coaching Manual*, 82–95.

7. BE (SELF-)REFLECTED

The ability to practice self-reflection is influenced by several variables: a leader's strong, healthy sense of self and identity; the practice of testing reality on a regular basis; the degree to which leaders control/contain their emotions/impulses, anxiety tolerance, and acceptance of their own limitations. These aspects help deal with the ambiguity that leadership brings: the moving back and forth between thinking, reflection, and action. Those who practice self-reflection have a much lower chance of adopting and/or exercising pathological behaviors or misusing power.[423]

Since most of an individual's behavior is automatic and repetitive, it is only the new, the unexpected, and the discomforting that triggers self-reflection and encourages change.[424]

DEVELOP (SELF-)REFLECTION

No athlete can exercise twelve hours a day. They all need recovery breaks, physically and mentally. In contrast, many executives do practice twelve hours a day or more. Or they think they can, having back-to-back meetings from morning until evening without taking the time to step back and reflect in between. And if there are no meetings planned, they keep themselves busy checking messages, talking on the phone, or busying themselves with other activities, rushing from one task to the next.

In today's hyperturbulent VUCA world, people run the risk of becoming victims of information. This overload leaves little or no time to look inside. Increased pressure both at work and in society asks for action taking, collaboration, stepping up and forward, and leaning in. "Doing nothing" is not allowed or well regarded. But it is crucial to

---

423 Kets de Vries, *Leaders, Fools and Impostors*, 113f.

424 Nelson and Hogan, "Coaching on the Dark Side," 14.

balance activity and inactivity, noise and quietness in order to explore the inner world and activate the wealth of inner resources.[425]

The equilibrium between action and reflection has become out of balance despite the fact that deceleration or even inactivity may be invaluable for mental health and/or as an incubator for future creativity. People are often unaware that "slacking off" can do a lot of good.[426]

The unconscious urge to be busy started early on in life. Probably most parents and teachers do not proclaim that doing nothing is good. And even later in life, how many people at work recommend inactivity and reflection? Indeed, the opposite is often true. It is considered good form to stay on the case, to work harder and longer, and to be busy.

Slacking off is associated with irresponsibility, laziness, and wasting time (or one's life). This is why people feel guilty when they are not active, or they get a kick out of being incredibly busy. Busyness can provide a temporary buzz, but it can also make people lose connection with both themselves and others. As a consequence, they alienate themselves from their feelings and needs and know less and less who they are, what and how they feel, what bothers them, and what is good for them.[427]

Moreover, busyness and the entailed estrangement can serve as an effective defense mechanism. Unwanted or uncomfortable feelings can be averted. Yet making unconscious thought processes conscious can be more fruitful and rewarding than the ongoing focus on solving issues or just staying busy.

Stress and exhaustion are frequent consequences, and increasingly, people do not even know if they are headed in the right direction. Noise and activities keep people from uncomfortable or even terri-

---

425 Manfred F. R. Kets de Vries, "Doing Nothing and Nothing to Do: The Hidden Value of Empty Time and Boredom," *Organizational Dynamics*, vol. 44 (2015), 169.

426 Manfred F. R. Kets de Vries, "The Case for Slacking Off," *Harvard Business Review* (December 11, 2013).

427 Ibid.

fying inactivity and quietness.[428] This saying brings it home: "Never get so busy making a living that you forget to make a life."[429]

As a consequence, busyness and stress disorders go hand in hand. Technology can provoke the feeling that busyness means effectiveness. The number of burnouts keeps increasing. Access to information, entertainment, and distraction is infinite, and busyness can be highly addictive. To stay physically and mentally healthy, it is important to include downtime and establish a balance of action and reflection.[430]

Reflection is different from thinking. While thinking is logical, rational, and systematic, it has its limitations. Thinking is important to oversee, review, make sense of, and decide on complex issues. In contrast, reflection is less rational, making use of preliminary thoughts, feelings, emotions, ideas, and intuitions.[431]

Busyness can create an illusion of control or purpose and a feeling of a buzz and thus avert demons of loneliness, worthlessness, depression, or fear of death. This is why doing nothing can bring doubts and anxieties to surface. More anxiety encourages more action. But instead of a feeling of relief, it further encourages activity.

Hyperactivity is not only considered good form, but it is even promoted, supported, and rewarded. Does more action automatically lead to higher productivity? Such an environment often incubates physical and mental health issues such as low morale, depression, substance abuse, relationship problems, and absence from the workplace.[432]

The best leaders balance action and reflection. They create space for downtime, which allows invaluable insights into the dark side of one's

---

428 Kets de Vries, "Doing Nothing and Nothing to Do," 170.

429 Ibid., 171.

430 Ibid., 170f.

431 Erik Van de Loo, Maszuin Kamarudin, and Jaap Winter, *Corporate Governance and Boards: System and Behavior* (Kuala Lumpur: Universiti Tun Abdul Razak, 2015), 232.

432 Kets de Vries, "Doing Nothing and Nothing to Do," 171.

personality and opens the opportunity to tap into a rich source of passion and energy. But this excursion requires courage. It sounds paradoxical that people shy away from doing nothing, even if they know that it adds to physical and intellectual health and boosts creativity. But the fear of bringing out existential anxieties is high.[433]

Checking the cell phone, laptop, or tablet stimulates the brain. The chemical signal, dopamine, is sent to the bloodstream, which creates a rush that is not easy to stop voluntarily. Neuroscientists have reported that when a task is performed, the left side of the brain is thought to process the majority of logical and sequential information, and the right side is thought to process the majority of visual information and to process information intuitionally, randomly, and holistically. The left hemisphere is an ally of busyness and therefore tends to overwrite the right side, which gets stimulated during periods of calm. Inactivity stimulates the right side of the brain and encourages unconscious thought processes. These processes can remain unconscious for a while before they enter the consciousness, for example, in the form of a sudden idea, brainwave, or insight. Very often, inactivity serves as a solver of complex problems that works unconsciously once the conscious focus on the issue is suspended. This explains why many issues get solved or ideas emerge in the shower, lying down, or while traveling. This state is called the "alpha state" of the brain.

The brain is an electrochemical organ. Brainwaves are a form of electrical activity emitted by the brain. Brainwaves are divided into four categories with a range from the most active to the least active. In the waking phase, a person's brain is in the beta state (strongly engaged mind, active conversation, arousal). When one drifts into sleep (just before sleep), the brain enters the alpha state (nonarousal) and then further drifts into delta theta (drowsy) and delta (sleep/dreaming or deep sleep/dreamless sleep).[434]

---

433 Ibid., 171.

434 Ned Herrmann, "What Is the Function of the Various Brainwaves?" *Scientific American*, December 22, 1997, https://www.scientificamerican.com/article/what-is-the-function-of-t-1997-12-22/; Suresh Behera, "What Is the Alpha State of Mind? What Are Its Benefits?" *Times of India*, September 14, 2003, https://timesofindia.indiatimes.com/What-is-the-alpha-state-of-mind-What-are-its-benefits/articleshow/180546.cms.

Since alpha brainwaves are slower and higher in amplitude than the other waves, the alpha state can be described as a very relaxed but focused and absorbing (almost hypnotic) state. In this state that is still considered conscious, the person is calm and able to receive new information and open up to new possibilities.[435] After completing a task, when sitting down, or when doing reflections before falling asleep, a person is often in an alpha state.[436]

In these alpha states, routine activities are absent so that the mind is taken off the prevalent problem. Such incubation time can be cultivated via relaxing, daydreaming, mindfulness, and meditation.

Numerous companies have introduced decompression time and offer meditation classes to raise employees' self-awareness, to improve self-management, and to encourage creativity: Procter & Gamble, Unilever, Nortel Networks, Comcast, Raytheon, 3M, and Pixar to name a few. The motto is to work smarter not harder.[437]

But also quite a few of the tech companies started to use this knowledge not only to the interest of their employees but also to their own. The Next Web (TNW) lists companies such as Facebook, Google, Pinterest, Dropbox, Eventbrite, Airbnb, Ask.com, Zynga, Automattic, and Twitter that foster creativity, productivity, and team building and apparently meet the needs of their employees. Offerings include: a yearly budget to travel anywhere in the world employees want to; a Ping-Pong table; in-office yoga, Pilates classes, and massage therapy (or at least wellness reimbursement); open vacation policy ("please rest and take some days off"); fully equipped music studio and game rooms; team sailing trips or outings at the trampoline park; the possibility to bring their pets to work.[438]

---

435 Behera, "What Is the Alpha State of Mind?"

436 Herrmann, "What Is the Function of the Various Brainwaves?"

437 Kets de Vries, "Doing Nothing and Nothing to Do," 173; S. A. Snell, S. S. Morris, and G. W. Bohlander, *Managing Human Resources* (Boston: Cengage Learning, 2015), 437.

438 Nancy Messieh, "12 Tech Companies That Offer Their Employees the Coolest Perks," TNW The Next Web, April 9, 2012, https://thenextweb.com/insider/2012/04/09/12-startups-that-offer-their-employees-the-coolest-perks/.

The mottos of Pinterest, "Whatever you need to be productive is what you should be using," and Ask.com, "We believe the best measure of success is what you accomplish, so we don't need to measure how much time you take off to enjoy life,"[439] underline the abovementioned "incubator for future creativity" and show why this is of interest to employers.

Meditation has also quietly made its way into corporate life. Prominent persons such as William Clay Ford Jr. (executive chairperson of Ford Motor Company), Michael Stephen (former chairperson of Aetna International), Robert Shapiro (ex-CEO of Monsanto), Oprah Winfrey (media proprietor, actress, and philanthropist), Arianna Huffington (co-founder of *Huffington Post* and Thrive Global), Bob Stiller (founder of Green Mountain Coffee), Russell Simmons (founder of Def Jam), Marc Benioff (founder, chairman, and CEO of Salesforce), Jeff Winer (CEO of LinkedIn), Michael Rennie (former senior partner and global leader of McKinsey's Organization Practice) swear by meditation and its benefits.[440] Indeed, Michael Rennie proclaimed, after fighting cancer, "I realized your mind can affect your body."[441]

Supported by clinical trials and allied with neuroscience, meditation has even penetrated the halls of high finance. Its long-time advocates include Ray Dalio (founder of Bridgewater, meditating since 1969), Lord Myners (former chairperson of Marks and Spencer and former financial services secretary of the UK finance ministry), Bill Gross (founder of PIMCO), Lord Leitch (former chairperson of Bupa), and Philipp Hildebrand (vice-chairperson of BlackRock and former head of Swiss National Bank), just to name a few.

---

439 Ibid.

440 Michael Carroll, *The Mindful Leader: Awakening Your Natural Management Skills Through Mindfulness Meditation* (Boston: Trumpeter, 2008), 2.

441 Kath Walters, "How My Cancer Changed My View of Leadership: McKinsey & Co's Michael Rennie," *SmartCompany*, October 19, 2012, http://www.smartcompany.com.au/people-human-resources/leadership/how-my-cancer-changed-my-view-of-leadership-mckinsey-a-cos-michael-rennie/; James Paine, "11 Wildly Successful Entrepreneurs Who Swear by Daily Meditation," *Inc.*, https://www.inc.com/james-paine/11-famous-entrepreneurs-who-meditate-daily.html.

Benefits of meditation range from increased focus to pulling back to see the bigger picture and finding a greater sense of serenity. The stilling of the mind not only helps save energy but also helps decrease confirmation bias, which is a tendency to search for, interpret, and prefer information that confirms one's prejudices while not valuing information that opposes them.[442]

"Learning without reflection is a waste, reflection without learning is dangerous."

—CONFUCIUS

GROUP REFLECTION (BOD, MANAGEMENT)

Reflection is not only a highly effective method for individuals but also for groups in business and could (or should) be introduced to management and board meetings. Most often, the goal of board and management meetings is to get as much done as possible as quickly as possible. The CEO or chairperson is praised if he or she manages to conclude the meeting before the scheduled time is up. Thus, there is no time for reflection. Even worse, reflection might undermine efficacy.

Another hurdle to creating reflective space is the fact that in many commercial organizations, this tool is still perceived as weak ("touchy-feely") and regarded as superfluous. Increased globalization, fast change, and the introduction of new technologies strengthen these defense mechanisms.[443]

Leaders play a crucial role in fostering reflective practices. People and organizations get transformed through novelty, insights, and findings, not by hanging on to the status quo.[444]

---

442 John Paul Rathbone, "Zen and the Art of Management," *Financial Times*, September 16, 2013, https://www.ft.com/content/32e0b9b4-1c5f-11e3-8894-00144feab7de.

443 James Krantz, "Work Culture Analysis and Reflective Space," in *Socioanalytic Methods: Discovering the Hidden in Organisations and Social Systems*, ed. Susan Long (London: Karnac, 2013), 37f.

444 Ibid., 41f.

Reflection opens space for new thoughts and ideas that can improve the system within which employees are functioning. Reflection in groups, organizations, or social contexts is incredibly powerful, as it helps to shed light on concerns and transform them into knowledge and purposeful action.

James Krantz defines such analysis as "a way of creating reflective space [...] to understand their own systems, to recognize unseen forces that affect their ability to accomplish work, and ultimately enable them to take action."[445] He further calls it "an array of intellectual technologies" with the goal to discover crucial and meaningful information about the shared work world. This information lies below the surface. The goal of these applied methods is to establish conditions for reflection to learn about and understand work cultures that form the organizations' unconscious background.[446]

Board and management teams must understand that reflective space serves as the oxygen for decision-making. The goal is not to think less but to create more space for reflection.[447] Reflective practices should be looked at and experienced as a normal element of work life.

IN SUM

Effective leaders possess as many of these skills as possible (most of them are closely related), combined with functional/technical skills, and are able to balance action and reflection to prepare for the long term. If they sincerely care about their own personal development and that of the people around them, if they practice introspection and follow their inner compass, chances for derailment can be minimized.

At the same time, leaders need to find their personal inner satisfaction so that they can become immune to other people's admiration and

---

445 Ibid., 24.

446 Ibid., 24f, 42f.

447 Van de Loo, Kamarudin and Winter, "Corporate Governance and Boards," 233.

appreciation. It is a matter of being a role model to their subordinates and not a hero. It takes focus and discipline to find and keep the appropriate mindset and to keep balance.

It is highly challenging for any leader to resist the temptations and seduction of power and to remain grounded. To help with this, all leaders need people they can trust and ask for feedback and advice, knowing they will speak the truth regardless of the leaders' status, function, title, or wealth. Most often, these people are spouses, friends, coaches, or mentors.[448]

Leaders must learn how to manage themselves so that they can help others cope with imbalance and get through periods of discomfort. Successful leaders are present and conscious of what is going on. This is how they discover the repetitive behavior patterns of others and are able to anticipate how they might be developing.

Leaders can be seen as mentors or coaches. Their core competencies include supporting their people in conquering their limitations and becoming more productive and effective.[449] In Krantz and Bridger's words, leaders are "enabling people to change the way they think about the problems around them, to alter their perspectives, and to discover new possibilities for action which can never occur to them as long as they remain on the secure rail tracks of their habitual mind-sets."[450]

The ability to strengthen the above-mentioned skills not only improves mental fitness and clarity and develops flexible and adaptive mind-sets, but also increases resilience and creativity. Higher self-awareness and better regulation of emotions also hones communication and listening skills and leads to better decision-making. All this improves people's motivation and commitment and, with it, productivity. The

---

448 Bill George, "Why Leaders Lose Their Way," Harvard Business School Working Knowledge: Business Research for Business Leaders, June 6, 2011, https://hbswk.hbs.edu/item/why-leaders-lose-their-way.

449 Robert Kegan and Lisa Lahey, "The Real Reason People Won't Change," Harvard Business Review, vol. 79, no. 10 (2001), 3.

450 Krantz, "Work Culture Analysis and Reflective Space," 34f.

result is lower fluctuation, better performance, and a company that thrives together with its people. All this will lead to fewer derailment of leaders.

CHAPTER 8

DETECTING AND AVOIDING DANGER

Looking at the many scandals described in chapter 1, the responsibility for these derailments is linked to the "magic triangle" with a focus on individuals in charge of operations: the C-Suite (the group of an organization's officers who have the word "chief" in their title). Many of the fraudulent individuals were driven by excessive narcissism, hubris, inflated ego, and greed to pursue their own interests—money, power, status—instead of performing their duties to uphold the interests of the company and other stakeholders.

As for the BoDs, several reasons kept them from complying with the duties to execute their responsibilities to the company and its stakeholders, which in many cases was shown in late or no action (inactivity). Reasons are ranging from wanting to keep the board seat to unfamiliarity with crises to lack of recruiting knowhow to sometimes the same reasons described for C-Suite and top executives: self-interest, hubris, greed for power.

In the latter case, it was predominantly the chairperson who derailed.

Sometimes, owners were involved too, either being passive and blaming BoDs and executives or, in some rare cases, engaging in harmful actions themselves, e.g., in the role of the CEO or chairperson.

The selection of the CEO is the job of the BoD. It appears, however, as if BoD have not been as effective in preventing individual and organizational derailment as they could or should have been. It is challenging, however, for directors to read the danger signs that follow consequences of accelerated change and increased pressure on leadership, both strong forces that increase derailment risk.

If leaders realize that the pool of corporate knowledge and wisdom resides in the gray matter of their employees, they understand the competitive advantage of putting sincere emphasis on leadership development and the selection, development, and retention of talent.[451]

In addition to the development of leaders, continuous monitoring of their behavior is crucial so that corrective interventions can be performed in time. This requires increased transparency on the introduction, application, and performance of checks and balances by the BoD. One of the ultimate goals is to make companies and industries hubris-proof, which will contribute to the reduction of derailment or even fraudulent behavior.[452] As the following sections will show, there are strategies to help fight hubris and other harmful conditions.

ASSESS CURRENT AND FUTURE LEADERS MORE THOROUGHLY

Every year, companies launch searches for new CEOs and other senior-level executives. The goal is to find the right candidate to interact with the BoD, increase profits, and improve on the effectiveness of the workplace culture.[453] It is vital to have the right leaders at the top!

---

451 Ibid., xivf.

452 Nixon, *Pariahs*, 97f.

453 Zak Stambor, "Psychologists Help Predict Potential Executives' Success," *American Psychological Association*, accessed May 27, 2018, http://www.apa.org/monitor/feb06/success.aspx.

This chapter focuses more on the CEO (also on the chairperson) than on the other parties within the magic triangle. Why the CEO?

First of all, it's the highest-ranking executive of an organization. Second, people in the CEO position are more often involved in derailment than those in other positions. Given the role and power of a CEO and their primary responsibilities such as decision-making, management of the overall operations and resources of a company, acting as the main point of communication between the BoD and operations, and often being the public face of the company, derailment of a CEO often causes the most harm to an organization. Finally, current CEOs are highly likely to be future board members and chairpersons. The CEO is appointed by the board if the BoD has the mandate to do so, which generally it does.

These leaders are very costly to hire, and their position is highly visible. Thus, if they fail, the negative impact on both cost and morale can be substantial. In recent decades, CEO pay has remained very high and has continued to grow much faster than the pay of any other employee. From 1978 to 2016, for example, in the US, CEO compensation is reported to have risen between 807 or 937 percent (depending on stock options granted or realized). Using the 937 percent figure, the rise of CEO pay has been 70 percent faster than the stock market, with both rates of growth dramatically greater than the 11.2 percent growth of a typical employee's annual compensation.[454]

One key way for hiring teams to reduce risks is to research their own companies to get to know the organizations' behavioral attributes. Another important element is to understand the interworking of the potential position, which adds to the position's layers of complexity: the company's market challenges, the position's operational needs, the demands of the BoD, and the company's culture.

---

454 Lawrence Mishel and Jessica Schieder, "CEO Pay Remains High Relative to the Pay of Typical Workers and High-Wage Earners," *Economic Policy Institute*, July 20, 2017, https://www.epi.org/publication/ceo-pay-remains-high-relative-to-the-pay-of-typical-workers-and-high-wage-earners/.

To know what goes into the position, one must investigate more than just the operational role. Since at the senior level most candidates are highly skilled at selling themselves, assessors need to get beyond the salesmanship to find out who the persons really are.[455]

Although many psychometric tests show a high level of sophistication, their effectiveness is around 80 percent.[456] Therefore, additional sophisticated methods need to be applied, such as extended interviews that help assess a candidate's career history, current role, position, vision, engagement, and thinking style—as described in detail in the previous sections. The combination of tests and methods helps connect the dots to find out the candidate's characteristics, which directly affect his/her leadership as well as the way the individual impacts others.

As described, there are numerous assessment and development tools that help maximize a leader's potential and increase the predictability for potential derailment. Several of them are combined and packed in a four-step process discussed below in the next section.

The questions raised in this next section can be asked in interviews by owners to assess current and potential directors as/and future chairpersons, by chairpersons and directors to assess current and future CEOs, and by CEOs (and BoDs) to assess current and future members of the management team. Given the content of the previous chapter, different questions may be appropriate, depending on the organizational structure, e.g., hierarchical vs. flat.

The four-step approach starts with the analysis of the organization/system to identify whether an issue is linked to the role or to its incumbent. A case study illustrates that approaches with focus on the person could be costly, time intensive, and ultimately misleading if the contamination lies with the system. Step two aims at getting to

---

455 Stambor, "Psychologists Help Predict Potential Executives' Success."

456 Ibid.

know the current/future leader and asking the right questions at the right time. Step three goes even further and helps identify the leader's definition and drivers of success and their origins. The fourth and last step offers additional tools to further assess the leader, including his/her environment to get as comprehensive and accurate of a picture as possible to lay a solid foundation for subsequent actions. Following the four steps, tools for development will be presented for overcoming resistance to change, the impact of coaching, and the value of a collaboration contract.

STEP 1: IS THE POISON IN THE BOTTLE OR IN THE SYSTEM?

As mentioned in chapter 6, it would be interesting to assess whether the CEO roles at Yahoo and HP and the chairperson role at HP were/are contaminated. These roles are "strong and effective" and thus the influence they have on their occupiers is likely to be significant, as is that on other roles and the organizations as a whole. The roles should be thoroughly evaluated against this background.

There are indicators that can help establish whether an issue lies with the role or with the occupier:[457]

1. Occupier issue—the occupier shows signs of confusion, frustration, denial, dishonesty, sabotage, fear, anxiety, anger (behavior or feelings that do not seem usual for that person)
2. Occupier issue—a feeling that the occupier is driven to corruptive behavior and does not seem to be him or herself
3. Role and occupier issue—an observation that the role and person attract problems (role and occupier)
4. Role issue—consistently corrupt behavior surrounding the role, e.g., role manipulation or objectification

Special importance is afforded to an organization's founding role in

---

457 Chapman and Long, "Role Contamination," 55–57.

terms of how its energy flows to the rest of the organization. Four types of power influence the founding role:

1. Personal power (shaped by the personality and patterns of the founder)
2. Structural power (its relation to the organizational structure)
3. The power of the role idea (perceptions and expectations of the founder, the founder's successors and others)
4. Ambient power (influence on and from other roles and their occupiers, from processes, structures, and cultural context)

Example of Poison in the System

The following case is altered from one described by Chapman and Long.[458]

Linda founded LindTech and led it as if she were the family head. Her son, Travis, who had previously worked in two companies in the same industry, joined the company after graduation from business school.

The company was acquired by a strategic partner that asked Linda to remain as CEO. Linda continued to apply the same leadership style: command and control. Thus, the internal system remained the same while the company's structure and strategy changed greatly. It now belonged to a bigger company with two different divisions for different businesses. The two were not in line.

Linda was still making decisions herself. But when the company's growth started to stagnate and profits decreased, she was replaced by Travis and she left. Travis applied a very different leadership style: collaborative and consultative. His decisions were based on thorough research of the company and its culture. He implemented new and sophisticated systems, and he intended to ensure alignment of policies, procedures, processes, and the corporate culture.

---

458 Ibid., 58–61.

Travis's long-time senior managers—all engineers and technicians by training—continued to "do their thing," which prevented Travis from driving internal change. During the annual meeting, everybody seemed to agree with Travis's new ideas, but afterward, they didn't carry through. This behavior was the outflow of a culture established under Linda—follow the micromanaging, controlling direction of the leader to avoid harmful outcomes.

Travis tried very hard to approach his role differently from his predecessor but could not crack the established culture of "absorb the role of the leader" instead of "collaborate with the leader." Travis's role corrupted other roles like the ones of the engineers and technicians. They were making decisions that unconsciously served their own needs and not those of the organization.

Because of a lack of development during the company's growth, the role of leader had become contaminated. This was worse than just having an improper leadership style or facing an overhead out of proportion with sales and services.

The way the founding role was shaped was so powerful that it was impossible for a new incumbent to succeed. It was as if it were still Linda's role.

Linda had good intentions for the organization when she founded and executed her role. She was not at all corrupt. However, the role became contaminated because of the entrenchment of a culture that prohibited open and clear conversations about emerging issues, that operated more like a family and not an organization with commercial objectives.

Travis inherited a corrupted role, which impacted how he could take up, shape, and develop it. As is typical for such role holders, Travis ended up being the scapegoat, as he was perceived to have failed to initiate a turnaround. The truth of the matter is that Travis was restricted by the system that resulted from an originally contaminated role.

Antidote to the Poison

It is almost impossible for a person to be successful in driving change if a contaminated role is inherited. The only solution is to examine and redefine the original role proactively so that both the role occupier and successor can benefit from the positive and eliminate the negative effects.

Hence, it is important to analyze how the role is being held by its occupier. It is possible for a person to examine one's own role, but only to some extent. The entire system needs to be assessed, as it supports the contamination of the role. An independent third party will be more able to look at the role from a disinterested perspective. It is crucial, however, to avoid blaming the occupier or the role, as guilt will further increase contamination of the role and the organization.

In order to increase success in decontaminating, a few requirements need to be met:[459]

1. Recognition of the interactivity of organizations. They are systems.
2. Recognition of role histories.
3. Recognition of the past.

Leaders cannot look at the future only, just because they:

1. Do not want to be linked to past failures or negative associations with the past
2. Intend to be perceived as the carrier of hope going forward
3. Want to avoid or heal negative feelings, pain or guilt that leaders or employees may have related to responsibility and accountability for past mistakes

By only looking to the future, a new role holder misses out on discovering the system's hidden dynamics. These root issues need to be uncovered and corrected.

---

459 Ibid., 62ff.

In order to avoid scapegoating, it is important to separate the person from the role, examine the organization and role histories, and the system.

QUESTIONS FOR THE ROLE OCCUPIERS

1. I'm challenged by my role and I don't seem to make progress in it. Can my own history and that of the role give me some hints regarding how I might overcome the challenge and make progress?
2. Are there repeating patterns in the role biography and in the way I tend to pick them up?
3. If there are patterns, what can I do about them?
4. Is it possible to reestablish the role history for myself, for my successor, and for all other affected roles and their occupiers?

The only way to change the impact of a role on a system is first to examine the occupier's "role experience." Attempts to simply redefine roles, responsibilities, systems, processes, structures, and specifications will fall short or will eventually fail as long as the occupier's experience of the role does not change. This would result in replication of the past.[460]

QUESTIONS TO ASK ABOUT THE SYSTEM

1. What can we learn from the history of this specific role, as well as all other roles, processes, and structures of the system?
2. Are there historical patterns, e.g., experiences associated with the role that resemble the experiences of today?
3. Can patterns of experience of role holding, e.g., particular feelings, wording, be detected?

Undoubtedly, role histories influence new occupants. Regardless of good intentions, poisoned roles cannot only impact role holders, but also their successors, other roles, and their occupants. Since organi-

---

460 Ibid., 65.

zations are closed systems, they tend to retain such features despite their toxic or dysfunctional effects.[461]

Only when this dynamic is understood (development of role) can a detoxification process have a chance for success. Failure to examine the role biography and history will put persons and systems at risk.

It is important to differentiate between systems and psychology. With the exception of social psychology, the focus of psychology lies with individuals and their characters or personalities. In contrast, systems focus on integrated rules, relations, and roles. Both elements need to be looked at with the role as the connecting element.

Roles are defined by the system and assumed, shaped, and developed by individuals. This interaction coshapes the system. The objective of Organizational Role Analysis (ORA; see sidebar) is the redefinition of roles in regard to behaviors, rules, and relations while respecting the personality of the person taking up the role. When analyzing and testing the role, the system needs to be scrutinized too.

ORGANIZATIONAL ROLE ANALYSIS (ORA)

As the management of change involves three elements (individual, role, and system), Irving Borwick created three main interventions: one related to the individual (the Mapping Exercise), one to the role (ORA), and one to the system (System Analysis). As the role links the individual with the system, it is pivotal for change management.[462]

The role of the individual in the system is examined and redefined by the ORA. The ORA helps role incumbents to explore, with the support of a third party, how their role is managed by the company and implemented by them. Individuals become their own observer,

---

461 Ibid., 66.

462 Borwick, "Organizational Role Analysis," 7–9.

with an outside perspective. For example, if leaders blame team members for low productivity on the basis that they are lazy, the leaders most probably believe this themselves. Based on how the leaders understand their role, their theory might be plausible. But on a deeper level, it is likely that the overt laziness is directly linked to systemic rules and relations that are again directly linked to how leaders understand their role. Third parties help them identify the system's underlying dynamic.[463]

Therefore, the goal of ORA is not to solve the problem but to understand how roles are assumed in the system. The main challenge is that leaders often try to solve the problems they know how to solve and not the ones they actually have. It is rather easy to find apparent/surface solutions, but it is challenging to differentiate between the symptom and the root problem. This is why many solutions do not work out. The ORA aims at going beyond the system to understand the real problem.[464] Therefore, it focuses on examining a role in regard to relations and rules. It takes place in a group and is not a one-on-one process.[465]

The organized process of ORA helps role incumbents understand their roles within the system. The process asks more for restraint than for action, meaning that facilitators do not provide the answers. The advantage is that once the role and its relations and rules have been uncovered and revealed, it is almost impossible to revert to previous roles. Thus, as the name ORA reveals, changes take place at the level of the system and not only or primarily at the personal level.[466]

---

463 Ibid., 9–11.

464 Ibid., 13.

465 Ibid., 19f.

466 Ibid., 28.

STEP 2: GET TO KNOW THE (CURRENT/POTENTIAL) LEADER

After having defined the context in which the organization operates, and examined the role and system for contamination, it is important that owners, BoD, and CEO assess the current or future leader(s) to evaluate the needed skills/qualities, and analyze the individual's personality and disposition.

To learn more about current leaders and/or potential candidates beyond written documents, it is essential to sit down with them and ask the right questions.[467] These will give a deeper insight into how they tick, maybe trigger causes for concerns (e.g., hubris, fraud) and give an indicator on their willingness and potential to develop.[468]

Employment discrimination laws (see sidebar) can vary from country to country, so it is important to consult human resources and legal experts on the laws that are pertinent in the respective jurisdiction.

US EQUAL EMPLOYMENT OPPORTUNITY COMMISSION (EEOC)

As a complex example of employment discrimination laws, the US EEOC enforces federal laws prohibiting unfair treatment because of race, color, religion, sex (including pregnancy, gender identity, sexual orientation), national origin, age (forty or older), disability, or genetic information.[469]

The EEOC prohibits discriminatory employment policies/practices concerning: job ads; recruitment; application/hiring; background checks; job referrals; job assignments/promotions; pay/benefits;

---

467 Kets de Vries, *Leaders, Fools and Impostors*, 114.

468 Ibid., 114; Manfred F. R. Kets de Vries, "Leadership Group Coaching in Action: The Zen of Creating High Performance Teams," *Academy of Management Executive*, vol. 19, no. 1 (2005), 66.

469 "Employees & Job Applicants," US Equal Employment Opportunity Commission, accessed June 11, 2018, https://www.eeoc.gov/employees/index.cfm.

discipline/discharge (including constructive discharge/forced resignation); employment references; reasonable accommodation for disability and/or religion; training/apprenticeship programs; harassment; terms and conditions of employment; preemployment inquiries; dress code.[470]

GENERAL QUESTIONS FOR THE LEADER

What do you do to maximize both performance and enjoyment in different aspects of your personal and professional life?

Is it easy or difficult for you to articulate your thoughts, feelings, emotions, and actions? Do you see and are you able to grasp their interrelation? What is your degree of willingness to learn and develop?

Please describe your personal background.

What major (personal or professional) events, situations, or incidents have had a significant impact on your career?

When were you at your best in your life? And when were you at your worst? Why do you think you were good/bad at that time? What was good/bad about what you were doing at that time? Why did events happen as they did?

If you had to choose, who would be your role model or idol? What types of people impress you and why? Has this perception changed from when you were a child?

Which accomplishment are you most proud of? Which one was the biggest in other people's eyes?

Please describe situations that make you feel angry, happy, and sad.

---

470 Prohibited Employment Policies/Practices," US Equal Employment Opportunity Commission, accessed June 11, 2018, https://www.eeoc.gov/laws/practices/index.cfm.

What would you have done differently in your life? Do you have any regrets?

Which three things in your life would you change if you could?

From a personal and professional standpoint, what does the future hold for you?

QUESTIONS TO ASK YOURSELF ABOUT THE LEADER IF THERE IS CAUSE FOR CONCERN REGARDING SOBS OR POTENTIAL DERAILMENT

Are there signs of losing touch with reality?

Does the leader more often than not blame others?

Does the leader tend to pass on the responsibility for his/her mistakes to others?

Does the leader strongly believe that people are either for or against him/her?

Are there indicators that people in the organization don't speak up because the leader shows strong negative reactions to bad news?

Does the leader tend to not involve others in the decision-making process and/or only promote people with a yea-sayer attitude?

Does the leader overly enjoy publicity and the spotlight?

Is the leader overly focused on his/her image in public?

Is the leader driven by outside signs of success?

Are there signs that the organizational culture is one of mistrust and suspicion?

Is there a feeling that the leader has become less approachable?

With what mindset is the leader approaching the topic of succession planning?

If a number of the above questions can be answered with yes, there is cause for concern for the organization. Chances are high that the leader's mental health is not well balanced. Thus, it is important to act quickly and try to identify and analyze potential signs of danger.

Here are a few possible statements made by leaders who might show danger signs, such as hubris:

1. Frequent reminders that "I'm the boss," especially to the subordinates.
2. Asking for extra reimbursement for minor expenses despite a high (above market or company standard) salary.
3. Minor (but frequent) lies. Observe the comfort level for lying, even if they just cancel a last-minute restaurant dinner table because they're not in the mood, e.g., "I'm stuck in traffic and won't make it" or "My father got sick."
4. Listen closely when you give them feedback for improvement, e.g., "Don't let the fame get to your head." If they answer, "This is what my spouse/partner keeps telling me," it might be deeper rooted than expected.
5. Statements to owners/shareholders such as, "Why don't you sell your shares or part of your business and enjoy life?" can reveal the need for "sole power" or exposure.
6. Voiced comparisons with owners/shareholders/chairperson in regard to salary, type of car owned, dividends can reveal envy or greed.

The fact that such a statement might come across subtly, charming, and/or in a humorous way should not obscure the possibility that there might be a cause for hubris concerns.

It is of utmost importance to identify questionable behavior early and to act upon it. The right reaction to fraudulent or illegal behavior seems obvious—uncover and assess it, probably dismiss the person right away, maybe even sue. It is less clear, however, what the response should be if the respective person(s) is/are involved in questionable actions that are not (yet) illegal.

There is no clearly defined catalogue of factors that help identify questionable behavior that should raise concerns. Nevertheless, it is crucial to investigate and identify allegations of arrogance, hubris, and excessive narcissism before (too much) harm is done.[471] This is why checks and balances are crucial. They can come in different forms, as described in the next section, after the following deep dive on the elaboration of the leader's inner drivers.

STEP 3: DIVE DEEPER INTO THE LEADER'S DEFINITIONS AND DRIVERS OF SUCCESS
Definitions of Success

Certain behaviors can provide insights into current or potential leaders' mental health, e.g., healthy leaders possess and demonstrate passion for their actions. Very often, they are also able to experience different feelings with few or zero blind spots. They take ownership of the events and incidents that have influenced their lives and thus do not feel the need to blame others. They are better than others at controlling their impulses and handling their own anxieties and potential internal contradictions.

Although it is normal for each human being to have experienced negative events and incidents in life, it matters how they deal with both positive and negative experiences.[472] If people have the ability to analyze and understand their own motivations in life, they can improve both themselves and the performance of their companies.

---

471 David F. Larcker and Brian Tayan, "Scoundrels in the C-Suite: How Should the Board Respond when a CEO's Bad Behavior Makes the News?" *Stanford Closer Look Series*, 2016, 1.

472 Kets de Vries, "Putting Leaders on the Couch," 7.

How leaders define success can give BoDs and owners valuable, additional insights. The definition of success is individual, as it depends on the person's upbringing. Consequently, the measurement of purpose and performance is also different. Perceptions of success can change over the course of a life, but some success indicators are more common than others, such as:[473]

1. Family: Because more leaders than might be assumed grew up in dysfunctional families, they may make it their mission early in life to provide their children with a different upbringing.

2. Wealth: In order to avoid experiencing again the same negative experience endured in childhood, e.g., deprivation, some leaders define success as achieving financial wealth. The perception of getting stuck can result from the feeling of having achieved a victory on one hand and being in a hamster wheel on the other hand. They are not able to stop. Many leaders are too obsessed with wealth as a success driver and go very far to reach their goals.

3. Recognition/fame: The thirst for recognition often originates in the search for approval from others, which stems from a lack of appreciation during upbringing. Such people have strong narcissistic traits, and thus the thirst for compensation helps boost their self-esteem.

4. Power: If success is understood as holding power, growth of that power is often sought. People who are obsessed with power have frequently experienced situations in life in which they were powerless. Power that is used in a healthy way fosters commitment and teamwork. If it is used in a harmful way, it can destroy companies and relationships. Referring to Lord Acton's warning that "power tends to corrupt, absolute power corrupts absolutely," power is not given up easily.[474] Or as another wise person put it (often attributed to Abraham Lincoln): "Nearly all men can stand adver-

---

473 Manfred F. R. Kets de Vries, "The Many Colors of Success: What Do Executives Want out of Life? *Organizational Dynamics*, vol. 39 (2010), 2ff.

474 Acton Institute, Lord Acton Quote Archive, accessed July 1, 2016, http://www.acton.org/research/lord-acton.

sity, but if you want to test a man's character, give him power."[475] This was tragically demonstrated by Joseph Stalin, who said, "The only real power comes out of a long rifle."[476]

5. Winning: In order to feel alive, winning at almost any price drives competitive leaders. There is a fine line between the positive and negative sides of competition, as a competitive spirit can turn toxic.

6. Friendships: There are leaders who define their success in life by having good friends because it shows them that they are good people who treat others well. Those leaders see friends as a means to an end, since friends indirectly help to reach goals and dreams.

7. Meaning: Leaders who define success by meaning ask themselves whether they have contributed to the improvement of the world and acted in a meaningful way often enough. Success is associated with the person and not with the leadership role.

When selecting leaders, owners and BoDs should ask their candidates about their reasons for and the purpose of their leadership. A warning light should be answers related to reputation, money, power, or fame (all objects of extrinsic success), as this indicates the candidate might be egotistical, self-centered, and not appreciative of others. The former chairperson and CEO of the Swiss multinational pharmaceutical company, Novartis, once told *Fortune*,

> For many of us, the idea of being a successful manager [...] is an intoxicating one. It is a pattern of celebration leading to belief, leading to distortion. When you achieve good results, you are typically celebrated, and you begin to believe that the figure at the center of all that champagne-toasting is yourself.[477]

The motivations described in the previous list may be acceptable if accompanied by more benevolent desires, e.g., serving something

---

475 "Quotes: Thoughts On The Business Of Life: Abraham Lincoln," *Forbes*, accessed March 5, 2018, https://www.forbes.com/quotes/76/.

476 "Joseph Stalin Quotes," BrainyQuote, accessed March 5, 2018 https://www.brainyquote.com/quotes/joseph_stalin_378367.

477 Bill George and Andrew McLean, "Why Leaders Lose Their Way," *strategy+business* vol. 35, no. 3 (2007).

bigger than themselves such as a greater purpose. Otherwise, leaders lose ground contact and become immune to criticism. They start to surround themselves with people who tell them what they want to hear, and in turn, other people learn quickly to tell such leaders what they want to hear.[478]

In sum, definitions of success can be marked by the internalization of anything learned during childhood and/or by severe incidents in the course of life. An illustrative example of this is Arnold Schwarzenegger, the former Austrian body builder, Hollywood actor, entrepreneur, and governor of California. He had a good relationship with his mother but not at all with his father, who preferred his older brother. His father was a very authoritarian policeman who apparently had an understanding of child rearing that bordered on child abuse. Arnold Schwarzenegger developed a strong desire to excel and prove himself to others. To be in control became his utmost goal so that his father would not be able to break his will. This is why he became a rebel and moved out of his home at a young age.[479]

People start defining success early on. Their main caregivers (most often parents, grandparents, and siblings) cowrite that script, which can make relevant a range of attitudes, from positive can-do ones to destructive ones characterized by limiting beliefs about the self. In his book, Bitz states, "Our parents shape us before we shape ourselves. They pass half their genes to us and teach us innumerable perspectives, practices, and prohibitions. They influence who we become and what we do more than anyone except for ourselves."[480]

The receipt of good care leads to an inner sense of self-efficacy, capacity for self-improvement, and feelings of security. In contrast, insufficient

---

478 Ibid.

479 Kets de Vries, "The Many Colors of Success," 5.

480 Bitz, *Winning Practices of a Free, Fit, and Prosperous People*, 120.

care marked by over- or understimulation or inconsistency can trigger serious psychological damage that is counterproductive for success.[481]

There are people, however, who have positive experiences despite suffering during childhood and who can overcome the negative aspects of their rearing. Their will to succeed, overcome inner insecurities, and become masters of their own destinies prepares them to take responsibility for their actions and not blame others for their fate. But there are many others who are not strong enough to prove their tormenting caregivers wrong, who develop a life theme of self-indulgence, self-destruction, and self-pity. The difference between people who are able to cultivate their own better nature to those who do not can be described as follows:[482]

1. Focus: Defining goals using imagination, fantasy, and thinking ahead; drawing a mental picture of wants.
2. Persistence: Actively pursuing success using determination and commitment, treating failure as a teacher. Excellence is the partner of persistence, and both require practice.
3. Self-mastery: Self-knowledge and mastery of thoughts is very hard, but it starts with recognizing and controlling attitudes toward what has occurred.

A common reason why individuals fail is a lack of faith in what they are able to accomplish. Once people start to interpret their own feelings and perceptions of success, they can choose their own paths and not let anybody else do so for them. And once they start to get to know themselves, they will also better understand the people around them. This is an important precondition to influencing, motivating, and guiding others in a mutually beneficial way.

It is not possible to change the way one's life started, but a new ending is entirely possible, starting now. Or as Orson Welles once said, "If

---

481 Kets de Vries, "The Many Colors of Success," 7–10.

482 Ibid., 7–10.

you want a happy ending, that depends, of course, on where you stop your story."[483]

DRIVERS OF SUCCESS

Opinions on what drives success are numerous. Common denominators, however, are passion, (hard) work, talent, and a portion of luck. Success is strongly related to people's interactions with each other.

Adam Grant[484] found that there are different types of interaction among people that relate to the characteristics of those involved. There are takers, matchers, and givers. Most people fall under the category *matcher* and instinctively try to maintain balance and fairness. Matchers strive for the long-term balance between give and take. Takers choose the dominant way, and it is their goal to control, be assertive, and earn respect. Very often, they feel superior to others. In the short term, they achieve success, as long as they are not dependent on others, such as leaders on the top company level who play out their power. As soon as change gets involved, they feel a threat to their power, and they might act unpredictably.

In contrast, givers—a rather rare category—either become the most successful and authentic leaders or are left behind. In the case of the latter, this is because they tend to be too self-sacrificing, as they constantly support others and oppress their own healthy interests and feelings. Successful givers put other people's interests ahead of theirs, but they never forget their own. They put on their own oxygen mask first so that they are better able to help others. Grant found that the style of giver significantly impacts success and happiness. Since the interaction style is not given but is a mindset, it can be learned.

---

483 Ibid., 7–10.

484 Adam Grant, *Give and Take: A Revolutionary Approach to Success* (London: Viking, 2013).

STEP 4: ASSESS LEADERS—LITERALLY

Research has provided evidence that there is a positive link between a dark personality and leader effectiveness. It was found that context is a determinant of whether dark personality traits will play a positive or negative role in the outcome of leadership effectiveness.[485] Based on the positive link between a dark personality and leadership effectiveness, narcissistic leaders, for example, tend to favor big, bold actions to grab attention. These actions, however, tend to have large consequences that can either be positive or negative: big wins or big losses. Consequently, their performance tends to be extreme and fluctuating and, hence, less stable than in organizations with leaders who score lower on narcissism.[486]

In common leadership selection processes, criteria such as experience, track record, IQ, and education are predominant. Criteria that can lead to a severe derailment, such as inner drivers and motivations, personal dysfunctions and disturbances, are downgraded or ignored.

Each individual has dysfunctional dispositions that reflect the dark side. They harm performance and cut into a person's strength potential. Interest in dark side characteristics has grown in the past twenty-plus years, as studies' findings have shown that the technical skills of derailed executives and successful executives are similar.[487]

However, analysis of managerial derailment has found that dark personality traits serve as an important precursor to leadership failure. One of the reasons why such individuals get into and manage to keep such high-level positions is that moral shortcomings are often ignored by their superiors in the evaluation process of the candidate's potential. In particular, problems with interpersonal relationship are often ignored and are consistent reasons for managerial derailment as they strongly overlap with a dark personality. Such interpersonal styles are

---

485 Harms, Spain, and Hannah, "Leader Development and the Dark Side," 501f.

486 Ibid., 8.

487 Eric Nelson and Robert Hogan, "Coaching on the Dark Side," *International Coaching Psychology Review*, vol. 4, no. 1 (2009), 9f.

characterized as insensitive, manipulative, demanding, authoritarian, aloof, critical, arrogant, volatile, excessively cautious, distrusting, perfectionist, and eager to please.[488]

As mentioned, mental models that are based on experiences early in life and unconscious to a large extent form the basis for weak interpersonal behaviors. Therefore, different individuals have different unproductive patterns. Most people are able to manage these patterns most of the time. But stress, too much work, strong emotions, fatigue, ambiguity, and organizational cultures can intensify and bring them to the surface.

These dispositions, however, can be assessed so that predictions of performance risk can be made.[489] For such an assessment, different researchers have identified leadership types and their respective unproductive patterns and describe how they can lead to overdrive and derailment.

Although research has found that a dark personality is a key culprit in issues that lead to managerial derailment in organizations, Harms, Spain, and Hannah[490] point out the importance of differentiating between those leaders that are simply ineffective/incompetent and those that are malicious, and those models of leadership that have destructive intentions and those that have destructive outcomes. For example, narcissists have a potentially destructive intention (elevate themselves, make others small), but it does not necessarily lead to negative outcomes. In contrast, leaders with histrionic tendencies have no intention to harm others, but their obsession for attention may lead to harm and negative outcomes.

The latter shows clearly that the attribute "dark" can be used twofold: one in its nature and the other in its effect.

---

488 Harms, Spain, and Hannah, "Leader Development and the Dark Side," 8.

489 Nelson and Hogan, "Coaching on the Dark Side," 9f.

490 Harms, Spain, and Hannah, "Leader Development and the Dark Side," 504.

The Dark Triad Test

The Dark Triad Test aims to measure the three socially undesirable traits: Machiavellianism, Narcissism, and Psychopathy.[491]

According to David Barrett,[492] CCO of cut-e (an Aon company), Machiavellians are good negotiators and people who are very strong at forming political alliances. At the same time, they are self-interested, cynical, manipulative, and without principles.

In comparison, narcissists tend to prefer big, bold actions that raise attention. Strong narcissists are egotists who use their charisma and superiority to reach their goal of influencing and dominating others.

And psychopaths are in possession of the most malicious traits. They usually lack empathy, show an impulsive behavior, are selfish, have no conscience, and do not shy away from taking very high risks.

Consequently, it is highly beneficial for any organization to select candidates who show low levels of the Dark Triad traits.

"Individuals with Dark Triad traits often self-sponsor their way into positions of leadership. They manage to fool the recruiters who appoint them—and charm the executives who promote them—because they come across as compelling and competent extroverts and they excel at interviews."

—DAVID BARRETT[493]

Therefore, Barrett has come up with seven steps that help protect from these candidates, in case a test has not or cannot be taken or to make sure a suited candidate with high scores on one or several traits can be kept at bay.

---

491 Jones and Paulhus, "Duplicity Among the Dark Triad," 1ff.

492 David Barrett, "Protect Your Organisation from Dark Triad Job Candidates," Human Resources Headquarters, accessed June 25, 2018, http://www.hrheadquarters.ie/protect-organisation-dark-triad-job-candidates/.

493 Ibid.

1. Assess the risk in context with your circumstances. Some jobs will require aspects of Dark Triad traits. Be clear about which and what levels of these traits are requested for the role to be filled.
2. Analyze the role thoroughly and identify not only the required competencies, abilities, knowledge, experience, attitude, and values but also the ideal personality and behaviors.
3. Make use of several assessment tools. Use a personality and values questionnaire and assess the candidate's motivation to reveal the person-job fit.
4. Design and lead structured interviews. A candidate with Dark Triad traits can be highly charismatic and tends to outsmart the interviewer and sometimes even tries to get in charge of the interview process. It is important for the interviewer to remain focused on competency-based questions that help them stay in charge and cover all elements of the role in question. Some interview guides help specifically check and verify the candidate's suitability so that outsmarting behavior can be offset.
5. Pay attention to those employed individuals whose traits are right below the "cut-off level" for the Dark Triad. Try not to assign several of them to the same team.
6. Identify, acknowledge, reward, and encourage good citizenship and the right behavior. Check whether and how your organization monitors and manages areas of performance that specifically relate to ethical and interpersonal behavior. Individuals with Dark Triad traits are able to thrive if moral shortcomings are ignored by the organization.
7. Appoint the right individuals. Make sure that the person's competencies and attributes are aligned with the role requirements.

720-Degree-Plus Feedback

The 360-degree feedback assessment is currently one of the most common human resource management practices.[494] It is a widely acknowledged process by which different sources such as subordi-

494 S. Jency, "720 Degree Performance Appraisal: An Emerging Technique," *International Journal of Informative & Futuristic Research*, vol. 3, no. 8 (2016), 2960.

nates, peers, direct bosses, customers, and even the individual under assessment give their feedback on a person's job performance. The goal is to gain an impartial, holistic, and balanced perspective and review of the individual's performance.[495]

On the other hand, the 720-degree performance appraisal as a human resource management tool aims at exceeding the usefulness of the 360-degree feedback by focusing more on development than performance.[496]

Why is it called 720-degree feedback? It is essentially a 360-degree survey that is done twice with each stakeholder asked. The first time sets the baseline to analyze performance results and define an action plan. The second time aims at measuring improvements. Therefore, a 720-degree feedback circle contains both preliminary and long-term feedback.[497]

This book takes it one step further by introducing *720-degree-plus* feedback, which overcomes the following flaws in the other assessments:

1. Top leaders often believe they are too high up the hierarchy to complete such a survey.
2. Often, feedback is not honest because the feedback givers are afraid of facing negative consequences.
3. Feedback surveys rarely include family and friends who could help provide a more holistic picture of the leader.
4. Since the ratings can be completed through online evaluation instruments, it is a rather bureaucratic, mechanical process.

First of all, the completion of a 720-degree-plus survey is mandatory

---

495 Silva Karkoulian, Guy Assaker and Rob Hallak, "An empirical study of 360-degree feedback, organizational justice, and firm sustainability," *Journal of Business Research*, vol. 69, no. 5 (2016), 1862-1864.

496 Jency, "720 Degree Performance Appraisal," 296If.

497 Anupama, Mary Binu, and Tapal Dulababu, "The Need of '720 Degree Performance Appraisal' in the New Economy Companies," *ZENITH International Journal of Multidisciplinary Research*, vol. 1, no. 4 (2011), 39ff. *English Oxford Living Dictionary*, "Morosoph," https://en.oxforddictionaries.com/definition/morosoph.

for the leader. Secondly, groups of feedback givers are assembled around a table to openly discuss the leader's or candidate's strengths and weaknesses. A neutral moderator must facilitate the discussion to arrange for the right setting (signed confidentiality agreement), describe the value of and overall goal of the initiative, and encourage openness to the situation, comfort to speak the truth, and benevolence with regard to their statements. This promotes honest feedback that is not impersonal or mechanical. It ensures a fruitful discussion that gives each participant the opportunity to support his/her opinion with arguments and experiences. Depending on the situation and the organization's culture, it might be advantageous for the facilitator to interview the feedback-givers individually. Thirdly, the questionnaire also includes feedback from family members, friends, and/or other persons who know the candidate well and outside of work (barring prohibitive laws in any given country or jurisdiction).

Despite the fact that such a process takes time and expense, it is worth the effort, as it helps reach the most accurate and comprehensive profile of the appraised candidate. It is much costlier to deal with negative outcomes.

As mentioned, many of those leaders who show a risk for derailment are so focused on themselves that they miss the opportunity to learn from others' feedback on their mistakes. They refuse to take responsibility for their actions. In addition to assessments, it is crucial to do whatever is needed, e.g., coaching, to help the leader become more self-aware and willing to develop. As we have seen, derailing/derailed leaders can seriously harm an organization's culture, productivity, and performance, or even the entire organization. This increases anxiety, fears, and hostility among subordinates.

(Further information on a selection of personality tests such as the Hogan Development Survey [eleven qualities that arise under pressure and can flip to the positive or negative side] or the Dark Triad Test [seven steps to protect from candidates with high level dark traits] that help recognize and mitigate performance risks before they become a problem can be found in this chapter.)

Encourage Reality Checks

Reality testing without immediately erecting defense mechanisms is challenging. Not many people manage to withstand the temptation to fall back on reflexes or succumb to the pressure of groupthink, and many fail to keep a clear head.

What can be done to help leaders realize the distortion of reality? What would be a good antidote to hubris? Back in history, this was the truth sayer, embodied by the jester (or wise fool or "morosoph"[498]) who served the purpose of giving honest feedback to the king.

It was the jester's job to keep the king constantly aware of the transience of his power. The jester shielded the king against the loss of reality in decision-making, preventing the power holder from foolish actions. The Romans were aware of the negative side of hubris. When a conqueror triumphantly entered Rome, there was either a slave sitting behind him constantly telling him, "You're human, Caesar. You're human, Caesar," or he was welcomed at the city gates by clowns and satyrs who shouted abusive words to him. This did not always work though.[499]

Erasmus, the philosopher, was even more aware of this and drew a differentiation between wise men, clowns, and fools. He wrote that unlike wise men and clowns, "fools have another gift which is not to be despised. They're the only ones who speak frankly and tell the truth, and what is more praiseworthy than truth?"[500]

Today, however, leaders need to find a source of feedback through

---

498 *English Oxford Living Dictionary*, "Morosoph," https://en.oxforddictionaries.com/definition/morosoph.

499 Kleiner, "The Thought Leader Interview," 5; Kets de Vries, "The Organizational Fool," 757.

500 Kets de Vries, "The Organizational Fool," 757f.

other ways, such as from employees and colleagues. But often, family and close friends are the ones best suited to this role. They can offer valuable insights into some of the leaders' unconscious drivers because they know them best, including their upbringing and background. However, it is important that leaders acknowledge this opportunity, because too often, their excessive workload leads them to sacrifice their personal needs, families, friends, and health for the job and the organization. Brigitte Ederer, former member of Siemens' management board, said it very clearly:

> The move to the top of the corporate pyramid brings changes with it that nobody knows how to deal with. You can no longer ask anybody because with certain decisions, you are the last authority and on your own. You ran the risk of becoming lonely. If you don't take care of your friends, they become fewer and fewer.[501]

Each leader needs to have people at their side whom they can both trust and ask for feedback and even advice. It is comforting to know that these people will speak up and tell them the truth regardless of the leader's position, title, or status, which is not always the case in business.

Clearly, identification with only the official/public leadership side that is positive and sunny is highly tempting. Disregard of the shadow side begins early on and lasts forever if not addressed. But if change is tackled, a tug-of-war between best intentions and most inner fears, between pride and shame is opened.[502] Too much pride (arrogance) can be a defense mechanism to avoid the experience of shame.[503]

People are more aware of the shadow sides of leadership on the political stage yet less so in business. As many practice examples show,

---

501 Roman Pletter, Peer Teuwsen, and Dorit Kowitz, Manager unter Druck", *Die Zeit*, February 6, 2014, https://www.zeit.de/2014/07/manager-selbstmord/komplettansicht.

502 De Haan, "The Leadership Shadow," 6.

503 Susan Long, "Images of Leadership," in *Psychoanalytic Perspectives on a Turbulent World*, ed. Halina Brunning and Mario Perini (London: Routledge, 2010), 6–7.

this perception needs to be adjusted.[504] Even extreme examples are numerous, as shown in previous chapters.

It is critical for a leader to resist temptation and not fall back on old, unproductive, if not destructive patterns triggered by impulses or give in to groupthink. It is not easy, however, to receive a reality check without instantly building a defense. All leaders need people at their side whom they can trust and ask for honest feedback and advice. They need to know that these people will tell them the truth regardless of their status or title, which is not all that common in business settings. Such feedback is vital, as it helps the leaders stay on track.

HELP (LEADERS) OVERCOME RESISTANCE TO CHANGE

The abilities to lead change and to coach and develop employees are crucial skills for successful leaders. But who's leading the leaders? Who is training the trainer? Are leaders subject to the same fears as their employees when change occurs? Can leaders—including persons exhibiting hubris—coach and be coached?

With the world changing faster and faster, new opportunities and challenges for organizations—and the accompanying new strategies, structures and processes—often bring resistance to change by employees, including leaders and aspiring leaders. This opposition can slow down productivity and performance. However, the real reasons behind it are often overlooked.

It is not change per se that people oppose. It is the fear of loss that comes with change, whether this is real or potential loss. Hence, many people prefer to stick to what they know and show resistance.[505] They establish various defenses and they unconsciously and actively hold on to hidden competing commitments, often despite a serious willingness to change. Thus, what looks like resistance to change could be seen as

---

504 Kippenberger, "The Dark Side of Leadership," 13.

505 Heifetz, Grashow, and Linsky, *The Theory Behind the Practice*, 10.

a personal immunity to change. It is these competing commitments that make employees act in inexplicable and unusual ways that frustrate their superiors.[506]

An example: Gloria is committed to advancing her career but behaves in ways that prevent her from getting promoted. She misses deadlines and delivers low-quality work. She was bullied when she was little and unconsciously resists taking on more power because she associates power with something negative, e.g., inflicting harm on those with less power. Therefore, if a supervisor were to put pressure on Gloria to advance or incentivize her or try to support her in other ways, Gloria would not make progress. She would fall back into her old patterns.

Gloria's story helps explain the phenomenon of immunity to change. There is a gap between her goals and intentions and her actions. Gloria is not just reluctant; she is almost paralyzed, which is characteristic of competing commitments. There is an unconscious and opposing agenda.

If leaders understand the concept of competing commitments, they are able to understand why people like Gloria, who are sincerely committed to their goals and to the changes leading to those goals, do not manage to act upon them.

Hidden Competing Commitments

Organizational psychologists and researchers Kegan and Lahey developed the Diagnostic Test for Immunity to Change. This four-stage process supports organizations and leaders in discovering the hindering blocks of change.[507] A trained coach can help guide the process.

1. The first step is to help steer an individual through a list of ques-

---

506 Kegan and Lahey, "The Real Reason People Won't Change," 2f.

507 Ibid., 4.

tions to discover their competing commitments and prompt them to select the one commitment they intend to work on.

2. The second step serves the purpose of helping identify the competing commitments that undermine change.
3. The third step involves the uncovering of underlying assumptions.
4. The fourth and last step aims at changing the resistant behavior.

The time needed for each step is not to be underestimated. It might sound like an easy and quick process, but it is not, since it fundamentally questions people's deeply rooted psychological beliefs that they have held on to for a very long time. Often, these beliefs are acquired in childhood. Questioning them may be very painful, uncomfortable, and embarrassing, and this is why they have not and would not acknowledge them or discuss them with anybody else. This being the case, some people might even choose to stick with their competing commitments rather than undergo the uncomfortable process of breaking up their immunity to change.[508]

It is crucial for leaders to guarantee that their employees' revelations will not be considered weaknesses and will not be used against them. In order to boost the change process, it is essential to support them in overcoming their immunity to change. The same is true for the leader's own process.

But as much as employees are subject to immunity to change, so are leaders. Thus, they also need to analyze their potential behavior against development goals and uncover their own long-held, underlying assumptions to find out how they might affect the change process and the people around them.[509]

---

508 Ibid., 2f.

509 Ibid., 9.

CASE STUDY

The protagonist of this case is Jerry.[510] Jerry is a CEO. He seems strong and self-confident and has risen naturally to positions of power which he seems to enjoy. He often initiates power games.

This image, however, does not correspond to his inner self. Inside, he is insecure, which he covers with arrogance and ignorance.

This game is stressful and increases the pressure, in addition to the one that the VUCA world already represents. His sleep quality has deteriorated, and the consequences of sleep deprivation are health problems—all of which have forced him to face the fact that he needs to change his behavior and attitude.

COMMITMENT TO A SINGLE CHANGE

Jerry created a list of desired changes and selected one commitment he wanted to work on. Jerry decided to overcome his insecurity, his fear of not being good enough, and framed it as an active endeavor:

> *I commit myself to actively accepting or initiating opportunities that nourish my self-confidence in a healthy way, and allow me to be approachable.*

EXAMINING COMPETING COMMITMENTS
What does Jerry do to work against himself?

Jerry did a whole series of things to stop himself from letting others in and trusting others. He was ambitious, and his tone was dominant.

To disguise his insecurity, he liked to brag. At the same time, he engaged in organizational politics to avoid any possible exposure of his insecurity or shortcomings.

---

510 Isabelle Nüssli, *Cockfighting: Solving the Mystery of Unconscious Sabotage at the Top of the Corporate Pyramid* (Leverage YourSelf AG, 2018), 132–137.

He rarely delegated and did not let others participate in the decision-making process.

While thirsting for compliments, he felt uncomfortable in the rare case that he received them. He believed that others were calculating or did not see the whole picture.

Why does Jerry work against himself?

The reflection led him to conclude that he was unsettled. Jerry felt dethroned by his younger brother Josh when Josh was born and was angry at his parents and brother. Jerry unleashed his anger on the BoD and the management team.

He tried to avoid the feeling he had as a child: not being good enough. He never understood why his parents wanted a second child and let his brother get away with everything. With him, they were always very strict.

Jerry was afraid to let go of power because others, like his brother, could invade his world and compete for attention. They could discover his insecurity and capitalize on it. They could consider him unqualified and lose interest in him. Therefore, he wanted to hold on to the feeling that gave him power—the feeling of esteem and supposed security.

UNCOVERING THE UNDERLYING BIG ASSUMPTION

Jerry's greatest assumption (and his fear) was that without power, he would not be important and would therefore be unloved and alone. Although he was aware that the actual chance of being alone was minimal, he realized that this unconscious belief prevented him from changing his behavior. As abstruse as it sounds, the fear of being unloved and alone is one of the two prevailing fears we have in everything we (don't) do. The other one is to be poor and in need (sleeping under bridges).

ACTION PLAN

Breaking habits and behaviors is not easy. A crisis can lead to an epiphany, but as valuable as an epiphany is to bring unconscious elements into consciousness, it alone is not enough. Sustainable changes occur only through small steps to improve.

What did Jerry do?

He started to practice active listening and he delegated more often.

He frequently asked for honest feedback, accepted it, and resisted the impulse to find arguments against it.

He checked in with himself and let go of the unpleasant feeling of giving up power. He played through the worst case and realized that it is not as bad as unconsciously thought.

The above activities, among others, helped Jerry work on genuinely strengthening his self-confidence based on solid ground and not on a cover-up for insecurity.

EFFECT

This exercise is an effective tool that can be applied to any change you want to achieve. While there may be relapses (if old habits break through, or if you do not adhere to the action plan), it should generally help move leaders forward.

It is impossible to press a button to change anything. The process requires trust and patience, especially with yourself, but also with others. Change does not happen in a single moment, but gradually through questioning and redefining deep-rooted, long-term beliefs, which can be painful or embarrassing to confront. This is why many people choose to hold on to their competing commitments instead of challenging themselves to reach the change and positive outcome they desire. The impulse to protect the self is human. But if change and positive outcomes are truly desired, it is important to work on over-coming these hurdles to redefine the beliefs that previously defined and held up the world. It is worth it.

LEARNING ANXIETY VS. SURVIVAL ANXIETY

In an interview with *Harvard Business Review* author Diane Coutu, Edgar H. Schein (Sloan Fellows Professor of Management Emeritus at MIT's Sloan School of Management and an expert on organizational development) proclaims that change in organizations requires trans-formational learning.[511] This can happen only if trust and openness are present, employees are empowered, and organizations become flatter. Such extensive change requires employees—including lead-ers—to let go of long-standing assumptions in order to acquire new ones. As the following text will show, the process of unlearning and relearning is very painful and takes time.[512]

According to Schein, learning comes with two types of anxieties: "learning anxiety" and "survival anxiety."[513]

Learning anxiety stems from the fear of trying out something new, as the experiment could be too challenging. It would mean letting go of old habits that have worked well in the past.

Individuals who are learning something new can feel like, or be per-ceived by others as, a dissenter of their tribe (group), which can harm those persons' self-respect and, in extreme cases, even identity.

Learning anxiety builds the foundation for resistance to change. In general, for individuals to try something new, a second form of anxiety needs to be experienced: survival anxiety.

---

511 Diane Coutu with Edgar Schein, "The Anxiety of Learning," *Harvard Business Review*, vol. 80, no. 3 (2002), 100–106.

512 Ibid., 68–75.

513 Ibid.

Survival anxiety is the dreadful awareness that one needs to change in order to survive. This form of anxiety imbeds deep hopelessness, which ends in opening up for learning. However, this process of emotional distress and despair cannot always be overcome, in which case the individual can remain in a state of discouragement.

Edgar Schein adds that many companies address these obstacles to change and learning by increasing survival anxiety. They bully employees into organizational learning with a message of learn it—"or else." This actually builds resistance to change.[514]

To help employees overcome all forms and roots of resistance to change and the associated learning, their "education" should start by leadership giving the employees a clear explanation of why the changes and learning are needed and how these will benefit the company and, in turn, the employees. The employees will be able to see that leadership trusts them by sharing what is going on, while demonstrating care and concern for their feelings and well-being. Then, acceptance can begin, and learning anxieties can continue to be overcome through user-friendly training, mentoring, rewards, and ongoing support.

In order for leaders to be equipped to lead change, they must first overcome their own anxieties. The CEO and other leaders usually feel most anxious about new learning, as it can trigger dysfunctional behavior. It is therefore crucial for leaders to set a good example, to become genuine learners, to recognize their vulnerabilities, weaknesses, and uncertainties. These preconditions are required to create a psychologically safe environment, which builds the basis for transformational learning. People in positions of power—leaders—have a higher tendency of finding excuses not to deal with personal work that can be emotionally painful. Complaints of people in all parts of the world regard the gap between what leaders say and what they do. This gap originates in an unawareness of their own inner theatre (see

---

514 Ibid.

chapter 5, "Key Driver Three: Leadership as an Accelerator," in the subsection "Influence of Upbringing on Leadership and Implications for Leadership Selection"). This lack of awareness makes them prisoners of their past, which steers their action.[515]

As this book has emphasized, it is not comfortable to uncover unconscious patterns. This process can provoke anxieties and even increase disorientation. However, if individuals dive deeper and change unproductive parts of their inner script, they will be able to tap unknown potential.[516] Coaching can help.

ENCOURAGE COACHING

Many issues encountered by executives are highly confidential, and many emotions they experience are highly personal. Where can they turn to discuss these in a confidential setting that allows for an outside perspective and coaching to help them work through the situation? Executive coaching can help the development of the executives and also the improvement of their relationship with others.

The difference between coaching and consulting is well explained by Kets de Vries:

> In contrast to consultancy, coaching focuses on individuals in their specific organizational context and does not come up with preconceived answers and solutions. The coach primarily enables executives to find their own solutions in order to create personally meaningful and fulfilling results.[517]

For example, when a CEO becomes silent and starts to sweat each time his much older chairperson stares at him with crossed arms and a frown on his forehead, a coach can help the CEO recognize *trans-*

---

515 Kets de Vries, *The Leader on the Couch*, xx.

516 Ibid., xi.

517 Manfred F. R. Kets de Vries, Konstantin Korotov, Elizabeth Florent-Treacy, *Coach and Couch: The Psychology of Making Better Leaders* (New York: Palgrave Macmillan, 2007), 4.

ference. In this case, the chairperson reminds the CEO of his father, a serious and strict man with a critical eye, who always signaled him that he could never live up to anyone's expectations. The goal is first to realize this unconscious pattern and, second, learn to overcome it.

This is how curious and motivated leaders manage to gain insights into their inner theatre, which they wouldn't otherwise. It not only helps them in their professional but also in their personal life. And the companies are better off. Coaches can further help shift focus, improve team development, and help create and implement succession plans.

Although coaching can be considered a relatively young field compared to other disciplines, it has gained substantial popularity in the past decade. Many researchers have found that coaching significantly helps leaders become better and more effective.[518]

It is the coach's task to discover and assess leaders' dysfunctional dispositions (which all people have as part of their personalities). Such assessments can have a considerable positive impact on leaders' self-awareness. The role of coaches is important, as they work with leaders to identify and agree on strategies, measures for development, and action plans.[519]

Coaches possess a large toolbox with the help of which they can identify signs of danger. The application of the right tools can help leaders rebuild the competencies required of them, as defined by the owner or the board, depending on the situation and context. Coaches support leaders in correcting flawed perceptions of themselves and their environments so that they can boost their self-awareness, emotional intelligence, and sensitivity in regard to interpersonal relationships.[520]

---

518 Nelson and Hogan, "Coaching on the Dark Side," 7.

519 Nelson and Hogan, "Coaching on the Dark Side," 7, 9.

520 Ibid., 12.

COACHING PEOPLE WITH HUBRIS

The experience and skills of seasoned board directors can help modify a narcissistic CEO's potentially destructive behaviors. However, if it becomes apparent that their efforts have had no impact, they will need to get professional help. But, as explained in chapter 5, reactive narcissists either tend to be unreceptive to professional help, or they know exceptionally well how to manipulate those providing it. It has been shown that these individuals are more likely to possess the two behaviors "self-promotion and talkativeness," both of which influence employability ratings ("not only benefit individuals in selection settings but also help these individuals self-promote their way into leadership positions").[521] Similarly, research has shown that individuals higher in Machiavellianism are more willing to not be honest in interviews.[522]

If they are open to coaching, it is most often because their personal pain is already advanced; it is a result of dissatisfaction with life, emptiness, lack of purpose, a sense of being involved in fraudulent actions, lack of meaningful relationships, absence of excitement in the job, or mood swings.[523]

As it is challenging to treat and/or remove persons exhibiting hubris (aka Seductive Operational Bullies, or SOBs), the best strategy is to identify them before they join the company. However, this is difficult because it is often the assumption of a position of power that causes them to become SOBs. Still, there are a few actions that might help prevent hiring or promoting SOBs.[524]

1.   A coach can try to access people such as spouses and close friends, who can cut through hubris, or to listen well to the SOB's subor-

---

521 Harms, Spain, and Hannah, "Leader Development and the Dark Side," 501.

522 Ibid.

523 Kets de Vries, *The Leader on the Couch*, 45–47.

524 Garrard and Robinson, *Intoxication of Power*, 99.

dinates, who often have a different perspective on their boss—but not necessarily. Remember, SOBs can be very charming.

2. If there is dual leadership in place, meaning the chairperson and the CEO are not the same person (see chapter 9, "Checks and Balances"), it is easier for the other directors to oversee the CEO who is not their chairperson at the same time. Thus, it is not easy to replace an SOB-CEO if that person is also their boss.

3. Counseling and coaching can help, although hubristic people do not like feedback and are good at telling coaches what they want to hear.

4. It can also help to ask what the candidate is curious, pleased, unsure, surprised, insecure, or mad about. What makes the person defensive? And what connects?

5. Conducting exit interviews with people who have left the company can be very revealing since they no longer fear retribution from SOBs.

Caution needs to be exercised to avoid displaying too much empathy toward SOBs, which can get in the way of their experiencing reality. It might be easier to create a leadership culture, structure, and processes of openness, transparency, mutual respect, and communication, given this is an environment in which an SOB will find it hard to thrive.[525]

Very often, the traditional institutional framework and checks and balances in big organizations are not designed to identify the elements of excessive narcissism. And if they do, it is often too late.[526] (Find more on checks and balances and how they can be assembled to help an organization become hubris-proof in chapter 9.)

As the numerous scandals around the world have shown, there are many leaders who indulge their egos and lust for power and who take extreme measures in pursuit of their goals. As has been extensively described in chapter 3, relationships based on different methods and

---

525 Ibid.

526 Kets de Vries, *Leaders, Fools and Impostors*, 25.

values accentuated by the impact of change can lead to disagreements on strategy. The dominant party wins and shapes the strategy process. The fight for power reveals the negative personality traits of the people involved. Better understanding of the values and methods of the persons involved and elaborating on their origins and how they have played out in a conflict of interest are crucial.

GROUP COACHING

Undoubtedly, one-on-one coaching is effective. However, combining it with group coaching can make it even more powerful. Changes in leadership behavior are longer-lasting when they are triggered in a group setting. Group coaching seems to increase accountability and trust and contributes to constructive conflict resolution.[527]

Group coaching helps each participant learn about and apply new interpersonal tools. Strong relationships are built on listening. Listening enhances understanding, which helps build trust and increases the motivation of participants, as they feel listened to and understood.[528]

In group coaching situations, people tend to take on a very similar role to that which they (used to) take on in their family of origin. But they are not aware of it. Common roles are those of mediator, clown, cheerleader, scapegoat, or hero.[529]

COACHING THE COACH—HELPING THE LEADER IMPROVE WORKFORCE ENGAGEMENT

According to Gallup, "Most of modern business relies on annual reviews to provide feedback and evaluate performance."[530] Conversely,

---

527 Kets de Vries, "Leadership Group Coaching in Action," 61.

528 Ibid., 68.

529 Ibid.

530 Jim Harter, "Dismal Employee Engagement Is a Sign of Global Mismanagement," Gallup Blog, accessed May 20, 2018, http://news.gallup.com/opinion/gallup/224012/dismal-employee-engagement-sign-global-mismanagement.aspx.

the modern workforce values development opportunities, ongoing exchange, and having a coach, rather than a "boss," who helps them tap their potential.

This is why it is important to help the leader become a better coach. And there are several ways to foster workforce engagement.

A start can be the assessment and audit of the current performance management system to detect the parts of the system that work *toward* an engaged workforce or *against* it. Furthermore, leaders must be trained in effective performance development conversations. (See chapter 7, "Crucial Leadership Skills (and How to Develop Them).")

Although performance reviews are still critical, they increase in value to both employees and organizations if they are linked to ongoing conversations that help manage expectations and foster development.

An organization's health depends on optimizing employee engagement. In addition to fixing problems within the current performance management system, it is crucial to develop awareness about the recruiting and promotion of the right leaders and build an adequate system for this process. Employee engagement starts at the top with inspiring leaders who foster a culture of inclusion, innovation, and excellence.

ENCOURAGE COLLABORATION CONTRACTS AMONG LEADERS

As described throughout this book, in leadership, context and relationships matter. Human beings hardly ever behave and act in isolation, but they are impacted by and affect others. This leaves fertile ground for conflict. But not all relational conflicts are bad—the business world often presents leaders with conflicts that ultimately help a company improve and grow. Interactions among the magic triangle as well as leadership assessment and development of the BoD and management by the shareholders and the BoD are frequent.

Based on interviews with leaders, personal business experience, and thorough research, the author of this book found that 95 percent of the interviewed leaders perceived that most relationships between chairpersons and CEOs do not work well.[531] When relationships are bad, especially between leaders at the top of a company, the conflicts they generate are counterproductive and can be ultimately destructive and lead to derailment, both in relation to the individuals involved as well as to the company.

It should be asked how the two leaders at the top can improve and nurture their relationship for the benefit of the organization's culture, productivity, and ultimately, performance. Power struggles and conflict at the top are strong forces that steer away focus from the business, the clients, the market product, and the employees. In turn, a powerful pairing at the top can make anything happen.

A substantial part of these upsides originates in the establishment of successful, high-functioning relationships. Although circumstances vary by organizations, by the end of the day, it comes down to how human beings operate in relationships, especially in which power adds to the dynamic.

There are tools and concepts that can help improve relationships between leaders at the top, whether it is between a chairperson and a CEO or between directors of the BoD or between members of the management.

PSYCHOLOGICAL CONTRACT

Not all agreements in business are and need to be transactional. They are relational and formed without written documentation or verbal expression. This describes the nature of a so-called psychological contract (PC).[532] The PC describes an employment relationship.

---

531 Nüssli, *Cockfighting*, 32–34.

532 Nüssli, *Cockfighting*, 32–34.

The concept was conceptualized in the 1960s by Dr. Chris Argyris, a psychologist. Denise Rousseau popularized the concept in the 1990s. In contrast to transactional contracts that are rather short-term oriented, have a certain duration, and focus on extrinsic factors, relational contracts are longer term, objective, broader in nature, and deal with intrinsic aspects. Their fulfillment calls for a high personal commitment.

Each employee, superior or subordinate, has a so-called psychological contract with their employer. Most people don't realize that they enter into such a contract when they join an organization. As the term reveals, it is not a written contract. Yet, since an organization cannot be party of such a contract, the contract is predominantly formed with the person at the other end of the table who personifies the organization. Generally, for the CEO, it is the chairperson; for an employee, his/her superior. Each of these parties has experience, expectations, and a belief in an obligation of reciprocity.

A person's attitude and behavior are reflected in a psychological contract in that they refer to expectations of promised exchanges. One individual expects to give something and to receive something in return. A breach of contract occurs when one person perceives that the other party has not met its promise. A violation of the contract happens when reactions are triggered that are strongly emotional. Contract breach and violation are negatively linked to job performance, satisfaction, and commitment.

Since experiences build the base of a psychological contract, it is subjective. When the perception emerges that the contract was violated, strong emotional reactions arise, such as the feeling of betrayal, anger, resentfulness, or a decrease in trust. These perceptions and the associated emotions are influenced by an individual's upbringing, experience, and personality.

Usually, people are not aware of their psychological contract with an organization or, in the form of a substitute, with a person. Because it happens unconsciously, trust is a key element to maintaining the health of a psychological contract. The absence of trust is associated with inferior quantity and quality of communication and cooperation as well as negatively linked to problem-solving and performance. Trust building creates togetherness, provides security, and impacts an individual's interpretations of social behavior.

This book has described how family upbringing shapes personality, which in turn shapes the way people develop their values, behavior, and actions. Therefore, it also shapes psychological contracts, the perception of and response to contract breach and violation. Someone's current environment predominantly serves to interpret and to reinforce the knowledge gained through early, formative childhood experiences. It is important to become aware of one's values and beliefs and their origin.

CREATE A LEADERS' ORAL COLLABORATION CONTRACT

An effective tool for any two leaders is to enter a "Leaders' Oral Collaboration Contract" (LOCC, based on what Nüssli calls "CCCC—Chairperson-CEO Collaboration Contract"). The CC can be considered as a type of psychological contract, which means that it's a verbal agreement between two or even more individuals that work together, be it a chairperson and a CEO, a CEO and a CFO, or others. A LOCC is not signed or written down, but rather, it's a process that is discussed and acknowledged by the involved parties. As a nontransactional agreement, the LOCC focuses on building trust, reframing instincts, and building a common language between the parties.

It increases clarity of roles by focusing on the how (how roles are assumed) instead of on the what (description of the role). It includes talking through the elements of roles with a coleader so that communication and clarity of roles can be improved. Consequently, trust can be (re)established and nurtured, which helps foster a healthier work environment and increases productivity.

A LOCC requests a high level of commitment of both parties. By framing the content and shaping another party's perception of the others' behavior, a breach of contract can be minimized. Increased trust leads to a lower likelihood of breach because it serves as a guideline that impacts an individual's interpretation of others' behaviors.

Discussing a LOCC is not an excessively personal discussion. It is more critical for the parties involved to show and share their human side, which will help improve mutual understanding and nurture trust.

FACILITATE THE CONVERSATION

It is recommended that the conversation be moderated, especially during the first meeting. The external facilitator could be a professional mediator, executive recruiter, executive coach, or an HR director—as long as the person does not have any bias toward one of the parties or feels any threat to his/her job security. Ideally, the facilitator is a neutral, trained professional who is used to working with leaders. It is also critical that the parties trust and feel good about the person chosen. The facilitator helps initiate the discussion, for example, by asking the parties how they would describe their relationship, what motivates them to discuss a LOCC, how they visualize an ideal outcome, and where this outcome could/would take them.

After an initial conversation, the facilitator will follow a rough structure around the conscious and unconscious elements that drive a relationship. A comprehensive version of the LOCC can be found in appendix 10. Here's an excerpt:

Conscious Drivers

Trust. How do you grant trust? Do you tend to give the benefit of the doubt, or do you harbor initial mistrust that improves with positive results? How are you going to increase and nurture trust in your relationship?

Role Clarity. Is there clarity about each of your roles? Have you ever discussed in depth how each of the roles should be filled? Is there a role history that influences role misinterpretations? How will you address and discuss potential issues and misunderstandings?

Unconscious Drivers

Corporate Governance That Is "Lived." Discuss each party's role (scope, interfaces, responsibilities). How aligned are your views, perceptions, and expectations? Where are overlaps of responsibilities and how are you going to tackle them? Who represents the company when and how? Which potential situations might be critical and could lead to conflicts?

Power

What does power mean to you? How would you describe the power balance between you two? Going forward, how can you agree to handle the division of power?

Time Spent

How much time do you spend together? Do you perceive it as too little, enough, or too much? Why? What would be an ideal frequency and amount of time to spend?

Only after these and a few other issues have been laid out and discussed do the parties take the written job descriptions and the organizational rules and charts into consideration. The newly gained insights and further increased trust support a fruitful discussion of the details of their roles, responsibilities, and balance of power.

This was the first part of the LOCC. The second part gives each party time for personal reflection to think deeply about their backgrounds, past experiences, and unconscious drivers. This happens individually. Neither content nor outcome are shared.

REMEMBER, IT IS NOT A TYPICAL CONTRACT

The LOCC is benefited by not being written down, which fosters the purpose of forming a new and improved psychological contract between the parties. The process of the individuals understanding each other's point of view is more important than the wording of a formal work agreement.

Sir Denys Henderson, the former chairperson of Britain's Imperial Chemical Industries, once stated, "The agreement [job description] should be put down in writing and eventually approved by the board. But the process of thoroughly understanding each other's viewpoint is more important than the final text."[533]

Going forward, it is strongly recommended that facilitating and even coaching become a standard part of "lived" corporate governance. If one party wishes to put a LOCC in place but for whatever reasons cannot or does not want to approach the other party directly, a good alternative can be to go through a more neutral party, such as the human resources department, independent directors of the board, a coach, or a common person of trust.

At first, innate defensiveness can make one party suspicious of or even resistant to discuss a LOCC. Still, it is essential for the person who initiates the discussion to not give up if the other party is not immediately receptive to the idea. But if one party continues to resist and is unwilling to form a LOCC, it might very well be a warning sign. Who would not want to develop, improve, and grow a relationship, if only for the benefit of the organization?

It is critical to ensure strict confidentiality. Sometimes, it helps if the parties sign a nondisclosure agreement before starting the discussion. Following the end of the formation of a LOCC, it is left to the parties whether they want to share their process with their colleagues and, if so, what information to share.

---

533 Ibid., 154.

Usually, the parties should expect the first meeting to be the most uncomfortable and challenging one, as they are attempting to break familiar patterns in their relationships. The parties may be defensive and reluctant to be the first to open up, but fortunately, these sessions do get much easier as they go on.

Frequency and number of sessions are up to the facilitator, the parties, the flow of the conversation, and the progress made in each session.

It is important that the parties be consistently reminded to trust both the process and themselves. It is normal to feel uncomfortable at points during the process or to not understand the point of view of the other party. It is often seen that as long as all individuals have a stake in the discussions, neither one will want to be the one who compromises the process or even gives up. It is by far more likely for the relationship to improve when all parties manage to press through the discomfort and trust the process.

There is no single right way to form a LOCC. The way the contract is carried out depends on the context and the situation surrounding the parties' relationships. Since human beings are complex and not entirely rational, it is not an exact science. The contract in appendix 10 serves as a guide and can be customized. Success depends on the acceptance of the unfamiliar, the trusting of the process, and the embracing of the outcome.

The higher the level of trust between and among the leaders at the top, the lower the likelihood for derailment. Chapter 9, "Checks and Balances," will further elaborate on the importance of building a culture of trust and how to do it.

BEWARE OF FOCUSING TOO MUCH OR TOO LITTLE ON THE LEADER

Leaders have a strong influence on the people, culture, and performance of their companies. Nevertheless, it is possible to overfocus or underfocus on the leader when analyzing business performance, assessing negative outcomes, or making vital decisions about hiring or accepting employment.

OVERFOCUSING ON THE LEADER

"Superheroes" in leadership have existed throughout human history. They lead organizations or nations into extraordinary outcomes. And they even do it with humility.

In turn, as we have seen, still too many leaders come with their own inner kryptonite, usually fear manifesting in hubris, greed, psychosis, and/or neurosis. They are fallible, even malevolent, actors in the stories of corporations or countries. They contradict themselves by trying to take sole credit for success but finding others to blame for failures.

Leaders can bring remarkable perspective, vision, and success to the organization or conversely inflict egregious harm. They do set the tone for the culture and strategies, and they do make a huge difference. But focusing on leadership as the only indicator or cause of a company's success and failure is dangerous for several reasons:[534]

1. It puts disproportionate (superhero) expectations on what an individual or a very small group can achieve. It is unlikely that the engine of a large, complex, international system can be completely overhauled just by changing the attitudes, behaviors, and actions of a small minority of the participants in the system.
2. Viewing leaders as the only source of changes and solutions presumes that all other participants have no impact or right to be heard. It does not pay respect to those who contribute to the functioning of the organization. In practice, these people are the custodians of the company's spirit, heart, and soul. They are closer to the customers, process operations, and root causes of problems than any individual leader could ever be.

---

534 Nixon, *Pariahs*, 231–233.

As described in chapter 5, hubris occurs in the context of power. For example, the former CEO of the Royal Bank of Scotland (RBS), Fred Goodwin, was not the only person displaying hubris in the financial market in 2008 or in RBS. Placing the blame for RBS's crisis on him alone overlooked the context. It was the responsibility of the BoD and the regulators to control and handle Goodwin's power. If they failed to do so, they were also to be blamed, as they did not stop the hubris from developing and thriving. In fact, they rewarded it.[535]

It is extremely difficult to establish the exact contribution of any individual leader to the success of their company. However, the general strong assumption is that leaders are very important for companies' performance in the long run.[536] The fact that stock prices can react very strongly after the announcement of a CEO's termination or appointment underlines this.

An example is Sika. When it was announced that its long-standing, successful CEO was leaving for LafargeHolcim, a leader in the building materials industry, many analysts considered his departure a setback for Sika during the takeover battle, in which he had been playing a key role. The analysts agreed, however, that his departure would not impact Sika's operating business. The day after the announcement, the share price dropped by 4 percent. From the perspective of Lafarge-Holcim, analysts deemed the change of personnel good news for the company and considered the CEO of Sika's good track record as a predictor of boosting profits. Consequently, LafargeHolcim's share price increased by 6.3 percent.[537]

An even more extreme example concerns Qi Lu, COO of the Chinese search engine company Baidu. When he announced that he was going to leave the company in May 2018 after a tenure of a year and a half,

535 Ibid., 23.

536 David F. Larcker, Stephen A. Miles, and Brian Tayan, "Succession 'Losers': What Happens to Executives Passed Over for the CEO Job?" *Stanford Closer Look Series*, 2016, 1.

537 Maurizio Minetti, Abrupter Beginn einer neuen Ära bei Sika, Luzerner Zeitung, http://www.luzernerzeitung.ch/nachrichten/wirtschaft/abrupter-beginn-einer-neuen-aera-bei-sika;art9642,1034175 (last visited July 28, 2017).

the price of the US-listed shares fell more than 10 percent, which accounted for the loss of market capitalization of $10 billion. Can a CEO be worth that much, even if (or because) the share price rose by 40 percent since he started, and he has an exceptional way of inspiring his teams to deliver top performance? And were the owners and the BoD aware of the risk embedded in this one leader?[538]

Economic and market analysts have to start somewhere, and it is logical to start at the top. But for owners, BoDs, CEOs, executive recruiters, and prospective employees to assess a leader, it is illogical or even dangerous to consider only their corporation's business performance record.

UNDERFOCUSING ON THE LEADER

The 2016 Gallup study *State of the Global Workplace* found that around 50 percent of all employees across all continents have once left their jobs because they wanted to get away from their bosses.[539]

Moreover, according to Gallup's 2017 *State of the Global Workplace* report, "85 percent of employees are not engaged or [are] actively disengaged at work. The economic consequences [...] are approximately $7 trillion in lost productivity. Eighteen percent are actively disengaged [...] while 67 percent are not engaged."[540]

There is huge, untapped potential in the two-thirds of the workforce who are not "actively" disengaged but simply not engaged. These people generally come to work with good intentions and a desire to contribute. They deliver reasonable performance. They give you their time—but not their hearts—because leadership hasn't inspired them or earned their loyalty or trust.

---

538 Krim Delko, Wenn Topmanager Milliarden wert sind, *NZZ Neue Zürcher Zeitung*, https://www.nzz.ch/finanzen/wenn-topmanager-milliarden-wert-sind-ld.1387658 (last visited May 24, 2018).

539 Manfred F. R. Kets de Vries, "Do You Hate Your Boss?" *Harvard Business Review*, vol. 94, no. 12 (2016), 98–102.

540 Harter, "Dismal Employee Engagement."

Motivated employees are a key driver for the success of a company. Reasons for disengagement are leadership issues such as micromanagement, bullying, conflict avoidance, shirking decision-making, stealing rewards for performance, withholding information, blaming, lack of listening, not serving as a role model, slacking, failing to develop the workforce, and fraud.[541]

These statistics about why employees leave and why they are disengaged reinforce the importance of the proactive, astute, thorough assessment and development of current and future leaders.

IN SUM

The goal of every organization is or must be to find the right leader who can interact with the BoD, increase profits, and improve on the quality and effectiveness of the workplace culture. This is especially true because in many scandals of the past decades, the key players were CEOs and top executives (and somewhat less often directors and sometimes owners). The past chapters have shown that who is at the helm is critical for any company.

Having shed light on the legal framework and the assessment of the three hidden key drivers (change, the human element, and leadership), this chapter offered solutions and provided a customizable toolbox to help detect and avoid danger while further driving change.

For example, it is critical to proactively examine whether the poison is in the bottle or in the system and—if necessary—redefine the original role so that both the role occupier and successor can harvest positive effects. It is a prerequisite for driving change. The case with Linda and Travis demonstrated that despite founder Linda's good intention, her role became contaminated. Travis inherited a corrupt role and ended up being the scapegoat for having failed to initiate the turnaround.

---

541 Kets de Vries, "Do You Hate Your Boss?"

After having defined the context in which the organization operates and having analyzed roles and systems for contamination, the next step is to assess the current or future leader to define the needed skills/qualities and assess the personality, disposition, and drivers for success. This is how warning signs can be detected early and how actions can be taken in a timely manner.

Different management practices complement the assessment, such as the 720-Plus Feedback, with the goal to reach an impartial, holistic, and balanced perspective and review of the individual's performance. Further, it is strongly recommended that the leader seek feedback by family and friends that serves as a reality check and antidote to hubris and helps them resist temptation to fall back on reflexes or succumb to the pressure of groupthink.

A LOOC between or among leaders nurtures trust, strengthens relationships, and lowers chances for derailment.

If a leader is willing and able to develop himself and his workforce and successfully lead through change, each individual will uncover hidden competing commitments to overcome unconscious immunity to change. Change does not happen instantly but gradually through questioning and redefining deep-rooted, long-term beliefs, which can be painful or embarrassing to confront. Individual and group coaching strongly boost such processes. Coaches provide tools that help the leaders rebuild the competencies required of them, defined by the owner or the BoD, depending on situation and context. Coaching not only helps leaders foster self-awareness, emotional intelligence, and sensitivity in interpersonal relationships but also helps them agree on strategies, measures for development, and action plans. Although it is almost impossible to successfully coach hubris, coaching practice can help detect and prevent hiring or promoting SOBs.

The process of analyzing, training, and developing a leader is not only an ongoing and crucial process but one that takes time. This requires patience from all parties involved. However, if good intentions and signs of development are noticeable, it is worth persisting. If not, it is worth taking action, such as separating the leader in question.

CHAPTER 9

CHECKS AND BALANCES

As the described cases of scandals demonstrated and based on ACFE's analysis, all too often, traditional institutional frameworks and checks and balances, especially in larger organizations, are not designed and/ or do not manage to identify important warning signs and triggers for derailments. And if they do, it is often too late.[542]

To make a company future proof, it is important to differentiate between human beings and systems, meaning between individuals and their characters, personalities, and relationships on the one hand, and integrated structure, mechanisms, and rules on the other hand, both sides need to be looked at. They are intertwined—comparable to a double helix—and complement each other. Therefore, when it comes to making a company ready to become derailment-proof, each of the two sides must contribute its part.

The previous chapter described the focus on the human element. Through the development and ongoing monitoring of leaders and their behavior, corrective interventions can be tackled in time.

---

542 ACFE, *Report to the Nations*.

The current chapter introduces a range of carefully selected frameworks, procedures, and concepts, such as good governance, a culture of trust, and a well-working whistleblowing system that must form an agile and reliable fine-meshed net that helps catch, develop, or dismiss (potential) leaders before they derail. Each of the tools can and should be customized and, together, thoughtfully orchestrated. Duties should be clearly defined and aligned, and cooperation encouraged so that no one person or unit ends up having absolute control over decision-making.

Therefore, aside from focusing on human beings, their assessment and development, it also requires increased transparency on the introduction, application, and performance of checks and balances within the system to minimize mistakes, prevent or reduce derailment, and make companies and industries derailment- and hubris-proof.

DEVELOP A CULTURE OF TRUST

When CEOs and chairpersons were asked what makes the relationship with their coleader work, the large majority of answers came down to one word: trust.[543] This raises the question of how trust can be built and nurtured.

Regarding reasons for derailment, an earlier study of European and US executives by the Center of Creative Leadership found that the groups had the same top two derailment factors, both of which undermine trust building:[544]

1. Having problems with interpersonal relationships
2. Not being able or willing to change or adapt

The amount of research and literature on the topic of trust is extensive, shedding light on different aspects (definitions of trust, creation of

543 Nüssli, Cockfighting, 38f.

544 Brittain Jean Leslie and Michael John Peterson, The Benchmarks Sourcebook: Three Decades of Related Research, (Greensboro, NC: Center for Creative Leadership 2011), 7, 45.

trust, situational trust, depth of trust, repairing trust), from different angles (trustor: someone that extends trust; trustee: someone that receives trust) and in various fields (business, law, philosophy, psychology, politics, science, sociology).

There is no universally accepted definition of trust. Oliver Eaton Williamson (an American economist, professor at the University of California, Berkeley, and recipient of the 2009 Nobel Memorial Prize in Economic Sciences, which he shared with Elinor Ostrom) described it as "Trust is a term with many meanings."[545]

However, it is commonly agreed upon that trust is key to all human relationships. "It is the basic currency of success [...] directly linked to the degree that top executives in the company are trusted."[546]

It is not easy for highly competitive executives to build trust. Therefore, trust can be looked at as a rare commodity in a lot of organizations. Trust is the glue that holds relationships together.

Trust is delicate. It can be broken in an instant. Although repairing trust is highly time- and energy-intensive, small steps can help. The restoration process requires patience, time, energy, and effort. Therefore, it is of supreme importance to care about and cultivate trust. But it is a mutual responsibility. Everyone has their own relationship with trust and recognizes it intuitively. Trust building creates togetherness, provides security, and affects people's interpretations of social behavior.

VIGNETTE

Roger and Sheena were chairperson and CEO, respectively.[547] When

---

545 Oliver E. Williamson, "Calculativeness, Trust, and Economic Organization," *Journal of Law and Economics of the University of Chicago*, vol. 36 (1993), 453.

546 Manfred F. R. Kets de Vries, *The Leadership Mystique*, 2nd ed. (Harlow, UK: Prentice Hall Financial Times, 2006), 161.

547 Adopted from Nüssli, *Cockfighting*, 103f.

Roger grew up, he perceived a constant mistrust in his family. As a result, he held trust in high regard and became highly sensitive to breach of trust. In contrast, Sheena grew up in a family where trust was very important and hence nurtured. Therefore, she also became sensitive to its breach.

Despite their shared belief in the importance of trust, Roger and Sheena withheld it from each other. When asked about their relationship, both stated that they gave the other person the benefit of the doubt. But Roger added that he needed to see proof quickly (an interesting dilemma because trust takes time to be built, but he was expressing an instant need for it) to be able to give someone the benefit of the doubt. This means that trust wasn't there.

Sheena could feel the absence of Roger's trust. Being expected to quickly provide "proof" undermined her ability to execute her plans. She felt like she was not able to meet the quality of work and level of planning that she was known for. She could not grasp why Roger didn't trust her more and realized she was getting less trustful of him. She started to wonder whether he had a hidden agenda.

As for Roger, he did not feel comfortable with the high level of trust he had granted his CEO, Sheena. To him, it was critical to be provided with results quickly. He began to wonder and worry whether Sheena would misuse the room he gave her, for example, attempting to dethrone him by using information against him.

Because of their mutual mistrust, they both decided that they didn't want to spend any more time with the other than necessary. The little communication they did have, they made sure was in written form in case they needed proof or protection.

If nurtured, trust not only fosters collaboration and decreases the likelihood for severe conflict, but it also strongly contributes to constructive conflict resolution, which in turn supports genuine commitment and increases mutual accountability. Chances for people to

trust each other are highly increased if they better know and understand each other (purpose of a LOCC).

Trust-Building Behaviors, Actions, and Strategies

Although trust is a complex topic, it appears to be hard to build and
is rather easy to distort. It is important to focus on which behaviors
and actions enhance trust building, especially since negative events
(trust breach or violation) carry more weight than positive ones (trust
building).[548]

Since (mis)trust breeds (mis)trust, there are a large number of behaviors and strategies that leaders can apply to help others (superiors
and subordinates) build trust in them—the BoD and workforce in
their CEO and the CEO in its BoD and workforce. All strategies and
behaviors involve human interactions in one way or the other.[549]

1. **Consistent behavior.** To increase credibility and predictability, it
   is important that leaders behave consistently on an ongoing basis.
2. **Integrity.** Leaders need to act upon their words.
3. **Shared and delegated control.** Leaders must include their subordinates in decision-making processes.
4. **Communication.** This should involve accurate and timely information, transparency, openness, and explanations for decisions
   (taken or to be taken).
5. **Addressing of concerns.** Good leaders protect their subordinates'
   interests and do not get involved in exploitative actions.
6. **Vision.** It is important for leaders to create and communicate a
   shared vision and collective values.

---

548 Paul Slovic, "Perceived Risk; Society for Risk Analysis," *Risk Analysis*, vol. 13, no. 6 (1993), 585–687.

549 Veronica Hope Hailey and Stephanie Gustafsson, "Experiencing Trustworthy Leadership" (Bath, UK: Chartered
Institute of Personnel and Development and University of Bath School of Management, 2014), 10.

Stephen M.R. Covey, author of *The Speed of Trust*, defines thirteen behaviors of a high-trust leader.[550]

Character behavior:

1. Talk straight (be honest and tell the truth)
2. Demonstrate respect (genuine care for others, show empathy)
3. Create transparency (be authentic, real, and open)
4. Right wrongs (make things right when you are wrong, apologize, and restitute swiftly)
5. Show loyalty (give appreciation and appraisal to others; be engaged)

Competence behaviors:

1. Deliver results (track record of good results)
2. Get better (improve on an ongoing basis; be a lifelong learner)
3. Confront reality (stand up, address, and tackle sensitive or difficult issues right away)
4. Clarify expectations (disclose and discuss them)
5. Practice accountability (hold yourself and others accountable and don't shirk responsibilities)

Character and competence behaviors:

1. Listen first (then speak)
2. Keep commitments (say what you are going to do and walk the talk; enter a LOCC)
3. Extend trust (show a propensity to trust)

Clearly, many of the skills and competencies listed in the chapter 7, "Crucial Leadership Skills (and How to Develop Them)," strongly contribute to trust building.

---

550 Stephen R. Covey, "The 13 Behaviors of a High Trusted Leader," CoveyLink, 2006, 2–6, https://resources.franklincovey.com/the-speed-of-trust/the-13-behaviors-of-high-trust.

It is essential that leaders and employees are allowed and able to show emotions and that doing so does not negatively impact their careers. It is also crucial for leaders to know how it feels to be a subordinate. This includes the fostering of self-awareness with regard to how they extend and receive trust. Referring to Erikson's eight stages of human development (see chapter 4), the first stage "trust versus mistrust" is critical to forming trust. During this stage, infants learn to trust if their caregivers meet their basic needs. If not, they may develop mistrust, suspicions, and anxiety.

Trust in a Virtual World

Trust building is even more important, although more difficult, in today's virtual world that brings forth increasing numbers of virtual teams. It is increasingly rare today that leaders work face-to-face with all their team members, which forces them to rely on different virtual communication channels. Team members display a broad range of disciplines, cultures, and experiences, which makes both clarity of communication and mutual understanding more challenging.[551]

It is not social media but personal contact and communication that helps build trust. Only if this higher degree of trust is established can collaboration among different people in different geographies be effective. In the absence of trust, teams do not function well, and virtual teams even less so or not at all.[552]

TRUST, POWER AND KNOWLEDGE SHARING

In the absence of trust, knowledge management projects cannot be(come) successful. Knowledge is closely linked with power and thus sharing gets more difficult. But when there is a certain level of trust, people are incentivized to share. Therefore, knowledge management projects cannot just be focused on data and data banks and leave out

---

551 Horney, Pasmore and O'Shea, Vol 33(4), "Leadership Agility: A Business Imperative for a VUCA World," People & Strategy, 2010, 4.

552 Kets de Vries, "Leadership Group Coaching in Action," 71.

the human element. It ultimately lies with people to acquire, increase, distribute, and manage, but also manipulate knowledge. Hence, good knowledge management is best if organizations create a culture of trust and make people understand the advantages of sharing knowledge.[553] Shared cultivation of knowledge undermines power and knowledge concentration with one person or unit.

CASE EXAMPLE: BERKSHIRE HATHAWAY

Berkshire Hathaway[554] is mainly known as an investment company and not as a company that has grown beyond its core operations. The corporation has invested time and energy in establishing a structure by which its entities are led. First of all, it is highly decentralized, and second, it grants a high degree of autonomy to the managers of its subsidiaries.

Warren Buffett (chairperson, president and CEO of the American multinational conglomerate) stated that in order to establish a seamless web of deserved trust, he gives each manager the following simple mission: run your business as if:

1. You were the 100 percent owner
2. The business was the one and only asset that you own or will ever own
3. You could not sell or merge it for at least the following 100 years

This seamless net of trust provides the corporation with the advantage of keeping a highly modest number of less than thirty headquarters staff (including Buffett), despite its roughly 400,000 employees around

---

553 Ibid.

554 David F. Larcker and Brian Tayan, "Trust and Consequences: A Survey of Berkshire Hathaway Operating Managers," *Stanford Closer Look Series*, 2015, 1–3.Jonathan Stempel, "Factbox: Warren Buffett, Berkshire Hathaway at a Glance," *Reuters*, May 1, 2019, https://www.reuters.com/article/us-berkshire-buffett-factbox/factbox-warren-buffett-berkshire-hathaway-at-a-glance-idUSKCN1S73NV; "Number of Employees at Berkshire Hathaway from 2010 to 2019," Statista, https://www.statista.com/statistics/787860/employees-of-berkshire-hathaway/.

the world.[555] The culture of the company is most often described as honest (absolutely crucial for the company's operations), having integrity, long-term oriented, and focused on caring for customers.

"Few things can help an individual more than to place responsibility on him, and to let him know that you trust him."

—BOOKER T. WASHINGTON

IMPACT OF TRUST ON STRESS-LEVEL, ENGAGEMENT AND PERFORMANCE

An HBR study showed that people working in high-trust companies perceived 74 percent less stress than people working in low-trust companies. In addition, they experienced 106 percent more energy at work, had 13 percent fewer sick days, reported 76 percent more engagement and a 29 percent higher satisfaction rate with their lives, linked to a 40 percent lower burnout rate. Increased performance is a consequence of these elements.[556] Implication: trust lies at the heart of a strong company culture.

Research found that monitoring systems, such as surveillance systems, increases extrinsic motivation and reduces intrinsic ones.[557] As this book has shown, the same holds true when mechanisms and guidelines such as corporate governance are considered and being treated as "the magic tools" to control behavior and performance. They provide valuable orientation and frame, but they also breed mistrust and resentment.

The key is to build a corporate governance system that is lived (here

---

555 Jonathan Stempel, "Factbox: Warren Buffett, Berkshire Hathaway at a Glance," *Reuters*, May 1, 2019, https://www.reuters.com/article/us-berkshire-buffett-factbox/factbox-warren-buffett-berkshire-hathaway-at-a-glance-idUSKCN1S73NV; "Number of Employees at Berkshire Hathaway from 2010 to 2019," Statista, https://www.statista.com/statistics/787860/employees-of-berkshire-hathaway/.

556 Paul J. Zak, "The Neuroscience of Trust," *Harvard Business Review*, vol. 95, no. 1 (2017), 84–90.

557 Roderick M. Kramer, "Trust and Distrust in Organizations: Emerging Perspectives, Enduring Questions," *Annual Review of Psychology*, vol. 50 (1999), 569–598.

is when the human takes center stage, once again) and is proactively adjusted. And, it needs to be based on trust.

A corporate governance system that is based on trust will be more cost effective than one that is focused on controls, rules, and regulations because it requires less bureaucracy, simplified processes, procedures, and increased productivity (research and literature show that relationships that are built on trust show higher productivity than those built on contracts.[558]). Realistically, however, corporate governance systems need both trust and rules. Seamlessly combining the two in a closely knit net will facilitate the detection of early warning signs and fraudulent behavior, prevent or reduce conflicts, reduce costs, and increase trust, engagement, and productivity.[559]

Regardless of the time, energy, and effort spent, building a reputation for trust and trustworthiness must be a key goal for any company. Building a culture of trust not only helps increase engagement, productivity, and performance, but it also prevents derailment. Actually, it should rather say "reduce" derailment because psychopaths, and to some extent persons exhibiting hubris, tick differently. They live on trust that other people place in them. Therefore, it is the seamless net of thorough leadership assessment and development and checks and balances—based on trust—that help make a company hubris proof. A good corporate governance system is indispensable.

IMPLEMENT GOOD (CORPORATE) GOVERNANCE

Balance and counterbalance and a constructive disequilibrium (not harmony at any price but critical discussions) need to be established and maintained so that conflicts and abuse of power by individuals or groups can be prevented.[560] It is not only about the right forms of governance. It is equally about the question of how it is lived—about

---

558 David F. Larcker and Brian Tayan, "Trust: The Unwritten Contract in Corporate Governance," *Stanford Closer Look Series*, 2013, 1–3.

559 Larcker and Tayan, "Trust: The Unwritten Contract in Corporate Governance," 2f.

560 Kets de Vries, *Leaders, Fools and Impostors*, 115.

the right operation of that governance. Even the most accurate and best designed system is of little help if diverging perceptions and interests are not discussed and aligned, or if the leaders recruited and in charge are prone to derailment.

In general, experts in corporate governance focus closely on issues that involve the BoD because of the directors' roles, liabilities, and responsibilities. Codes of best corporate governance practices ask BoDs to comply with their recommendations relating to shareholder and stakeholder relationships, compositions, and independence of the BoD, as well as procedures and internal control systems.

It is the BoD's duty to make sure that adequate internal controls and risk management procedures are in place. Some of the mentioned practices are dictated by regulators and stock exchange requirements; others are urged by corporate governance experts and practitioners.[561] Examples follow.

BOARD OF DIRECTORS

The answer to "What makes a board highly effective?" has changed in the past ten to twenty years as a consequence of corporate scandals and the financial crisis, and it needs to change further. It is common for BoDs to consist of former CEOs who have lengthy industry experience and successful track records in both general and risk management. However, board effectiveness is not a sum of the board members' accomplishments.

Other factors are also critical, such as the dynamic and functioning of the team, diversity, the general background of the directors, board size, tenure, independence, committees, leadership structure, evaluation, number of board seats, succession planning, and leadership structure. All these factors will be described in the next sections.

---

561 Larcker and Tayan, "Seven Myths of Boards of Directors," 1.

SPECIFIC BOARD EXPERIENCE
Recruiting, Succession Planning, and Talent Development

In the selection process of a CEO, considerable weight is put on measurable skills.

In the CEO evaluation process, BoDs often focus too much on financial performance and not enough on nonfinancial aspects. How can it still be that only a CEO with industry experience can be considered as a viable candidate? Does this not lead to inbreeding? Rather than look only for those with experience in their industry, BoDs should consider CEOs who did not start their business career in that particular industry and who can always be trained in key technical risks.[562]

Research shows that more than 20 percent of BoDs admit that they know their CEO's strengths and weaknesses only poorly or moderately. So it is not surprising that directors show weak skills in evaluating potential CEOs. If the former CEO was not successful, they tend to look for very different skills. Furthermore, only a little more than half of all directors seem to know the strengths and weaknesses of the executive one level below the CEO. Two thirds of the directors do not even take part in the performance evaluations of senior executive teams, and only 7 percent assume a formal mentoring role to them.[563]

Insufficient succession planning and talent development negatively affect a company's performance. The more time a company takes to come up with a successor, the worse its subsequent performance is compared to peers. Directors need more frequent contact with internal candidates so that they can appreciate or help improve their leadership potential.[564]

Consequently, BoDs need to have directors with talent management and succession experience. These directors can support the BoD and

---

562 Nixon, *Pariahs*, 97f.

563 Larcker, Miles, and Tayan, "Seven Myths of CEO Succession," 3.

564 Ibid., 3f; Larcker, Miles, and Tayan, "Succession 'Losers,'" 1.

the management team with best practices for talent development and succession planning, which in the first place requires the thorough selection of directors either by the owners or by the BoD via the GA. As this book has frequently stated, directors must learn how to discover warning signs that are linked with possible destructive behavior, and they must be willing to impose restrictions if the CEO shows resistance. It cannot be emphasized enough that BoDs must guard against collusion between a CEO's predisposition (hubris) and current position (power) and draw and defend the respective boundaries.[565]

Of course, the same is true for owners and shareholders in regard to the directors and the chair of the BoD. The optimal selection of directors and a chairperson by the owners/shareholders (direct or via the nomination committee) is vital. It is not only essential that the directors be committed and know the company well, but also that they not be guided by their egos or put their own interests before the ones of the company (arguing that they act in the company's best interests).

Hence, the BoD has to provide a platform for different interests to be addressed in order to facilitate the strategy formation process and anticipate the potential impact on and adjustment of the corporate governance model. Since this is a proactive process, the BoD must consist of directors who can both handle such a process and ensure that the selected executives can do so too.

Active CEO Position Questionable

There still is a wide belief among shareholders that active CEOs form the best directors because of their operations knowledge. It is assumed that these CEOs strongly contribute to strategy, risk management, succession planning, performance evaluations, and the relationship with shareholders and stakeholders. Yet empirical research shows less positive evidence regarding their performance.[566]

---

565 Kets de Vries, *The Leader on the Couch*, 45–47.

566 Larcker and Tayan, "Seven Myths of Boards of Directors," 3.

For example, there's strong evidence that an outside CEO-director has neither a positive nor a negative impact on the company.[567] Moreover, directors who are active CEOs contribute to a higher CEO compensation of the company for which they serve as director.[568]

The question to ask here is whether an outside CEO can truly add value, both in terms of experience and regarding their personality. Shareholders and owners should not be blinded by publicity, exposure, title, status, and focus on the (potential) true contribution of the outside CEO-director.

Team Size

It is fallacious to believe that bigger teams perform better than small teams because of the amount of resources. The links that need to be managed among team members grow exponentially with the growth of the team itself. And this is the core reason for issues in teams.

In general, team size should not reach double digits. The ideal working team size is six persons. A very big senior leadership team can be worse than no team at all.[569] However, admittedly, the size of the BoD team is not independent on the size and reach of a company. With an increasing number of committees, the number of members to be assigned to these committees needs to increase. Still, this should not serve as an excuse for the BoD to have twenty board members, where the complexity increase is likely to cut into efficiency and effectiveness. Thus, it is recommended for shareholders and directors to honestly ask themselves if its board size is in line with needs and not related to power and fear of loss of seats (status).

---

567 Rüdiger Fahlenbrach, Angie Low, and René M. Stulz, "Why Do Firms Appoint CEOs as Outside Directors? *Journal of Financial Economics*, vol. 97, no. 1 (2010), 30.

568 Haidan Li and Yiming Qian, "Outside Ceo Directors on Compensation Committees: Whose Side Are They On?" *Review of Accounting and Finance*, vol. 10, no. 2 (2011), 110; Olubunmi Faleye, "CEO Directors, Executive Incentives, and Corporate Strategic Initiatives," *Journal of Financial Research*, vol. 34, no. 2 (2011), 251.

569 Diane Coutu, "Why Teams Don't Work," *Harvard Business Review*, vol. 87, no. 5 (2009), 99–105.

In addition to the size of the team, trust among team members is vital. Trust needs time to be built and nurtured. Increased team size is not conducive to trust building.

In order to contribute to a board's performance and functioning, chairpersons need to spend far more time than they actually do on aspects that make teams function well. This task is one of the most important duties of the chairperson.[570]

Diversity

It is widely accepted that the best BoDs consist of a portfolio of different skills and experiences. It is as challenging as it is fundamental for BoDs to build diverse skillsets and knowledge pools. The advantages of diversity (diversity in all regards) are manifold: fresh thinking, new insights, and different perspectives on clients, markets, and best practices. BoDs that are too homogeneous can run the risk of having blinds spots and missing out on trends and issues inside and outside the company.

Diversity, including skills, experience, gender, race, age, and tenure helps a company better compete on an international level. Based on research that included 2,000 public companies over a time span of thirteen years, more diverse BoDs were prone to less risk-taking and were more likely to pay dividends than comparable homogenous peer groups, because different views on potential outcomes include different perspectives on risks.[571]

Aside from the many advantages of having a diverse BoD, diversity can also entail disadvantages if not sourced and managed (for inclusion) well.[572]

---

570 Nixon, *Pariahs*, 65–68.

571 Elena Bajic, "Why Companies Need to Build More Diverse Boards," *Forbes*, August 11, 2015, https://www.forbes.com/sites/elenabajic/2015/08/11/why-companies-need-to-build-more-diverse-boards/#5798d758662c.

572 Daniel Ferreira, "Board Diversity," *Corporate Governance: A Synthesis of Theory, Research, and Practice*, ed. Kent H. Baker and Ronald Anderson (London: London School of Economics, 2010), 227f.

Advantages

1. Increased creativity and different views
2. Increased access to different resources and networks
3. Better public relations and investor relations, and higher legitimacy

Disadvantages

1. Increased conflict, teamwork, and communication are lacking (diversity needs inclusion[573])
2. Directors that add to diversity but don't have sufficient skills, experience, or qualifications, or they do but don't have time to meet their obligations and duties
3. Potential conflicts of interest

Tenure

Board tenure (also called board refreshment) for an individual to serve as director is defined in bylaws and can be adjusted by the BoD. Tenure limits are still not widely defined. Not rarely, directors serve indefinitely, which can make the BoD stale and no longer open to new perspectives, inputs, and ideas coming from new members.

Since such limits are not required by law, quite a few companies either do not follow them, adjust the statutes when the limit is up, or simply ignore the guidelines.[574]

The setting of and compliance with term limits would add urgency to each individual's role and motivate the best use of their time. This would also support the importance of initiating and leading through change processes. Despite this guideline, each member should be regularly assessed in regard to potential change of behavior, action,

---

573 Frances X. Frei and Anne Morriss, "Begin with Trust," *Harvard Business Review* (May–June 2020), 1.

574 Frederick E. Allen, "Sarbanes-Oxley 10 Years Later: Boards are Still the Problem," *Forbes*, July 29, 2012, https://www.forbes.com/sites/frederickallen/2012/07/29/sarbanes-oxley-10-years-later-boards-are-still-the-problem/#762381202345.

interests with length, or accumulation of power, competencies, and contribution (see the section "Board Evaluation").

Number of Board Seats

Many board members who hold several board seats are "always" open for more seats. Often, the same publicly known individuals get asked by well-known companies to join their boards.

With the increased focus on corporate governance, directors' responsibility and liability, especially in public companies, have been brought closer to center stage. This is why such mandates are generally well compensated (especially in listed companies) and lead many board members to give up their daily jobs to become professional board members.[575]

During crises and scandals, the amount of time required to complete one's board-related duties rises dramatically, making it more complicated for professional board members who sit on many different boards to properly fulfill their duties by participating in emergency, short-notice meetings. Thus, directors should keep in mind the time needed in case of crisis of companies on whose boards they sit and limit or align the number of board seats accordingly. They need to be willing (and hopefully able, which previous relevant experience tells; otherwise, time will) to potentially serve as "bad-weather pilots" and prepare in good times for it. In today's VUCA world, such experience, qualities, and preparation are more valuable than ever.

Independence

What is the role of the BoD aside from its formal role of directing and supervising the affairs of the company, setting the company's strategic goals, and evaluating management performance within a

---

575 Ibid.

framework of prudent and effective controls?[576] Whom does it serve: the shareholder or the company?

As previous chapters have shown, the strategy formulation process includes more politics than usually expected and planned for because it depends on the underlying values and methods of the actors involved. This is why Korine and Gomez recommend that corporate governance be tested against changes and, hence, the BoD must ask during strategy formation, "Whom is the strategy for?" rather than, "Which is the best strategy?"[577]

BoDs' legal responsibilities and liabilities differ, depending on the jurisdiction. In most countries, the BoD is obligated to act in the best long-term interests of the company. But who or what constitutes the company? And what are its best long-term interests? Practice shows over and over again that differing interests make it almost impossible for BoDs to serve the best interests of companies.[578]

In the US, this means that it is the directors' obligation to focus on shareholder value. Switzerland has a similar approach, although Art. 717(1) CO states it is the BoD's duty to act in the company's best interest and to refrain from any actions that could cause harm.[579]

But as elaborated at length in chapter 3, "Key Driver One: Change as a Triggering Element," one must also consider that there are different types of shareholders, and that different shareholder groups have different interests. Although directors have a legal duty to act in the best interests of their companies, Higgs found that it has long been acknowledged that this is not sufficient in itself to provide a guarantee

---

576 Derek Higgs, *Review of the Role and Effectiveness of Non-Executive Directors* (London: Department of Trade and Industry, 2003), 21, https://ecgi.global/sites/default/files//codes/documents/higgsreport.pdf.

577 Korine and Gomez, *Strong Managers, Strong Owners*, 7.

578 Ibid., 6.

579 Sommer, Die Treuepflicht des Verwaltungsrats, 17.

that potential conflicts will not harm the objectivity of the board's decision-making.[580]

After the scandals of the 1990s and 2000s, and with reference to corporate governance codes, there has been an increased call for nonexecutive directors. This led to the establishment of the Higgs Committee in 2001 and the Higgs Report in 2003. In its report, the Committee emphasizes the importance and effectiveness of nonexecutive directors.[581]

A nonexecutive director (also external or outside-director) is a board member who is not part of the executive management team, meaning the director is neither employed by the company nor affiliated with it and does not take part in the company's day-to-day management. The counterpart is the inside or executive director. Nonexecutive directors are expected to challenge and monitor the performance of executive directors and management, taking into account the best interests of the company and its stakeholders. These directors add a different and fresh perspective to the BoD. Despite their contact with management and need to be well-informed, they must retain independence of mind and be willing, capable, and courageous enough to raise their voice, to question, and to challenge.[582]

But nonexecutive does not automatically mean independent. As much as the definition of nonexecutive is similar around the world, the definition of independent differs. It is not defined by the law and different codes, and expert opinions give different definitions.[583] According to the Higgs Report, "independent means that all directors have to take decisions objectively in the interests of the company."[584]

---

580 Higgs, The Department of Trade and Industry, 2003, 35.

581 Ibid., 17.

582 Ibid., 35.

583 *Investopedia*, "Non-Executive Director," http://www.investopedia.com/terms/n/non-executive-director.asp (last visited July 31, 2017).

584 Higgs, The Department of Trade and Industry, 2003, 36.

The EU Commission provides the following definition: "A director should be considered to be independent only if he is free of any business, family or other relationship, with the company, its controlling shareholder or the management of either, that creates a conflict of interest such as to impair his judgement."[585] The commission provides criteria to assess the status of directors' independence, but the determination of what it means in the different jurisdictions of its member states is to be defined on a case-by-case basis by the board. The EU Commission sees a trend toward independent directors. However, the different definitions make standards uneven. For example, the requirement of independence from the majority shareholder has not been fully accepted by all member states.[586]

According to Higgs, independent nonexecutive directors are "independent of management and free from any business or other relationship which could materially interfere with the exercise of their independent judgement, leaving it to boards to identify which of its nonexecutive directors are considered to meet this test." But this definition does not give much guidance to BoDs as to what this test involves. In the UK alone, more than a dozen of such definitions of independence exist, and they all provide different criteria.[587] The tricky question remains whether the definition should be defined in the code of best practice for corporate governance (the same for all) or in a company's statute (depending on the company's circumstances).

In any case, in order to increase transparency and manage expectations and hence avoid conflicts (of interest), it is strongly recommended that (in)dependence be discussed both when new directors get hired and throughout their tenure. It is up to the shareholder and the BoD to define the process.

---

585 European Commission, "Commission Recommendation on the Role of Non-Executive or Supervisory Directors of Listed Companies," *Official Journal of the European Union* (February 25, 2005), 56f, https://eur-lex.europa.eu/LexUriServ/LexUriServ.do?uri=OJ:L:2005:052:0051:0063:EN:PDF.

586 Ibid.

587 Higgs, The Department of Trade and Industry, 2003, 35f.

Board Committees

The BoD establishes the board committees and appoints its members. Being assigned with specific tasks, the committees help fulfill the BoD's diverse range of responsibilities. The most common committees and their general function (depending on various factors such as size and structure of the company) are:

Nomination and Governance Committee

Larcker and Tayan found that the level to which a company defines the rigor of its control systems is a consequence of the level of self-interest within the company. Today's corporate governance systems reveal the degree to which self-interest exists. In general, requirements are extensive, which confirms that self-interest within companies is high. A large amount of money is spent annually on fees for internal and external auditors, and compliance to meet legislators' and market requirements consisting of numerous rules, regulations, and procedures.[588]

The nomination committee is the board's "voice on governance"[589]—how to shape the company's governance policies and practices. Aside from periodically reviewing the company's charter, bylaws, and policies on ethics and compliance matters, their duties include board succession planning and the recruiting, recommending, education, and self-evaluations of board directors. Many companies prefer delegating risk management to their nomination and governance committees.

It is critical that the members of the committee make sure the corporate governance system is adjusted proactively and that it is lived. Consequently, leaders in charge must be thoroughly selected and/or developed.

---

588 Larcker and Tayan, "Trust: The Unwritten Contract in Corporate Governance," 1.

589 Nick Price, "What Is the Role of the Nomination Committee?" BoardEffect, April 15, 2019, https://www.boardeffect.com/blog/what-role-nomination-committee/.

Remuneration/Compensation Committee

The variety in level and extent of compensation between companies and within industries is high. The challenges lie in the complexity of finding the right balance between rewarding top talents and aligning compensation with performance, which requires the BoDs to have all information needed to make an informed decision.[590]

BoDs should constantly review and question whether the right actions, behaviors, and outcomes are rewarded and whether the right compensation mechanisms are in place so that goals are aligned with aims and values.[591]

Short-term rewards should be limited. Leaders who are obsessed with power, ego, money, and status might be prone to hubris. Therefore, if a CEO or a chairperson refuses a fair, adequate, or merchantable compensation package, this person might not be the right leader. It is worth looking for the right leader who still wants to assume the job.[592]

Corporate governance systems exist to prevent self-interested behavior. Each person's interests strongly influence decision-making in daily business life. Economists see this as an incentive problem. People are more incentivized to work for their own advantage than for the benefit of their employers. A framework consisting of contracts, controls, processes, and procedures, together with recruiting, should realign the imbalance by aligning the different interests of insiders with those of shareholders.[593]

It is important to focus on the alignment of rewards and performance, taking into account systems and people.

---

590 Nicholas J. Price, "Role of the Remuneration Committee in Corporate Governance," Diligent Insights, February 19, 2019, https://insights.diligent.com/compensation-committee/role-of-the-remuneration-committee-in-corporate-governance.

591 Ibid., 112f.

592 Nixon, *Pariahs*, 98f.

593 Larcker and Tayan, "Trust: The Unwritten Contract in Corporate Governance," 1.

Audit Committee

The main purpose of an audit committee is the oversight of the financial reporting and the audit process, the system of internal controls as well as compliance with laws and regulations.[594]

A key component of an effective corporate governance system is an effective audit committee.

In order to achieve high efficacy, the audit committee and the auditors have to keep an ongoing and open dialogue independent of the members of the BoD and the executive team.

Although auditors do not bear direct corporate governance responsibility, their contributions to information checks on aspects of corporate governance are important, e.g., the check for misstatements.

Special attention: referring to some of the companies that ran into scandals, the responsibility for these scandals was linked to gatekeepers (auditors), aside from the magic triangle. Hence, a well-working audit committee plays a critical role in overseeing and controlling the auditor's contributions to information checks on corporate governance aspects.

Auditors have a public responsibility that is more important than their contracts with companies. During an audit, it is of utmost importance that the audit committee and ultimately the BoD receives accurate and relevant information from the auditors to meet its shareholder obligations, which requires a transparent and open dialogue with the auditors.[595]

Board Evaluation

The goal and the purpose of self-evaluations (comprehensive assess-

---

594 "Audit Committee Role & Responsibilities," CFA Institute, https://www.cfainstitute.org/en/advocacy/issues/audit-committee-role-practices.

595 Broadley, "Auditing and Its Role in Corporate Governance," 5, 10, 13ff, 19; "Audit Committee Role & Responsibilities."

ments of the BoD's activities, both conduct and process) can be summarized as follows: "to determine whether they are functioning effectively [...] to ensure that boards are staffed and led appropriately, that board members are effective in fulfilling their obligations, and that reliable processes are in place to satisfy important oversight requirements."[596]

It is good news that investors, regulators, and other stakeholders are requesting greater board effectiveness and accountability, which is reflected in their increasing interest in board evaluation processes and outcomes. But also, BoDs themselves are looking to enhance their board evaluation processes and disclosures to better address stakeholder interest and enhance their own effectiveness.[597]

In the US, the New York Stock Exchange requires BoD and board committees of public corporations to conduct a self-evaluation at least once per year. However, although most BoDs are not required to do regular performance reviews, many BoDs do so, not least because most codes of best practices for Corporate Governance recommend an annual self-assessment of the BoD and its committees.

Despite this good news, however, research found that many evaluations of BoD are not adequate. For example, most evaluations fail to spot and course-correct poor performance of individual directors. Only 55 percent of the analyzed companies also evaluate individual directors, and a low number of 36 percent thinks that their company does a good job of assessing an individual's performance accurately. Generally, directors are quite considerably dissatisfied with the dynamics in their boardrooms; for example, only 64 percent is convinced that the BoD is open to new points of view, around 50 percent believes that not all skills of the directors are leveraged, less than 50 percent think that dissent is well received, and 44 percent share the

---

596 David Larcker et al., "How Boards Should Evaluate Their Own Performance," *Harvard Business Review,* (March 1, 2017).

597 Ibid.

belief that personal and/or past experiences dominate fellow directors' perspectives.[598]

Why these alarming numbers? Research found that the root cause of the problem lies in the evaluation process itself. The first part of the evaluation (BoD) is standard, but the second part (contribution of individual directors; interpersonal and group dynamics) is more difficult. However, it adds more value. Typically, though, the second part either lacks rigor or is left out completely.[599] For example, survey evidence indicates that 53 percent of board members think that fellow board members don't voice their honest opinion when management is present.

Therefore, good evaluation processes include both BoD and individual self-evaluations. Ideally, they also include a third step, which collects feedback on the chairperson. The implementation of the evaluations should be accompanied or even facilitated by an outside party to enhance honest and open answers. It is critical for BoDs to compile, share, and discuss the outcome of the evaluations so that they can improve their collaboration and overall performance.

The evaluation process is more than just an assessment of whether the BoD, its members, and committees have performed their required responsibilities and duties to satisfaction. Rather, this process should be designed in a way that rigorously assesses whether, among others, the strategy and business, board dynamics and processes, composition and diversity, monitoring and risk management are effective in the short and long term, and for both the company and its business environment.[600]

---

598 Ibid.

599 Ibid.

600 Steve Klemash, Rani Doyle, and Jamie C. Smith, Effective Board Evaluation (Cambridge, MA: Harvard Law School Forum on Corporate Governance, 2018), https://corpgov.law.harvard.edu/2018/10/26/effective-board-evaluation/; Fianna Jurdant, Austin Tyler, and Erik Vermeulen, "Board Evaluation: Overview of International Practices" (OECD, 2018).

The fact that many BoDs suffer from poor group dynamics indicates room for improvement. For a company to grow, thrive, and reach its full potential, a well-functioning board is key. To achieve this, BoDs must be committed, alert, and inquisitive.

Numerous evaluation templates exist. They serve as a valuable guide. However, since each company is unique, questions should be assessed and customized to meet the company's needs.

LEADERSHIP STRUCTURE

Chapter 1 initiated the discussion of the leadership structure, whether the chairman and CEO roles should be combined or separated. Details, advantages, and disadvantages of each leadership structure are summarized hereafter.

Reasons for Combination of Roles (Single Leadership)

In decisions to combine the chairman and CEO roles, 91 percent take place as routine, orderly successions. This leaves only a small percentage involving a specific event such as a merger, sudden resignation, or governance issue. In nine out of ten combinations, the incumbent CEO takes on the additional chairperson title.[601]

Reasons for Separation of Roles (Dual Leadership)

Hundreds of shareholder-sponsored proxy proposals calling for a separated leadership structure have been submitted to S&P 500 companies over the past decade. Compared to today's 50 percent, a decade ago, more than 70 percent of the S&P 500 companies had dual leadership, and fifteen years ago 77 percent. As with combinations, most separations (78 percent) take place during an orderly succession. A temporary separation of the roles is far more common in large companies. Smaller companies prefer permanent separation. Boeing, for

---

601 David F. Larcker and Brian Tayan, "Chairman and CEO: The Controversy Over Board Leadership," *Stanford Closer Look Series*, Stanford Graduate School of Business, 2016, 2.

example, separated the two roles after facing a procurement scandal in 2003. UnitedHealth did so after facing a stock option backdating scandal in 2006, and Freddie Mac was forced to do so in 2008, following conservatorship.[602]

What are the advantages and disadvantages of separating the chairperson and CEO roles? The following points are extracted from different studies by Larcker, Miles, and Tayan.

Advantages of Separation

1. There is a clear distinction between the strategic and operation levels. The chairperson has the authorization to speak on behalf of the BoD.[603]
2. Conflict in regard to performance evaluation, CEO compensation, succession planning on both board and management levels can be reduced.[604]
3. In a combined role, it is more challenging for the other directors to oversee the CEO, who is their chairperson at the same time. Thus, it is not easy to replace a CEO who shows poor performance if that person is also their boss.

Disadvantages of Separation

1. Artificial separation in the case of a successful dual leadership structure might not bring the expected outcome or may even lead to negative consequences.[605]
2. A separation can lead to a duplication of leadership, worsened decision-making, and confusion within the company, especially in cases of emergency or crisis.[606]

---

602 Larcker, Miles, and Tayan, "Seven Myths of CEO Succession," 1.

603 Larcker and Tayan, "Chairman and CEO," 1.

604 Ibid., 1.

605 Larcker and Tayan, "Chairman and CEO," 1.

606 Ibid., 1.

Separation Followed by Combination

One-third of the companies studied by Larcker and Tayan intended to permanently separate the leadership structure but later recombined it. Case examples are Best Buy (thirteen years later), General Motors (eight months later), Bank of America (five years later), and Walt Disney (nine years later). The separation of the two roles due to pressure from shareholder proposals happened predominantly in large companies. This may indicate that the targeted companies might not necessarily be the ones with the most severe governance issues but those that are most visible to the public.[607]

Despite the vast amount of literature on the topic, there seems to be little to no empirical evidence that combined leadership roles are better or worse for future performance or governance quality,[608] leading to the following questions:

1. In which situations is it beneficial to have separated leadership?
2. What are the criteria for a BoD to decide on the leadership structure?

This book's extensive elaboration on the hidden key drivers (especially the human element) help find answers to these questions.

The advantages and disadvantages of having an independent chairperson depend on the situation because it is about people and therefore about the chairperson and/or CEO's competences, experiences, personalities, drivers, and leadership skills that all strongly influence the decision of whether the role is combined or separated.

If one person has a dysfunctional relationship with power, or even is equipped with hubris syndrome, a combined role will further increase the danger and potential harm caused to the organization and its workforce by derailment. But in case of a separation of roles, if the

---

607 Ibid., 2f.

608 Ibid., 1.

two leaders at the top get involved in power games, with or without hubris involved, reason for concern is also given.

On the other hand, if an individual has a clear understanding of him/herself, his/her dispositions, strengths, and weaknesses and is self-reflective, the person knows how and when to wear the two different hats and lead the BoD and the management team accordingly. This can support the advantages listed above.

But also, if the two roles are assumed by two different individuals and each of them is self-aware and knows how to lead himself/herself and others, and role clarity is given (even a LOCC agreed), a powerful duo at the top not only meets increasing corporate governance guidelines but also adds to effectiveness and efficiency on all ends. Consequently, the answers to the two questions raised depends on the people involved and the context given. Inner drivers and motivations, personal dysfunctions, and disturbances must not be downgraded or ignored. The price to pay is too high.

This decision and selection process is a critical one, as bad leadership is more than a lack of common skills. The dysfunction of disposition can override valuable skills. Ultimately, the observation and assessment of leaders' behavior patterns induced by a person's interests can help discover and predict dysfunctionalities but also provides valuable information on that person's potential for development.

The pressure on leadership is immense. Awareness of the situation is the first step toward a constructive discussion. This raises further awareness and helps the respective person(s) in charge make the right decision. Reflection is an ongoing process.

CEO SUCCESSION PLANNING

Successful companies are forward-oriented with regard to their succession planning.

Based on a study conducted by Heidrick and Struggles and the Rock Center for Corporate Governance at Stanford University in 2010, only slightly more than half of the companies studied stated that they had a specific CEO successor in the pipeline if an immediate replacement were necessary. Almost 40 percent reported that they did not have viable internal candidates. Succession should not be considered as an event but as a continuous and ongoing process.[609]

According to a survey conducted by PricewaterhouseCoopers in 2013, 86 percent of shareholders considered CEO succession planning to be one of the most important tasks of BoDs, together with strategy, risk management, and CEO compensation.[610]

But action seems to lag. Findings of a study of Nordic companies conducted by the Boston Consulting Group and EZI (Egon Zehnder International) Nordic companies and published in 2019 found a need for BoD to raise their game when it comes to succession planning. The study states that "many boards approach succession planning as an art, with the chairperson's instinct often driving the process." Although the study included Nordic only companies (value creation by Nordic companies has strongly exceeded the global average of companies in other regions, and their market indexes have consistently outperformed those in the US, UK, and continental Europe in regard to total shareholder return in the past thirty years), BCG and EZI "believe that their findings are relevant globally."[611] This also speaks to the effectiveness of the nomination committee.

What about the process of succession planning? For example, should

---

609 Larcker, Miles, and Tayan, "Seven Myths of CEO Succession," 1–4.

610 Larcker, Miles, and Tayan, "Seven Myths of CEO Succession," 2; Larcker, Miles, and Tayan, "The Handpicked CEO Successor," *Stanford Closer Look Series*, 2014, 1.

611 Ketil Gjerstad et al., "Bringing Science to the Art of Ceo Succession Planning," (BCG Boston Consulting Group: Corporate Development & Finance, Corporate Strategy, 2019).

CEOs choose their own successors? The main advantages and disadvantages can be summarized as follows:[612]

Advantages

CEOs generally know internal candidates best and are therefore in a good position to assess those candidates and pick a successor from them. This is what former Baxter International CEO, William Graham, did. Also, William Spoor at Pillsbury, Donald Kendall at PepsiCo, and Jack Welch at GE all chose their own successors after completing long CEO tenures.

Departing CEOs can positively impact the succession process if they are open and fully transparent about the ultimate result, and if they manage to distance themselves from their personal biases.

Disadvantages

It is the fiduciary duty of BoDs to select CEOs. Therefore, directors are expected to be committed and deeply involved in succession planning, which requires a thorough concept of developing internal executives and creating a reliable evaluation process. BoDs must try to be objective regarding internal candidates' skills compared to the external market.

The perspectives of BoDs differ from those of CEOs.

It is arguably impossible for CEOs to remain objective in evaluating internal talents. They are prone to biases and preferences that have been established over time.

CEOs often lack experience and expertise in discovering and assessing CEO potential in others.

---

612 Larcker, Miles, and Tayan, "Seven Myths of Ceo Succession," 2; David F. Larcker, Stephen A. Miles, and Brian Tayan, "The Handpicked CEO Successor," *Stanford Closer Look Series*, 2014, 1.

Oftentimes, CEOs are too focused on their personal legacy, which gets in the way of an objective evaluation.

It is not uncommon for CEOs to think that it is their right to select their successor, and they often choose candidates who demonstrate skills and characteristics that are similar to their own.

As much as the selection of the BoD is a crucial process to be undertaken by the owners or the shareholders, the selection of the CEO is a crucial process to be undertaken by the BoD. It is imperative that the BoD have the ability and impartiality to choose the right person to be in charge of far reaching decisions that will impact the company's productivity and performance, including its strategy and organizational design. This includes the BoD's skill in evaluating the CEO's personal leadership style that will strongly influence people, culture, and again, ultimately tie into performance.

The BoD will be able to respond more effectively to the fast-changing dynamic environment and generate significant value on all ends *if* its members combine their experience-based judgments with a disciplined and structured approach. If the decision whether to involve the current CEO in the selection process or not is thoroughly thought through and discussed out, the defined answer will contribute to a successful process and ultimately to a desired outcome.

LIVING CORPORATE GOVERNANCE

Summarizing the most important elements of a corporate governance system, it can be said that weak governance is probably the most dangerous condition and the most difficult to identify and treat quickly enough. Hubris can grow if governance is weak so that governance can easily be undermined. Hence, both regulators and active and strong BoD who are attentive to warning signs can help prevent hubris.[613]

---

613 Ibid., 57.

This is an ongoing process and needs time, energy, commitment, focus, and self-reflection.

Even the highly praised German two-tier system was not able to prevent the Volkswagen emissions scandal. The key point does not lie only with the right structure of a corporate governance system (which, as laid out in chapter 2, "Flaws of Traditional Frameworks," needs to be regularly updated) but with the way it is lived. How governance is operationalized is fundamental. It is not sufficient to simply have the right system or even the right people on the BoD if its directors do not ask the right questions and hold the CEO to account, or lack the courage to speak the truth because they are, for example, intimidated by a strong chairperson or CEO. "To live" governance refers to a key point of this book that emphasizes the importance of moving the human factor into the center. The recommendations and advice found in this book will help improve governance operations and reduce or prevent derailment and hence negative outcomes.

WHISTLEBLOWING

Whistleblowing is not the only tool used to help detect and correct inappropriate and illegal behavior, but it can contribute to the ethical and legal health of organizations and governments. Examples of wrongdoing include corruption, bribery, illegal surveillance, misuse of organizational resources, or illegal conspiracies.

The following are justifications for a company to set up a whistleblowing program:[614]

1. To police itself. Whistleblowing can serve as an alternative channel for individuals if the organization's internal mechanisms or chains of command impede the reporting of illegal or inappropriate behavior.

---

614   David Schultz and Kachik Harutyunyan, Volume 1, issue 2, "Combating Corruption: The Development of Whistleblowing Laws in the United States, Europe, and Armenia," *International Comparative Jurisprudence*, vol. 1, no. 2 (2015), 88.

2. To correct or reform organizations, as they can develop seriously bad behavior or even pathologies. Whistleblowing contributes to exposing such behavior in public, which can strongly increase the pressure to change.
3. To expose wrongdoing that needs to be corrected or brought to the public's attention.
4. To hold wrongdoers to account for their behavior and thereby promote justice.

These reasons contribute to increasing recognition of whistleblowing as a necessary and important element in correcting unethical and illegal wrongdoing. The trend toward whistleblowing is fostering countries' and organizations' adoption of legislation that legalizes or supports such reporting, which contribute as follows:[615]

1. They create mechanisms to encourage (specifically anonymous) whistleblowing.
2. They can force organizations to promote whistleblowing processes.
3. They may financially incentivize whistleblowing and increase encouragement of it.
4. They can provide protection for whistleblowers from punishment.

COMPARISON BETWEEN THE US AND EUROPE

The US is likely to spearhead the ranking in regard to innovation and export of whistleblowing laws. Through this, the country has a strong influence on international organizations such as the World Bank and the OECD but also on the domestic laws of other countries.[616]

The US has influenced Europe to adopt whistleblower laws similar to its own. The goal is the same: to encourage individuals to report wrongdoing and protect them when they do. This contributes to the recognition of whistleblowing as both an ethical and a legal action.

---

615 Ibid., 88.

616 Ibid., 89.

Since most European countries are unused to a culture where reporting wrongdoing is seen as positive, whistleblowers are often labeled as traitors. This negative association prevents the correction of wrongdoing.[617]

Insufficient awareness of whistleblowing can harm the health, safety, and lives of people and organizations.[618] In a survey led by the European Commission, 74 percent of those interviewed admitted to not reporting unethical or illegal behavior they had witnessed or experienced themselves.[619] This result raises cause for concern. If 74 percent of EU citizens do not report illegal or unethical behavior, what are the rates like in emerging economies or in countries where democracy is not in place?[620]

Whistleblowing laws, culture, and practice are more advanced in common law countries than in civil law countries because of their early phase of emergence. Consequently, the legal processes for protecting whistleblowers and the availability of reporting channels are much less developed in continental European countries.[621] The EU aims to close this gap.

On October 7, 2019, the Council of the European Union approved a directive[622] aimed to protect whistleblowers against retaliation. The new rules officially entered into force on December 16, 2019, and require the installment of safe channels for reporting both within an organization—private or public—and to public authorities. Member states of the EU are given two years to transpose the directive into

---

617 Ibid., 89.

618 Ibid., 92.

619 European Commission, *Corruption,* (Brussels: European Commission, 2014), 100, https://ec.europa.eu/commfrontoffice/publicopinion/archives/ebs/ebs_397_en.pdf; Schultz and Harutyunyan, "Combating Corruption," 92.

620 Schultz and Harutyunyan, "Combating Corruption," 92.

621 Ibid., 95.

622 European Parliament and the Council, "Directive (Eu) 2019/1937" *Official Journal of the European Union*, November 26, 2019, https://eur-lex.europa.eu/legal-content/en/TXT/?uri=CELEX%3A32019L1937.

their national law.[623] This directive will have a big impact given the fact that in 2019, only ten EU countries (out of twenty-eight) had comprehensive legislation in place to protect whistleblowers (only four countries in 2013).[624]

PROCESS FOR ESTABLISHING A WHISTLEBLOWER PROGRAM

An organization that considers establishing a whistleblowing program should ask itself the following questions:[625]

1. What statutory mandates call for a whistleblower program?
2. What wrongdoing behavior can be addressed through whistleblowing?
3. Can whistleblowing have a substantial impact on the workforce?
4. Should the policy include other stakeholders such as suppliers, customers, and business partners?
5. Should anonymity of the report and the individual be promoted?
6. Who within the organization should be in charge of the whistleblowing policy?
7. Should the report be forwarded to the audit committee?

If the respective report concerns regulatory noncompliance, how should the affected team remain objective and handle the situation?

What should an organization do with reports that are proven wrong?

Whistleblowing policies are one of many possible tools organizations can use to police unethical and illegal behavior. The implementation of such programs is both crucial and challenging. Therefore, aspects

---

623 Daida Hadzic "European Union—New Measures for Protection of Whistleblowers," KPMG, November 13, 2019, https://home.kpmg/xx/en/home/insights/2019/11/flash-alert-2019-169.html.

624 Ibid., 93.

625 Mahajan Rohit, Jayant Saran, and Veena Sharma, "Setting Up a Whistleblowing Program: 10 Frequently Asked Questions," Deloitte, https://www2.deloitte.com/content/dam/Deloitte/in/Documents/finance/in-fa-setting-up-a-whistleblowing-mechanism-noexp.PDF (last visited May 7, 2018).

such as reporting mechanisms, education, and awareness, support for whistleblowers by leaders, response mechanism, record retention, assessment of the program, and international issues, e.g., data privacy and legal compliance, should be considered.[626]

In the ACFE report,[627] the most popular detection schemes were tips, regardless of whether a hotline existed or not; 47.3 percent of the organizations in which schemes were detected had hotlines; 28.2 percent lacked one.[628]

With regard to the channel through which tips were submitted, telephone hotlines accounted for 39.5 percent and the internet for almost 60 percent (consisting of email, 34.1 percent, and web-based/online forms, 23.5 percent).[629]

ADDITIONAL CONSIDERATIONS FOR WHISTLEBLOWING

The pros and cons of whistleblower systems need to be considered and managed.[630]

Pros:

1. Improper behavior gets exposed.
2. It is usually an ethically correct decision to make.
3. There are legal protections in place.
4. There is often financial compensation.

Cons:

---

626 Jim Ratley, "Creating an Effective Whistleblower Program," *Security*, August 1, 2012, http://www.securitymagazine.com/articles/83343-creating-an-effective-whistleblower-program.

627 ACFE, Report to the Nations, 27.

628 Ibid., 27.

629 Ibid., 28.

630 Mike Bothwell, "Pros and Cons of Whistleblowing in the Workplace," Bothwell Law Group, August 14, 2017, http://whistleblowerlaw.com/whistleblowing-in-the-workplace/.

1. Not everyone sees whistleblowing as a positive decision.
2. There are personal and career risks.
3. Reports may not hold up under the law or facts.
4. The process can take years.
5. It might harm relationships with others.

A typical factor in companies with a hubristic culture is that people who tell challenging truths are not listened to. Companies such as Enron, WorldCom, Lehman Brothers, BP, Shell, and others that were involved in famous scandals all had internal whistleblowers who were trying to tell senior executives about concerning issues. But these truth tellers were either ignored or suppressed.[631]

In a video message, Sir John Andrew Likierman, Dean of the London Business School brings the topic to the point:

> In my view, any organization which has a whistleblower ought to start from the supposition that they are right, there is an issue to address until proved to the contrary. And when I say proved, I do mean proved. [...] In most cases, there is an element of truth about any whistleblowing allegation. It may not be absolutely true but it may indicate something that is a problem. Perhaps not exactly the problem indicated and that in itself paradoxically is valuable to an organization. What we know from history, is that in quite a lot of cases people blew the whistle, nobody paid any attention. It would have been a lot better if the whistleblower had been listened to. [...] Actually, scandals coming to the open may be a very healthy sign. [...] I'm rather an optimist in terms of the general trend. Will there always be ethical issues? I think there will. The borderline in terms of what is ethical and not ethical shifts all the time. And we are not all the same as people. We are very different. [...] It's unreasonable to believe that everybody will behave in the same way. So, is there an ultimate answer? Will we all behave ethically? No. The question is "are the mechanisms there to bring limit to the open and to

---

631 Nixon, *Pariahs*, 95–96.

cope with them and not to eliminate them." Because we will never do that; but to minimize their harmful effects.[632]

IMPLICATIONS

One-third of the ACFE survey respondents confirmed that a lack of internal antifraud controls was the main organizational weakness that led to frauds. In 20 percent of the cases, reason number two was the overriding of existing internal controls by the offender.[633]

According to the ACFE, external audits, codes of conduct, and internal audit departments are the most commonly implemented antifraud control measures (mechanisms in place when fraudulent behavior happened) across locations and organization types and sizes.[634] However, the top three means to discover fraudulent behavior in all measured countries were tips, internal audits, and management reviews. Where such control measures were in place, wrongdoing got detected more quickly, and its size was smaller.[635]

Precaution is always more efficient and economical than cleaning up after the event, e.g., investigations and repair of wrongdoing such as fraudulent behavior. In the worst case, the latter even causes reputation damage.[636]

Although a code of conduct, as a tool of corporate governance, was among the three most frequently implemented control measures in place when fraud occurred, it was not among the top means of fraud detection. This could be an indicator of the reactive character of the

---

632 John Andrew Likierman, "Pros and Cons of Whistleblowing," Asia-Pacific Economics Blog, February 3, 2015, https://apecsec.org/pros-and-cons-of-whistleblowing/.

633 ACFE, Report to the Nations, 46.

634 Ibid., 38.

635 Ibid., 5, 21.

636 Matthias Schmid, Compliance, „Was tun gegen Korruption und Betrug? Mehr Prävention und Kontrolle als Gegenmittel, persorama," Magazin der Schweizerischen Gesellschaft für Human Resources Management (Spring 2016), 45.

corporate governance system (as explained in chapter 2, "Flaws of Traditional Frameworks"). Therefore, the corporate governance system and the code of conduct as a tool of corporate governance must proactively and regularly be adjusted.

The outcome of ACFE's report also underlines the importance of a trust culture (trust fosters daring to give tips, the number one means to discover wrongdoing) and of management reviews (as one of the top three detection means). In contrast, external audits have not contributed much to fraud detection (see analysis of scandals described throughout this book).

Aside from a well-functioning governance, risk-management, and compliance structure, it is also critical to have management systems in place that are fraud-proof and safe from manipulation. Thus, it is essential to clearly define and discuss the processes, codes, guidelines, policies, and directives, as they not only serve as a regulatory framework but also serve as a communication tool and have a deterrent effect.[637] Aside from these systems, it is essential to have the right leaders at the top.

Even in combination (though more so than in isolation) these two parts—systems and human beings/leadership—might not guarantee full protection against fraud and/or derailment. But together, they form a strong and agile fine-meshed net that reliably contributes to derailment reduction, at least by raising important early warning signs, decreasing the detection time, contributing to the mitigation of losses and serving as a deterring factor for potential offenders.

IN SUM

The previous sections have described at length the importance of establishing checks and balances such as a culture of trust and good corporate governance. The establishment of checks and balances is not

---

637 Atteslander and Cromm, Jürgen, Methoden der empirischen Sozialforschung, 13. neu bearb. und erw., Berlin 2010, 45, 47.

enough. A culture of trust and governance systems must also be lived and continuously improved so that opportunities for wrongdoing and derailment can be minimized.

These two might sound contradictory, but they mustn't be. The key lies in balancing trust and control. It is a fine but crucial line that needs constant attention and adjustment by all parties involved. A well-lived culture of trust allows for the necessary checks and balances.

The checks and balances described serve as safeguards that help keep organizations and their leaders in line. But it would be incorrect to believe that even the best-designed mechanisms and systems will fully prevent greedy and dishonest people, whose self-interests overrule those of their companies, from abusing their power. This brings us back to the previous chapter.

A leader is anyone who has power of information, role, function, or status. The leadership style of any leader and the way authority and power are dealt with depends on the individual's personality. This will have been influenced by the leader's upbringing, regardless of culture, jurisdictions, rules, and regulations. The same is true for subordinates, their personalities, their attitudes toward authority, and how they behave and act within systems and rules.

It is of utmost importance for BoDs and owners to get to know current and potential leaders because the wrong person can cause serious harm. In this context, it is also essential to assess how well the leaders are aware of their conduct and whether they are willing to work on their behavior or not.

But it is also important for individuals in power to be required to hold themselves accountable and manage their lives responsibly. This leadership task requires a great portion of the leadership competencies discussed in chapter 7 such as emotional intelligence as well as an understanding of dynamics such as hidden commitments, transference, leadership shadows, and human irrationality. Leaders must become aware of the concern for and responsibility of nurturing, guiding, and contributing to the next generation (generativity, as Erikson coined it). They must not attach their identity to any role or position; it is ephemeral. They must understand and foster organizational learning. And so, they must remain agile and be adaptive.

For leaders and organizations to be successful, it is essential that leaders learn how to critically analyze their own performance. Self-reflection boosts self-awareness, which increases self-knowledge. Self-knowledge helps one, for example, to realize that power can be addictive and thus understand its destructive side. Leaders who are able to do this are true leaders who will leave positive legacies associated with trust, respect, sane admiration, and affection.

The previous chapter put the human element center stage. Thorough selection, development, and ongoing coaching of leaders help intervene in a timely manner.

The current chapter introduced a number of customizable frameworks that, if orchestrated, will help minimize mistakes and prevent or reduce derailment.

The following chapter will provide practical advice to different stakeholders (BoD, management, executive search firms, investors, judges) and help reach the planned result when orchestrating and implementing the tools and concepts described in this chapter.

CHAPTER 10

AUTHOR'S ADVICE

As accompanying recommendations for action, this smaller chapter provides a list of advice.

Specifically, this section builds on explanations and provides advice to key decision-makers, opinion leaders, and influencers in the fields of business and law and lists positive outcomes that can be achieved. Insights from business, law, and social science must be integrated. Derailment prevention is about real, effective, and responsible leadership within a solid legal framework in a constantly changing environment.

The author's following advice is organized into three sections: for business, for law, and for the decision-making processes of high-performance organizations.

AREA OF BUSINESS

In everything, awareness and perspective are key. In business, the goal is to thrive, not just survive, in a globalized economy and a world where rapid sociopolitical and technological changes open up all kinds of new opportunities and threats—for both innovation and potential derailment. New challenges and chances require proactive new awareness and perspectives for all actors involved. Directives include:

1. Anticipate/manage the impact of any type of change on people/power balance, among the magic triangle and in corporate governance.
2. Become aware of the overwhelming importance and impact of the human element (self and others) in organizations.
3. Understand hidden dynamics (organizational and personal) that can lead to conflict, especially in the magic triangle of owner, BoD, and management.
4. Learn how to spot early warning signs for misuse of power in order to redirect and develop the directors and CEOs who display those tendencies.

Some high-level business outcomes that can be achieved are:

1. Better leadership performance through development of future-proof competencies such as agility, increased self-awareness, and trust building that lead to people becoming better change agents.
2. Better overall business performance and agility through awareness and conflict reduction, particularly in the magic triangle.
3. Better leadership (development): better people/subordinate development, engagement, performance, and organizational alignment (better recruiting, change leadership, lived corporate governance).

ADVICE TO OWNERS, BODS, AND CEOS

Understanding change, the human element, leadership, and hidden dynamics helps define and execute the owner's strategy and leads to better communication. A better selection process for both BoD and the CEO helps reduce conflicts and potential for derailment while increasing performance.

Increased self-awareness leads to better leaders and change agents, better understanding and selection of management, higher performance, and fewer negative outcomes.

Whoever is in charge of the search process needs to own it. They need to provide a clear description of the organization's context, including change and its impact, and of the required leadership skills, and take full responsibility for the decision.

ADVICE TO BODS ONLY

1. Adjust the corporate governance system more frequently and pro-actively.
2. Create a healthy balance between support and challenge: more often than not, the BoD puts too much trust in the CEO and forgets to remain politely skeptical. The BoD should create a healthy tension with its CEO. Mutual trust is key.[638]
3. Establish the right BoD culture and effectiveness.

The definitions of culture and effectiveness differ from BoD to BoD. BoDs should systematically review their stakeholder groups' perspectives and interests. Staying close to them helps BoDs receive early warning signs and deeper and different opinions of their own performance and that of the CEOs, e.g., the potential development of hubris and toxic cultures. If the BoD runs the risk of becoming hubristic (especially the chairperson), it is the owner's responsibility to take action…quickly.

1. The BoD should define and develop an open culture that encourages honest feedback and independent thought. It needs to allow for diversity of opinions and stretch a company's leadership by scrutinizing traditional and current knowledge and wisdom.
2. The BoD must be strong and active, consisting of the right personalities, experiences, and skills (and their best mix) that will be best suited to perform its task.
3. The BoD should focus on creating a dispute platform for healthy, constructive conflict among shareholders, BoD, and management, for situations where it seems impossible to bridge the divide

---

638 Nixon, *Pariahs*, 65–68.

between various interests. This will minimize the risk of derailment and create healthy checks and balances within the magic triangle.

4. The BoD needs to establish a system of checks and balances and define policies and procedures aimed at preventing bad leadership on all levels. These practices include setting time limits on CEOs' and directors' tenures, implementing regular performance reviews and evaluations of the BoD and management, and holding the BoD and CEO accountable for their performance. Clear and open criteria for selection and a thorough recruitment process help strengthen the BoD and increase its independence.

ADVICE TO EXECUTIVE SEARCH FIRMS

With no doubt, the appointment of the right directors (one of whom may potentially become the chairperson) and CEO is crucial for any organization. Executive search firms specialize in recruitment services, and BoDs and owners should make use of their extensive expertise.

Although the BoD must own the search process, it is important that search firms also (let) gather extensive information about a candidate outside of work, e.g., by asking them and testing their reaction or by requesting interview(s) with family (always within the confines of hiring laws). Not only the information provided but also the way it is presented (tone, easiness vs. hesitation, nonverbal cues) can provide important hints. This is how patterns might be detected, self-awareness tested, the potential for development evaluated, and chances for early warning signs increased.

The goal is to gain a better understanding of key drivers for derailment such as change, the human element, and leadership, which may strongly increase the quality of the selection process and lead to both better performance and a stronger reputation. A successfully completed search process, of course, not only benefits the organization but also helps the executive search firm establish deeper, longer, and better relationships with owners, BoD, CEOs, and executives, which is especially beneficial to the leadership development process, a scope of services that becomes more and more common among executive search firms.

Referring to the critical competence to have the courage to speak the truth if there is even the slightest doubt that a candidate might be the perfect fit—regardless of the advanced stage in the process—it is vital to speak up and—depending on the situation—to start all over. It would be the lesser evil compared to the potential damage a miscast leader could cause.

ADVICE TO INVESTORS

Ideally, a well-governed company is one whose leaders serve the best interests of both the company and its shareholders, while maximizing long-term value creation and minimizing risk. In contrast, a company that is poorly governed is understood as one whose leaders make poor decisions and put their own interests before those of shareholders so that value gets destroyed.[639] It remains a challenge for outside shareholders and investors to assess quality of governance. As shown in this book, too often, poor governance is detected only after the outcomes of decisions become known.

Shareholders and investors play a key role, as they have the potential to put pressure on companies to move toward better government and responsible leadership. Therefore, they are well advised to require new indicators of where to invest which helps foster companies with well-functioning governance, leaders, and workforces—key factors for long-term success.

1. Assess whether companies have systems of accountability in place to encourage stakeholders to take part in decision-making in order to prevent oligarchic corporate structures, in which a single person

---

639 Larcker and Tayan, "Governance Aches and Pains," 1.

(often the CEO, but not seldom also the chairperson) has full control of the agenda.

2. Appraise if checks and balances (e.g., culture of trust and a proactive governance system that is lived) are established and well-managed.

3. Have a close look at who is at the helm of the company before they decide on a potential investment. Leadership is one of the most critical aspects. The quality of leadership reflects the quality of the company's management and is a key success factor. There is no one recipe for quality of leadership, but the prevalence of solid leadership assessment and development methods and concepts are strong indicators of the importance of and focus on leadership.

Consequently, the value of the company must not be based on financial performance only and increasingly on intangibles. Investors and shareholders must care about and pay close attention to the quality of a company's culture, corporate governance, strategy, sustainability, reputation, and innovation as strong performance indicators. Research of more recent years has found that successful long-term investors recognize the impact of leadership on a company's performance.[640] Leadership needs to further gain momentum as a key discipline in a company's valuation.

It might still be challenging for many investors to shift focus from short-term success and financial rewards (that, as shown in this book, might eventually entail derailment and value destruction), to long(er)-term holistic success. But what it yields in ultimate benefit for all stakeholders will be larger, and the impact on the economy and society will be bigger than one can conceive.

AREA OF LAW

Discoveries from business and social sciences can and should be transferred to and incorporated in the world of law. In large part, business,

---

640 Mohamad Ridhuan Mat Dangi et al., "Leadership Quality and Competency Towards Investor Valuation and Firm Performance," *Journal of Advanced Research in Business and Management Studies*, vol. 7, no. 2 (2017), 55–68.

economics, and classic law assume that shareholders, directors, and managers are rational.[641] Leaders' egos often appear to be bigger drivers for decisions and judgments than pure rationality. Why then does the assumption persist that leadership is a rational task executed by rational people focusing on rational organizational goals?

Human beings are not entirely rational. Organizations tend to link their successes to the brilliance, foresight, and calculation of their leaders, and their failures are associated with leaders' stupidity, mistakes, and carelessness. These explanations are based on the assumptions that leaders are rational. But leaders, like anybody else, may be driven by strong and entrenched impulses, emotions, desires, or fantasies that can seriously and dangerously impact how they operate. Very often, a leader's personality manifests in the organization's strategy, processes, structure, and culture. Therefore, unstable personalities can lead to unstable organizations.[642]

When organizations nurture the confidence of a leader, it can easily get inflated and turn into overconfidence. Overconfidence almost always leads to reduced risk perception and consequently to more risk-taking.[643]

In order for the legal world to accept and incorporate discoveries from organizational psychology into corporate (and security) law, a few hurdles first need to be overcome.[644]

The answer to the question "How will a director or CEO think or behave in a particular situation?" might be, "It depends." This answer, however, is not well qualified for a legal analysis.

People do not share the same predictable cognitive traits or biases.

---

641 Donald C. Langevoort, "The Behavioral Economics of Mergers and Acquisitions," *Tennessee Journal of Business Law* (Spring, 2011), 3.

642 Kets de Vries and Miller, *Unstable at the Top*.

643 Langevoort, "The Behavioral Economics of Mergers and Acquisitions," 5.

644 Ibid., 2.

Thus, it is not enough to know the context of the actor's situation. One needs to know about the person's personality and disposition.

Even if it were proven and accepted that there are behavioral traits such as overconfidence or emotionally driven risk-taking, this might impact leaders' or managers' judgment and decision-making but not necessarily negatively impact the firm.

If lawmakers and judges accepted that people in business sometimes behave in irrational ways, what would their interventions look like?

Behavioral explanations should not serve as an excuse. Remedies should teach the person or organization a painful lesson so that they can learn from their mistakes. But cognitive bias should be considered in the judgment process, as it might help shed light on the decision from a different angle.

The following two challenges make the situation more complex:[645]

1. Lawmakers and lawyers want scientific certainty and are therefore willing to draw conclusions (generalizations) based on even incomplete behavioral information and data. Social scientists, on the other hand, do not like to generalize too quickly, even if statistics show some relevance, because there are often other risks and explanations on which further research would help shed more light.
2. Corporate law uses state-of-mind principles such as intent, good faith, and gross negligence. These are conscious and cognitive. Patterns/biases such as overconfidence, hubris, or the winner's curse are unconscious.

There are quite a few Delaware corporate law cases in which judgments at both the chancery and supreme court levels have recognized and included psychological discoveries/outcomes, demonstrating

---

645 Ibid., 6f.

awareness of biases, egotistical behavior, and consequences, and the influence these can have on high-risk judgments and decisions. For example:

1. Oracle Corporation: 824 A. 2d 917, 938 (Del. Ch. 2003): Considering possible motivations that led to judgments of others: "Delaware law should not be based on a reductionist view of human nature that simplifies human motivation on the lines of the least sophisticated notions of the law and economics movement." The vice chancellor considers that people's interests are more than just economic in nature: "Homo sapiens is not merely homo economicus [economic human]."[646]

2. Chesapeake Crop. vs. Shore, 771 A.2d 293, 297: "There is always the possibility that subjectively well-intentioned, but nevertheless interested directors, will subconsciously be motivated by the profoundly negative effect a takeover could have on their personal bottom lines and careers."[647]

3. Unocal Crop vs. Mesa Petroleum Co., 493 A.2d 946, 958: "Because of the omnipresent specter that a board may be acting primarily in its own interests, rather than those of the corporation and its shareholders, there is an enhanced duty which calls for judicial examination at the threshold before the protections of the business judgment rule may be conferred."[648]

4. Revlon, Inc. vs. MacAndrews & Forbes Holdings, Inc., 506 A.2d 173, 185: "We must conclude that under all the circumstances the directors allowed considerations other than the maximization of shareholder profit to affect their judgment, and followed a course that ended the auction for Revlon, absent court intervention, to the ultimate detriment of its shareholders."[649]

---

646 Meredith M. Brown, *Takeovers: A Strategic Guide to Mergers and Acquisitions* (New York: Aspen Publishers Online, 2010), 9–23.

647 Delaware, Chesapeake Corp. v. Shore.

648 Delaware, Unocal Corp. v. Mesa Petroleum Co.

649 Delaware, Revlon, Inc. v. MacAndrews & Forbes Holdings.

ADVICE TO LEGISLATORS

As demonstrated by the Delaware corporate law cases, rationality in corporate judgment should not be presumed.

Auditing is key: the cost of accounting and audit failures is very high. Audit firms must be perceived as independent contractors, and they must be inspected (compliance, independence) in order to increase public confidence and integrity.[650]

For example, the US-based Public Company Accounting Oversight Board (PCAOB) is a private sector, nonprofit corporation created by the Sarbanes-Oxley Act of 2002 to oversee the audits of public companies and other issuers/entities. More examples of such protectors of the public interest are the Canadian Public Accountability Board (CPAB) and the Australian Securities & Investments Commission (ASIC).[651]

ADVICE TO JUDGES

There are limits to judges' ability and willingness to incorporate behavioral insights into law. However, as the Delaware corporate law cases demonstrate, they might be well advised to learn more about behavioral economics, for example, about the high possibility of irrationality in organizational decision-making and judgments.

What about the judges themselves? As chapter 5, "Key Driver Three: Leadership as an Accelerator," has shown, perceptions are based on personal experiences. Thus, it is impossible for judges to make interpretations without using these personal lenses shaped by their pasts. They are at least unconsciously biased.

Concluding from the discoveries that human beings are not entirely

---

650 Broadley, "Auditing and Its Role in Corporate Governance," 2006, 26f.

651 "Audit Inspection and Surveillance Programs," Australian Securities & Investments Commission, http://asic.gov.au/regulatory-resources/financial-reporting-and-audit/auditors/audit-inspection-and-surveillance-programs/ (last visited March 8, 2018).

rational, judges as human beings cannot be entirely rational either. "Legal formalism" presumes that judges apply legal reasoning in assessing the facts of a case in a rational, almost mechanical, way. Legal realists, however, believe that the rational use of legal reasoning does not fully account for judges' decisions, as psychological, political, and social variables also impact judicial rulings, which the following studies underline.

A Judge's Breakfast

Danziger, Levav, and Avnaim-Pesso[652] analyzed the mockery that justice is "what the judge ate for breakfast." Their data comprised 1,112 judicial rulings compiled over a period of fifty days in a ten-month period and concerned eight Israeli judges who each chaired two different parole boards that served four major Israeli prisons. Each judge ruled fourteen to thirty-five cases per day.

Danziger et al. demonstrated that the percentage of positive rulings decreased continuously from 65 percent to almost zero within each decision-making session and jumped back to 65 percent after the break. These findings hint that judicial rulings might be influenced by factors other than legal reasoning.

Earlier research by Muraven and Baumeister[653] implies that repeated judgments or decisions deplete individuals' cognitive control and mental resources, which can impact succeeding decisions. This research suggests that making repeated rulings is more likely to lead to the simplification of judges' decisions. However, cognitive control can be partly restored and mental fatigue overcome by the following actions: taking a short rest, raising the body's glucose levels (e.g., eating), taking a walk outside, thinking positively.

---

652 Shai Danziger, Jonathan Levav, and Liora Avnaim-Pesso, "Extraneous Factors in Judicial Decisions," proceedings of the National Academy of Sciences, 2011.

653 M. Muraven and R. F. Baumeister, "Self-Regulation and Depletion of Limited Resources: Does Self-Control Resemble a Muscle?" *Psychological Bulletin*, vol. 126 (2000), 256.

In the study by Danziger et al.,[654] neither the severity of the crime, the time served in prison, nor the defendant's gender or ethnicity seemed to influence the ruling. The assumption that a certain type of prisoner, e.g., a recidivist, could be more likely to show up right before a judge's break can be ruled out because the judges determined the break time during the course of the proceedings and did not know the details of the subsequent cases.

In addition, one might assume that judges follow a specific proportion of judgments that they expect to be positive and that once this number is reached, rejections will follow. But the opposite appears to be true: the more positive rulings judges made, the more they tended to rule favorably in succeeding cases.

Although they did not study changes in judges' moods or mental resources over time, these findings show that extraneous factors can influence judicial decisions, which supports the increasing body of evidence that experienced judges are prone to psychological biases.

IMPLICATIONS

These findings imply that there might feasibly be other situations, business- or non-business-related decisions, where experts' judgments are affected by extraneous factors.

Like leaders, judges are well advised to start with themselves. If they practice self-reflection and become aware of their emotions, perceptions, and patterns—and their origins—they will be able to increase their decision-making abilities in two ways: discovering when and how their personalities influence their decision-making, and better understanding other people's motives and drivers.

Along with all individuals engaged in leadership and decision-making—owners, BoDs, CEOs, management, accountants, and

---

654 Danziger, Levav, and Avnaim-Pesso, "Extraneous Factors in Judicial Decisions."

regulators—judges play a role in the same game. Their contribution to improving the health of that game can certainly benefit all parties involved.

DECISION-MAKING PROCESSES OF HIGH-PERFORMANCE ORGANIZATIONS

This book has shown the complexity of the interrelation among the three hidden key drivers for derailment and offered an approach to a solution, including many tools and supporting pieces of advice. To help keep an overview of the different aspects to consider and tools to apply, the following section offers a short checklist, which can help owners and board members think through the process.

Checklists save time, ensure a consistent approach, and keep one on course. They can also be customized for specific, current needs and easily adjusted for changing/future needs. The following is in chronological order.

CHECKLIST FOR OWNERS AND BOARD OF DIRECTORS
Hard Law and Soft Law

1. Familiarize yourself with corporation laws and regulations that apply to your organization.
2. Familiarize yourself with your country's corporate governance (CG) code.
3. Use your country's CG code as a basis to create an outline of your organization's CG model.
4. Conduct a comparative analysis of your country's CG with your organization's current and projected needs and strategies in order to design your organization's CG system.
5. Assign an individual or team to proactively anticipate, recognize, analyze, and report external and internal changes that can impact CG, on an ongoing basis. Secure and analyze their recommendations and adjust your CG system accordingly.
6. Put checks and balances in place.

Change Leadership

1. Stay adaptive and make necessary changes in ownership, management, and strategy.
2. Identify parties' different interests and consider potential shifts in the balance of power.
3. Watch out for persons exhibiting hubris and other dangerous actors. Do not get tricked by them.
4. Ensure the BoD creates a platform for open discourse relating to diverging interests.
5. Establish a company culture of trust, transparency, and openness.
6. Share and celebrate successes.

Leadership Selection, Alignment/Realignment, and Succession

1. Thoroughly plan and execute recruitment and succession processes.
2. Create a shared definition of the context and define the required skillset for current and future leaders.
3. Invest time, energy, and money in proven, unbiased experts to manage the selection process.
4. Measure candidates' skills, qualities, and traits and detect patterns through:
    - business performance track record
    - interviews
    - psychometric assessments
    - psychological evaluation/coaching
    - references
    - background checks
    - online reviews and digital dirt

Measure candidates' cultural fit through:

1. A comparison of their industry and corporate experience with your organization.
2. Research/analysis of prior corporate cultures they fostered.

3. Engage a coach to help analyze and develop current and future leaders.
4. Check whether the right personalities are in power, particularly in the CEO/chairperson roles.
5. Encourage LOCCs between leaders to foster relationships and nurture trust.
6. If necessary, make personnel adjustments quickly.

IN SUM

The advice from this chapter and checklist for key decision-makers, opinion leaders, and influencers in the fields of business and law aim at recommending focused action when applying the learning and tools provided.

In particular, they highlight the most important aspects such as the anticipation/management of change on people/power balance, the understanding of hidden dynamics (organizational and personal) or ways and means to spot early warning signs.

The more careful the tools are selected, customized, and orchestrated, the higher the chance for success—better leadership and better overall business performance.

Each party involved can contribute its part to success:

1. Owners/shareholders via better defining and executing the owner's strategy, improving communication, and optimizing the selection of board members.
2. BoD through an improved CEO selection process, frequent and proactive adjustment of the corporate governance system, and the providence of a platform for open dialogue.
3. Investors by putting pressure on companies to move toward better governance and responsible leadership. It has become common knowledge that a company's value is not only based on financial performance.

4. Regulators and judges by understanding why rationality in corporate judgment should not be presumed. It is not about replacing remedies with behavioral explanations but about understanding and practicing self-reflection to become aware of emotions, perceptions, and patterns, which helps improve decision-making twofold: discover when and how one's own decision-making is influenced, and better understand third parties' drivers and motives.

Application and implementation, however, needs practice. It is not easy to shift focus from short-term to long(er)-term holistic success. But it ensures consistency and comprehensiveness. It also trains the parties involved in speaking the same language, which motivates to take common action. What it yields in ultimate benefit for all stakeholders will be larger, and the impact on economy and society will be bigger than one can conceive. An improved health of this "game" benefits all parties involved.

Given this, organizations will be able to navigate change and flourish long term, driven by motivated and encouraged leaders and employees.

CONCLUSION

CORPORATE GOVERNANCE

Conflicts, lapses in judgment, excesses, and fraud within the owner-corporate board-management magic triangle precipitate many governance failures. Media exposure helps uncover but also magnifies their negative effects, and complicates their resolution, which destroys value on all ends.

Although corporate laws (hard law) and corporate governance (soft law) might have contributed to transparency and facilitated corporate governance up to a point, they don't seem to have managed to significantly decrease or even prevent derailment and negative outcomes. Instead, stricter laws and more regulations have led to increased pressure, more lawsuits, and higher liability coverages. Reasons for the falling short of corporate governance can be found in its structural and systematic flaws and challenges but more strongly in the three hidden key drivers and their interrelations: change, the human element, leadership.

Change: Too often, the legal framework of most companies is reactive and only modified after conflicts and scandals. The pace of change in today's world has accelerated. External change necessitates internal change. A forward-looking perspective could help companies preempt and prevent these crises.

Shifts in power within the magic triangle create fertile soil for conflicts. Since interests between owners and executives differ, changes in ownership or management affect the strategy-formation process, which in turn impacts corporate governance. Following the anticipation and adaption to change, shifting interests must be surfaced and openly dealt with.

The human element: Shifts in power are root causes of conflicts. They accentuate interests and lead to unpredictable behavior by those who are gaining and losing power. Contrary to the common perception that we cannot foresee how shifts in power will affect people, we can often foresee trouble brewing if we take the time to consider people's past experiences and behaviors under stress. Childhood experiences, especially, hardwire in early life and affect adult behavior.

Owners, directors, and executives must consider the human element if they are going to fill their leadership positions with leaders who put the interests of their stakeholders first, establish trust, inspire people, and effectively lead their companies.

Leadership: New technologies, fast-changing environments, globalization, and stakeholders' expectations place enormous pressure on leaders. Personalities of leaders affect company cultures, team members, and performance. It is critical to have the right person at the helm. Leadership is the third key driver of conflict and an accelerator of it.

Usually, owners and directors use common selection criteria that includes education, IQ, technical and social skills, and past performance. They consider the company's context and environment but often shy away from exploring people's developmental histories. The toolkit featured in this book may be used by owners and directors to assess and develop leaders as well as implement customized checks and balances. The latter includes building a culture of trust, periodically and proactively adjusting corporate governance, and establishing a whistleblowing mechanism. Each practice aims at cultivating responsible leadership and prevents governance derailments.

All the factors affecting corporate governance come together at the highest levels of power—in government, corporations, and societies. Preventing negative outcomes requires another triad: awareness, perspective, and proactivity. To foresee and prevent derailments, owners, directors, and executives must keep their eyes out for hubris, anticipate change, be agile, adaptive, and focused on the best interests of the stakeholders and the organization.

MEASUREMENT OF SUCCESS

How can derailment reduction/prevention be measured? There is no easy answer because it is not an exact science. However, there are various informative indicators. To begin with, rates of reported fraud and conflict can be compared pre- and post-intervention, as was done at the outset of this book with regard to the widespread introduction of corporate governance guidelines. Comparisons can be made at the individual, team, company, sector, and national levels, depending on the intervention.

Surveys and 720-degree-plus feedback regarding the performance of executives by owners, boards, and the reports to key executives are helpful. The same holds true for measurable concepts like EQ. The thoughts of directors and executives and those with whom they interact about their development can be considered and used to ascertain whether identified developmental behaviors are improving. The agreement on a LOCC offers a further valuable tool that not only shows the good intention of the parties involved but also their ability to discuss critical topics like roles, trust, power, and the quality of communication and relationships.

REMAINING QUESTIONS

This book attempts to shed light on a range of topics regarding corporate governance failures and derailment, their causes, and their reduction. In doing so, it raises many questions:

1. How can shareholders and investors more effectively assess the performance of boards and directors? What information do they need?
2. The boards' responsibilities are largely a product of requirements imposed by laws and regulatory agencies. Why do companies fail to take these requirements more seriously? Why aren't more governance practices optional, at the discretion of companies and their shareholders, instead of being inflicted by rigid standards? Would flexible models result in better market outcomes or in more failures?
3. Would fewer controls and efforts to build higher levels of trust in organizations lead to better governance quality?
4. How can we distinguish between bad decisions that result from bad leadership, governance failure, and/or those resulting from unpredictable market changes?
5. How can we determine the main cause of a company's poor decisions and problems? Is it the owners, directors, or executives, or a combination? Responsibilities must be clearly defined to trace the antecedents of conflict and hold people accountable.
6. How is it possible for shareholders to distinguish between a temporary setback and systemic trouble? How can they identify the tipping point when the company begins to get off track? And how much time and leeway should be given to successful boards and CEOs to correct personal and governance shortcomings once they are detected?

FURTHER CONSIDERATIONS

Starting early: The sooner people learn about the effects of childhood and upbringing on leadership, the sooner they may initiate corrective measures. Teaching students to be more self-aware before they attend college and enter the workforce would be advantageous.

Behavioral patterns are acquired early in life. Parents, caregivers, and teachers play crucial roles in shaping children's behavior. Since children tend to imitate behaviors, these figures are important role models. Once children start school and spend time with their peers, it becomes increasingly difficult to shape children's behaviors.

As with adults in business, disruptive children can derail groups. They do not know how to recognize and regulate their behavior. Teachers and support staff who have learned how to recognize and correct counterproductive behavior patterns like bullying can intervene. Dysfunctional behaviors are symptoms of larger problems. It is critical to understand what is behind them as these behaviors are never merely random.[655]

Studies indicate that psychopathic traits are difficult to change once people reach maturity. Early intervention can have a significant positive impact. Adequate nutrition and specialized professional care can positively affect trajectories at the age of three, which is when many behavioral tendencies start to become apparent.[656]

There is relatively little information available on how upbringings shape the behaviors and leadership styles of female leaders. This is largely due to there being far fewer female leaders than male. More female executives need to be given the chance to move up the ladder and included on corporate boards. Adding female leaders to predominately male leadership groups improves decision-making, performance, and innovation. Encouraging girls at an early age is fundamental to this endeavor.

Business schools: Economics, politics, and corporate environments drive business schools to a large extent. They only recently have started to talk about the value of emotions in domestic and corporate life.

---

655 Nancy Rappaport and Jessica Minahan, "Breaking the Behavior Code," ASCD Inservice, June 7, 2012, http://inservice.ascd.org/behavior-code/ (last visited May 7, 2018).

656 Niels Birbaumer, Frankfurter Allgemeine Zeitung, http://www.faz.net/aktuell/wissen/leben-gene/hirnforschung-mit-straftaetern-das-boese-beginnt-im-gehirn-13649029.html?printPagedArticle=true#pageIndex_2 (last visited May 6, 2018).

It is time to supplement the traditional rationale and technological curriculum with emotionally intelligent curriculum.

In mission statements of top business schools, developing responsible and thoughtful leaders who can create value for their organizations and communities is a common theme. And several schools offer business ethics classes. But to what extent do business schools work to develop executives and positively impact their cultures and staffs? Many of the leaders responsible for the scandals described in this book graduated from the world's top business schools. Apparently, the current curriculum does not always develop leaders who have the best interests of their stakeholders and organizations at heart.

Business schools must help their students learn how successfully lead their organizations. This might include lessons on how to temper envy and greed, handle power, be humble and accountable, and show gratitude. These skills are not easily measurable but are important. For business schools to become truly transformational, they need to teach these skills so that their students learn how to handle the more irrational aspects of their professional lives.

The world needs leaders who can look beyond the short term, care about the common good, and are aware of the impact of their own actions. Business schools need to make sure they offer a holistic approach to business education. Technocracy is no longer the sole answer if it ever was.

Good leaders understand how to balance actions and reflection so that they move forward and stop periodically to reflect on where they are heading.

"Remember, if you're headed in the wrong direction, Life considers U-turns to be legal, in all jurisdictions."

—B. T. HENDERSON

The selection process: The time and energy we should invest into selecting leaders is usually underestimated. A successful selection process requires the sort of respect, preparation, time, and money that companies typically spend on strategy and corporate acquisition research.

The selection and development of a board chair or CEO should be done with care. Founding owners cannot be selected (although one can choose whether to work for/with them, their company and culture), but directors and executives can. It is both important to help leaders develop and maintain a sense of the larger picture, purpose, and some humility.

Corporate culture: An increased awareness and the inclusion of EQ measures at the board and top executive level facilitates the development of a culture that includes humility and humanity and helps to prevent derailment. A culture characterized by transparency, openness, and trust, as well as one that requires candid feedback periodically at all hierarchical levels helps companies walk the fine line between the positive and negative use of power.

CONCLUDING REMARKS

Corporate governance systems need to clarify complex relationships among owners, directors, and executives. They must regularly be updated as ownership, personnel, and strategy change. The board of directors should add this task to their responsibilities to ensure the corporate policies are effective.

The most important task of owners and shareholders is to select the right directors, and similarly, the most important task of the directors is to select the right CEO. Boards must find the right balance between being supportive and skeptical of their CEOs, ask the right questions, and provide constructive feedback. The same holds true for the owners vis-à-vis their directors (especially the board chair) and for the CEOs vis-à-vis members of their management team (as potential successors).

Although everyone agrees honest, able, and effective leaders are needed at the top of organizations, it is not easy to identify and employ them. A substantial portion of one's personality and behaviors are genetic, and most of the rest of them are shaped in childhood. Owners and directors need to explore board chairs and CEO candidates' personality, past, and behavioral tendencies in the recruitment process, even though it is not easy to ascertain them. When questioned, many candidates may not be willing to reveal certain details, or they may not even be aware of how childhood experiences have affected them. Nevertheless, a lot can be achieved if hidden dynamics are considered and if energy is devoted to a thorough selection and development process.

Our early experiences provide valuable insights into our personalities, leadership styles, and areas to develop. But we must be ready to probe the shadow sides and want to use the discovered insights to become better leaders. The effects of these shadows emerge most when we are under pressure. If we do not detect these shadows and manage them, they can ultimately lead to conflict and derailment. The more people learn about themselves, the better they can handle themselves and the more able they are to lead and develop others.

Leaders and business owners can improve business adaptation and performance by becoming aware of the human element and hidden dynamics of conflict. Such awareness helps us work with leaders who are at risk, anticipate their tendencies and impacts, and initiate change within a solid legal framework.

This book has explained how change, the human factor, and leadership affect corporate governance, how derailments develop, the damage they do, and what solutions are available. A lot can be done to prevent and minimize negative outcomes, but serious commitment is essential.

The corporate governance scandals recounted early in this book call for owners and boards to think more about universal values, moral standards, and the virtues of humility, temperance, truthfulness, humanity, personal accountability, knowledge, courage, wisdom, and justice.

Leaders must think more about their personal and organizational purposes. Leaders often do not do what they say. The reason for this might be that these leaders lack an awareness of their own inner motivations and outer behaviors. When owners and boards do not encourage and expect such an awareness, many leaders will not take the time to develop it and inadvertently derail the organization. The information and approaches in this book can help prevent this.

Many people with power find excuses for why they are unable to devote time and energy to this introspection that might be emotionally challenging. The process of detecting unconscious forces and related patterns can be new and uncomfortable. It can cause anxiety and be disorienting. And many people transfer and blame the consequences of their own inadequacies onto others. Leaders must find the time to take a step back. Discovering one's blind spots provides valuable insights into one's life and leadership, and it positively impacts an entire workforce and organization.

As described, the fields of law and business assume that human beings are rational, yet evidence suggests they are more emotional than rational. Interestingly, rational, pragmatic, and objective thinking are still considered superior to feeling. This assumption negatively affects outcomes and limits us, as our feelings are the primary source of the energy that fuels us (or determines our action).

Management scholars and practitioners are increasingly realizing that organizations are systems that have their own dynamics. Only some of these dynamics are conscious and rational; many of them are unconscious and irrational.

The clinical paradigm sheds much-needed light on unconscious processes and underlying reasons for people's behaviors. To gain a more comprehensive understanding of what is going on in organizations, it is critical to be aware of dynamics of the interrelationships between leaders and their teams, as well as processes and structures that impact individuals, groups, and entire companies.

It is impossible to define universal ways to prevent derailment, but it is comparatively easy to spot the danger signs when one knows where to look. Cultures of feedback and trust and checks and balances are important, but the major ingredient for individual and organizational success is awareness.

Given this, organizations will be able to navigate change and flourish long term, driven by motivated and encouraged leaders and employees.

TABLES

APPENDICES

TYPES OF DERAILMENT

Since this book focuses on derailment within organizations, especially among the magic triangle of owner, BoD, and management, it is necessary to understand how the term is used. Here, derailment is explained and divided into: (a) severe conflict, (b) excess(es), (c) fraud, (d) corporate scandal. All have undesirable consequences (negative outcomes) for one or all parties involved, for other stakeholders, and for the company.

This means that severe conflict, excesses, fraud, and scandal are derailments. They are not the consequences of derailment, because the consequences of any kind of derailment are lawsuits, bankruptcy, jail time, worthless pensions, etc. Neither is derailment something that triggers severe conflict, excesses, fraud, and scandal, because the triggers are what this book describes at length: change, narcissism, hubris, etc.

Derailment can be defined as "the obstruction of a process by diverting it from its intended course."[657]

---

657 *Oxford Dictionary,* "derailment," https://en.oxforddictionaries.com/definition/derailment (last visited September 20, 2018).

For the organization as a whole, the process being obstructed is the execution of the mission and performance of the business itself.

In the case of management derailment, the obstruction causes the executive to be diverted from doing the job successfully. The reasons are multifold because of either personal failure or conditions triggered by external factors. For example, an executive makes a serious mistake, such as excess or even fraud, that leads to dismissal from the position. Another example describes external conditions such as economic downturn that force a BoD to lay off the CEO. A third and common reason is rooted in the executive's inability to create and nurture effective working relationships due to deeply rooted fears, inflexibility, or personality clashes with others.[658]

What follows is a more detailed description of the different types of derailment, as they will emerge in a number of cases throughout the book. Each of these derailments obstruct a process by diverting it from its intended course.

SEVERE CONFLICT

Conflicts involve differing and/or opposing opinions, principles, and beliefs. The term itself has a negative connotation, even though "good conflict" does exist (chapter 7, "Crucial Leadership Skills (and How to Develop Them)").

In practice, people generally consider conflicts to be negative, time- and energy-consuming, neither pleasant nor productive, and not viewed as opportunities. This is certainly true in the context of derailment in business.

In an ideal world, everybody would have a positive attitude toward conflict and see it as a learning opportunity. Unfortunately, however, people often get worn down or impacted negatively by conflict.

---

658 Brian Bass, "What Is Management Derailment?" *Houston Chronicle*, https://smallbusiness.chron.com/management-derailment-31849.html (last visited September 20, 2018).

Thus, it is worth considering how organizational dynamics, in addition to broad individual attitudes, contribute to negative experiences of conflict. Chronic bad conflicts tend to involve unresolved issues relating to proper and open communication, power (imbalances), felt injustice, confused role identities, ill-managed disputes, a lack of inclusion, etc.[659]

Conflicts within the magic triangle often arise between people in dominant roles or political positions who have differing views, values, and interests affecting the execution of power and status involving power games and the prevalence of ego. (Freud originally described the ego as the conscious part of the mind; however, today it is generally understood as self-esteem or self-interest.)[660]

All too often, power is mishandled or abused, which can lead to excess, fraud, or scandal (see following subsection). But not all people are prone to this. Conflict can bring out the best in a person, or the worst. What drives people to allow conflicts to arise—or even to actively promote bad conflicts—as well as why people tend to deal with conflicts in a certain way.

EXCESS(ES)

The *Cambridge Dictionary* defines *excess* as "an amount that is more than acceptable, expected, or reasonable," and *excesses* as "actions far past the limit of what is acceptable."[661] In this book, excesses include greed and actions such as excessive remuneration or borrowing. These not only harm companies but hint at a person's inner drivers. Although excessive actions might be legal (in contrast to fraud), they are not socially or ethically acceptable.

---

659 Ken Johnson, "The Good and Bad of Conflict," August 2014, Mediate.com, http://www.mediate.com/articles/JohnsonK6.cfm (last visited February 23, 2017).

660 Sarah Wilson, "The ego, the superego and the id," *The Guardian*, March 6, 2009, https://www.theguardian.com/lifeandstyle/2009/mar/07/ego-superego-id-sigmund-freud.

661 *Cambridge Dictionary*, "excess," http://dictionary.cambridge.org/de/worterbuch/englisch/excess (last visited October 8, 2017).

FRAUD

The *Cambridge Dictionary* defines *fraud* as "the crime of getting money by deceiving people."[662] The Association of Certified Fraud Examiners (ACFE) describes occupational fraud as "the use of one's occupation for personal enrichment through the deliberate misuse or misapplication of the employing organization's resources or assets."[663]

In its global analysis of 114 countries and 2,140 cases between January 2014 and October 2015, the ACFE discovered that 83 percent of occupational fraud cases involved asset misappropriation. However, this type of fraud accounted for the smallest median loss. In contrast, financial statement fraud happened in 10 percent of the cases but accounted for the highest median loss. Corruption—defined by Transparency International as "the abuse of entrusted power for private gain"[664]—was in the middle of both percentage of cases and median loss.[665]

According to the ACFE, occupational fraud happens every day in the 114 analyzed countries. The report describes in great length how occupational fraud takes place, the characteristics of the people who enact fraudulent behavior, and the types of organizations that become victims. It also gives a summary of expert opinions on organizational revenue lost to fraud.[666]

In large organizations, corruption accounts for the highest fraud risk. In contrast, smaller companies witnessed check tampering, skimming, payroll fraud, and cash larceny schemes far more often.[667]

---

662 *Cambridge Dictionary*, "fraud," https://dictionary.cambridge.org/de/worterbuch/englisch/fraud (last visited May 4, 2019).

663 ACFE, "Report to the Nations," 6.

664 "What Is Corruption?" Transparency International, http://www.transparency.org/what-is-corruption/#define (last visited March 18, 2017).

665 ACFE, "Report to the Nations," 4.

666 Ibid., 6.

667 Ibid., 4.

CORPORATE SCANDAL

The complexities of scandal place it into a unique category of derailment, as a multitiered obstruction containing both actions and consequences and originating with conflict, excess(es) and/or fraud.

Dictionary.com's definitions include:[668]

1. "a disgraceful or discreditable action, circumstance, etc." (action and consequence]
2. "an offense caused by a fault or misdeed" (consequence]
3. "damage to reputation; public disgrace" (consequence]
4. "defamatory talk; malicious gossip" (action and consequence]

The *Cambridge Dictionary* definition calls *scandal* "a situation that is extremely bad" or "an action or event that causes a public feeling of shock and strong moral disapproval."[669]

Scandal begins with disgraceful action(s) taken by executive(s) and is also referred to as "organizational misconduct." This leads to initial, undesirable consequences (public outrage, criminal charges/convictions) that lead ultimately to great harm to all stakeholders and/or collapse of the organization.

WebFinance Inc.'s Business Dictionary defines scandal this way:

> Set of questionable, unethical, and/or illegal actions that a person or persons within a corporation engage in. This often becomes a wide public incident. Typically there are questions about the corporation's actions, which are either allegedly illegal or actually proven to be illegal. Corporate scandals are therefore brought about from allegations about ethical practices or behaviors, by legal action or decisions, or a combination of

---

668 Dictionary.com, "scandal," https://www.dictionary.com/browse/scandal?s=t (last visited November 6, 2019).

669 *Cambridge Dictionary*, "scandal," http://dictionary.cambridge.org/de/worterbuch/englisch/scandal (last visited October 8, 2017).

the two. They may also be due to persons within a corporation acting on their own behalf with or without regard for the company.[670]

---

670 WebFinance Inc. Business Dictionary, "corporate scandal," http://www.businessdictionary.com/definition/corporate-scandal.html (last visited November 6, 2019).

LEGAL FRAMEWORKS CONSISTING OF HARD LAW AND SOFT LAW

OBJECTIVES OF LEGAL FRAMEWORKS

To understand the legal frameworks surrounding organizational conflict and conduct, and to define the characteristics of hard and soft law, one first needs to look at their objectives. Why are there laws and guidelines to regulate and police organizations?

Governments are interested in the well-being of companies, and thus, they face the challenge of balancing companies' entrepreneurial freedom with the protection of shareholders, other stakeholders, and the public. Since most governments do not intend to, and cannot get directly involved in companies' decision-making processes, it is left to the companies themselves to find the best solutions. Concurrently, governments aim to ensure that companies are effective in terms of management, control, accountability, transparency, and responsibility.[671]

---

671 Bühler, "Corporate Governance," *und ihre Regulierung in der Schweiz, ZGR Zeitschrift für Unternehmens- und Gesellschaftsrechtn* 41. nos. 2–3 (2012): 229.

Governments therefore face significant challenges in defining the ideal balance between regulation and freedom.[672] For example, in Switzerland, the hard law leaves a decent amount of freedom to companies with respect to corporate governance. The Swiss Code of Best Practice for Corporate Governance (Swiss Code or SCBP) outlines soft law duties of corporations and recommends concrete proposals regarding legal scope of action.[673]

HARD LAW (CORPORATE LAW) AS A FRAMEWORK FOR CORPORATE GOVERNANCE
CORPORATE LAW

A company is a legal entity that is treated as a legal person by the law. It can both sue and be sued, distinct from its shareholders.[674] Corporate law can be defined as follows: "Corporate law deals with the formation and operations of corporations and is related to commercial and contract law."[675]

Different organizations have similar legal characteristics and face similar legal problems that cut through jurisdictions. These characteristics are legal personality, limited liability, transferable shares, delegated management under a board structure, and investor ownership. Because these basic legal characteristics are common to today's organizations, corporate law needs to address them.[676]

Corporate law has two key functions:[677]

---

672 Ibid., 229.

673 Ibid., 228.

674 John Armour, Henry Hansmann, and Reinier Kraakman, "The Essential Elements of Corporate Law: What Is Corporate Law?" Harvard Law and Economics Research Paper No. 643, July 21, 2009, 9, http://www.law.harvard.edu/programs/olin_center/papers/pdf/Kraakman_643.pdf.

675 HG.org, Corporate Law: Definition, State Laws, Publications, Organizations, HG.org Legal Resources, https://www.hg.org/corporate-law.html (last visited November 14, 2017).

676 Armour, Hansmann, and Kraakman, "The Essential Elements of Corporate Law," 2.

677 Ibid., 3.

1. Establish the corporate form of the company per se
2. Reduce the ongoing costs of doing business via the established corporate form.

These functions can be exercised by facilitating coordination between people involved in organizations and by reducing opportunism. Corporate law does this by addressing three types of conflicts: between shareholders and managers, among shareholders, and between shareholders and other stakeholders, including creditors and employees.

In addition to the objective of defining the corporate form and containing conflicts among participants, the overall goal of corporate law is to serve the interests of society as a whole. More particularly, the goal is to accumulate the welfare of all who are impacted by a company's activities, e.g., shareholders, employees, suppliers, customers, third parties. Economists call this "the pursuit of overall social efficiency."[678]

EVOLUTION AND IMPLICATIONS OF CROSS-COUNTRY CORPORATE LAW

Corporate law around the globe has evolved with a cross-country convergence followed by an increased divergence. The initial set of rules was simple and imitated existing charters of corporations. But it did not predict or reflect innovations that led to industrialization, isolated socioeconomic changes within individual countries, or weaknesses uncovered in the structure of corporate law.

Pistor, Keinan, Kleinheisterkamp, and West[679] provide a comprehensive analysis of the evolution of corporate law and its international roots.

Pistor et al. defined the following key elements in the development of

---

678 Ibid., 25.

679 Pistor et al., "Evolution of Corporate Law: A Cross-Country Comparison," 791–871.

corporate law: (1) the demand for corporate law, (2) the institutional context and the level to which legal systems develop complementary control mechanisms, and (3) market and regulatory competition. These are mutually dependent and imbedded in the socioeconomic and political situation of the respective country and the level of competition.

Their analysis of corporate law's evolution starts in the early nineteenth century. It includes the jurisdictions of France, Germany, the UK, and the US—origin countries—and Chile, Colombia, Israel, Japan, Malaysia, and Spain—transplant countries that adopted their corporate laws from the four origin countries, directly or indirectly.

DIFFERENT LEGAL SYSTEMS OF DIFFERENT COUNTRIES

The most common legal systems that countries follow are either common law or civil law.[680] The foundational difference between these two systems is the main source of the law.

COMMON LAW

In general, common law is not codified, meaning that there is no comprehensive collection of legal statutes and rules. Although it does rely on legislative decisions (scattered statutes), it largely abides by precedents (judicial decisions made in similar previous cases). Such precedents are historically documented in collections of case law and maintained over time via court records. In the decision of each new case, it is the presiding judge who applies these precedents, which gives him or her a powerful role in shaping the law. Before the judge decides on the appropriate sentence, it is a jury of ordinary people without legal training that decides on the facts of the case and that ultimately provides the judge with its verdict.

---

680 "The Common Law and Civil Law Traditions," The Robbins Collection: School of Law (Boalt Hall), University of California at Berkeley, https://www.law.berkeley.edu/library/robbins/CommonLawCivilLawTraditions.html (last visited March 27, 2018); S. B., "What Is the Difference Between Common and Civil Law?"

CIVIL LAW

In contrast, civil law (often called European Continental Law) is codified. This means that nations that apply civil law systems have comprehensive legal codes that are continually updated. They specify all matters that can be brought before a court, the procedure to be applied, as well as the adequate punishment for each offense. Unlike common law systems, in civil law countries, it is the role of the judge to determine the facts of a case and to apply the provisions of the applicable code. Because the framework within which he or she works is based on a comprehensive, codified set of laws, the judge's decisions are less influential for the shaping of civil law than the decisions of legislators and legal scholars who interpret the codes. Importance is not attached to past judgments. Since the objective of codes and statutes is to cover all eventualities, the judge's role in applying the law to the prevalent case is more limited.

According to the *CIA World Factbook*,[681] approximately 150 out of 230 countries apply civil law systems. Common law is in force in eighty countries that are mainly former English colonies.

What role does corporate law play for corporate governance? What is its relevance to corporate reality? Does legislative action tend to follow, rather than precede, economic change? Is it impossible for law to foresee situations that have never happened before? Or is corporation law as much influenced by corporate practice as the other way around, thus indicating a reciprocal dependency (or interrelationship) rather than an effect of one area on the other? It will be demonstrated here that it is not primarily law that influences corporate reality.

SOFT LAW (CORPORATE GOVERNANCE)

Since the field of corporate governance is very broad, there is no uniform academic definition or model for it. The most widely accepted definitions and models will now be outlined.

---

681 CIA, "The CIA World Factbook," 2017, xxi.

Definition

There are numerous definitions of corporate governance, for example:

1. Shleifer and Vishny: "The ways in which suppliers of finance to corporations assure themselves of getting a return on their investment."[682]
2. Organization for Economic Cooperation and Development (OECD): "Procedures and processes according to which an organization is directed and controlled. The corporate governance structure specifies the distribution of rights and responsibilities among the different participants in the organization [...] and lays down the rules and procedures for decision-making."[683]
3. Cadbury: "The system by which business corporations are directed and controlled."[684] This definition is underpinned by Hilb, who coined the term "New Corporate Governance" as "a system by which companies are strategically directed, integratively managed and holistically controlled in an entrepreneurial and ethical way."[685]

History

The widespread belief is that corporate governance was first described by Berle and Means in 1932[686] before the term was coined by Jensen and Meckling in 1976.[687] While acknowledging this early coining, in fact, a type of corporate governance could already be recognized in the business regulation of the Swiss Kreditanstalt (now Credit Suisse) as far back as 1859.[688]

---

682 Andrei Shleifer and Robert W. Vishny, *A Survey of Corporate Governance*, NBER working paper series: 5554 (Cambridge, MA: National Bureau of Economic Research, 1996), 10, https://www.nber.org/papers/w5554.

683 OECD, Glossary of Statistical Terms, "corporate governance," https://stats.oecd.org/glossary/detail.asp?ID=6778 (last visited June 14, 2016).

684 Stephen Bloomfield, *Theory and Practice of Corporate Governance: An Integrated Approach* (Cambridge, UK: Cambridge University Press, 2013), 8.

685 Martin Hilb, *New Corporate Governance: Successful Board Management Tools* (New York: Springer, 2012), 7.

686 Berle and Means, *The Modern Corporation and Private Property*.

687 Jensen and Meckling, "Managerial Behavior, Agency Costs and Ownership Structure."

688 Jung, "Alfred Escher," 242.

Corporate governance evolved around what economists call "agency problems." Berle and Means discovered that the interests of shareholders (principals) and executives (agents) diverge when ownership and control are separated, which often leads to conflict. They presumed that since the agents do not own the company, they do not bear the full costs of their actions. They have advantages over the principals, e.g., knowledge over other parties (asymmetric information) that may be misused to serve their own objectives and interests in such areas as compensation, bonuses, job security, status, and power.[689] In contrast, shareholders focus on maximizing shareholder value and on profitability and calculated risk.[690]

Both parties are driven by their self-interest, but the growth of a corporation tends also to involve the growth of managers' (agents') power. Following the scandals of the 1990s and 2000s, corporate governance experienced an upswing and has been widely discussed since.

Clarification

In contrast to laws and statutes, corporate governance regulations are not strictly binding and thus cannot be enforced. This is why they are called soft law.[691] These regulations are created and developed outside the sphere of national legislation and thus, they are built on the understanding of self-regulation.[692]

Corporate governance cements fundamental principles that are described by law. It presents corporate bodies with recommendations on how they should design their legal margins for maneuver. Good corporate governance can be considered as well-understood corporate law.[693]

---

689 Mahler and Andersson, "Corporate Governance: Effects," 6.

690 Lüpold, Der Ausbau der "Festung Schweiz," 16; Berle and Means, *The Modern Corporation and Private Property*.

691 Jackson, "Global Corporate Governance," 44.

692 Sommer, „Die Treuepflicht des Verwaltungsrats," 6.

693 Bühler, "Corporate Governance," 237.

The goal of corporate governance is the avoidance of dubious practices that can entail short-term profits at the expense of long-term profits, which can potentially damage a company's reputation.[694]

The problems and conflicts that corporate governance addresses are common in stock corporations. For example, corporate governance describes the interactions between companies and their shareholders, e.g., the right to having a say, transparency, dividends; their executives, e.g., management and control, compensation; other stakeholders, e.g., employee participation, tax, and market interests.[695]

The Cadbury Report published in the UK in 1992 is considered a breakthrough in corporate governance. Many other countries followed and launched their own governance codes. The objective of these codes is for corporate governance to serve as a set of instruments for self-regulation as well as a reliable system based on control mechanisms, checks, and balances. The main steps of corporate governance's international development can be recapped as follows:[696]

1. 1992 in the UK: Cadbury Report (the 1999 Combined Code)
2. 1995/99 in France: Viénot Report
3. 1998 and 2004 by the OECD: Principles of Corporate Governance
4. 2002/03 in Germany: Deutscher Corporate Governance Kodex (DCGK)
5. 2002 in Switzerland: Swiss Code of Best Practice (SCBP)
6. 2002 in US: Sarbanes-Oxley Act (SOX)
7. 2017: more than 120 different corporate governance codes exist

As this list demonstrates, many countries published their first sets of law and guidelines around the same time. Corporate governance became the subject of an international debate. Although different codes are based on different national laws and have faced different

---

694 Jackson, "Global Corporate Governance," 44.

695 Lüpold, Der Ausbau der "Festung Schweiz," 1.

696 "Index of Codes," ECGI (European Corporate Governance Institute), http://www.ecgi.org/codes/all_codes.php (last visited June 4, 2016).

developments, they are quite similar. However, their areas of focus are different.[697]

CORPORATE GOVERNANCE MODELS

Within corporate governance literature, a common distinction is made between "insider" governance systems and "outsider" governance systems. These models show differences regarding:[698]

1. Ownership structure (concentrated vs. dispersed)
2. Executive management (direct or indirect control/one- or two-tier systems)
3. Orientation (banking market vs. stock exchange)
4. Control mechanisms

To further explain:

1. *Insider systems:* concentration of ownership stakes and direct representation of the major stakeholders on the boards (and sometimes also on management) that monitor management.
2. *Outsider systems*: dispersion of ownership stakes (shares) and indirect control by owners on management by having representatives, elected by them, on the monitoring boards.

In this context, there are three dominant models, one of which refers to the outsider system and two refer to the insider system:

1. Within the outsider, the most important examples of countries are the US, Great Britain, and Canada, which use the Anglo-Saxon

---

697 Rolan Müller, Lorenz Lipp, and Adrian Plüss, Der Verwaltungsrat: Ein Handbuch für die Praxis, 596ff.

698 Gregory Francesco Maassen, An International Comparison of Corporate Governance Models: A Study on the Formal Independence and Convergence of One-Tier and Two-Tier Corporate Boards of Directors in the United States of America, the United Kingdom and the Netherlands (Amsterdam: Spencer Stuart, 1999), 42; Klaus Gugler, Dennis C. Mueller, and Burcin B. Yurtoglu, "Corporate Governance and Globalization," Oxford Review of Economic Policy, vol. 20, no. 1 (2004), 130f; Daliborka Becic, "Comparative Analysis of Corporate Governance Systems," Annals of DAAAM for 2011 and Proceedings of the 22nd International DAAAM Symposium, vol. 22, no. 1 (2011), 1361f; Gregory Jackson and Andreas Moerke, "Continuity and Change in Corporate Governance: comparing Germany and Japan," Corporate Governance: An International Review, vol. 13, no. 3 (2005), 351f.

or Anglo-American model. Aside from the low concentration of capital, which gives management a main role, it is also characterized by its large and liquid stock market, high-level minority shareholder protection, dominant role of institutional investors, and its one-tier board (described in the next section). It is also known as the shareholder system.

2. In countries with insider models, two different forms of governance structure can be found:
    ○ In Germany, Switzerland, and a few other continental European countries, these models are called the Continental European model or German model, in which control is typically unidirectional. Aside from corporate concentrated ownership among strategically oriented banks and industrial companies, it has a two-tier board (described in the next section). It is also known as the stakeholder system.
    ○ The Japanese model is similar to the European model in the concentration of ownership among banks and industrial companies. In contrast, several companies are linked together via so-called interlocking directorships (cross-shareholding of debt and equity). It has a two-tier system and is also known as the stakeholder system.

ONE-TIER AND TWO-TIER CORPORATE SYSTEMS

In general, there are two categories of systems: If a company is governed by just one corporate body (top management and supervisory together) that occupies both the management and monitoring functions, it is called a monistic (one-tier) system. If the two functions are separated, it is called a dual (two-tier) system.

One-Tier Board

Both executive directors and nonexecutive directors function together in one organizational level. Not only can the domination of the board lie with either the majority of executive directors or nonexecutive directors but also the board can have a leadership structure that separates or combines its CEO and chair positions.[699]

Two-Tier Board

In this two-tier model, a second organizational layer has been created that separates the board's executive function from its monitoring function. The upper layer is the supervisory board. It consists of non-executive supervisory directors who may be representatives of labor, the government, and/or institutional investors. The lower level is the management board. It generally consists of executive managing directors. The leadership structure holds formal independence from the executive function of the board because the CEO does not hold a seat in the supervisory board.[700]

The US system is monistic, and the German is dualistic.[701]

Future Convergence vs. Divergence of Corporate Governance

The question remains whether convergence or divergence of corporate governance will prevail. As seen above, approaches to governance vary. One relevant driver can be the internationalization of financial markets and, therefore, of an investor's portfolio.[702] Opinions seem to differ. Arguments in favor of convergence are reflected in common international standards and regulations (e.g., market integration and accounting standards) because of pressure from international companies, the stock market, securities regulators, and international institutions such as the International Monetary Fund and the World Bank. Arguments in favor of divergence are related to hindering

---

699 Maassen, An International Comparison of Corporate Governance Models, 15.

700 Ibid., 15.

701 Cornelia Geissler, "ein Board?" *Harvard Business Manager* (February 2006).

702 Berthold Leube and George L. Davis, "The Next Stage of Globalization: The Convergence of Corporate Governance Practices," *The Focus Magazine*, vol. 14, no. 2 (2011), 36ff, https://www.egonzehnder.com/insight/the-next-stage-of-globalization.

factors such as culture, resistance, ownership structures, economic progress, politics, and religion, e.g., Islamic Sharia's view of certain Western practices as unethical or immoral.[703]

---

703 Davies, "Globalisation of Corporate Governance," 49; Sasan, "Corporate Governance: Convergence vs. Divergence," 24ff.

APPENDIX 3

SCANDALS RELATED TO CORPORATE GOVERNANCE

SCANDALS *BEFORE* CORPORATE GOVERNANCE WAS PUT ON THE MAP

The list of companies and organizations that had run into/experienced a scandal is long. What follows is an extract.[704]

1998: WASTE MANAGEMENT

1. Public, US-based waste management company
2. Fake earnings of $1.7 billion—intentional false increase of depreciation time length for fixed assets on the balance sheets
3. Key players: founder, chairperson, CEO, and other top executives

2001: ENRON

1. US-based commodities, energy, and services corporation
2. Huge debts kept off balance sheet; overstatement of earnings by

---

704 Bloomfield, *Theory and Practice of Corporate Governance*, 5ff; "The 10 Worst Corporate Accounting Scandals of All Time"; Balkhi, "25 Biggest Corporate Scandals Ever"; Farrell, "The World's Biggest Accounting Scandals."

several hundred million dollars; shareholders lost $74 billion; many employees lost jobs; thousands of employees and investors lost their savings

3. Largest American bankruptcy at the time[705]
4. Key players: CEO, CFO, and former CEO

2001: HIH INSURANCE

Australia's second-largest insurance group before provisional liquidation in 2001.

1. Total losses $5.3 billion by false or misleading statements, and failure to discharge the duties as a board's director in good faith and in the company's best interests
2. Key player: former CEO, top executives, director (former CEO of a company acquired by HIH not long before the collapse)

2002: ABB

1. Swedish-Swiss multinational conglomerate; one of the world's largest engineering companies
2. CHF 233 million in pension and retirement benefits to the chairperson and CEO despite company's loss of CHF 691 million and CHF 4 billion of debt
3. Key players: CEO and chairperson[706]

2002: WORLDCOM

1. Second largest, US-based telecommunications company before filing for Chapter 11; later MCI, Inc.
2. Artificially inflated assets of $11 billion with $3.8 billion in fraudulent accounts, inflated revenues, underreported line costs, fake accounting entries, hiding the truth about the company's decreas-

705 Peregrine, "Enron Still Matters, 15 Years After Its Collapse."

706 "About ABB," www.abb.com; "Barnevik's Bounty."

ing operating performance from investors; 30,000 employees lost their jobs; investors lost $180 billion

3. Key players: founder/CEO, CFO

2002: TYCO

1. US-based, diversified manufacturing conglomerate (electronic components, healthcare, fire safety, security, and fluid control)
2. Inflated company income by $500 million, $150 million stolen, much of it for private use. Unapproved loans and fraudulent stock sales. Money taken out of company disguised as executive compensation.
3. Key players: CEO and former CFO

2003: HEALTH SOUTH

1. US's largest publicly traded healthcare company
2. Fictitious transactions and accounts to inflate company's earnings by $1.4 billion; subordinates were told to make up numbers and transactions
3. Key player: CEO

2003: FREDDIE MAC

1. Public, US-based, federally backed home loan mortgage-financing giant
2. Intentional misstatement and understatement of $5 billion in earnings
3. Key players: COO/president, CEO/chairperson, ex-CFO, former senior executives

2003: PARMALAT

1. Leading Italian global producer of milk and other food
2. €14 billion ($18.6 billion) hole in accounting records; selling

credit-linked notes to itself and diverting the company's funds elsewhere[707]

3. Key players: founder, CFO, and executives[708]

SCANDALS *AFTER* CORPORATE GOVERNANCE WAS PUT ON THE MAP

2004: ROYAL DUTCH SHELL

1. Anglo-Dutch oil group
2. Breached market abuse provisions in relation to the calculation of its oil reserves. The overbooking of proven reserves in its oil fields accounted to 4.5 billion barrels—almost one quarter of its total, destroying billions of pounds of market value. It subsequently downgraded its reserves three more times.
3. Key players: chairperson, CEO oil and gas, CFO[709]

2005: AMERICAN INTERNATIONAL GROUP (AIG)

1. One of the largest global insurance and financial service corporations, US based
2. Accounting fraud of $3.9 billion, together with bid-rigging and manipulation of stock price; loans booked as revenues; steering customers to insurers with whom AIG had payoff agreements; ordered traders to inflate stock price
3. Key players: CEO, CFO

2008: LEHMAN BROTHERS

1. Global financial services company, US-based before bankruptcy and one year after

---

707 Ilaria Polleschi, "Parmalat Founder Sentenced in Company's Collapse," Reuters, December 9, 2010, https://www.reuters.com/article/us-parmalat/parmalat-founder-sentenced-in-companys-collapse-idUSTRE6B84AJ20101209.

708 "Parmalat Founder Given Eighteen-Year Jail Term over Fraud," *BBC News*, December 9, 2010, http://www.bbc.com/news/business-11958133.

709 Mark Tran, "Shell Fined over Reserves Scandal," *The Guardian*, July 29, 2004, https://www.theguardian.com/business/2004/jul/29/oilandpetrol.news.

2. Fortune Magazine ranked the company number one "most admired securities firm"
3. Over $50 billion in loans were hidden and disguised as sales, selling toxic assets to Cayman Island banks (to be bought back eventually); company made believe that it had $50 billion more cash and $50 billion less in toxic assets than in reality
4. Key players: CEO, executives

2008: ROYAL BANK OF SCOTLAND

1. Scotland-based, one of the world's largest banks before it faced the biggest bank bailout in history
2. Loss of £24 billion (the biggest loss in Britain's corporate history) caused by excessive borrowing, which led to a £45 billion government bailout. The year before, it had reported a record operating profit of £10.3 billion.
3. Key player: CEO, who had been knighted in 2004[710]

2009: SATYAM

1. India's fourth-largest outsourcing IT services provider and back-office accounting firm
2. False inflation of revenue by 28 percent and earnings by $125 million (by end September 2008) and cash balances by $1.5 billion; incurring a $253 million liability on funds personally established
3. Key player: founder/chairperson[711]

---

710 Jill Treanor, "RBS Sale: Fred Goodwin, the £45bn Bailout and Years of Losses, *The Guardian*, August 3, 2015, https://www.theguardian.com/business/2015/aug/03/rbs-sale-fred-goodwin-bailout-years-of-losses; Gordon Rayner, "Banking Bailout: The Rise and Fall of RBS," *The Telegraph*, January 20, 2009, http://www.telegraph.co.uk/finance/newsbysector/banksandfinance/4291807/Banking-bailout-The-rise-and-fall-of-RBS.html; "RBS Posts Biggest Loss in U.K. Corporate History," *NBC News*, February 26, 2009, http://www.nbcnews.com/id/29403447/ns/business-world_business/t/rbs-posts-biggest-loss-uk-corporate-history/; Jill Treanor, "Losses of £58bn Since the 2008 Bailout—How Did RBS Get Here?" *The Guardian*, February 24, 2017, https://www.theguardian.com/business/2017/feb/24/90bn-in-bills-since-2008-how-did-rbs-get-here-financial-crisis-.

711 Dennis Howlett, "Satyam Scandal—The Fallout," *The Guardian*, January 15, 2009, https://www.theguardian.com/technology/2009/jan/15/satyam-computer-services.

2011: OLYMPUS

1. Japanese camera and medical equipment firm
2. Overstating earnings by almost $2 billion over many years
3. Key players: former chairperson, senior executives[712]

2014: TESCO

1. UK's biggest retailer
2. Overstatement of estimated profits by £263 million by overestimating revenues paid by suppliers as well as annual pretax loss of £6.4 billion
3. Key players: senior executives, possibly including former CEO[713]

2015: FÉDÉRATION INTERNATIONALE DE FOOTBALL ASSOCIATION (FIFA)

1. International governing body of football
2. $150 million in bribes for broadcasting rights; corruption, money laundering
3. Key players: FIFA president, officials, CFO, general secretary, UEFA president[714]

2015: TOSHIBA

1. Multinational conglomerate operating in diverse industries, based in Japan
2. Overstating operating profit by $1.2 billion

---

712 "Olympus Scandal: Former Bosses to Pay $529m over Fraud," *BBC News*, April 28, 2017, http://www.bbc.com/news/business-39741921.

713 Graham Ruddick and Julia Kollewe, "Tesco to Pay £129m Fine over Accounting Scandal," *The Guardian*, March 28, 2017, https://www.theguardian.com/business/2017/mar/28/tesco-agrees-fine-serious-fraud-office-accounting-scandal; Sarah Butler, "Former Tesco Directors Charged with Fraud over Accounting Scandal," *The Guardian*, September 9, 2016, https://www.theguardian.com/business/2016/sep/09/sfo-charges-former-tesco-directors-with-fraud.

714 Alice Molan, "FIFA Corruption Scandal Continues," *The Laundromat*, June 27, 2017, http://thelaundromat.kwm.com/fifa-corruption-scandal-continues/.

3. Key players: president and CEO and vice chairperson[715]

2015: BARCLAYS

1. One of the world's largest banks, based in the UK
2. Libor manipulation tied to financial contracts and derivatives worth trillions of dollars
3. Key players: CEO and senior executives[716]

2016: VOLKSWAGEN

1. German car maker
2. Falsification of emissions data on nearly 600,000 diesel cars, pretending they were more environmentally friendly; installation of software into car computers (called "defeat device") that detects when the car is being checked
3. Key players: former CEO, senior executives[717]

2017: ODEBRECHT

1. South America's construction giant, based in Brazil
2. Bribery in exchange for contracts in Brazil and ten other countries
3. Key players: Group CEO, other executives[718]

2018/2019: THE ABRAAJ GROUP

1. Biggest private equity dealmaker of the Middle East and North Africa; one of the most influential emerging-market investors
2. Inflation of the value of the firm's holdings; misappropriating hun-

715 Du, "5 Things to Know about Toshiba's Accounting Scandal," *Wall Street Journal*, July 21, 2015, https://blogs.wsj.com/briefly/2015/07/21/5-things-to-know-about-toshibas-accounting-scandal-2/.

716 Jill Treanor, "Barclays Bank Reaches $100m US Settlement over Libor Rigging Scandal," *The Guardian*, August 8, 2016, https://www.theguardian.com/business/2016/aug/08/barclays-libor-100m-us-settlement.

717 Burden, "VW to Pay $2.8B Fine"; Iovino, "VW Can't Dodge 2nd Securities Action."

718 Daniel Gallas, "Brazil's Odebrecht Corruption Scandal," *BBC News*, April 17, 2019, http://www.bbc.com/news/business-39194395.

dreds of millions of USD from the healthcare fund; fraud, bribe, and conspiracy

3. Key players: CEO/founder, two managing partners[719]

2020: LUCKIN COFFEE INC

1. Chinese coffee company and coffeehouse chai; 4,500 locations in China—more than Starbucks; listed on NASDAQ
2. Fabricated transactions amount to around $310 million
3. Key players: COO, executives reporting to COO[720]

719 Simon Clark and William Louch, "Third Abraaj Executive Arrested," *Wall Street Journal*, April 18, 2019, https://www.wsj.com/articles/third-abraaj-executive-arrested-11555585989; Luke MacGregor, "Top Abraaj Executives Arrested on US Fraud Charges," *CNBC*, April 12, 2019, https://www.cnbc.com/2019/04/12/top-abraaj-executives-arrested-on-us-fraud-charges.html.

720 Joshua Franklin, Harry Brumpton, and Julie Zhu, "Starbucks' China Challenger Luckin Raises $561 Million in U.S. IPO," *Reuters*, May 16, 2019, https://www.reuters.com/article/us-luckin-coffee-ipo/starbucks-china-challenger-luckin-raises-561-million-in-u-s-ipo-idUSKCN1SM2SH; Amelia Lucas, "Shares of China's Luckin Coffee Plummet 80 Percent after Investigation Finds COO Fabricated Sales," *CNBC*, April 2, 2020, https://www.cnbc.com/2020/04/02/luckin-coffee-stock-plummets-after-investigation-finds-coo-fabricated-sales.html.

LAWSUITS RELATED TO THE CASES DESCRIBED

The following list of lawsuits, in relation to the cases of scandals described in Appendix 3, sheds light on the legal ramifications of derailment.[721] This list shows the involvement of the parties within the magic triangle.

1998: WASTE MANAGEMENT

Waste Management settled a shareholder class-action suit for $457 million. Accounting firm Arthur Andersen was fined $7 million by the US Securities and Exchange Commission (SEC) for its involvement.

2001: ENRON

The former chairperson/CEO died during the process; the former vice-chairperson committed suicide. The CEO was sentenced to jail for twenty-four years and the CFO for four years, charged with securities

---

721 Bloomfield, *Theory and Practice of Corporate Governance*, 5ff; "The 10 Worst Corporate Accounting Scandals of All Time"; Balkhi, "25 Biggest Corporate Scandals Ever"; Farrell, "The World's Biggest Accounting Scandals."Michael J. Jones, *Creative Accounting, Fraud and International Accounting Scandals*, (West Sussex, UK: Wiley, 2011).

fraud, wire fraud, mail fraud, money laundering, and conspiracy. The company filed for bankruptcy. Accounting firm Arthur Andersen was found guilty of fudging Enron's accounts and for obstructing justice by shredding audit documents.

2001: HIH

The former CEO was sentenced to four years and six months in prison with a nonparole period of two years nine months.[722]

2002: ABB

The chairperson agreed to pay back CHF 90 million and the CEO's pension and benefits were reduced by CHF 47 million.[723]

2002: WORLDCOM

The CFO was fired, the financial controller resigned, and the company filed for bankruptcy. The CEO received a twenty-five-year prison sentence, and the CFO received five years for fraud, conspiracy, and filing false documents with regulators.

2002: TYCO

The CEO and the CFO were sentenced to eight to twenty-five years in jail. Tyco was forced by a class-action lawsuit to pay out $2.92 billion to investors.

2003: HEALTH SOUTH

The CEO was sentenced to prison for seven years for bribing Alabama's governor but was acquitted of all thirty-six counts of accounting fraud.

---

722 Michael J. Jones, *Creative Accounting, Fraud and International Accounting Scandals*, (West Sussex, UK: Wiley, 2011).

723 "Former ABB CEOs to Pay Back SFr137 Million," SWI swissinfo.ch, March 10, 2002, http://www.swissinfo.ch/eng/former-abb-ceos-to-pay-back-sfr137-million/2591332.

2003: FREDDIE MAC

The company received a fine of $125 million; the president/COO, chairperson/CEO and ex-CFO were fired.

2003: PARMALAT

The founder was accused of questionable accounting practices and sentenced to eighteen years in jail. The court ordered executives to pay €2 billion back to the firm and reimburse investors.[724]

2004: ROYAL DUTCH SHELL

The chairperson and CEO of Oil and Gas and the CFO resigned, and the company agreed to pay $120 million (£65.7 million) to the US SEC and £17 million to its British counterpart, the Financial Services Authority.[725]

2005: AMERICAN INTERNATIONAL GROUP (AIG)

Settlement with the SEC for $10 million in 2003 and $1.64 billion in 2006, with one pension fund for $115 million and with three others for $725 million. The CEO was fired but did not face criminal charges. In 2008, the company experienced a $61.7 billion quarterly loss—the largest in history—and after securing a bailout with taxpayer money, its executives paid themselves bonuses of $165 million-plus.

2008: LEHMAN BROTHERS

Lehman Brothers was forced into bankruptcy—the largest in US history. As the SEC did not have enough evidence, it stopped its prosecution in 2013.

---

724 "Parmalat Founder Given Eighteen-Year Jail Term over Fraud."

725 Tran, "Shell Fined over Reserves Scandal."

2008: ROYAL BANK OF SCOTLAND

In 2017, fines and legal costs have risen to £15 billion, including the bill for the Protection of Personal Information Act (PPI) for mis-selling payment protection insurance. The bill from the industry has topped £30 billion. In 2017, RBS has made provision of £5.9 billion to settle with the US Department of Justice regarding the scandal in the US over toxic mortgages. In 2013, RBS was fined for the manipulation of the Libor (£390 million) and foreign exchange markets (£800 million).[726]

2009: SATYAM

The founder/chairperson and his brother were charged with breach of trust, conspiracy, cheating, and records falsification but were released because the Central Bureau of Investigation failed to file charges in a timely manner.[727]

2011: OLYMPUS

Tokyo's court found the former chairperson and five executives liable for $529 million. They got suspended jail sentences.[728]

2014: TESCO

Settlement of £235 million of investigations by the Serious Fraud Office and Financial Conduct Authority. The former CFO of Tesco UK, the former managing director of Tesco UK, and the former commercial director for food faced charges of fraud by abuse of position and false accounting. The former CEO did not face charges.[729]

---

726 Treanor, "Losses of £58bn Since the 2008 Bailout—How Did RBS Get Here?"

727 Howlett, "Satyam Scandal—The Fallout."

728 "Olympus Scandal: Former Bosses to Pay $529m over Fraud."

729 Ruddick and Kollewe, "Tesco to Pay £129m Fine over Accounting Scandal"; Butler, "Former Tesco Directors Charged with Fraud over Accounting Scandal."

2015/2018: FIFA

FIFA's Ethics Committee banned the FIFA and UEFA presidents for eight years from all football-related activities. A Swiss criminal investigation is continuing as of early 2018, including additional former FIFA executives. Individuals continue to show up before US courts in relation to corruption charges (members of the FIFA Audit and Compliance Committee included). The US Department of Justice has extended its investigation involving the FBI, the IRS, and Interpol.[730]

Swiss authorities continue their investigations, analyzing fifty-three possible incidents of money laundering and 104 cases of suspicious activity linked to Swiss bank accounts in context with the awarding of the hosts of the 2018 and 2022 FIFA World Cup tournaments.

2015: TOSHIBA

Sixteen members of the BoD resigned, which was half its size. Only one quarter of the sixteen directors came from outside Toshiba. The Financial Services Agency imposed a $60-million fine on the company—the largest ever in Japan for accounting related violations. Toshiba announced job cuts and restructuring measures to get up again after the scandal.[731]

2015: BARCLAYS

A $450-million fine was imposed by UK regulators and others for manipulation in 2012. In addition, Barclays had to pay $100 million for settlement with more than forty states in the US for fraudulent and anticompetitive conduct in 2016. The CEO had to resign.[732]

---

730 Molan, "FIFA Corruption Scandal Continues."

731 Du, "5 Things to Know about Toshiba's Accounting Scandal"; Kyodo, "Toshiba Fined Record ¥7.3 Billion over Accounting Scandal," *Japan Times*, December 25, 2015, http://www.japantimes.co.jp/news/2015/12/25/ business/corporate-business/toshiba-fined-record- percentC2 percentA57-3-billion-over-accounting-scandal/#. WX4ej7puJPY.

732 Treanor, "Barclays Bank Reaches $100m US Settlement"; Balkhi, "25 Biggest Corporate Scandals Ever."

2015/2018: SIKA

The majority owning family holding had filed a liability claim against three directors for excessive spending on avoidance of change of control. In turn, one major shareholder submitted a liability claim against the representative of the founding family and Sika board member for negotiating with Saint-Gobain without consulting the other directors.[733]

The Sika family challenged certain decisions of the extraordinary GA 2015, the ordinary GA 2015, and the two subsequent GAs: the voting restriction regarding the reelection of five board members and the nonelection of another board member.

The Cantonal Court decided in October 2016 that the voting right restriction at the GA 2015 was legal and denied the family's requests. The family appealed against this judgment. Before the decision on the appeal was taken by the Superior Court of the Canton of Zug and the two other challenges by the family regarding certain elections at the GA 2016 and 2017 before the Cantonal Court, the parties reached a complex deal in May 2018 over a three-year hostile legal dispute.

2016: VOLKSWAGEN

A $2.8 billion fine and three years of probation were issued after Volkswagen pleaded guilty to three criminal charges for its ten-year conspiracy. In addition, civil penalties of $1.5 billion were imposed. Volkswagen also agreed to pay $11.2 billion to buy back or repair diesel vehicles in the US and to contribute $4.7 billion to federal pollution reduction. In 2018, six current and former Volkswagen executives (including the former CEO) were accused in criminal cases (conspiracy to defraud the United States, to commit wire fraud, and to violate the Clean Air Act), and international arrest warrants were issued. In

---

733 awp/dpa, Drei Sika-Verwaltungsräte sehen sich Verantwortlichkeitsklage gegenüber, *NZZ*, https://www.nzz.ch/wirtschaft/newsticker/drei-sika-verwaltungsraete-sehen-sich-verantwortlichkeitsklage-gegenueber-1.18543256 (last visited July 31, 2017).

2019, five of them (including the former CEO) were charged with serious fraud in Braunschweig, Germany.[734]

2017: ODEBRECHT

In June 2015, the Group's CEO was arrested. Since then, not only the CEO but also seventy-six other executives have been sent to jail. Odebrecht entered deals with Brazilian investigators, agreeing to admit to crimes and to point out corrupt officials in exchange for reduced prison time. Odebrecht agreed to pay $2.6 billion (the world's largest fine of its kind) and signed a leniency deal with US and Swiss authorities.[735]

2018/2019: THE ABRAAJ GROUP

After being arrested in April 2019, Abraaj Group founder has been released on bail four weeks later after paying $19 million—a record security in the judicial history of the UK. Two former senior executives who were arrested in April, were released on bail earlier. In total, six former executives (founder/CEO, CFO, managing partners) are facing racketeering and securities-fraud charges, having defrauded investors, inflated the value of the firm's holdings, and stolen hundreds of millions of dollars. One of them admitted he lied to investors around the globe to hide losses and raise more funds. He pleaded guilty to conspiracy and agreed to cooperate with US prosecutors. His sentencing got postponed to at least late 2020, pending the outcome of an extradition request of the founder/CEO. The latter denied any wrongdoing. Two Abraaj Group companies were fined a combined

734 Burden, "VW to Pay $2.8B Fine"; Pending Criminal Division Cases: Volkswagen Diesel Engine Vehicle Matters, The United States Department of Justice (2018); Karin Matussek, "VW's Former Ceo Charged in Germany over Diesel Rigging," *Bloomberg*, April 15, 2019, https://www.bloomberg.com/news/articles/2019-04-15/ex-vw-ceo-winterkorn-charged-in-germany-over-diesel-rigging.

735 Gallas, "Brazil's Odebrecht Corruption Scandal."

$315 million by the Dubai Financial Services Authority for deceiving investors and misappropriating funds.[736]

2020: LUCKIN COFFEE INC

The investigation found that the COO and several executives reporting to him (all of them suspended by now), had engaged in misconduct, including fabricating sales. Luckin reported it will take legal action against the responsible individuals.[737]

An internal investigation still is at a preliminary stage and the estimate of the fabricated sales still needs to be verified by the independent auditor. The independent outside counsel and the independent forensic accounting expert have been engaged already (status quo April 2020).

736 Erik Larson, "Abraaj's Abdel-Wadood Pleads Guilty, Will Cooperate in Probe," *Bloomberg*, June 28, 2019, https://www.bloomberg.com/news/articles/2019-06-28/abraaj-executive-abdel-wadood-pleads-guilty-to-conspiracy; Kristin Ridley, "Abraaj Founder Faces February Extradition Hearing on U.S. Fraud Charge, *Euronews*, June 26, 2019, https://www.euronews.com/2019/06/26/abraaj-founder-faces-february-extradition-hearing-on-us-fraud-charge; Arif Sharif, "What's Been Learned and Who's Charged in Abraaj Collapse," *Bloomberg*, August 7, 2019, https://www.bloomberg.com/news/articles/2019-08-07/what-s-been-learned-who-s-charged-in-abraaj-collapse-quicktake; Lubna Hamdan, "Sentencing for Former Abraaj Md Abdel-Wadood Adjourned to August," *Arabian Business*, January 14, 2020, https://www.arabianbusiness.com/banking-finance/437555-sentencing-for-former-abraaj-md-abdel-wadood-adjourned-to-august; Case: U.S. v. Naqvi, 19-cr-00233, U.S. District Court, Southern District of New York (Manhattan).Franklin, Brumpton, and Zhu, "Starbucks' China Challenger Luckin Raises $561 Million"; Lucas, "Shares of China's Luckin Coffee Plummet 80 Percent."

737 Franklin, Brumpton, and Zhu, "Starbucks' China Challenger Luckin Raises $561 Million"; Lucas, "Shares of China's Luckin Coffee Plummet 80 Percent."

APPENDIX 5

POSITIONS OF NATIVISTS AND ENVIRONMENTALISTS

The following research is representative of nativist positions in psychology.

Bowlby's theory of attachment and loss. He claimed that infants cling to their mothers due to a survival instinct (nature) and not because mothers offer love and care (nurture, environment).[738]

Chomsky's universal grammar theory proposes that children are born with an innate, genetically determined capacity for the learning and development of language: a universal grammar.[739]

Freud's instinct theory of aggression describes two primitive forces: the life and death instincts. Both are driven innately by nature. They oppose each other in the subconscious and thus serve as the origin of desires to aggress.[740]

---

738 John Bowlby, *Attachment and Loss* (New York: Basic Books, 1969), xii—xv.

739 Noam Chomsky, *Aspects of the Theory of Syntax* (Cambridge, MA: MIT Press, 1969), 3–62.

740 Ben Karr, "Freudian Aggression Theory: Two Hypothesis," *Psychotherapy: Theory, Research and Practice*, vol. 8, no. 4 (1971).

REPRESENTATIVES OF ENVIRONMENTALIST POSITIONS

Bandura's social learning theory argues that a person learns aggression through observation, imitation, and modeling and, thus, from the environment (nurture).[741] His famous Bobo doll experiment (1961–1963) constituted an empirical approach to testing his theory that behavior can be acquired.[742]

Skinner's conceptualization of verbal behavior believed that language is learned behavior from other people via behavior-shaping techniques and thus under the control of eventualities.[743]

---

741 Albert Bandura, *Social Learning Theory* (Englewood Cliffs, NJ: Prentice Hall, 1977), 22.

742 A. Bandura, D. Ross, and S. A. Ross, 63(3), 575–582, "Transmission of Aggression Through Imitation of Aggressive Models," *Journal of Abnormal and Social Psychology*, vol. 63, no. 3 (1961), 575, 582.

743 B. F. Skinner, *Verbal Behavior* (New York: Appleton-Century-Crofts, 1957), 1–10.

LEADERSHIP

HISTORY AND DEVELOPMENT

Why is leadership one of the most widely researched and described activities in business literature? There is a mystique and fascination about leadership roles that might be rooted in the fact that they are often aspired to but rarely obtained. This could be why leadership triggers various emotions, feelings, and attitudes. These may involve associations with power, authority, heroism, celebrity, and idolization, and also perceptions of support for and care of subordinates, service, and commitment.[744]

The personality of a leader, e.g., a CEO, can have a very strong impact on a company's culture, its people and, consequently, its performance. Various theories regarding leadership qualities have emerged within the fields of psychology, management and anthropology. Although these theories differ in focus and perspective, they agree on one key point: organizations need the right leaders. But which criteria are necessary for a person to qualify as "right?"

---

744 Long, "Images of Leadership," 1.

DEFINITIONS AND THEORIES OF LEADERSHIP

Many leadership training courses focus on the traits, skills, and/or behavior of leaders. Yet there is a wide range of opinions on what leadership is and what leadership traits, skills, and behaviors are. This raises questions about how such training can be effective.

Leadership definitions and quotes are numerous and include:[745]

1. Simplified: "Managers are people who do things right and leaders are people who do the right thing." (W. G. Bennis & B. Nanus)
2. Related to success and influence: "Leadership is measured by success and effectiveness. A leader is successful when the person he or she is trying to influence demonstrates the desired behavior." (P. Forbes)
3. Confused with management: "Successful leaders and managers must use power—to influence others, to monitor results, and to sanction performance." (D. G. Winter)
4. Linked to authority: "Leadership has traditionally been synonymous with authority, and authority has traditionally been understood as the ability to command others, control subordinates and make all the truly important decisions yourself." (J. R. Katzenbach and D. K. Smith)

Philosophers, scholars, practitioners, and leaders have all tried to develop leadership models, approaches, and theories in order to improve leadership practices.[746] The next section will provide an overview of the main approaches to the study of leadership that are found in the scientific literature of the past century. The list is not comprehensive but intended to provide an overview based on a compilation of the work of a long list of leadership researchers and authors.

---

745 Richard A. Barker, "How Can We Train Leaders If We Do Not Know What Leadership Is?" *Human Relations*, vol. 50, no. 4 (1997), 343f.

746 Kilburg and Donohue, "Toward a 'Grand Unifying Theory' of Leadership," 8–11; Stippler et al., Führung, 11.

FIRST APPROACHES: PERSON-CENTERED THEORIES OF LEADERSHIP

The oldest leadership theories place the person at the center. There are three person-centered leadership theories: Great-Man Theory (focused on personality), Trait Theory (focused on traits that are stable across time and situations), and Skills Theory (focused on capabilities). In these theories, the influence of subordinates and context are not regarded as important. The first two approaches consider the major factors responsible for successful leadership as innate. Skills Theory, on the other hand, takes the view that capabilities can be developed and trained.[747]

LEADERSHIP STYLES

Next came research on leadership styles. Key approaches include Situational Leadership, Contingency Theory, and Goal Path Theory. These refute the assumption that characteristics can be consistently applied to good effect, and they acknowledge that leadership success is dependent on the personality of the leader plus the situation. They also consider leaders' behavior. In particular, they assume that situations can strongly influence if/how specific behaviors lead to success.[748]

However, leadership styles can be looked at from different angles. For example, if the focus lies on decision-making, styles can range from autocratic to democratic. If the interest lies in the way situations are dealt with by the leader, the descriptions can be charismatic, participative, situational, transactional, transformational, adaptive, quiet, or servant-like. Another way of looking at leadership styles is with a focus on task vs. people orientation.[749]

---

747 Stippler et al., Führung, 15.

748 Ibid., 19.

749 Robertson, "Leadership Theory vs. Leadership Style."

SYSTEMIC LEADERSHIP THEORIES

Other approaches focused not only on personality and behavior but also on organizations as a whole, as systems.[750]

From such perspectives, organizations are considered to be social systems that self-regulate and are not controllable/steerable from outside. Systemic leadership approaches have been particularly popular in the German-speaking world.

Another leadership theory that involves all employees in an organization is co-intrapreneurship. This aims to encourage self-initiative and self-responsibility among all employees so that they contribute to the execution of the corporate strategy.

Systemic approaches are fundamentally different from traditional management concepts that represent the view of leaders actively and effectively steering an organization's activities.

Four different schools base their approaches on this basic idea/understanding.[751] The oldest approach is the St. Gallen Management Model. It was first developed in the 1960s and has been further developed since. Other schools are the Wittener Approach, the Munich Approach, the Wiener Approach, and an approach developed by Daniel Pinnow.

RELATIONAL LEADERSHIP, TRANSFORMATIONAL LEADERSHIP, VALUES AND ETHICS

In the next category of theories, relationships between leaders and their teams move into the foreground.

TRANSFORMATIONAL LEADERSHIP THEORY

The theory of Transformational Leadership was first described in

---

750 Stippler et al., Führung, 33f.

751 Ibid., 34.

1978 by political scientist James MacGregor Burns and has remained popular since. Bernard Bass strongly influenced Burns's work, which assumes that leadership is based on shared visions and ethical-moral changes, and it is a process that transforms both leaders and subordinates, which enhances productivity and moral behavior. During the transformational process, a charismatic leader is responsible for recognizing and meeting the team's needs with the aim of developing a shared vision. The popularity of this theory is based on the inclusion of intrinsic motivation and the development of team members as well as their leaders.[752]

The leader is in charge of developing a vision for the entire organization that is meaningful, is based on the organization's basic values, and is long term. Another crucial aspect of Transformational Leadership is empowerment of employees to actively participate in achieving the company's vision and its related goals and collective purpose.[753]

Charisma is seen as an important leadership trait for transforming team members. Bass, however, emphasizes team members' needs, especially emotional ones, and believes that people need strong role models, and thus charisma is not sufficient.[754]

Critics such as Northouse state that this theory has no conceptual clarity and might lead to hero-worshipping. In addition, it can be argued that the approach of focusing on a leader's charisma might be aligned with Trait Theory. It also suggests that changes are instigated purely by leaders instead of leaders and teams. Team members might tend to blindly follow and not challenge the thoughts and actions of charismatic leaders. Last but not least, finding successors for charismatic leaders can be challenging as prospects may not have

752 Ibid., 54ff; Michael E. Brown and Linda K. Treviño, "Ethical Leadership: A Review and Future Directions," *Leadership Quarterly*, vol. 17 (2006), 598f; Shukurat Moronke Bello, "Impact of Ethical Leadership on Employee Job Performance," *International Journal of Business and Social Sciences*, vol. 3, no. 11 (2012), 229.

753 Stippler et al., Führung, 54ff; Brown and Treviño, "Ethical Leadership," 598f; Bello, "Impact of Ethical Leadership," 229.

754 Stippler et al., Führung, 54ff.

sustainable structures for keeping organizations alive through their engaging personalities.

Transformational leadership is often described as demarcation and contrasted to transactional leadership.

TRANSACTIONAL LEADERSHIP THEORY

According to Burns, transactional leadership is based on meeting the needs of the individual rather than general interests. It is founded on a reward-penalty system between leaders and those they lead. The leader controls both the path—enhance or impede—and the goal—provide or hold back rewards.[755]

VALUES AND ETHICS

There are also theories that especially include ethical behavior, values, and principles such as:

1. *Authentic Leadership:* Avolio, Luthans, and Walumbwa defined authentic leaders as "those individuals who are deeply aware of how they think and behave and are perceived by others as being aware of their own and other's values/moral perspective, knowledge, and strengths; aware of the context in which they operate; and who are confident, hopeful, optimistic, resilient, and high on moral character."[756]
2. Spiritual Leadership: Fry calls this, "The values, attitudes, and behaviors that are necessary to intrinsically motivate one's self and others so that they have a sense of spiritual survival through calling and membership."[757]
3. Ethical Leadership (see section)
4. Bad Leadership (see section)

---

755 Ibid., 55.

756 Bruce J. Avolio, Fred Luthans, Fred O. Walumbwa, "Authentic Leadership: Theory Building for Veritable Sustained Performance" [working paper, Gallup Leadership Institute, University of Nebraska-Lincoln, 2004, 4]).

757 Louis W. Fry, "Toward a Theory of Spiritual Leadership," *Leadership Quarterly*, vol. 14 (2003), 711.

ETHICAL LEADERSHIP

Probably the most well-known definition of ethical leadership comes from Brown, Teviño, and Hartman, and defines it as "the demonstration of normatively appropriate conduct through personal actions and interpersonal relationship, and the promotion of such conduct to followers through two-way communication, reinforcement, and decision-making."[758]

Similarities with transformational, authentic, and spiritual leadership are concern for others, ethical decision-making, integrity, and role-modeling. Common differences are that ethical leaders highlight moral management, which is more transactional. Individual differences are that authentic leaders accentuate self-awareness and authenticity; spiritual leaders emphasize visioning, hope/faith, and work as vocation; and transformational leaders point out intellectual stimulation, vision, and values.[759]

BAD LEADERSHIP

According to Barbara Kellerman, there are two categories of bad leadership: ineffective and unethical, with seven subgroups:[760]

1. Ineffective leadership. Incompetent (lack of will or skill to maintain effective action)
2. Rigid (may be competent but are stiff and unyielding, and unable or unwilling to adapt to new perspectives and different ideas)
3. Intemperate (lack of self-control which is supported by the followers)
4. Unethical leadership

---

758 M. E. Brown, L. K. Treviño, and D. A. Harrison, 97(2), 117–134., "Ethical Leadership: A Social Learning Perspective for Construct Development and Testing," *Organizational Behavior and Human Decision Processes*, vol. 97, no. 2 (2005), 120.

759 Brown, Treviño, and Harrison, "Ethical Leadership," 598.

760 Barbara Kellerman, *Bad Leadership,* (Boston: Harvard Business School Press, 2004), 38–48; Brown, Treviño and Harrison, "Ethical Leadership," 38–48.

5. Callous (not caring or not kind, ignores or devalues others' wishes and needs)
6. Corrupt (lies, cheats, or steals, sometimes supported by followers)
7. Insular (disregard for others' health and well-being outside of their group or organization)
8. Evil (commitment of atrocities, severe harm to others, pain as instrument of power)

CLASSICAL MODERNISM

Representatives of Classical Modernism[761] such as Warren Bennis, Peter Drucker, and Edgar Schein address holistic leadership. Most of these models ask for a holistic understanding of the self, including one's own values, strengths, and weaknesses. They postulate that leaders who have undergone a hard, genuine, thorough process of self-realization are better prepared to establish deep, collaborative relationships with their teams.

For many leaders, it is crucial to develop a clear identity. Bennis postulates that "becoming a leader is synonymous with becoming yourself. It's precisely that simple, and it's also that difficult." He further states that leadership is a constant, lifelong process during which leaders develop a clear picture of their inner voice, passions, values, and personal goals.

Bennis adds that a leader's inner voice emerges during a crisis. In *Geeks and Geezers* (together with Robert Thomas), he bases this claim on the results of interviews with leaders older than seventy (geezers: seventy to eight-two) and younger than thirty-five (geeks: twenty-one to thirty-four).[762] The results show that most leaders have had a drastic, life-changing and often difficult incident in their life that led to the acquisition of new skills. They have discovered a higher

---

761 Stippler et al., Führung, 13, 83ff.

762 "Geeks and Geezers: How Era, Values, and Defining Moments Shape Leaders," *Publishers Weekly*, https://www. publishersweekly.com/978-1-57851-582-0 (last visited August 22, 2017).

meaning and vision, and have developed the ability to include others in this higher meaning.

In addition, they have developed learning and leadership tools that cannot be explained by mere intelligence. One of these crucial skills is the adaptability to continue life despite its changes and losses. This ability allows them to handle difficult challenges without being marked by them. They actively try to acquire new skills during crises.

Drucker, Bennis, and a few others consider self-management as one of the most important tasks of a leader. In one of his works, Drucker describes five key skills leaders require to reach their goals: time management; deciding which contributions to the organization are most relevant; knowing one's own strengths and weaknesses; setting the right priorities; and choosing the right strategy. These capabilities are based on effectiveness (meaning doing the right things) that can be reached by a continuous perception of one's values and productive and unproductive behaviors.

All of these relatively recent approaches view holistic leadership as an important component for the success of an organization. The best leaders reduce their dependence on the status quo, consider personal and shared values, invite members and stakeholders of an organization to participate, regard the organization within a bigger system, and develop creative, adaptive processes to solve problems and work toward a joint, socially responsible future.

FOLLOWERSHIP AND LEADER-FOLLOWER INTERACTIONS AND THEORIES
WHAT ARE FOLLOWERS AND WHY DO THEY FOLLOW?

Leadership is a relationship. Without followers, there would be no relationship and, thus, no leadership. If there were a leadership equation, leaders would be on one side, and followers on the other side. Followers, like leaders, all have their own personalities and senses of identity. They are human beings with emotions, values, thoughts, and personal stories.

This section focuses not on leaders, but on those who are led: followers or subordinates. While some treat these two terms interchangeably, others believe that leaders have followers and managers have subordinates.[763] In this book, the two terms will be used interchangeably.

Followership exists in every aspect of life: in sports, politics, military, and religion, followership has a long-standing tradition. When it comes to being or becoming a leader, however, the importance of followership often gets neglected or undervalued. No organized effort can be sustained without the contribution of followers.[764]

Followers are often underestimated or forgotten in discussion of the leadership puzzle, yet their personalities and actions strongly influence their leaders. Similar to exploring different leadership styles, researchers and others have come up with constructs for assessing followership. Robert Kelley quoted in Blackshear,[765] for example, states that it is not enough to understand motivations and perceptions that lead to effective followership. He examined the behavior that leads someone to perform better or worse.

The two underlying dimensions measure followers' independent critical thinking and assess their activity/passivity. He identified the following five patterns and types of followers based on their behavior and thinking:

1. **Sheep or Passive Followers**: Passive do as they are told and do not think critically.
2. **Yes People or Conformist Followers**: More participative than pas-

---

763 Vineet Nayar, "Three Differences Between Managers and Leaders," *Harvard Business Review,* (August 2, 2013).

764 Patsy B. Blackshear, "The Followership Continuum: A Model for Increasing Organizational Productivity," *Innovation Journal: The Public Sector Innovation Journal,* vol. 9, no. 1 (2014), 3.

765 Peter Baker Blackshear, "A Model for Increasing Organizational Productivity," *The Public Sector Innovation Journal* 9, no. 1 (2004): 4.

sive followers, but rather deferential if not servile and thus do not provide particular challenges.

3. **Alienated Followers**: Deep and independent thinkers who do not willingly commit to any leader. But they are passive and often cynical. They prefer passive resistance instead of offering inputs.

4. **Effective or Exemplary Followers**: Ideal in almost all ways, excelling at all tasks, engaging strongly with the group and providing intelligent yet sensitive support and challenge to the leader. They are liked for being risk-takers, self-starters, and independent problem solvers. They can even be successful without strong leadership. They are able to manage themselves well, show high commitment to an organization, purpose, principle, or person, build their competencies, and show courage, honesty, and credibility.

5. **Survivor or Pragmatic Followers**: Positioned in the very center of the above four quadrants, they are middling in their independence, engagement, and general contribution. They are adept in surviving change.

Kelley's typology raises the question of whether the followers depend on the circumstances or inherent, enduring traits. Nor does it explain how a follower can develop and thus move from one category into another.

It would be interesting and helpful to analyze how the five follower types interact with different leadership styles. For example, why would an alienated follower, as an independent thinker, become a follower? Structural factors are missing.

Other critical remarks are provided by Wilkinson.[766] On the positive side of Kelley's model, he sees the usefulness to distinguish between leaders and followers and the possibility to define a strategy for each follower type. The model helps foster the discussion of work effort and thinking effort, about independence and depth of thought. He acknowledges that critical, autonomous, and creative thinking and

---

766 David Wilkinson, "Kelly's Typology of Followership," *Ambiguity Advantage*, June 23, 2008, http:// ambiguityadvantage.blogspot.ch/2008/06/kellys-typology-of-followership.html (last visited March 9, 2018).

behavior are crucial for organizational development, which is not present in organizations that encourage control, compliance, and obedience.

However, Wilkinson argues that categorizing people triggers a tendency of typecasting them. He further addresses that many leaders use such models to manipulate people.

According to Kellerman, there are different reasons why people follow. Human beings have a need for simplicity and stability. Leaders offer a sense of order and certainty, which can be provided even by bad leaders. A leader is perceived as someone who takes responsibility for what is happening. Obedience to authority helps to keep things simple, especially under stress.[767]

TRANSFERENCE
WHY FOLLOWERS BEHAVE IN CERTAIN WAYS AND LEADER-FOLLOWER INTERACTION

Followers have their own identities that are shaped by things other than their leaders. As with every human being, followers can be irrational and difficult to control and lead. Psychoanalysts might argue that this is because followers unconsciously project their thoughts and emotions in interactions with their superiors.[768] From this perspective, such behavior is based on what Freud refers to as transference (a false connection).[769]

Transference is "a displacement of patterns of feelings, thoughts, and behavior, originally experienced in relation to significant figures during childhood, onto a person involved in a current interpersonal relationship. Transference represents a confusion of time, person, and

---

767 Kellerman, *Bad Leadership*, 22f.

768 Michael Maccoby, "Why People Follow the Leader: The Power of Transference," *Harvard Business Review*, vol. 82 (2004), 2.

769 Kets de Vries, "Putting Leaders on the Couch," 5; Kets de Vries et al., *Coach and Couch*, 233.

place."[770] In this case, followers might misinterpret the reality of their situations in the way they respond to their leaders. They act as if the leader is an important authority person from childhood, such as a parent. Followers then project former hopes and dreams onto the leader.[771]

The basis for transference is the need to deal with feelings of helplessness that stem from childhood experience.[772] Transference comes in two complementary forms: mirroring and idealization.

MIRRORING

The word *mirror* originates in the Latin word *mirare* and means "to look at, to wonder, or to admire."[773] The person, e.g., a leader, looks for his or her own reflection in another person, e.g., a follower, to boost self-esteem.[774]

Winnicott said in 1971 that the mother's face can be considered the first mirror that a baby looks at. Therefore, the baby sees itself. The mirror's/mother's reflection/reaction is crucial. Changes that babies notice in their mothers' faces affect the quality of the development their emotions. This is a process that never stops in life. It helps explain why people see their own fears, desires, failures, and successes in others. Positive reactions from a mother to her infant's narcissistic displays can get retriggered in leadership positions. These unconscious behavior patterns are common to all leaders and can lead to what Kets de Vries calls "mirror hunger" in extreme cases: a hunger for ongoing appreciation and approval from subordinates, which helps keep the equilibrium of the psyche.[775]

---

770 M. G. Thompson, *The Ethic of Honesty: The Fundamental Rule of Psychoanalysis* (Rodopi, 2004), 80.

771 Kippenberger, "The Dark Side of Leadership," 12.

772 Kets de Vries, "The Organizational Fool," 756.

773 Kets de Vries, *Leaders, Fools and Impostors*, 7.

774 Manfred F. R. Kets de Vries, "Dysfunctional Leadership," *INSEAD: Faculty & Research*, vol. 58 (2003), 5f.

775 Kets de Vries, "The Organizational Fool," 756.

This is also why subordinates displace their hopes and fantasies onto their present leaders and interpret their behaviors in light of images they have created of them. It is a seduction for leaders to think that they really are the illusory species their followers have created. But being a leader involves much more than just serving as a mirror on which others project their hopes and fantasies.[776]

Mirroring can also have advantages. During crisis or change, it helps create a common vision and commitment to aligned action. Most leaders are not averse to mirroring, and admiration by subordinates can be highly satisfactory.[777]

IDEALIZING

Idealizing is the opposite of mirroring. Idealization is when a person, e.g., a follower, looks for another person, e.g., a leader, to idealize and admire so that he or she feels powerful and protected.[778]

Subordinates may try to deal with feelings of helplessness they experienced in their infancy. By idealizing their leaders, they can reinforce their own power position. Their wishful thinking is to become one with or be part of the leader who possesses all the great and almost celestial qualities they themselves would like to have.[779]

Mirroring and idealizing reinforce each other. They can lead to positive or destructive consequences. In the positive case, they can create and enhance group cohesion and orientation. However, if this dynamic remains unrecognized, it can become too powerful and flip into the negative. For example, leaders may harm others if unable

---

776 Kets de Vries, "Leaders, Fools and Impostors," 10.

777 Ibid., 14.

778 Kets de Vries, "Dysfunctional Leadership," 5f.

779 Kets de Vries, "The Organizational Fool," 756.

to do a reality check or lacking a secure sense of self, due to being unaware of what they are doing.[780]

Leaders who show strong narcissistic traits enjoy admiration, which might lead to a dependency on this emotional fix. Mutual admiration can become dangerous because of selective—distorted—perception (seeing and hearing what you want to).[781]

If a follower decides not to participate in a task assigned by the leader, the latter can interpret such behavior as a personal attack, which might call back feelings of humiliation or helplessness from the past and evoke frustration, anger, or rage. It is not uncommon that people get anxious and regress into childhood behaviors if they feel intimidated. They activate defense mechanisms by identifying with anger displayed by the leader. Thus, they can move from the target object to the threatening one. Given transference, there are only two options available: to be in favor of or against a leader. Independent thinking is absent.[782]

POSITIVE AND NEGATIVE TRANSFERENCE

Positive transference can have an impact on productivity, e.g., when employees see their superiors as parent figures and do everything possible to demonstrate maximal commitment and make them happy. This happens unconsciously.[783]

But such dynamics can change suddenly if employees believe that their expectations are no longer met, for example if they feel they were passed over for promotion. This can reopen long-forgotten childhood wounds, e.g., a sibling being preferred to oneself despite one's perceived superiority. Therefore, *negative transference* happens when employees see reflections in their bosses that unconsciously

---

780 Ibid., 756f.

781 Kippenberger, "The Dark Side of Leadership," 12.

782 Ibid., 12.

783 Maccoby, "Why People Follow the Leader," 4.

remind them of negative experiences with a parent. Therefore, they fight their bosses.

When external factors such as stress or crisis change an organization's dynamic, transference can strongly impact relationships. Leaders might be too occupied with change and fail to take enough care of their followers, who, as a result, may start to behave irrationally (e.g., being reminded of lack of appreciation from a parent).

Transference cuts through culture, age, and gender. It can get very complicated. For example, a male superior can be the subject of maternal transference and does not need to be seen as a father figure.

Images that are projected are shaped by family cultures. Changing family structures relating to divorce, single parenthood, both parents working, etc., alter the impact that parents have on a child. It can be a child's sibling, grandparent, or nanny who leaves the most significant mark. This tendency may have a positive impact in emerging flat-hierarchical organizational structures, as they call for greater teamwork. For instance, sibling leaders, especially middleborns, are theoretically used to negotiating and mediating, and so may be well placed to lead companies that focus on team-oriented project business.

It is possible for a person to have multiple transferences. For example, an employee could experience his direct superior as his mother when he was a child and the company's overall CEO whom he has never met (but seen or heard of) as his father when he was a baby (as an ideal yet distant parent). And to add complexity to the concept, transference is very often mutual, which means that not only do the followers project their childhood emotions onto their bosses, but their bosses might do the same to them. One example would be an employee who sees her boss as her favorite brother, whom she has idealized. In turn, her boss can see her as his withholding mother. This situation is called countertransference.[784]

---

784 Ibid., 4.

Because transference can be a double-edged sword, it is crucial for leaders to try to understand and analyze the concepts of both transference and countertransference. They then need to discuss their relationships with their subordinates so that objectivity can be reestablished. Leaders who work in cross-cultural environments should keep in mind that different cultures have different understandings of parents' roles. This alters the face of the transference (authority vs. obedience, loyalty vs. coaching, empowerment vs. independence). With continuing globalization and increased diversity, stereotyping becomes less and less accurate, which makes it even more crucial for leaders to understand employees' individual motivations.[785]

As long as followers' motivation to follow their bosses is present and works, it is not important whether this motivation is real (based on a realistic assessment of the current relationship) or not (related to an experience with an authority figure from the past because of transference). But it is an advantage if leaders know their own transferences so that they can positively influence their followers to increase mutual understanding. An outside view can help, for example, a qualified coach who is trained in this specific field as described in chapter 8 (more on coaching in chapter 8, "Detecting and Avoiding Danger").

---

785 Ibid., 4.

APPENDIX 7

HOGAN DEVELOPMENT SURVEY (HDS)

As described in chapter 5, the word *dark* refers to the primitive, negative, unconscious emotions and impulses of human beings, such as striving for power, greed, envy, selfishness, or rage.

The overreliance on the five-factor model, or Big Five, called for research that went beyond the five dimensions of personality (extroversion, neuroticism, agreeableness, conscientiousness, and openness to experience). Most modern research involving dark personality focuses on the Dark Triad (discussed in chapter 5 and chapter 8) and the DSM-IV Axis II disorder.

The DSM-IV Axis II disorder emphasizes the dark side as negative characteristics—qualities that can disrupt relationships, damage reputations, and derail peoples' chances of success. They arise in times of increased strain. The subclinical versions of the DSM-IV Axis II disorder are often measured with the Hogan Development Survey (HDS), which identifies eleven interpersonal themes. Each of these dispositions has a positive (bright) and negative (dark) side. If the positive side is not handled well, it flips into the negative or even destructive.

INTIMIDATION (MOVING AWAY)
EXCITABLE

1. Positive: enthusiastic; excited about people, the organization and tasks.
2. Negative: volatile, easy to disappoint, disposed to anger and frustration, need for respect and understanding, moody, irritable, hard to satisfy.
3. Childhood: experienced disappointment or exploitation by others.
4. Consequence: Looking for clues of rejection, shows emotional outbursts or withdrawal. Strong emotions are illusionary. They believe they are in control and at the same time keep distance from others to avoid a potential threat.

SKEPTICAL

1. Positive: shrewd.
2. Negative: does not trust others and doubts their plans; in turn, expects to be mistreated; cynical, insensitive to criticism, irritable.
3. Childhood: experienced lack of trust or mistreatment.
4. Consequence: retreats from others to increase control; often shows anger or pugnacity; sensitive to politics.

CAUTIOUS

1. Positive: careful.
2. Negative: cautious, cannot accept criticism, experiences feelings of rejection, afraid of making a mistake, immune to positive feedback, rule-bound.
3. Childhood: learned that unsuccessful experiences are related to a defect that makes them different from others.
4. Consequences: does everything to prevent unpredictable situations, including social interactions and taking decisions.

RESERVED

1. Positive: independent.
2. Negative: prefers working alone over working in a group, socially insensitive, highly rational, self-focused, and self-sufficient.
3. Childhood: n/a.
4. Consequence: immune to any type of feedback and does not provide feedback; welcomes others calling them tough, resilient, and independent.

LEISURELY

1. Positive: focused.
2. Negative: does not express strong feelings such as frustration directly, perceived as incompetent, envious and resentful toward successful people, inflexible, stubborn.
3. Childhood: socialization experienced early in life.
4. Consequence: has own (hidden) agenda.

FLIRTATION AND SEDUCTION (MOVING AGAINST)
BOLD

1. Positive: confident, leaves a strong first impression.
2. Negative: arrogant, believes in own uniqueness and exceptionality, ignores weaknesses, opinionated.
3. Childhood: experienced overpampering and did not learn to accept boundaries and discipline.
4. Consequence: insensitive to the effects of own behavior; believes in two-class systems of leaders and subordinates and sees self as belonging to the first.

MISCHIEVOUS

1. Positive: vivacious, charming, good first impression.
2. Negative: dramatic, antisocial, risk-taker, tests the limit and crosses borders, does not like to comply with social norms, manipulative, impulsive, more hot air than substance.

3. Childhood: n/a.
4. Consequences: hard to advise, does not think through the consequences of actions.

COLORFUL

1. Positive: amiable, extrovert, good performance on public stage, has a positive aura, perceived as charismatic and competent.
2. Negative: they tend to confuse attention with accomplishment; are self-centered, impulsive, over committed, doubt their abilities.
3. Childhood: experienced that charm and talent to entertain (and not competence and accomplishment), lead to attention and approval.
4. Consequence: they do not trust their own capabilities; are afraid that others might uncover their weaknesses; show exhibitionistic and entertaining elements under pressure instead of effectiveness and productivity.

IMAGINATIVE

1. Positive: creative, imaginative.
2. Negative: eccentric, socially insensitive but enjoys interaction with others; they believe they are unique and show a need to emphasize creativity over practicality.
3. Childhood: n/a.
4. Consequence: immune to negative feedback, criticism and even rejection.

COMPLIANCE (MOVING TOWARD)
DILIGENT

1. Positive: hard working, organized, diligent.
2. Negative: perfectionist; prefers rules, standards, and guidelines, as does not trust independent thinking when it comes to performance; cannot delegate; critical.
3. Childhood: experienced a high level of performance orientation in which work below a certain standard was not acceptable.

4. Consequence: thinks in black or white (either you are perfect, or you fail), so cannot objectively evaluate a given assignment.

DUTIFUL

1. Positive: pleasant, agreeable, dutiful.
2. Negative: has not learned to think independently, no sense of competence and self-efficacy, does not believe in own strengths, looking for approval, pleaser, indecisive.
3. Childhood: experienced a high level of nurturing as a child, in which caregivers did not decrease the nurturing level when the child became more self-sufficient.
4. Consequence: does not know the experience of mastery; dependent on others for decision-making.

GENDER GAP

President Geun-hye Park of South Korea was the first democratically elected leader in her country to be forced from office.[786] The parliament impeached Park after mass demonstrations calling for her to be removed because of a scandal concerning her long-time friend, Samsung heir Choi Soon-sil. She was detained in custody right after she was dismissed. She was accused of eighteen charges, including bribery (over $50 million), coercion, and abuse of power regarding government favors toward tycoons such as Samsung heir Lee Jae Yong (also put on trial), and sentenced to twenty-four years in prison.[787]

Is there a difference in gender when it comes to derailment? Do women behave differently from men if increased pressure or change shifts the power balance and endangers their authority? Do they utilize valves other than fraud, excess, or conflicts? How do their unconscious

---

786 South Korea's presidential scandal, *BBC News*, http://www.bbc.com/news/world-asia-37971085 (last visited July 28, 2017).

787 "Sentencing of South Korea Ex-Leader Park Geun Hye and Samsung Heir May Go Live on TV," *Straits Times*, July 26, 2017, http://www.straitstimes.com/asia/east-asia/sentencing-of-south-korea-ex-leader-park-geun-hye-and-samsung-heir-may-go-live-on-tv; Choe Sang-Hun, "Park Geun-hye, South Korea's Ousted President, Gets 24 Years in Prison," *New York Times*, April 6, 2018, https://www.nytimes.com/2018/04/06/world/asia/park-geun-hye-south-korea.html.

patterns acquired in childhood play out in leadership positions? Do women have different leadership styles from men?

WOMEN IN SENIOR MANAGEMENT ROLES (C-LEVEL)

Grant Thornton, an international organization of independent assurance, tax, and advisory companies, publishes an annual survey. Based on 5,526 interviews of listed and nonlisted companies in thirty-six economies, their 2017 results revealed the proportion of women in senior business positions rose from 22 percent in 2015 to 24 percent in 2106 to 25 percent in 2017, the highest number ever reached. Concurrently, the percentage of businesses with no women also increased: from 32 percent in 2015 to 33 percent in 2016 to 34 percent in 2017. In terms of diversity in leadership, developing countries outperformed major economies.[788]

According to further findings in the survey, in the G7 countries (Canada, France, Germany, Italy, Japan, UK and US), 39 percent of businesses had no women at senior levels (same as 2016). With only 22 percent of senior business positions being filled by women (same as 2016), these seven countries performed worse than many others. These low numbers were present despite widespread public proclamations of support for equality and research evidence that diversity adds to performance. Moreover, in the survey, it was found that reports from Eastern Europe of 38 percent and the Association of Southeast Asian Nations (ASEAN) of 36 percent showed the highest percentage of women in leadership positions. In Eastern Europe, only 9 percent of businesses had no women in senior positions.[789]

In the ultimate decision of selecting a CEO, it might be reasonable to assume that BoDs feel more comfortable selecting candidates who have behavioral attributes that match typical CEO profiles. However,

---

788 Dina Medland, "Today's Gender Reality in Statistics, Or Making Leadership Attractive to Women," *Forbes*, March 7, 2016, https://www.forbes.com/sites/dinamedland/2016/03/07/todays-gender-reality-in-statistics-or-making-leadership-attractive-to-women/#58e2ae2a6883; Grant Thornton, *Women in Business: New Perspectives on Risk and Reward*, Grant Thornton International, 2017, 1–12.

789 Medland, "Today's Gender Reality in Statistics"; Thornton, *Women in Business*, 1–12.

behavioral attributes are evaluated differently depending upon who displays them.[790] Female executives can receive a negative evaluation for traits that, in a man, are seen as positive, e.g., action-orientation, decisiveness, and a leader-like attitude.[791]

People tend to feel more comfortable with behavior that is in line with stereotypes or perceived roles (refer to the Stereotype Content Model developed by Fiske, Cuddy, Glick, and Xu[792]). Women who are seen as exhibiting rather masculine leadership traits may be perceived as violating expected behavioral norms. At the same time, however, women demonstrating so-called feminine traits may be perceived as less competent than their male counterparts. This is a double-edged sword that might work against the success and/or development of female executives. A similar pattern can be found with ethnic minorities.[793]

WOMEN ON BODS

According to EZI Egon Zehnder International's Global Board Diversity Analysis, in 2018, still only 20.4 percent of the board directors in the forty-four countries studied were women—at least up from 13.6 percent in 2012. During the same time span, the number of board director positions held by women in Western Europe has increased from 15.6 percent to 29 percent. Percentages vary, but there has been a clear trend toward more women on boards.[794]

790 Larcker, Miles, and Tayan, "Seven Myths of CEO Succession," *Stanford Closer Look Series*, 2014, 4.

791 Laurie A. Rudman and Peter Glick, "Feminized Management and Backlash Toward Agentic Women: The Hidden Costs of Women of a Kinder, Gentler Image of Middle Manager," *Journal of Personality and Social Psychology*, vol. 77, no. 5 (1999), 1004–1010.

792 Fiske et al., "A Model of (Often Mixed) Stereotype Content: Competence and Warmth Respectively Follow From Perceived Status and Competition," *Journal of Personality and Social Psychology*, vol. 82, no. 6 (2002), 899.

793 Gruenfeld, "Having Power and Influence," *TrendHunter*, https://www.trendhunter.com/about-trend-hunter (last visited November 3, 2017).

794 Global Board Diversity Tracker published by Egon Zehnder International, Inc., 2018, 'Who's Really on Board?' information from page 5.

WHY THE GENDER GAP?

Although there are more women in nonexecutive director positions, the number of women in top management has not increased much. This is despite trends of organizations moving toward service orientation and cross-cultural business in which women have demonstrated stronger skills than men.[795]

Kets de Vries critically questions the "many explanations given" regarding the gender gap in business, referring primarily to the idea that "anatomy-is-destiny," e.g., there is a biological basis for gendered behavior. He acknowledges that there may be truth to this account but suggests other possible explanations, as follows:[796]

1. Pregnancy and childrearing (the responsibility for which typically falls on women) can happen during critical career phases and thus get in the way of career planning and development.
2. Women may not want to give in to the compromises and sacrifices that top management positions may ask.
3. Some men prefer being among men and are less comfortable with women in a group.
4. Some men do not feel comfortable with a female boss, who might remind them of their mother.
5. Heterosexual men may not find it easy to mentor women. They may be afraid of potential feelings, the reaction of their spouse, or in some countries, a potential sexual harassment case.

All of those theories aside, Kets de Vries is convinced that diversity adds to better decision-making and problem solving. A gender balance can provide different perspectives and insights that help encourage healthy debates. Homogenous groups might run the risk of groupthink and making consensus prematurely.[797]

---

795 Kets de Vries, "The Leadership Mystique," 257.

796 Ibid., 258–260.

797 David F. Larcker and Brian Tayan, "Pioneering Women on Boards: Pathways of the First Female Directors," *Stanford Closer Look Series* at Stanford Graduate School of Business, 2013, 1.

Pittinsky, Bacon, and Welle disapprove of differentiating women's and men's leadership styles, as it encourages stereotypical thinking. They recommend a degendering of leadership so that no gender is associated with a specific leadership style.[798]

Therefore, the much smaller percentage of women in CEO or board positions compared to their male counterpart might explain the fewer cases of derailment that include a female leader. In order to underline or oppose this reason, further research and studies are needed.

In regard to female leaders, it is difficult to draw generalizations about the link between their success and their upbringing since there are not yet enough female leaders in business. But according to Kets de Vries, many of today's successful female leaders seem to have been their fathers' favorite "sons."[799]

798 Stippler et al., Führung, 98.

799 Kets de Vries, "Putting Leaders on the Couch," 2.

APPENDIX 9

CEO AND CHAIRPERSON TURNOVER AT YAHOO AND HEWLETT-PACKARD

YAHOO

1. Terry Semel, chairperson and CEO, resigned in 2007.
2. Jerry Yang, co-founder of Yahoo, took over as CEO in 2007 and replaced Terry Semel.
3. Carol Bartz took the CEO position in 2009 following Yang's resignation after he received only 66 percent support at the annual meeting.
4. Yahoo's BoD replaced Bartz two-and-a-half years later with former PayPal executive, Scott Thomson, after she failed to achieve the performance targets.
5. Five months later, it came out that Thomson had misrepresented his educational records. He resigned and was replaced by Marissa Mayer, a former Google executive.
6. In 2017, Mayer was forced out and replaced by Thomas J. McInerney after the acquisition by Verizon.

What was left of Yahoo was renamed Altaba.

HEWLETT-PACKARD

CEOS

1. Carly Fiorina: CEO from July 1999 to February 2005. Fiorina was forced out (she technically resigned) after a merger with Compaq failed. During her tenure, the company's stock price fell by 50 percent.
2. Robert Wayman: interim CEO from February 2005 to March 2005.
3. Mark Hurd: CEO from April 2005 to August 2010. Hurd was forced out after submitting false expense reports, apparently to hide a relationship with a former employee.
4. Cathie Lesjak: interim CEO from August 2010 to September 2010.
5. Léo Apotheker: (president and) CEO from September 2010 to September 2011. During his tenure, his financial outlook was cut back three times so that the BoD lost confidence that the company could reach its sales targets. Raymond J. Lane (executive chairperson from September 2011 to April 2013) stated that Apotheker lacked execution and communication.
6. Meg Whitman: (president and) CEO of HP from September 2011 to November 2015; CEO of HPE from November 2015 to January 2018.
7. Dion Weisler: CEO of HP Inc. from November 2015 to present (as of April 2018).
8. Antonio Neri: (president since June 2017) and CEO of HPE from February 2018 to present (June 2020).

CHAIRPERSONS OR PRESIDENTS

1. Michael Capellas: president from May 2002 to November 2002.
2. Pattie Dunn: nonexecutive chairperson from February 2005 to September 2006. Dunn was let go after it was found that she was involved in a secret attempt to stop boardroom media leaks by spying on fellow directors and journalists.
3. Mark Hurd: chairperson from September 2006 to August 2010.

4. Léo Apotheker: president (and CEO) from September 2010 to September 2011.
5. Raymond J. Lane: executive chairperson from September 2011 to April 2013.
6. Ralph V. Whitworth: nonexecutive chairperson from April 2013 to July 2014.
7. Meg Whitman: chairperson of HP Inc. from November 2015 to July 2017.
8. Chip Bergh: chairperson of HP Inc. from July 2017 to present (October 2020).

LOCC: LEADERS' ORAL COLLABORATION CONTRACT

PART I: BRIEFING

A LOCC is a type of Psychological Contract between any two leaders. Thus, it is a relational contract that, by its nature, is subjective, long term, broad, and focuses on intrinsic factors. A LOCC requires a high personal commitment and has a higher tendency of violation than other agreements because of inherent ambiguity (diverging interpretations of promissory obligations). Therefore, it needs to be clearly discussed.

The LOCC is an orally discussed contract and therefore not to be signed. It focuses on the "how" (how roles need to be filled) and not only on the "what" (mere descriptions of the roles). The "how" brings the "what" to life. It is a process of talking out one's own and the counterpart's roles.

EXTERNAL FACILITATOR

It is important that a third party lead the discussion, so the leader among the two involved in the LOCC who either is the superior in line or usually wins the power game cannot exercise more power over the process than the other. The focus lies on the discussion.

- The facilitator could be a mediator, an executive coach, an executive recruiter, or an HR director.
- It needs to be someone both parties trust and select together.

FORM

- It is important this is a strictly oral discussion. There is no note taking or written recording because that would make it too transactional. The focal point is the communication between the two team members.
- Most often, the first session is the most uncomfortable. It gets easier with practice, but two to three additional sessions might be needed.

CONFIDENTIALITY

- Strict confidentiality is of utmost importance.
- It is recommended the commitment to confidentiality be in written form.
- At the end of the process, the parties can agree on what information they want to share with others.

LOCATION

- The sessions should take place in a neutral environment—not in one of the leaders' offices and, ideally, not in one of the commonly used meeting rooms.

FREQUENCY

- Number and frequency of the sessions are defined by the parties and the facilitator, depending on the flow of the conversation, the content covered, and the progress made.

OUTPUT

- It is strongly recommended the completion of the process be shared with the board of directors (BoD) and the management team to increase public commitment and the incentive for each party to live up to their word. It also is a strong signal to the workforce, which most likely positively impacts the company's culture and productivity.
- It is up to the parties whether they want to share further details on certain discussion items.
- The parties need to discuss possible worst cases before they start; for example, how should the relationship be lived (e.g., communication, trust) in the rare case the process gets stopped or interrupted?

GOAL

A LOCC helps both parties do the following:

- Improve the frequency and quality of communication.
- Reach clarity on roles and define the power balance.
- Reestablish and nurture trust, a key element for a healthy LOCC.
- Positively influence the various conscious and unconscious elements described.
- Avoid contract breach, which occurs when one party perceives the other party has failed to fulfill their promises. Breach is perceived.
- Prevent contract violations, which are displayed through strong emotional reactions to breaches (e.g., feelings of betrayal, anger, resentfulness). Violation is felt.
- Positively impact the leaders' relationship, which helps increase their psychological and physical health, improve company culture and working environment, and increase productivity and, ultimately, performance.
- Have a healthy relationship not only in good times but especially during crisis and times of pressure.

PART II: TEMPLATE OF DISCUSSION POINTS

CONSCIOUS DRIVERS

Trust

- How do you define trust? What does trust mean to you?
- How do you grant trust? Do you tend to initially give the benefit of the doubt or mistrust that improves with positive results?
- How would you describe the level of trust between you two?
- How are you going to increase and nurture trust in this relationship?

Role Clarity

- Is there clarity about each of your roles?
- Have you ever discussed in depth the chairperson and CEO roles (the "what" and the "how"—how the roles are fulfilled)?
- Is there a role history that influences role misinterpretations?
- How will you address and discuss future issues and misunderstandings?
- Going forward, agree on whose job it is to ensure role clarity.

UNCONSCIOUS DRIVERS

Corporate Governance That Is Lived (the "how," not just the "what")

- Discuss the leadership (e.g. Chairperson's) role (scope; interfaces; responsibilities; who is in charge of what, when, and how).
- Discuss the counterpart's (e.g. CEO's) role (ditto).
- Compare and contrast: How aligned are your views, perceptions, and expectations? Do your former roles influence your perspectives of your current roles? Where are overlaps of responsibilities, and how are you going to tackle them?
- Intensely discuss the two roles until you reach clarity and feel comfortable with your understandings of them.
- Who represents the company when and how? Which potential situations might be critical and lead to conflicts?

Power

- How do you define power?
- What does power mean to you?
- How would you describe the power balance between you two?
- Going forward, agree on how to handle the division of power.

Time Spent

- How much time do you spend together, and how do you spend that time? Do you perceive it as too little, enough, or too much? Why?
- What would be an ideal frequency and amount of time to spend together?
- Going forward, agree on where you are going to spend this time together (office versus neutral location; or go for lunch, dinner, a drink, or a hike).

Other

- Goals: What are your goals professionally and personally? Role clarity seems to increase the (legitimacy of) power to achieve goals. For this, a mutual understanding and alignment of goals are essential.
- Success: What does success mean to you?
- Communication: How would you describe the nature and quality of the communication between you two? Going forward, agree on how you are going to define and handle communication.
- Is there anything else you would like to share, discuss, or ask?

Pick up your company's job descriptions, organizational rules, and functional charts, if existent. Discuss them in the light of the newly gained insight and the trust further built. Draft necessary changes, and discuss and finalize them in the next board meeting.

PART III: SELF-REFLECTION (NOT TO BE DISCUSSED)

CONSCIOUS

(Anti-)Role Model

- Who was/is your role model or anti-role model?
- How has s/he shaped the way you perceive and exercise leadership?
- What type of role model do you want to be yourself?

UNCONSCIOUS

Transference

"a displacement of patterns of feelings, thoughts, and behavior originally experienced in relation to significant figures during childhood onto a person involved in a current interpersonal relationship"[800]

- Which authority figure from your past does your counterpart remind you of, if any? Take time to think about it. Is the transference positively or negatively connoted?
- How has transference unconsciously impacted your relationship with your counterpart? Is your perception still accurate and your behavior productive, or can and should they be changed?

Family Origin

- How has your family and upbringing impacted you? What is the earliest memory of your childhood that comes to your mind?
- Has there been a life-changing incident that has marked you?
- Which values were held high in your family? Do they differ from the ones you hold high and promote today?
- What are your patterns and worldview? Where do they originate?
- What emotional reactions are you known for? What situations trigger these emotions?
- Do you interpret your environment in a way that reinforces and confirms your prior knowledge, attitudes, or beliefs?
- How much do you know about your counterpart's upbringing?

---

800 American Psychoanalytic Association, *Psychoanalytic Terms and Concepts*, edited by B.E. Moore and B.D. Fine (New Haven: Yale University Press, 1990), 196.

INTENSIFIERS
Birth Order

- What was your niche in your family? What role did you play?
- How has your birth-order rank marked you? And your siblings?
- How would you describe your role in your family today, and what is the relation of your family role to the role you play in business?
- How were your relationships with your sibling(s) and parents when you were growing up? And how are they today?
- How do your behavioral patterns impact family and friends?

(Self-)Awareness

- How would you rate your level of (self-)awareness? Why?
- How do you rate your counterpart's level of (self-)awareness?
- How can your (self-)awareness be improved?
- Is (self-)reflection part of your routine? How often do you reflect, how, and for how long? Thinking (reviewing, strategizing, overseeing, deciding) and reflecting (making use of preliminary thoughts, emotions, ideas) are not the same.
- Have you ever had or considered a coach? Why (not)?
- How do you want to be remembered? Do you live your life accordingly?
- Are you going to assume responsibility for your actions and behavior? What would you like to change? When and how?

ACKNOWLEDGMENTS

Along the winding road to writing this book, there is a long list of people who inspired, guided, and supported me.

I thank Oana Baloi, Simon Berger, Martin Bidermann, Susanne Giger, Doug Harbison, Adrian Kaegi, Dr. Thomas Ladner, Spiros Margaris, Olivia Mathijsen, Alex Miescher, Mariana Moura, Franziska Müller-Tiberini, Rajesh Ramani, Martin Schneider, Matthias Schmid-Huberty, Thomas Sieber, Fleur Smeets-Tonies, Amelia La Spada, Guy Spier, Walter Thurnherr, Dr. Jürg Wittwer, and Mascha Wolf for being such inspiring conversation partners, offering valuable insights, experiences, feedback, and ongoing encouragement.

My deep appreciation goes to the early readers of my work: Mark Bitz, Veit Dengler, Michelle Goldstone, Dr. Martin Neese, Ngaio and Brad Parker, Marike Schipper, and Patrick Villiger who provided critical feedback that helped me adjust my compass early on.

I'm indebted to the four institutions of which I am a proud master alumnae that have influenced, encouraged, and supported my research, presentations, and teaching: the Kellogg School of Management (Katie Nowak for opening many doors for me to speak and engage with curious, engaging students, executive education participants, and alumni), INSEAD (Professors Dr. Manfred Kets de Vries, Dr. Roger Lehman, and Dr. Erik van de Loo for their invaluable insights), Indian School of Business (ISB), and the University of St. Gallen (Professor Dr. Dr. h.c. Carl Baudenbacher for sharing his exceptional expertise, and my supervisor PD, Dr. Thomas Werlen, for his early guidance and precious support).

During the course of researching and writing, I've met with board members, business leaders, executive search consultants, and researchers from different fields and backgrounds who shared insights and helped me validate my own findings and experiences.

This work would not have been possible without my editors: Rose Lobban who provided editorial feedback. A very special thanks goes to Judy Smyer for her extraordinary and tireless work improving the coherence, consistency, and stringency of this book. The critical final round is owed to the exceptional work of Hal Clifford and Jane Borden. They and their team at Scribe Media, especially Kayla Sokol, have helped turn the manuscript into an actual book.

Finally, my deepest gratitude goes to my family: my husband Heinrich, my parents Gertrud and Niklaus, my brother Andreas, and my (step) children Alexia and Simon. Their emotional support and encouragement of my writing throughout this long journey kept me going.

ABOUT THE AUTHOR

As an international senior executive, **ISABELLE NÜSSLI** has lived it. Throughout her career, Isabelle's entrepreneurial mindset, strategic focus, and cross-cultural communication have connected her with a broad range of complex challenges in national and international business leadership.

With this diversified experience, Isabelle brings personal insights and strategic vision to her practice as a leadership and personal coach. As "chief energizing officer" of Leverage YourSelf AG, she directs a team of experts in business strategy, corporate governance, and applied psychology. She and her team support business leaders and startups in navigating changes and transformations, developing strong organizational dynamics at the human level, and capitalizing on their full potential.

Isabelle is the co-founder and chairperson of Responsible Leadership AG and its online learning platform and offline conference series "Self-Leadership-Days." She is a mentor at the startup incubator and accelerator F10, focusing on fintech, regtech, and insurtech. She is a partner at evitive ag, which specializes in strategic innovation and corporate venturing and accelerating. She serves on national and international academic and business boards and committees.

Isabelle is the author of *Cockfighting: Solving the Mystery of Unconscious Sabotage at the Top of the Corporate Pyramid*, an Amazon bestseller in the categories of corporate governance, communication in management, and business ethics.

She has held senior management positions in Switzerland and abroad. She was chairperson of NUSSLI Group, Switzerland, a leading international provider of infrastructures for sport and cultural events, such as the Olympics and World Expositions. Earlier roles with the company included global key account manager as well as CFO of the US subsidiaries.

Isabelle earned a master of business administration (MBA) from the Kellogg School of Management at Northwestern University, an executive master of European and international business law (E.M.B.L.-HSG) from the University of St. Gallen, and an executive master in consulting and coaching for change (EMCCC) from INSEAD.

BIBLIOGRAPHY

"31 Inspiring, Make-You-Think Travel Quotes," *HuffPost*, January 16, 2017, https://www.huffingtonpost.com/entry/31-inspiring-make-you-think-travel-quotes_us_5877e9f2e4b077a19d180c42.

ABB, "About ABB," www.abb.com (last visited May 7, 2018).

"ABI Research Corporate Governance Pays for Shareholders and Company Perfomance," ABI Association of British Insurers, February 2, 2008, https://www.abi.org.uk/News/News-releases/2008/02/ABI-Research-Corporate-governance-pays-for-shareholders-and-company-perfomance.

ACFE (Association of Certified Fraud Examiners), *Report to the Nations on Occupational Fraud and Abuse: 2016 Global Fraud Study.*

Acton Institute, Lord Acton Quote Archive, http://www.acton.org/research/lord-acton (last visited July 1, 2016).

Acton Institute, Lord Acton Quote Archive, http://www.acton.org/research/lord-acton (last visited May 1 2019).

"Adaptive Leadership Definition," TeamworkDefinition.com, http://teamworkdefinition.com/adaptiveleadership/ (last visited May 8, 2018).

Allen, Frederick E., "Sarbanes-Oxley 10 Years Later: Boards are Still the Problem," *Forbes*, July 29, 2012, https://www.forbes.com/sites/frederickallen/2012/07/29/sarbanes-oxley-10-years-later-boards-are-still-the-problem/#762381202345.

Allianz Global Corporate & Specialty, *Global Claims Review: Liability in Focus*, 2017.

Altman, Neil, "Wilfred Bion: From World War I to Contemporary Psychoanalysis," *International Journal of Applied Psychoanalytic Studies*, vol. 13, no. 2 (2016), 163–178.

Alvarez, Luis, "Could the CEO be Replaced by a Robot?" World Economic Forum, January 13, 2017, https://www.weforum.org/agenda/2017/01/could-the-ceo-be-replaced-by-a-robot/ (last visited April 17, 2017).

American Psychological Association, "The Road to Resilience: What Is Resilience?" http://www.apa.org/helpcenter/road-resilience.aspx (last visited November 27, 2017).

Anderson, Susan Leigh, "If Hollywood Has Taught Us Anything, It's That Robots Need Ethics," World Economic Forum, https://www.weforum.org/agenda/2016/12/robot-ethics-doing-the-right-thing-as-well-as-not-doing-the-wrong-thing (last visited April 17, 2017).

Anupama, Mary Bintu T.D., and Tapal Dulababu, "The Need of 720 Degree Performance Appraisal in the New Economy Companies," *ZENITH International Journal of Multidisciplinary Research*, vol. 1, no. 4 (2011).

APA/dpa, Fussball: FIFA-Präsident Infantino: Kämpfte als Baby um mein Leben, Tiroler Tageszeitung, http://www.tt.com/home/11183804-91/fußball-fifa-präsident-infantino-kämpfte-als-baby-um-mein-leben.csp (last visited June 4, 2016).

Armour, John, Henry Hansmann, and Reinier Kraakman, The Essential Elements of Corporate Law: What Is Corporate Law? 2009.

Aronson v. Lewis 473 A.2d 805, 812 (1984).

Aronson, Bruce, "The Toshiba Corporate Governance Scandal: How Can Japanese Corporate Governance be Fixed?" JURIST, August 10, 2015, http://www.jurist.org/forum/2015/08/bruce-aronson-toshiba-scandal.php.

Atkins, Ralph, "Suicide Highlights Swiss Executive Stress," SWI swissinfo.ch, June 1, 2016, http://www.swissinfo.ch/eng/zurich-insurance_suicide-highlights-swiss-executive-stress/42194504.

Atteslander, Peter, and Jürgen Cromm, Methoden der empirischen Sozialforschung, 13. neu bearb. und erw., Berlin 2010.

"Audit Committee Role & Responsibilities," CFA Institute, https://www.cfainstitute.org/en/advocacy/issues/audit-committee-role-practices.

"Audit Inspection and Surveillance Programs," Australian Securities & Investments Commission, http://asic.gov.au/regulatory-resources/financial-reporting-and-audit/auditors/audit-inspection-and-surveillance-programs/ (last visited March 8, 2018).

Authentic Leadership: Theory Building for Veritable Sustained Performance, 2004.

Avolio, Bruce J., Fred Luthans, and Fred O. Walumbwa, "Authentic Leadership: Theory Building for Veritable Sustained Performance," working paper, Gallup Leadership Institute, Universtiy of Nebraska-Lincoln.

Avolio, Bruce J., Fred O. Walumbwa, and Todd J. Weber, "Leadership: Current Theories, Research, and Future Directions," *Annual Review of Psychology*, vol. 60 (2009), 421–449.

awp/dpa, NZZ, Drei Sika-Verwaltungsräte sehen sich Verantwortlichkeitsklage gegenüber, https://www.nzz.ch/wirtschaft/newsticker/drei-sika-verwaltungsraete-sehen-sich-verantwortlichkeitsklage-gegenueber-1.18543256 (last visited July 31, 2017).

Bacal, Robert, "Organizational Conflict—The Good, the Bad & the Ugly," World of Work, http://work911.com/articles/orgconflict.htm (last visited February 23, 2017).

Bajic, Elena, "Why Companies Need to Build More Diverse Boards," *Forbes*, August 11, 2015, https://www.forbes.com/sites/elenabajic/2015/08/11/why-companies-need-to-build-more-diverse-boards/#5798d758662c.

Balkhi, Syed, "25 Biggest Corporate Scandals Ever," *List 25*, October 29, 2018, http://list25.com/25-biggest-corporate-scandals-ever/.

Bandura, A., D. Ross, and S. A. Ross, "Transmission of Aggression through Imitation of Aggressive Models," *Journal of Abnormal and Social Psychology*, vol. 63, no. 3 (1961), 575–582.

Bandura, A., Social Learning Theory, 1977.

Barker, Richard A., "How Can We Train Leaders If We Do Not Know What Leadership Is?" *Human Relations*, vol. 50, no. 4 (1997).

Barmettler, Stefan, and Ohanian Mathias, Der stille Schaffer, Handelszeitung, June 2, 2016.

"Barnevik's Bounty: Scandal and Poor Performance Have Forced ABB to Open Up," *The Economist*, February 28, 2002, http://www.economist.com/node/1011457.

Barrett, David, "Protect Your Organisation from Dark Triad Job Candidates, Human Resources Headquarters, http://www.hrheadquarters.ie/protect-organisation-dark-triad-job-candidates/ (last visited June 25, 2018).

Bass, Brian, "What Is Management Derailment?" *Houston Chronicle*, https://smallbusiness.chron.com/management-derailment-31849.html (last visited September 20, 2018).

Baudenbacher, Carl, Uniform Liability Standards for the Private and the Public Sector—Lessons from the Hypo Alpe Adria Debacle, EMBL-HSG University of St. Gallen, 2016.

Bawany, Sattar, "Leading Change in Today's VUCA World: Leadership Excellence Essentials," HR.com, February 2016.

Becic, Daliborka, "Comparative Analysis of Corporate Governance Systems," Annals of DAAAM for 2011 and Proceedings of the 22nd International DAAAM Symposium, vol. 22, no. 1 (2011).

Behera, Suresh, "What Is the Alpha State of Mind? What Are Its Benefits?" *Times of India*, September 14, 2003, https://timesofindia.indiatimes.com/What-is-the-alpha-state-of-mind-What-are-its-benefits/articleshow/180546.cms.

Bello, Shukurat Moronke, "Impact of Ethical Leadership on Employee Job Performance," *International Journal of Business and Social Sciences*, vol. 3, no. 11 (2012).

"Benjamin Franklin Quotes," BrainyQuote, https://www.brainyquote.com/quotes/benjamin_franklin_151593 (last visited January 1, 2018).

Bennis, Warren and James O'Toole, "Don't Hire the Wrong CEO," *Harvard Business Review*, vol. 78 (2000).

Berglas, Steven, "Rooting Out Hubris, before a Fall," *Harvard Business Review*, April 14, 2014, https://hbr.org/2014/04/rooting-out-hubris-before-a-fall.

Berle, Adolf A., and Gardiner C. Means, *The Modern Corporation and Private Property* (New York: Macmillan, 1932).

Bernasconi, Alessandro, and Melanie Koller, Universität Zürich, Aspekte der aktienrechtlichen Verantwortlichkeit nach OR 754, 2013.

Bertram, Christopher, "Jean Jacques Rousseau," Stanford Encyclopedia of Philosophy, May 26, 2017, https://plato.stanford.edu/entries/rousseau/ (last visited October 17 2017).

Beyer, Anne, Larcker, David F. and Tayan, Brian, "Does the Composition of a Company's Shareholder Base Really Matter?" *Stanford Closer Look Series*, 2014.

Bill, George, and Andrew McLean, "Why Leaders Lose Their Way," *strategy+business*, 2007.

Birbaumer, Niels, Frankfurter Allgemeine Zeitung, Hirnforschung mit Straftätern: Das Böse beginnt im Gehirn, http://www.faz.net/aktuell/wissen/leben-gene/hirnforschung-mit-straftaetern-das-boese-beginnt-im-gehirn-13649029.html?printPagedArticle=true#pageIndex_2 (last visited May 6, 2018).

Birkinshaw, Julian , "Beware the Next Big Thing," *Harvard Business Review*, vol. 92, no. 5 (2014), 50–57.

Bitz, Mark, *Winning Practices of a Free, Fit, and Prosperous People*, Naples, FL: Flourish Books, 2019.

Blackshear, Patsy B., "The Followership Continuum: A Model for Increasing Organizational Productivity," *Innovation Journal: The Public Sector Innovation Journal*, vol. 9, no. 1 (2014).

Bleidorn, Wiebke, Christian Kandler, and Avshalom Caspi, "The Behavioural Genetics of Personality Development in Adulthood—Classic, Contemporary, and Future Trends," *European Journal of Personality*, vol. 28 (2014), 244–255.

Bloomfield, Stephen, *Theory and Practice of Corporate Governance: An Integrated Approach*, Cambridge, UK: Cambridge University Press, 2013.

Bloomsbury Business Library—Business & Management Dictionary, "Johari Window," http://web.b.ebscohost.com.ezproxy.insead.edu/ehost/detail/detail?vid=11&sid=d985d7c3-0901-4a09-919b-3e6502484002percent40sessionmgr103&bdata=JnNpdGU9ZWhvc3QtbGl2ZQ percent3dpercent3d#AN=26742018&db=bth (last visited July 14, 2017).

Blum, Adrian, "Sika-VRP Hälg: 'Wir haben fair analysiert,'" *Finanz und Wirtschaft*, August 12, 2014, http://www.fuw.ch/article/sika-vrp-halg-wir-haben-fair-und-unvoreingenommen-analysiert/.

Boiger, Michael, Eva Ceulemans, Jozefien De Leersnyder, Yukiko Uchida, Vinai Norasakkunkit, and Batja Mesquita, Beyond Essentialism: Cultural Differences in Emotions Revisited, Emotion, 2018.

Bonnefon, J. F., A. Shariff, and I. Rahwan, "Moral Machine—Human Perspective on Machine Ethics," MIT Massachusetts Institute of Technology, http://moralmachine.mit.edu/ (last visited April 18, 2017).

Borwick, Irving, "Organizational Role Analysis: Managing Strategic Change in Business Settings." In *Coaching in Depth: The Organizational Role Analysis Approach*, London, New York: Karnac Books, 2006.

Bothwell, Mike, "Pros and Cons of Whistleblowing in the Workplace," Bothwell Law Group, August 14, 2017, http://whistleblowerlaw.com/whistleblowing-in-the-workplace/.

Bowlby, J., Attachment and Loss, 1969.

Brehm v. Eisner 746 A.2d 244 (2000).

Bridges, William and Susan Mitchell, "Leading Transition: A New Model for Change." In *Leader to Leader 2: Enduring Insights on Leadership from the Leader to Leader Institute's Award Winning Journal*, edited by Frances Hesselbein and Alan R. Shrader. San Francisco: Jossey-Bass, 2008.

Broadley, Derek, "Auditing and its Role in Corporate Governance," FSI Seminar on Corporate Governance for Banks, OECD.org/Deloitte, 2006.

Brown, M. E., L. K. Treviño, and D. A. Harrison, "Ethical Leadership: A Social Learning Perspective for Construct Development and Testing," *Organizational Behavior and Human Decision Processes*, vol. 97, no. 2 (2005), 117–134.

Brown, Meredith M., *Takeovers: A Strategic Guide to Mergers and Acquisitions*, New York: Aspen Publishers Online, 2010.

Brown, Michael E. and Linda K. Treviño, "Ethical Leadership: A Review and Future Directions," *Leadership Quarterly*, 17 (2006), 595–616.

Bühler, Christoph B., "Corporate Governance und ihre Regulierung in der Schweiz," *ZGR Zeitschrift für Unternehmens- und Gesellschaftsrecht*, Band 41, Heft 2–3 (2012), 228–245.

Bültel, Nadine, Starmanager: Medienprominenz, Reputation und Vergütung von Top-Managern, 2011.

Buranyi, Stephen, "Rise of the Racist Robots—How AI Is Learning All Our Worst Impulses," *The Guardian*, August 8, 2017, https://www.theguardian.com/inequality/2017/aug/08/rise-of-the-racist-robots-how-ai-is-learning-all-our-worst-impulses.

Burden, Melissa, "VW to Pay $2.8B Fine, Gets 3 Years Probation," Detroit News, April 21, 2017, http://www.detroitnews.com/story/business/autos/foreign/2017/04/21/volkswagen-emissions-scandal/100736014/.

Burton, Chris, *A Study into Motivation and Engagement—Why We Really Do the Things We Do…*(London: Engage for Success, 2012–2013).

Burton, Neel, "What's the Difference between a Feeling and an Emotion?" *Psychology Today*, December 19, 2014, https://www.psychologytoday.com/us/blog/hide-and-seek/201412/whats-the-difference-between-feeling-and-emotion.

BusinessDictionary, "conflict," http://www.businessdictionary.com/definition/conflict.html (last visited October 8, 2017).

Butler, Sarah, "Former Tesco Directors Charged with Fraud over Accounting Scandal," *The Guardian*, September 9, 2016, https://www.theguardian.com/business/2016/sep/09/sfo-charges-former-tesco-directors-with-fraud.

Calhoun, Amy, "Gore Again Named One of the 100 Best Companies to Work For," March 30, 2016, W. L. Gore Company, https://www.gore.com/news-events/press-release/enterprise-press-release-fortune-100-list-2016-us.

CALIDA Holding AG, *Corporate Governance Report 2015*, CALIDA Group, 2016.

Cambridge Advanced Learner's Dictionary & Thesaurus, "conflict," Cambridge University Press, http://dictionary.cambridge.org/dictionary/english/conflict (last visited February 23, 2017).

Cambridge Dictionary, "excess," http://dictionary.cambridge.org/de/worterbuch/englisch/excess (last visited October 8, 2017).

Cambridge Dictionary, "fraud," https://dictionary.cambridge.org/de/worterbuch/englisch/fraud (last visited May 4, 2019).

Cambridge Dictionary, "scandal," http://dictionary.cambridge.org/de/worterbuch/englisch/scandal (last visited October 8, 2017).

Cambridge Dictionary, "technocracy," https://dictionary.cambridge.org/us/dictionary/english/technocracy (last visited July 14, 2019).

Cambridge Dictionary, "whistle-blower," http://dictionary.cambridge.org/de/worterbuch/englisch/whistle-blower (last visited March 17, 2017).

Campbell, Sherrie, "The 10 Benefits of Conflict," *Entrepreneur*, July 28, 2016, https://www.entrepreneur.com/article/279778.

Carroll, Michael, *The Mindful Leader: Awakening Your Natural Management Skills Through Mindfulness Meditation*, Boston: Trumpeter, 2008.

Caulkin, Simon, "Gore-Tex Gets Made without Managers," *The Guardian*, November 1, 2008, https://www.theguardian.com/business/2008/nov/02/gore-tex-textiles-terri-kelly.

Chadra, Shruti, "VUCA World: Provoking the Future," *Human Capital*, vol. 20, no. 8 (2017) 14–18.

Chapman, Jane, and Susan Long, "Role Contamination: Is the Poison in the Person or in the Bottle," *Socio-Analysis: The Journal of the Australian Institute of Socio-Analysis*, vol. 11 (2009), 53–66.

Charan, Ram and Colvin, Geoffrey, "Why CEOs Fail: It's Rarely for Lack of Smarts or Vision. Most Unsuccessful CEOs Stumble Because of One Simple, Fatal Shortcoming," *Fortune* magazine archive, June 21, 1999.

Chesapeake Corp. v. Shore, CourtListener.com, 771 A.2d 293 (Del. Ch. 2000).

Chomsky, N., Aspects of the Theory of Syntax, 1969.

CIA, *The CIA World Factbook*, 2017.

Clark, Simon, and William Louch, "Third Abraaj Executive Arrested," *Wall Street Journal*, April 18, 2019, https://www.wsj.com/articles/third-abraaj-executive-arrested-11555585989.

Collins, Stuart, "Global Claims Review 2014: Loss Trends and Emerging Risks for Global Businesses," *Global Risk Dialogue Magazine*, 2014, https://www.agcs.allianz.com/content/dam/onemarketing/agcs/agcs/reports/AGCS-Global-Claims-Review-2014.pdf.

Counter, Rosemary, "The Case for Telling the Honest Truth," *Canadian Business*, 2016.

Coutu, Diane, "The Anxiety of Learning," *Harvard Business Review*, vol. 80, no. 3 (2002), 100–106.

Coutu, Diane, "Why Teams Don't Work," *Harvard Business Review*, vol. 87, no. 5 (2009), 99–105.

Covey, Stephen M. R., "The 13 Behaviors of a High Trusted Leader," CoveyLink, 2006.

Dahinten, Jan, and Andrew Marc Noel, "Sika, Saint-Gobain Sign Deal to End Bitter Takeover Battle," Bloomberg, May 11, 2018, https://www.bloomberg.com/news/articles/2018-05-11/saint-gobain-sika-reach-deal-ending-three-year-legal-standoff?in_source=video_page.

Dahlitz, Matthew, "Basic Psychological Needs," *The Neuropsychotherapist*, http://www.neuropsychotherapist.com/basic-psychological-needs/ (last visited April 18, 2017).

Dangi, Mohamad Ridhuan Mat, et al., "Leadership Quality and Competency Towards Investor Valuation and Firm Performance," *Journal of Advanced Research in Business and Management Studies*, vol. 7, no. 2 (2017), 55–68.

Danziger, Shai, Jonathan Levav, and Liora Avnaim-Pesso, "Extraneous Factors in Judicial Decisions," proceedings of the National Academy of Sciences, 2011.

Davies, Adrian, The Globalisation of Corporate Governance: The Challenge of Clashing Cultures, 2011.

Davis, Nicholas, Finanz und Wirtschaft, Learning from Luther about Technological Disruption, https://www.fuw.ch/article/learning-from-luther-about-technological-disruption/ (last visited July 21, 2019).

De Haan, Erik, "The Leadership Shadow: How to Recognise and Avoid Derailment, Hubris and Overdrive," *Leadership*, (2015), 1–9.

De Neve, Jan-Emmanuel, and James H. Fowler, *Journal of Economic Behavior & Organization*, vol. 107, part B (2014), 428–439.

De Smet, Aaron, Michael Lurie, and Andrew St. George, *Leading Agile Transformation: The New Capabilities Leaders Need to Build 21st-Century Organizations*, McKinsey & Company, 2018.

DeCanio, Stephan J., "Robots and Humans—Complements or Substitutes?" *Journal of Macroeconomics*, vol. 49 (2016), 280–291.

Delko, Krim, NZZ Neue Zürcher Zeitung, Wenn Topmanager Milliarden wert sind, https://www.nzz.ch/finanzen/wenn-topmanager-milliarden-wert-sind-ld.1387658 (last visited May 24, 2018).

Deloitte LLP, The State of the State Report 2016–17: Brexit and the business of government, 2016.

Diamond, Stephen A., "Essential Secrets of Psychotherapy: What Is the 'Shadow'?" *Psychology Today*, April 2012, https://www.psychologytoday.com/blog/evil-deeds/201204/essential-secrets-psychotherapy-what-is-the-shadow (last visited October 8, 2017).

Dictionary.com, "behavior pattern," http://www.dictionary.com/browse/behavior-pattern (last visited May 7, 2017).

Dictionary.com, "scandal," https://www.dictionary.com/browse/scandal?s=t (last visited November 6, 2019).

"Directive (Eu) 2019/1937" *Official Journal of the European Union*, November 26, 2019, https://eur-lex.europa.eu/legal-content/en/TXT/?uri=CELEX%3A32019L1937.

Dotlich, D. L. and Cairo, P. C., *Why CEOs Fail: The 11 Behaviors That Can Derail Your Climb to the Top—And How to Manage Them*, San Francisco: Jossey-Bass, 2007.

Drath, Karsten, Resilienz in der Unternehmensführung: Was Manager und ihre Teams stark macht, 2014.

Du, Lisa, "5 Things to Know about Toshiba's Accounting Scandal," *Wall Street Journal*, July 21, 2015, https://blogs.wsj.com/briefly/2015/07/21/5-things-to-know-about-toshibas-accounting-scandal-2/.

Dunsch, Jürgen, Frankfurter Allgemeine Zeitung, Swissair-Pleite: Luftnummer, http://www.faz.net/aktuell/wirtschaft/swissair-pleite-luftnummer-1411598.html (last visited March 9, 2018).

EC, European Commission, Special Eurobarometer 397: Corruption Report, 2014. *Journal of the European Union, https://eur-lex.europa.eu/LexUriServ/LexUriServ.do?uri=OJ:L:2005:052:0051:0063:EN:PDF*

Elfenbein, Hillary Anger, Manas K. Mandal, Nalini Ambady, Susumu Harizuka, and Surender Kumar, "Cross-Cultural Patterns in Emotion Recognition: Highlighting Design and Analytical Techniques," *Emotion*, vol. 2, no. 1, (2002) 75–84.

"Emotional Intelligence in Leadership: Learning How to Be More Aware," Mind Tools, https://www.mindtools.com/pages/article/newLDR_45.htm (last visited April 30 2017).

"Employees & Job Applicants," US Equal Employment Opportunity Commission, https://www.eeoc.gov/employees/index.cfm (last visited June 11, 2018).

English Oxford Living Dictionary, "ego," https://en.oxforddictionaries.com/definition/ego (last visited April 26, 2018).

English Oxford Living Dictionary, "hubris," https://en.oxforddictionaries.com/definition/hubris (last visited April 26, 2018).

English Oxford Living Dictionary, "morosoph," https://en.oxforddictionaries.com/definition/morosoph (last visited April 2, 2017).

English Oxford Living Dictionary, "narcissism," https://en.oxforddictionaries.com/definition/narcissism (last visited April 26, 2018).

"Erik Erikson, 91, Psychoanalyst Who Reshaped Views of Human Growth, Dies," *New York Times,* May 13, 1994, http://www.nytimes.com/books/99/08/22/specials/erikson-obit.html.

Erikson Institute, "Erik H. Erikson," https://www.erikson.edu/about/history/erik-erikson/ (last visited July 28, 2017).

Erikson, Erik H., *Childhood and Society,* 3rd ed., New York: W. W. Norton, 1993.

Erikson, Erik H., *Identity, Youth and Crisis,* New York: W. W. Norton, 1968.

Erikson, Erik H., *The Life Cycle Completed: A Review,* New York: W. W. Norton, 1981.

European Commission, "Commission Recommendation on the Role of Non-Executive or Supervisory Directors of Listed Companies," *Official Journal of the European Union* (February 25, 2005), 56f, https://eur-lex.europa.eu/LexUriServ/LexUriServ.do?uri=OJ:L:2005:052:0051:0063:EN:PDF.

EZI, Global Board Diversity Analysis, 2017.

"F. Scott Fitzgerald Quotes," BrainyQuote, https://www.brainyquote.com/quotes/f_scott_fitzgerald_100572 (last visited March 5, 2018).

Fahlenbrach, Rüdiger, Angie Low, and René M. Stulz, "Why Do Firms Appoint CEOs as Outside Directors?" *Journal of Financial Economics,* vol. 97, no. 1 (2010), 12–32.

Faleye, Olubunmi, "CEO Directors, Executive Incentives, and Corporate Strategic Initiatives," *Journal of Financial Research,* vol. 34, no. 2 (2011), 241–277.

Farrell, Sean, "The World's Biggest Accounting Scandals." *The Guardian*, July 21, 2015, https://www.theguardian.com/business/2015/jul/21/the-worlds-biggest-accounting-scandals-toshiba-enron-olympus.

Feldges, Dominik, NZZ Neue Zürcher Zeitung, Sika muss sich die neu gewonnene Freiheit teuer erkaufen, https://www.nzz.ch/wirtschaft/sika-muss-sich-die-neu-gewonnene-freiheit-teuer-erkaufen-ld.1385114 (last visited June 10, 2018).

Fernández-Aráoz, Claudio, Great People Decisions: Why They Matter So Much, Why They are So Hard, and How You Can Master Them, Hoboken, NJ: John Wiley & Sons, 2007.

Ferreira, Daniel, "Board Diversity," London School of Economics, 2010.

Fiske, Susan T., Amy J. C. Cuddy, Peter Glick, and Jun Xu, "A Model of (Often Mixed) Stereotype Content: Competence and Warmth Respectively Follow from Perceived Status and Competition," *Journal of Personality and Social Psychology*, vol. 82, no. 6 (2002), 878–902.

Folkman, Joseph, "The '8 Great' Accountability Skills For Business Success," *Forbes*, November 14, 2014, https://www.forbes.com/sites/joefolkman/2014/11/14/how-do-you-score-the-8-great-accountability-skills-for-business-success/#345085893c11.

Forbes (@forbes) "Learning without reflection is a waste, reflection without learning is dangerous—Confucius," Twitter, July 5, 2014, 9:45 a.m., https://twitter.com/forbes/status/485434337614397441?lang=de.

"Former ABB CEOs to Pay Back SFr137 Million," SWI swissinfo.ch, March 10, 2002, http://www.swissinfo.ch/eng/former-abb-ceos-to-pay-back-sfr137-million/2591332.

Foucault, Michel, "Discourse and Truth: the Problematization of Parrhesia," University of California at Berkeley, Oct.–Nov. 1983, https://foucault.info/doc/documents/parrhesia/foucault-dt1-wordparrhesia-en-html (last visited January 4, 2018).

Franklin, Joshua, Brumpton, Harry, and Zhu, Julie, "Starbucks' China Challenger Luckin Raises $561 Million in U.S. IPO," *Reuters*, May 16, 2019, https://www.reuters.com/article/us-luckin-coffee-ipo/starbucks-china-challenger-luckin-raises-561-million-in-u-s-ipo-idUSKCN1SM2SH.

Frei, Frances X. and Morriss, Anne, "Begin with Trust," *Harvard Business Review* (May–June 2020), 1.

Fry, Louis W., "Toward a Theory of Spiritual Leadership, *Leadership Quarterly*, vol. 14 (2003), 693–727.

Furnham, Adrian, "Current Development in Psychometric Tests," *European Business Review*, September 20, 2019, https://www.europeanbusinessreview.com/current-development-in-psychometric-tests/.

Gallas, Daniel, "Brazil's Odebrecht Corruption Scandal," *BBC News*, April 17, 2019, http://www.bbc.com/news/business-39194395.

García-Castro, Roberto, Miguel A. Ariño, Miguel A. Rodriguez, Silvia Ayuso, "A Cross-National Study of Corporate Governance and Employment Contracts," *Business Ethics: A European Review*, vol. 17 (2008), 260.

Gardner, Howard, *Multiple Intelligences: The Theory in Practice*, New York: Basic Books, 1993.

Garrard, Peter, and Graham Robinson, *The Intoxication of Power*, London: Palgrave MacMillan, 2016.

Garton, Eric, "How to Be an Inspiring Leader," *Harvard Business Review*, 2017.

"*Geeks and Geezers: How Era, Values, and Defining Moments Shape Leaders*," *Publishers Weekly*, https://www.publishersweekly.com/978-1-57851-582-0 (last visited August 22, 2017).

Geissler, Cornelia, Ein Board? *Harvard Business Manager*, 2006.

"Genetic Inheritance—AQA," Bitesize, BBC, http://www.bbc.co.uk/schools/gcsebitesize/science/add_aqa_pre_2011/celldivision/inheritance1.shtml (last visited February 24, 2018).

"George Will Quotes," BrainyQuote, https://www.brainyquote.com/quotes/george_will_104463 (last visited January 1, 2018).

George, Bill, "Becoming a More Authentic Leader," *Harvard Business Review*, 2015.

George, Bill, "Leading a Global Enterprise," Harvard Business School alumni webinar, 2013.

George, Bill, "The Truth About Authentic Leaders," Harvard Business School Working Knowledge, 2016.

George, Bill, "Why Leaders Lose Their Way," Harvard Business School Working Knowledge, 2011.

Ghoshal, Sumantra, "Bad Management Theories Are Destroying Good Management Practices," Advanced Institute of Management Research (AIM), UK, vol. 4, no. 1 (2005), 75–91.

Gjerstad, Ketil, et. al., "Bringing Science to the Art of Ceo Succession Planning," (BCG Boston Consulting Group: Corporate Development & Finance, Corporate Strategy, 2019).

Goldman, David, "HP CEO Apotheker Fired, Replaced by Meg Whitman," *CNN Money*, September 22, 2011, http://money.cnn.com/2011/09/22/technology/hp_ceo_fired/index.htm.

Goleman, Daniel, "Emotional Intelligence," http://www.danielgoleman.info/ (last visited April 30, 2017).

Goleman, Daniel, "Social Skills," http://www.danielgoleman.info/social-skills-and-eq/ (last visited July 14, 2017).

Goleman, Daniel, "What Makes a Leader," *Harvard Business Review*, vol. 76, no. 6 (1998), 93–102.

Goodman, Peter S., "Failure Offers Lessons Japan Would Rather Forget," *New York Times*, September 6, 2009, http://www.nytimes.com/2009/09/06/weekinreview/06goodman.html?_r=2.

Goodreads, Albert Einstein: Quotes, https://www.goodreads.com/quotes/7718768-once-you-stop-learning-you-start-dying (last visited February 26 2018).

Graham, Kenny, "Your Company's Purpose Is Not Its Vision, Mission, or Values," *Harvard Business Review*, vol. 9 (2014).

Grant, Adam M., *Give and Take: A Revolutionary Approach to Success*, London: Viking, 2013.

Green, Charles H., "The New Leadership is Horizontal, Not Vertical," Trusted Advisor, http://trustedadvisor.com/articles/the-new-leadership-is-horizontal-not-vertical (last visited May 7 2018).

Greenleaf, Robert K., "Start Here: What Is Servant Leadership?" Robert K. Greenleaf Center for Servant Leadership, https://www.greenleaf.org/what-is-servant-leadership/ (last visited May 7, 2018).

Grohol, John M., "Differences Between a Psychopath vs Sociopath," Psych Central (blog), https://psychcentral.com/blog/differences-between-a-psychopath-vs-sociopath/ (last visited February 26, 2018).

Gruenfeld, Deborah, "Having Power and Influence," TrendHunter, https://www. trendhunter.com/about-trend-hunter (last visited November 3, 2017).

Gugler, Klaus, *Corporate Governance and Economic Performance*, New York: Oxford University Press, 2001.

Gugler, Klaus, Dennis C. Mueller, and Burcin B. Yurtoglu, "Corporate Governance and Globalization," *Oxford Review of Economic Policy*, vol. 20, no. 1, 129–56, 2004.

Gwen, Coach, "Levels of Listening," LeaderWhoLeads.com, http://www. leaderwholeads.com/levels-of-listening.html (last visited May 2 2017).

Hadzic, Daida, "European Union—New Measures for Protection of Whistleblowers," KPMG, November 13, 2019, https://home.kpmg/xx/en/home/ insights/2019/11/flash-alert-2019-169.html.

Haller, Max, Organhaftung und Versicherung. Die aktienrechtliche Verantwortlichkeit und ihre Versicherbarkeit unter besonderer Berücksichtigung der D&O-Versicherung, 2008.

Hamdan, Lubna, "Sentencing for Former Abraaj Md Abdel-Wadood Adjourned to August," *Arabian Business*, January 14, 2020, https://www.arabianbusiness.com/ banking-finance/437555-sentencing-for-former-abraaj-md-abdel-wadood- adjourned-to-august.

Harms, P. D., Seth M. Spain, and Sean T. Hannah, "Leader Development and the Dark Side of Personality," *Leadership Quarterly*, vol. 22 (2011), 495–509.

Harrell, Eben, "Succession Planning: What the Research Says," *Harvard Business Review*, vol. 94, no. 12 (2016), 70–74.

Harter, Jim, "Dismal Employee Engagement Is a Sign of Global Mismanagement," Gallup Blog, http://news.gallup.com/opinion/gallup/224012/dismal-employee- engagement-sign-global-mismanagement.aspx (last visited May 20, 2018).

Hayward, Mathew L. A., Rindova, Violina P. and Pollock, Timothy G., Believing One's Own Press: The Causes and Consequences of CEO Celebrity, 2004.

Heifetz, Ronald, Grashow, Alexander and Marty, Linsky, *The Theory Behind the Practice: A Brief Introduction to the Adaptive Leadership Framework*. Harvard Business Press, 2009.

Hern, Alex, The Guardian, Self-driving cars don't care about your moral dilemmas, https://www.theguardian.com/technology/2016/aug/22/self-driving-cars-moral-dilemmas (last visited April 18 2017).

Herrmann, Ned, "What Is the Function of the Various Brainwaves?" *Scientific American*, December 22, 1997, https://www.scientificamerican.com/article/what-is-the-function-of-t-1997-12-22/.

Hespe, Franz, Homo homini lupus—Naturzustand und Kriegszustand bei Thomas Hobbes, VS Verlag für Sozialwissenschaften, Wiesbaden 2011.

HG.org Legal Resources, "Corporate Law: Definition, State Laws, Publications, Organizations," https://www.hg.org/corporate-law.html (last visited November 14 2017).

Higgs, Derek, Department of Trade and Industry, Review of the Role and Effectiveness of Non-Executive Directors, 2003.

Higgs, Malcolm, and Deborah Rowland, "What Does It Take to Implement Change Successfully? A Study of the Behaviors of Successful Change Leaders," *Journal of Applied Behavioral Science*, vol. 47 (2011), 309.

Hilb, Martin, *New Corporate Governance: Successful Board Management Tools*, New York: Springer, 2012.

Hilti, "About Us," https://www.hilti.com/content/hilti/W1/US/en/company/about-hilti/company-profile/about-us.html (last visited November 2, 2017).

Hirschhorn, Larry and Gilmore, Thomas, "The New Boundaries of the 'Boundaryless' Company, *Harvard Business Review*, vol. 70, no. 3 (1992), 104–115.

Hobbes, T. and Gaskin, J. C., *The Elements of Law, Natural and Politic*, Oxford 1999.

Hofstede, Geert, "Power Distance Index," Clearly Cultural, http://www.clearlycultural.com/geert-hofstede-cultural-dimensions/power-distance-index/ (last visited July 28, 2017).

Hogan, Hogan Development Survey: The Dark Side of Personality, https://www.hoganassessments.com/assessment/hogan-development-survey/ (last visited June 25 2018).

"Holacracy: A Complete System for Self-Organization," HolacracyOne, http://www.holacracy.org/ (last visited April 10, 2017).

Holwerda, Tjalling Jan, Dorly J. H. Deeg, Aartjan T. F. Beekman, Theo G. van Tilburg, Max L. Stek, Cees Jonker, and Robert Schoevers, "Feelings of Loneliness, but Not Social Isolation, Predict Dementia Onset: Results from the Amsterdam Study of the Elderly (AMSTEL)," *Journal of Neurology, Neurosurgery, and Psychiatry*, vol. 85 (2014), 135–142.

Hope Hailey, Veronica, and Gustafsson, Stefanie, Chartered Institute of Personnel and Development and University of Bath School of Management, Experiencing Trustworthy Leadership, 2014.

Horgan, John, *The End of War*, n.p.: McSweeney, 2012.

Horney, Nick, Bill Pasmore, and Tom O'Shea, "Leadership Agility: A Business Imperative for a VUCA World," *People & Strategy*, vol. 33, no. 4 (2010).

Howlett, Dennis, "Satyam Scandal—The Fallout," *The Guardian*, January 15, 2009, https://www.theguardian.com/technology/2009/jan/15/satyam-computer-services.

Hug, Daniel and Pfister, Franziska, NZZ Neue Zürcher Zeitung, Der Kampf wird immer kostspieliger, http://www.nzz.ch/nzzas/nzz-am-sonntag/uebernahmeschlacht-um-sika-der-kampf-wird-immer-kostspieliger-ld.14399 (last visited July 1 2016).

Hughes, Shayne, "What Does My Childhood Have to Do with My Leadership?" HuffPost, August 1, 2013, http://www.huffingtonpost.com/shayne-hughes/what-does-my-childhood-ha_b_3678394.html.

Huston, Matt, Scott McGreal, Jonathan D. Rasking, and Grant Hilary Brenner, "Big 5 Personality Traits," *Psychology Today*, https://www.psychologytoday.com/us/basics/big-5-personality-traits (last visited August 11, 2019).

Ibarra, Herminia, "The Authenticity Paradox," *Harvard Business Review*, 2015.

"Index of Codes," ECGI (European Corporate Governance Institute), http://www.ecgi.org/codes/all_codes.php (last visited June 4, 2016).

Iovino, Nicholas, Courthouse News Service, VW Can't Dodge 2nd Securities Action Over Emissions Scandal https://www.courthousenews.com/vw-cant-dodge-2nd-securities-action-emissions-scandal/ (last visited July 2017).

Isaac, Mike, "Uber's C.E.O. Plays With Fire," *New York Times*, April 23, 2017, https://www.nytimes.com/2017/04/23/technology/travis-kalanick-pushes-uber-and-himself-to-the-precipice.html.

Iwakabe, Shigeru, "Psychotherapy Integration in Japan," *Journal of Psychotherapy Integration*, vol. 18, no. 1 (2008).

Jackson, Gregory, and Andreas Moerke, "Continuity and Change in Corporate Governance: comparing Germany and Japan," *Corporate Governance: An International Review*, vol. 13, no. 3 (2005).

Jackson, Kevin, Global Corporate Governance: Soft Law and Reputational Accountability, *Brooklyn Journal of International Law*, January 1, 2010.

Jacobs, Katie, "Is Psychometric Testing Still Fit for Purpose?" People Management, February 22, 2018, https://www.peoplemanagement.co.uk/long-reads/articles/psychometric-testing-fit-purpose.

Jami, Criss, "Killosophy Quotes," Goodreads, https://www.goodreads.com/work/quotes/43973648-killosophy?mobiright-demo=anchor&page=5 (last visited January 1, 2018).

Jency, S., "720 Degree Performance Appraisal: An Emerging Technique," *International Journal of Informative & Futuristic Research*, vol. 3, no. 8 (2016), 2956–2965.

Jensen, Michael C., and William H. Meckling, "Theory of the Firm: Managerial Behavior, Agency Costs and Ownership Structure," in Peter M. Jackson (ed.), *Economics of Organisation and Bureaucracy*, vol. 1, Cheltenham, UK: Edward Elgar, 2013.

Johansen, Bob, and James Euchner, "Navigating the VUCA World," *Research Technology Management*, vol. 56, no. 1 (2013), 10–15.

"Johari Window Model and Free Diagrams," Businessballs, https://www.businessballs.com/self-awareness/johari-window-model-and-free-diagrams-68/ (last visited May 6, 2018).

John, Oliver P., Laura P. Naumann, and Christopher J. Soto, "Paradigm Shift to the Integrative Big Five Trait Taxonomy: History, Measurement, and Conceptual Issues," 2008.

Johnson, Ken, "The Good and Bad of Conflict," Mediate.com, August 2014, http://www.mediate.com/articles/JohnsonK6.cfm (last visited February 23, 2017).

Johnson, Sandhya, "Competency Confusers #3: Agility and Adaptability," LinkedIn, https://www.linkedin.com/pulse/competency-confuser-3-agility-adaptability-sandhya-johnson/ (last visited July 23, 2019).

Jolly, Richard, and Randall S. Peterson, "Going Nowhere Fast: Executive Derailment and How to Avoid It," London Business School, March 6, 2017, https://www.london.edu/faculty-and-research/lbsr/going-nowhere-fast#. WSQIUYVOJPY.

Jones, Daniel N., and Delroy L. Paulhus, "Duplicity among the Dark Triad: Three Faces of Deceit," *Journal of Personality and Social Psychology*, vol. 113, no. 2 (2017), 329–342.

Jones, David, "From Wedding Singer to FIFA's Godfather: The Hidden Secrets of Sepp Blatter, *Daily Mail*, June 4. 2011, http://www.dailymail.co.uk/sport/football/article-1394109/Sepp-Blatter-remarkable-rise.html.

Jones, Michael J., *Creative Accounting, Fraud and International Accounting Scandals*, (West Sussex, UK: Wiley, 2011).

"Joseph Stalin Quotes," BrainyQuote, https://www.brainyquote.com/quotes/joseph_stalin_378367 (last visited March 5 2018).

Jung, C. G., *Aion: Researches into the Phenomenology of the Self*. In *Collected Works of C. G. Jung*, vol. 9, part 2, Princeton, NJ: Princeton University Press, 1968.

Jung, Joseph, "Alfred Escher (1819–1882): Aufstieg, Macht, Tragik," In Nzz Libro (Zürich Verlag Neue Zürcher Zeitung, 2014).

Jurdant, Fianna, Tyler, Austin, and Vermeulen, Erik, "Board Evaluation: Overview of International Practices" (OECD, 2018).

Kahn, Marc Simon, Coaching on the Axis: Working with Complexity in Business and Executive Coaching, New York: Karnac Books, 2014.

Kaiser, Rob, "Linking Personality and 360 Assessments to Coach and Develop Leader," Symposium at the 28th Annual SIOP Conference, Houston, TX, 2013.

Karkoulian, Silva, Guy Assaker, and Rob, Hallak, "An Empirical Study of 360-Degree Feedback, Organizational Justice, and Firm Sustainability, *Journal of Business Research*, vol. 69, no. 5 (2016), 1862–1867.

Karr, Ben, "Freudian Aggression Theory: Two Hypothesis," *Psychotherapy: Theory, Research and Practice*, vol. 8, no. 4 (1971).

Katrin, Stefanicki, "Clarification on the Rights and Duties of the Board of Directors in a Recent Court Judgement—A General Overview," *Deloitte*, May 14, 2018, https://blogs.deloitte.ch/tax/2018/05/clarification-on-the-rights-and-duties-of-the-board-of-directors-in-a-recent-court-judgement-a-gener.html.

Kegan, Robert and Lisa Lahey, "The Real Reason People Won't Change," *Harvard Business Review*, vol. 79, no. 10 (2001).

Kellerman, Barbara, *Bad Leadership*, Boston: Harvard Business School Press, 2004.

Kelley, Robert, "In Praise of Followers," *Harvard Business Review*, 1988.

Kent, H. W., *Bibliographical Notes on One Hundred Books Famous in English Literature*, New York: Grolier Club, 1903.

Kets de Vries, Manfred F. R. and Danny Miller, *Unstable at the Top*, Boston: Dutton, 1988.

Kets de Vries, Manfred F. R., "Coaching the Toxic Leader," *Harvard Business Review*, published https://hbr.org/2014/04/coaching-the-toxic-leader?cm_sp=Article-_-Links-_-Comment April 2014,

Kets de Vries, Manfred F. R., "Do You Hate Your Boss?" *Harvard Business Review*, 2016.

Kets de Vries, Manfred F. R., "Doing Nothing and Nothing to Do: The Hidden Value of Empty Time and Boredom, *Organizational Dynamics*, vol. 44, 2015.

Kets de Vries, Manfred F. R., "Dysfunctional Leadership," *INSEAD: Faculty & Research*, vol. 58 (2003).

Kets de Vries, Manfred F. R., "Finding Balance in Business Education," INSEAD Knowledge, 2017, https://knowledge.insead.edu/blog/insead-blog/finding-balance-in-business-education-4346.

Kets de Vries, Manfred F. R., "Knowledge, The Epitaph Question," INSEAD, 2017.

Kets de Vries, Manfred F. R., "Leadership Group Coaching in Action: The Zen of Creating High Performance Teams, *Academy of Management Executive*, vol. 19, no. 1 (2005).

Kets de Vries, Manfred F. R., "Putting Leaders on the Couch," *Harvard Business Review*, vol. 82 (2004).

Kets de Vries, Manfred F. R., "The Case for Slacking Off," *Harvard Business Review*, 2013.

Kets de Vries, Manfred F. R., "The Many Colors of Success: What Do Executives Want Out of Life?" *Organizational Dynamics*, vol. 39 (2010).

Kets de Vries, Manfred F. R., "The Organizational Fool: Balancing a Leader's Hubris," *Human Relations*, vol. 43, no. 8 (1990), 751–770.

Kets de Vries, Manfred F. R., "The Personality Audit," INSEAD, 2006.

Kets de Vries, Manfred F. R., "The Psycho-Path to Disaster: Coping with SOB Executives," *Organizational Dynamics*, 43, 2014.

Kets de Vries, Manfred F. R., Konstantin Korotov, Elizabeth Florent-Treacy, *Coach and Couch: The Psychology of Making Better Leaders*, New York: Palgrave Macmillan, 2007.

Kets de Vries, Manfred F. R., *Leaders, Fools and Impostors*, revised edition, iUniverse, 2003.

Kets de Vries, Manfred F. R., *The Leader on the Couch: A Clinical Approach to Changing People and Organisations*, Jossey-Bass, 2006.

Kets de Vries, Manfred F. R., *The Leadership Mystique*, 2nd ed., Harlow, UK: Prentice Hall Financial Times, 2006.

Kilburg, Richard R. and Marc D. Donohue, "Toward a 'Grand Unifying Theory' of Leadership: Implications for Consulting Psychology," *Consulting Psychology Journal*, vol. 63, no. 1 (2011), 6–26.

Kippenberger, T., "The Dark Side of Leadership: What Drives People to Become Leaders?" *The Antidote*, vol. 2, no. 3 (1997), 11–13.

Kitayama, Shinobu, Hazel R. Markus, and Masaru Kurokawa, "Culture, Emotions and Well-Being: Good Feelings in Japan and the United States," *Cognition and Emotion*, 2000.

Kleiner, Art. "The Thought Leader Interview: Manfred F.R. Kets De Vries." *strategy+business*, no. 59 (2010).

Klemash, Steve, Doyle, Rani, and Smith, Jamie C, *Effective Board Evaluation* (Cambridge, MA: Harvard Law School Forum on Corporate Governance, 2018), https://corpgov.law.harvard.edu/2018/10/26/effective-board-evaluation/.

Knorr, Andreas, and Arndt, Andreas, *Swissair's Collapse—An Economic Analysis*, vol. 28, IWIM (Institute for World Economics and International Management) at Universität Bremen, 2003, http://www.iwim.uni-bremen.de/files/dateien/1444_w028.pdf.

Korine, Harry, and Gomez, Pierre-Yves, *Strong Managers, Strong Owners: Corporate Governance and Strategy*, New York: Cambridge University Press, 2014.

Kowalsky, Marc, Carsten Schloter: Tod eines CEO, BILANZ, http://www.bilanz.ch/unternehmen/carsten-schloter-tod-eines-ceo (last visited March 26, 2017).

Kowalsky, Marc, Was den deutschen Topmanager in den Tod trieb, Die Welt, https://www.welt.de/wirtschaft/article119750051/Was-den-deutschen-Topmanager-in-den-Tod-trieb.html (last visited March 28 2017).

KPMG LLP, Nomination & Remuneration Committee—Terms of Reference 2017.

Kramer, Roderick M., "Trust and Distrust in Organization: Emerging Perspectives, Enduring Questions," *Annual Reviews*, vol. 50 (1999), 569–598.

Krantz, James, "Work Culture Analysis and Reflective Space," in *Socioanalytic Methods: Discovering the Hidden in Organisations and Social Systems*, London: Karnac, 2013.

Kurvinen, Matti, Töyrylä, Ilkka and Murthy, D. N. Prabhakar, *Warranty Fraud Management: Reducing Fraud and Other Excess Costs in Warranty and Service Operations*, John Wiley & Sons 2016.

Kyodo, "Toshiba Fined Record ¥7.3 Billion over Accounting Scandal," *Japan Times*, December 25, 2015, http://www.japantimes.co.jp/news/2015/12/25/business/corporate-business/toshiba-fined-record- percentC2 percentA57-3-billion-over-accounting-scandal/#.WX4ej7puJPY.

Langevoort, Donald C., "The Behavioral Economics of Mergers and Acquisitions," *Tennessee Journal of Business Law* (Spring, 2011).

Larcker, David F., and Brian Tayan, "Chairman and CEO: The Controversy over Board Leadership," *Stanford Closer Look Series*, Stanford Graduate School of Business, 2016.

Larcker, David F., and Brian Tayan, "Governance Aches and Pains: Is Bad Governance Chronic?" *Stanford Closer Look Series*, 2016.

Larcker, David F., and Brian Tayan, "Pioneering Women on Boards: Pathways of the First Female Directors," *Stanford Closer Look Series* at Stanford Graduate School of Business, 2013.

Larcker, David F., and Brian Tayan, "Scoundrels in the C-Suite: How Should the Board Respond when a CEO's Bad Behavior Makes the News?" *Stanford Closer Look Series*, 2016.

Larcker, David F., and Brian Tayan, "Seven Myths of Boards of Directors," *Stanford Closer Look Series* at Stanford Graduate School of Business, October 12, 2015, https://www.gsb.stanford.edu/insights/seven-myths-boards-directors.

Larcker, David F., and Brian Tayan, "Trust and Consequences: A Survey of Berkshire Hathaway Operating Managers," *Stanford Closer Look Series*, 2015.

Larcker, David F., and Brian Tayan, "Trust: The Unwritten Contract in Corporate Governance," *Stanford Closer Look Series*, 2013.

Larcker, David F., Stephen A. Miles, and Brian Tayan, "Seven Myths of CEO Succession," *Stanford Closer Look Series*, March 19, 2014, https://www.gsb.stanford.edu/sites/gsb/files/publication-pdf/cgri-closer-look-39-seven-myths-ceo-succession.pdf.

Larcker, David F., Stephen A. Miles, and Brian Tayan, "Succession 'Losers': What Happens to Executives Passed Over for the CEO Job?" *Stanford Closer Look Series*, 2016.

Larcker, David F., Stephen A. Miles, and Brian Tayan, "The Handpicked CEO Successor," *Stanford Closer Look Series*, November 18, 2014, https://www.gsb.stanford.edu/faculty-research/publications/handpicked-ceo-successor.

Larcker, David, et. al., "How Boards Should Evaluate Their Own Performance," *Harvard Business Review,* (March 1, 2017).

Larson, Erik, "Abraaj's Abdel-Wadood Pleads Guilty, Will Cooperate in Probe," Bloomberg, June 28, 2019, https://www.bloomberg.com/news/articles/2019-06-28/abraaj-executive-abdel-wadood-pleads-guilty-to-conspiracy.

Leming, M.R. and Dickinson, G.E., *Understanding Dying, Death, and Bereavement*, 2015.

Leslie, Brittain Jean and Peterson, Michael John, *The Benchmarks Sourcebook: Three Decades of Related Research*, (Greensboro, NC: Center for Creative Leadership 2011), 7, 45.

Leube, Berthold, and George L. Davis, "The Next Stage of Globalization: The Convergence of Corporate Governance Practices," Egon Zehnder, *Focus Magazine*, vol. 14, no. 2 (2011).

Lewis, Michael, "The Self in Self-Conscious Emotions," *Monographs of the Society for Research in Child Development*, vol. 57 (1992), 85–95.

Li, Charlene, "3 Things All Engaged Leaders Have in Common," *FastCompany*, March 20, 2015, https://www.fastcompany.com/3043688/3-things-all-engaged-leaders-have-in-common.

Li, Haidan and Qian, Yiming, "Outside Ceo Directors on Compensation Committees: Whose Side Are They On?" *Review of Accounting and Finance*, vol. 10, no. 2 (2011), 110.

Lichtenberg, J.D., *Psychoanalysis and Motivation*, Hillsdale, NJ 1989.

Likierman, John Andrew, "Pros and Cons of Whistleblowing," Asia-Pacific Economics Blog, February 3, 2015, https://apecsec.org/pros-and-cons-of-whistleblowing/.

Lim, Nangyeon, "Cultural Differences in Emotion: Differences in Emotional Arousal Level between the East and the West," *Integrative Medicine Research*, vol. 5, no. 2 (2016).

Livermore, David, "Customs of the World: Using Cultural Intelligence to Adapt, Wherever You Are," The Great Courses, 2013.

Lloyd, Harold Anthony, "Law and the Cognitive Nature of Emotion: A Brief Introduction," *Wake Forest Law Review* 54, no. 4 (2019).

Locke, J., *Second Treatise of Government*, New York, 1690.

Long, James G., "Psychopathy and Politics," December 26, 2014, American Thinker, http://www.americanthinker.com/articles/2014/12/psychopathy_and_politics.html.

Long, Susan, "Drawing from Role Biography in Organizational Role Analysis." In *Coaching in Depth: The Organizational Role Analysis Approach*, London, New York: Karnac Books, 2006.

Long, Susan, "Images of Leadership." In *Psychoanalytic Perspectives on a Turbulent World*, London: Routledge, 2010.

Long, Susan, "Transforming Experience in Organisations: A Framework for Organisational Research and Consultancy." In *The Transforming Experience Framework*, Karnac Books 2015.

Long, Susan, and Maurita Harney, "Socioanalytic Interviewing." In *Socioanalytic Methods: Discovering the Hidden in Organisations and Social Systems*, London, 2013.

Lorsch, Jay W., and Rakesh Khurana, "Changing Leaders: The Board's Role in CEO Succession," *Harvard Business Review*, vol. 77 (1999).

Lucas, Amelia, "Shares of China's Luckin Coffee Plummet 80 Percent after Investigation Finds COO Fabricated Sales," *CNBC*, April 2, 2020, https://www.cnbc.com/2020/04/02/luckin-coffee-stock-plummets-after-investigation-finds-coo-fabricated-sales.html.

Luna, Des, "Marissa Mayer out, Thomas Mcinerney in as Yahoo CEO after Verizon Acquisition," *TechTimes*, March 15, 2017, https://www.techtimes.com/articles/201596/20170315/marissa-mayer-out-thomas-mcinerney-in-as-yahoo-ceo-after-verizon-acquisition.htm.

Lüpold, Martin, Der Ausbau der "Festung Schweiz": Aktienrecht und Corporate Governance in der Schweiz, 1881–1961, 2008.

Lyons, Minna, "Machiavellianism: Introduction to the Dark Triad," *Science Direct*, https://www.sciencedirect.com/topics/psychology/machiavellianism.

Maassen, Gregory Francesco, An International Comparison of Corporate Governance Models: A Study on the Formal Independence and Convergence of One-tier and Two-tier Corporate Boards of Directors in the Unites States of America, the United Kingdom and the Netherlands, 1999.

Maccoby, Michael, "Why People Follow the Leader: The Power of Transference," *Harvard Business Review*, vol. 82 (2004).

MacGregor, Luke, "Top Abraaj Executives Arrested on US Fraud Charges," *CNBC*, April 12, 2019, https://www.cnbc.com/2019/04/12/top-abraaj-executives-arrested-on-us-fraud-charges.html.

Mackenzie, Mindy, *The Courage Solution: The Power of Truth Telling with Your Boss, Peers, and Team*, Austin: Greenleaf Book Group, 2016.

Macnow, Alexander Stone, ed., *MCAT Behavioral Science Review: Created for MCAT 2015*, New York: Kaplan, 2014.

Maher, Maria, and Thomas Andersson, *Corporate Governance: Effects on Firm Performance and Economic Growth*, Paris: Organisation for Economic Co-operation and Development, 1999, https://www.oecd.org/sti/ind/2090569.pdf.

Maiello, Suzanne, "Prenatal Experiences of Containment in the Light of Bion's Model of Container/Contained, *Journal of Child Psychology*, vol. 38, no. 3 (2012), 250–267.

Margaris, Spiros, "Machine Learning in Financial Services: Changing the Rules of the Game," SAP, August 2017.

MarketsandMarkets, Artificial Intelligence Market worth $190.61 billion by 2025 with a Growing CAGR of 36.6 percent, https://www.marketsandmarkets.com/PressReleases/artificial-intelligence.asp (last visited July 23 2019).

Matussek, Karin, "VW's Former Ceo Charged in Germany over Diesel Rigging," *Bloomberg*, April 15, 2019, https://www.bloomberg.com/news/articles/2019-04-15/ex-vw-ceo-winterkorn-charged-in-germany-over-diesel-rigging.

Mawson, Chris, "Wilfred Bion," Melanie Klein Trust, http://www.melanie-klein-trust.org.uk/bion (last visited November 29, 2017).

McFadden, Christopher, "The Invention and History of the Printing Press," Interesting Engineering, https://interestingengineering.com/the-invention-and-history-of-the-printing-press (last visited July 21 2019).

McGregor, Jena, "Travis Kalanick May Have Resigned as Uber's CEO—but He Isn't Going Away, *The Washington Post,* June, 22, 2017, https://www.washingtonpost.com/news/on-leadership/wp/2017/06/22/travis-kalanick-may-have-resigned-as-ubers-ceo-but-he-isnt-going-away/?utm_term=.e18ad923836c.

McGregor, Jena, "Why a Toxic Workplace Is Now a Much Bigger Liability for Companies," *Washington Post*, February 24, 2017,https://www.washingtonpost.com/news/on-leadership/wp/2017/02/24/why-a-toxic-workplace-is-now-a-much-bigger-liability-for-companies/?tid=a_inl&utm_term=.96cb71d7cc44.

McKenna, Eugene F., *Business Psychology and Organisational Behaviour: A Student's Handbook* (Philadelphia: Psychology Press, 2000), 45–47.

McKnight, D. Harrison and Norman L. Chervany, "The Meaning of Trust," University of Minnesota, Carlson School of Management, 1996, http://www.misrc.umn.edu/workingpapers/fullpapers/1996/9604_040100.pdf.

McLeod, Saul, "Erik Erikson," *SimplyPsychology*, http://www.simplypsychology.org/Erik-Erikson.html (last visited November 2, 2017).

McLeod, Saul, "nature vs nurture in psychology," *SimplyPsychology*, https://www.simplypsychology.org/naturevsnurture.html, (last visited May 7, 2017).

McLeod, Saul, "psychoanalysis," *SimplyPsychology*, http://www.simplypsychology.org/psychoanalysis.html (last visited February 27, 2017).

McMillan, Lori, "The Business Judgment Rule as an Immunity Doctrine," *William & Mary Business Law Review*, vol. 4, 2013.

Medland, Dina, "Today's Gender Reality in Statistics, Or Making Leadership Attractive to Women," *Forbes*, March 7, 2016, https://www.forbes.com/sites/dinamedland/2016/03/07/todays-gender-reality-in-statistics-or-making-leadership-attractive-to-women/#58e2ae2a6883.

"Meg Whitman Steps Off HP Inc. Board of Directors; Company Appoints Chip Bergh as Chairman," Press Center, HP, July 26, 2017, https://press.ext.hp.com/us/en/press-releases/2017/meg-whitman-steps-off-hp-inc--board-of-directors--company-appoin.html.

Meier, Ernst, BAAR: Sika-Streithähne bleiben stur, Luzerner Zeitung, https://www.luzernerzeitung.ch/wirtschaft/baar-sika-streithaehne-bleiben-stur-ld.85797 (last visited September 9, 2018).

Meier, Ernst, So dreckig war die Schlammschlacht um Sika, Basler Zeitung, https://bazonline.ch/wirtschaft/unternehmen-und-konjunktur/so-dreckig-war-die-schlammschlacht-um-sika/story/25817052 (last visited June 10, 2018).

Messieh, Nancy, "12 Tech Companies That Offer Their Employees the Coolest Perks," TNW The Next Web, April 9, 2012, https://thenextweb.com/insider/2012/04/09/12-startups-that-offer-their-employees-the-coolest-perks/.

Mestel, Rosie, "Does the 'Aggressive Gene' Lurk in a Dutch Family?" *New Scientist*, October 30, 1993, https://www.newscientist.com/article/mg14018970-600-does-the-aggressive-gene-lurk-in-a-dutch-family/ (last visited April 9 2018).

Meyer, Erin, "Navigating the Cultural Minefield," *Harvard Business Review*, vol. 92, no. 5 (2014), 119–123.

Meyer, Maren, Das Ende der Hierarchien: Holacracy schafft den Chef ab, BILANZ, December 21, 2016.

Miller, Michael C., "Unconscious or Subconscious?" *Harvard Health Blog*, Harvard Health Publications, August 1, 2010, http://www.health.harvard.edu/blog/unconscious-or-subconscious-20100801255.

Minetti, Maurizio, Luzerner Zeitung, Abrupter Beginn einer neuen Ära bei Sika, http://www.luzernerzeitung.ch/nachrichten/wirtschaft/abrupter-beginn-einer-neuen-aera-bei-sika;art9642,1034175 (last visited July 28, 2017).

Mischel, W., *The Marshmallow Test: Mastering Self-Control*, Boston: Little, Brown, and Company, 2014.

Mishel, Lawrence, and Jessica Schieder, "CEO Pay Remains High Relative to the Pay of Typical Workers and High-Wage Earners," *Economic Policy Institute*, July 20, 2017, https://www.epi.org/publication/ceo-pay-remains-high-relative-to-the-pay-of-typical-workers-and-high-wage-earners/.

Molan, Alice, "FIFA Corruption Scandal Continues," *The Laundromat*, June 27, 2017, http://thelaundromat.kwm.com/fifa-corruption-scandal-continues/.

Moles, Peter and Nicholas Terry, Cadbury Committee on the Financial Aspects of Corporate Governance (UK) Cadbury Committee, 2005.

Moneycab, Sika zieht Schlussstrich unter Streit mit der Eignerfamilie, May 17, 2018, https://www.moneycab.com/2018/05/17/sika-zieht-den-schlussstrich-unter-den-streit-mit-der-eignerfamilie/.

Morris, C.W., *The Social Contract Theorists: Critical Essays on Hobbes, Locke, and Rousseau*, 1999.

Morrison, Alan D. and Wilhelm, Jr., William J., "The Demise of Investment-Banking Partnerships: Theory and Evidence," Oxford Financial Research Centre Working Paper, AFA 2006 Boston Meetings Paper, July 24, https://ssrn.com/abstract=569109 or http://dx.doi.org/10.2139/ssrn.569109.

Motivational Wizard, 55 Short Inspirational Quotes About Life Lessons And Moving On, http://motivationalwizard.com/short-inspirational-quotes-life-lessons/ (last visited March 9, 2018).

Müller, Roland, Lorenz Lipp, and Adrian Plüss, Der Verwaltungsrat: Ein Handbuch für die Praxis, Zürich 2007.

Muraven, M. and Baumeister, R. F., "Self-Regulation and Depletion of Limited Resources: Does Self-Control Resemble a Muscle?" *Psychol Bull*, vol. 126 (2000), 247–259.

Nayar, Vineet, "Three Differences Between Managers and Leaders," *Harvard Business Review*, 2013.

Nelson, Eric, and Robert Hogan, "Coaching on the Dark Side," *International Coaching Psychology Review*, vol. 4, no. 1 (2009).

Niiya, Yu, Phoebe C. Ellsworth, and Susumu Yamaguchi, "Amae in Japan and the United States: An Exploration of a 'Culturally Unique' Emotion," *Emotion*, vol. 6, no. 2 (2006), 279–295.

Nixon, Matt. *Pariahs: Hubris, Reputation, and Organisational Crises*. Libri Publishing, 2016.

"Non-Executive Director," Investopedia, http://www.investopedia.com/terms/n/non-executive-director.asp (last visited July 31, 2017).

"Number of Employees at Berkshire Hathaway from 2010 to 2019," Statista, https://www.statista.com/statistics/787860/employees-of-berkshire-hathaway/.

Nüssli, Isabelle, *Cockfighting: Solving the Mystery of Unconscious Sabotage at the Top of the Corporate Pyramid*, Leverage YourSelf AG, 2018.

Oatley, K. and Jenkins, J.M., *Understanding Emotions*, n.p.: Wiley, 1996.

Obholzer, Anton, "Psychoanalytic Contributions to Authority and Leadership Issues," *Leadership and Organization Development Journal*, vol. 17, no. 6 (1996), 53–56.

OECD, "Glossary of Statistical Terms: Corporate Governance," European Central Bank, 2004, Annual Report: 2004, ECB, Frankfurt, https://stats.oecd.org/glossary/detail.asp?ID=6778 (last visited June 14 2016).

Oehler, Ken, Stomski, Lorraine and Kustra-Olszewska, Magdalena, What Makes Someone an Engaging Leader, *Harvard Business Review* (November 2014).

"Olympus Scandal: Former Bosses to Pay $529m over Fraud," *BBC News*, April 28, 2017, http://www.bbc.com/news/business-39741921.

Orsagh, Matt, "Dual-Class Shares: From Google to Alibaba, Is It a Troubling Trend for Investors?" *Market Integrity Insights* (blog), CFA Institute, April 1, 2014, https://blogs.cfainstitute.org/marketintegrity/2014/04/01/dual-class-shares-from-google-to-alibaba-is-it-a-troubling-trend-for-investors/.

Oxford Dictionary, "derailment," https://en.oxforddictionaries.com/definition/derailment (last visited September 20, 2018).

Oxford Dictionary, "pathology," https://www.oxfordlearnersdictionaries.com/definition/english/pathology (last visited August 10, 2019).

Oxford Reference, "ignorantia juris non excusat," http://www.oxfordreference.com/view/10.1093/oi/authority.20110803095957244 (last visited July 25, 2017).

Pacer, Nathan, "Artificial Intelligence (AI) Q4 2017 Startup Highlights," LinkedIn, 2018.

Paine, James, "11 Wildly Successful Entrepreneurs Who Swear by Daily Meditation," *Inc.*, https://www.inc.com/james-paine/11-famous-entrepreneurs-who-meditate-daily.html.

"Parmalat Founder Given Eighteen-Year Jail Term over Fraud," *BBC News*, December 9, 2010, http://www.bbc.com/news/business-11958133.

Peevy, Jeff, "Holding Staff Accountable," *ABRN Magazine*, July 2017.

Peregrine, Michael W., "Enron Still Matters, 15 Years after Its Collapse." *New York Times*, December 1, 2016, https://www.nytimes.com/2016/12/01/business/dealbook/enron-still-matters-15-years-after-its-collapse.html.

Perry, Christopher, "The Shadow," The Society of Analytical Psychology, https://www.thesap.org.uk/resources/articles-on-jungian-psychology-2/about-analysis-and-therapy/the-shadow/ (last visited July 28, 2017).

Pistor, Katharina, Yoram Keinan, Jan Kleinheisterkamp, and Mark D. West, "Evolution of Corporate Law: A Cross-Country Comparison," *University of Pennsylvania Journal of International Law*, vol. 23, no. 4 (2002).

Pletter, Roman, Peer Teuwsen, and Dorit Kowitz, DIE ZEIT, Manager unter Druck, https://www.zeit.de/2014/07/manager-selbstmord/komplettansicht (last visited September 15, 2018).

Prabhat, S., "Difference Between Temperament and Personality," Differencebetween.net, http://www.differencebetween.net/language/words-language/difference-between-temperament-and-personality/ (last visited February 24, 2018).

Price, Nicholas J., "Role of the Remuneration Committee in Corporate Governance," Diligent Insights, February 19, 2019, https://insights.diligent.com/compensation-committee/role-of-the-remuneration-committee-in-corporate-governance.

Price, Nick, "What Is the Role of the Nomination Committee?" BoardEffect, April 15, 2019, https://www.boardeffect.com/blog/what-role-nomination-committee/.

Prime, Jeanine, and Elizabeth Salib, "The Best Leaders Are Humble Leaders," *Harvard Business Review* (2014).

"Prohibited Employment Policies/Practices," US Equal Employment Opportunity Commission, https://www.eeoc.gov/laws/practices/index.cfm (last visited June 11, 2018).

"Projective Identification," Melanie Klein Trust, http://www.melanie-klein-trust.org.uk/projective-identification (last visited April 23 2018).

Püntener, Carmen, FAA-HSG University of St.Gallen, Vertrauen am Arbeitsplatz: Den Pudding an die Wand nageln, 2016.

"Quotes: Thoughts on the Business of Life: Abraham Lincoln," *Forbes*, https://www.forbes.com/quotes/76/ (last visited March 5, 2018).

Quotes Codex, "That which we do not bring to consciousness appears in our lives as fate," https://www.quotescodex.com/that-which-we-do-not-bring-to-consciousness-appears-in-our-lives-as-fate-carl-jung-178996/ (last visited November 3, 2017).

Quotes, The Web's Largest Resource for Famous Quotes & Sayings, http://www.quotes.net/quote/16774 (last visited November 3, 2017).

Rappaport, Nancy, and Jessica Minahan, "Breaking the Behavior Code," ASCD In Service, June 7, 2012, http://inservice.ascd.org/behavior-code/.

Rathbone, John Paul, "Zen and the Art of Management," *Financial Times*, September 16, 2013, https://www.ft.com/content/32e0b9b4-1c5f-11e3-8894-00144feab7de.

Ratley, Jim, "Creating an Effective Whistleblower Program," *Security*, August 1, 2012, http://www.securitymagazine.com/articles/83343-creating-an-effective-whistleblower-program (last visited May 7, 2018).

Rayner, Gordon, "Banking Bailout: The Rise and Fall of RBS," *The Telegraph*, January 20, 2009, http://www.telegraph.co.uk/finance/newsbysector/banksandfinance/4291807/Banking-bailout-The-rise-and-fall-of-RBS.html.

"RBS Posts Biggest Loss in U.K. Corporate History," *NBC News*, February 26, 2009, http://www.nbcnews.com/id/29403447/ns/business-world_business/t/rbs-posts-biggest-loss-uk-corporate-history/.

Revlon, Inc. v. MacAndrews & Forbes Holdings, Justia US Law, 506 A.2d 173, 1986.

Richards, Leigh, "How Can Conflict Be Good for an Organization?" *Houston Chronicle*, March 6, 2019, http://smallbusiness.chron.com/can-conflict-good-organization-741.html.

Ridley, Kristin, "Abraaj Founder Faces February Extradition Hearing on U.S. Fraud Charge," *Euronews*, June 26, 2019, https://www.euronews.com/2019/06/26/abraaj-founder-faces-february-extradition-hearing-on-us-fraud-charge.

Robertson, Tanya, "Leadership Theory vs. Leadership Style," *Houston Chronicle*, http://smallbusiness.chron.com/leadership-theory-vs-leadership-style-32967.html (last visited November 15, 2017).

Roche, Bryan and Dermot, Barnes-Holmes, "Behavior Analysis and Social Constructivism: Some Points of Contact and Departure," *Behavior Analyst*, vol. 26, no. 2 (2003), 215–231.

Rohit, Mahajan, Jayant Saran, and Veena Sharma, "Setting Up a Whistleblowing Program: 10 Frequently Asked Questions," Deloitte, https://www2.deloitte.com/content/dam/Deloitte/in/Documents/finance/in-fa-setting-up-a-whistleblowing-mechanism-noexp.PDF (last visited May 7, 2018).

Ruddick, Graham, and Julia Kollewe, "Tesco to Pay £129m Fine over Accounting Scandal," *The Guardian*, March 28, 2017, https://www.theguardian.com/business/2017/mar/28/tesco-agrees-fine-serious-fraud-office-accounting-scandal (last visited July 25 2017).

Rudman, Laurie A. and Glick, Peter, "Feminized Management and Backlash Toward Agentic Women: The Hidden Costs of Women of a Kinder, Gentler Image of Middle Manager," *Journal of Personality and Social Psychology*, vol. 77, no. 5 (1999).

Rust, John, "Psychometrics 1889," Cambridge Judge Business School at the University of Cambridge, https://www.psychometrics.cam.ac.uk/about-us/our-history/first-psychometric-laboratory.

S. B., "What is the Difference Between Common and Civil Law?" The Economist Explains, *The Economist*, July 17, 2013, https://www.economist.com/blogs/economist-explains/2013/07/economist-explains-10.

Sang-Hun, Choe, "Park Geun-hye, South Korea's Ousted President, Gets 24 Years in Prison," *The New York Times*, April 6, 2018, https://www.nytimes.com/2018/04/06/world/asia/park-geun-hye-south-korea.html.

Sasan, Mehrani/Moradi, Mohammad/Eskandar, Hoda, "Corporate Governance: Convergence vs. Divergence," *British Journal of Economics*, vol. 9, no. 1 (2014).

Saudino, Kimberly J., "Behavioral Genetics and Child Temperament," *Journal of Developmental and Behavioral Pediatrics*, vol. 26, no. 3 (2005), 214–223.

Schmid, Matthias, Compliance—Was tun gegen Korruption und Betrug? Mehr Prävention und Kontrolle als Gegenmittel, persorama—Magazin der Schweizerischen Gesellschaft für Human Resources Management (Spring 2016).

Schmutz, Christoph G., Calida will eine neue Ära einläuten, NZZ Neue Zürcher Zeitung, http://www.nzz.ch/wirtschaft/calida-will-eine-neue-aera-einlaeuten-1.18717501 (last visited May 7, 2018).

Schrage, Michael, "When Authenticity Does More Harm than Good," *Harvard Business Review* (2015).

Schreiner, Erin, "Five Types of Conflict Resolution Strategies," *Houston Chronicle*, http://smallbusiness.chron.com/five-types-conflict-resolution-strategies-19251.html (last visited May 7, 2018).

Schultz , Stefan, "VW-Chef Müller blamiert sich beim," *Der Spiegel*, January 12, 2016, http://m.spiegel.de/wirtschaft/unternehmen/a-1071573.html.

Schultz, David, and Khachik Harutyunyan, "Combating Corruption: The Development of Whistleblowing Laws in the United States, Europe, and Armenia," *International Comparative Jurisprudence,* vol. 1, no. 2 (2015).

Schumpeter, Joseph, "The Holes in Holacracy: The Latest Big Idea in Management Deserves Some Scepticism," *The Economist*, July 5, 2014, https://www.economist.com/news/business/21606267-latest-big-idea-management-deserves-some-scepticism-holes-holacracy.

Schürpf, Thomas, Völlig verhärtete Fronten, NZZ Neue Zürcher Zeitung, http://www.nzz.ch/wirtschaft/unternehmen/fall-sika-jetzt-haben-wieder-die-aktionaere-das-wort-ld.13274 (last visited May 7, 2018).

Scott, John T. (ed), *Jean-Jacques Rousseau: Human Nature and History*, vol. 2 (Routledge: London and New York, 2006).

"Sentencing of South Korea Ex-Leader Park Geun Hye and Samsung Heir May Go Live on TV," *Straits Times*, July 26, 2017, http://www.straitstimes.com/asia/east-asia/sentencing-of-south-korea-ex-leader-park-geun-hye-and-samsung-heir-may-go-live-on-tv.

Sharf, R. S., *Theories of Psychotherapy and Counseling: Concepts and Cases*, Boston: Cengage Learning, 2015.

Sharif, Arif, "What's Been Learned and Who's Charged in Abraaj Collapse," *Bloomberg*, August 7, 2019, https://www.bloomberg.com/news/articles/2019-08-07/what-s-been-learned-who-s-charged-in-abraaj-collapse-quicktake.

Sheldon, Kennon M. and Gunz, Alexander, "Psychological Needs as Basic Motives, Not Just Experiential Requirements," *Journal of Personality*, vol. 77, no. 5 (2009).

Shleifer, Andrei, and Robert W. Vishny, A Survey of Corporate Governance, 1996.

Sika AG, Sika Geschäftsjahr 2015: Corporate Governance, 2015.

Sika AG, Sika Geschäftsjahr 2016: Corporate Governance, 2016.

SIKA General Assembly of April 12, 2016, livestream SIKA Website 2016.

Sika, Corporate Governance: Bekenntnis zu Offenheit und Transparenz, http://www.sika.com/de/group/investors/corporate-governance.html (last visited June 4, 2016).

Skinner, B.F., Verbal Behavior, 1957.

Slovic, Paul, Perceived Risk; Society for Risk Analysis, Risk Analysis; Trust, and Democracy, vol. 13, no. 6 (1993).

Smolaks, Max, "HP Completes Separation into Two Companies," November 2, 2015, Datacenter Dynamics, http://www.datacenterdynamics.com/content-tracks/design-build/hp-completes-separation-into-two-companies/95130.fullarticle.

Snell, S. A., S. S. Morris, and G. W. Bohlander, *Managing Human Resources*, Boston: Cengage Learning, 2015.

Sommer, Christa, Die Treuepflicht des Verwaltungsrats gemäss Art. 717 Abs. 1 OR, Zürich 2010.

"South Korea's Presidential Scandal," *BBC News*, April 6, 2018, http://www.bbc.com/news/world-asia-37971085.

Spence, Susan H., "Social Skills Training with Children and Young People: Theory, Evidence and Practice," *Child and Adolescent Mental Health*, vol. 8, no. 2 (2003), 84–96.

Stambor, Zak, "Psychologists Help Predict Potential Executives' Success," *American Psychological Association*, http://www.apa.org/monitor/feb06/success. aspx (last visited May 27, 2018).

Starr, Julie, *The Coaching Manual: The Definitive Guide to the Process, Principles and Skills of Personal Coaching*, 2nd edition, New York: Pearson Education, 2007.

Stein, Steven J. and Book, Howard E., *The EQ Edge: Emotional Intelligence and Your Success*, Mississauga, ON: John Wiley & Sons, 2011.

Stempel, Jonathan, "Factbox: Warren Buffett, Berkshire Hathaway at a Glance," *Reuters*, May 1, 2019, https:// www.reuters.com/article/us-berkshire-buffett-factbox/ factbox-warren-buffett-berkshire-hathaway-at-a-glance-idUSKCN1S73NV.

Stippler, Maria, Sadie Moore, Setz Rosenthal, and Tina Dörffer, Führung— Überblick über Ansätze, Entwicklungen, Trends, 4, Verlag Bertelsmann Stiftung 2014.

Surbhi, S., "Difference between Motivation and Inspiration," Key Differences, April 8, 2016, http://keydifferences.com/difference-between-motivation-and-inspiration.html.

Sutherland, Diana, "Are Dichotomies Like Nature vs Nurture Useful for Understanding the History and Philosophy of Development?" Birkbeck, University of London, 2013.

Suvák, V., *Care of the Self: Ancient Problematizations of Life and Contemporary Thought*, Leiden and Boston: Brill-Rodopi, 2017.

Sweney, Mark, "Murdoch Family Defeat Shareholder Revolt over News Corp Voting Structure," *The Guardian*, November 18, 2014, https://www.theguardian. com/media/2014/nov/18/murdoch-family-news-corp-shareholder-revolt.

"The 10 Worst Corporate Accounting Scandals of All Time," *Accounting Degree Review*, http://www.accounting-degree.org/scandals/ (last visited March 9, 2018).

"The Gore Story," https://www.gore.com/about/the-gore-story#overview (last visited August 12 2018).

The Higher Standard, Board Governance for Early Stage Technology Companies, 2016.

The Robbins Collection: School of Law (Boalt Hall), University of California at Berkeley, The Common Law and Civil Law Traditions, https://www.law.berkeley.edu/library/robbins/CommonLawCivilLawTraditions.html (last visited March 27, 2018).

The Web's Largest Quotes & Sayings, Bruce Lee, http://www.quotes.net/mquote/26503 (last visited November 3, 2017).

Thompson, M. G., *The Ethic of Honesty: The Fundamental Rule of Psychoanalysis*, Rodopi, 2004.

Thornton, Grant, *Women in Business: New Perspectives on Risk and Reward*, Grant Thornton International, 2017.

Tracy, J. L., R. W. Robins, and J. P. Tangney, *The Self-conscious Emotions: Theory and Research*, New York: Guilford Press, 2007.

Tran, Mark, "Shell Fined over Reserves Scandal," *The Guardian*, July 29, 2004, https://www.theguardian.com/business/2004/jul/29/oilandpetrol.news (last visited July 25 2017).

Traub, Stephen, "HP CFO Wayman to Retire," CFO, December 11, 2006, http://ww2.cfo.com/human-capital-careers/2006/12/hp-cfo-wayman-to-retire/.

Treanor, Jill, "Barclays Bank Reaches $100m US Settlement over Libor Rigging Scandal," *The Guardian*, August 8, 2016, https://www.theguardian.com/business/2016/aug/08/barclays-libor-100m-us-settlement.

Treanor, Jill, "Losses of £58bn Since the 2008 Bailout—How Did RBS Get Here?" *The Guardian*, February 24, 2017, https://www.theguardian.com/business/2017/feb/24/90bn-in-bills-since-2008-how-did-rbs-get-here-financial-crisis-.

Treanor, Jill, "RBS Sale: Fred Goodwin, the £45bn Bailout and Years of Losses, *The Guardian*, August 3, 2015, https://www.theguardian.com/business/2015/aug/03/rbs-sale-fred-goodwin-bailout-years-of-losses.

Trickey, Geoff, and Gillian Hyde, *A Decade of the Dark Side: Fighting our Demons at Work*, n.p.: Psychological Consultancy Ltd., 2009, http://www.psychological-consultancy.com/wp-content/uploads/DarkSideReport-1.pdf.

Tse, Tomoeh Murakami, "CIT's Bankruptcy Raises New Questions about Bailout," *The Washington Post*, November 15, 2009, http://www.washingtonpost.com/wp-dyn/content/article/2009/11/15/AR2009111502280.html.

Unocal Corp. v. Mesa Petroleum Co., JUSTIA US Law, 493 A.2d 946 (1985).

Van de Loo, Erik, Maszuin Kamarudin, and Jaap Winter, "Corporate Governance and Boards," UNIRAZAK, Malaysia 2015.

Verhoeven, Floor E. A., et. al., "The Effects of Maoa Genotype, Childhood Trauma, and Sex on Trait and State-Dependent Aggression," *Brain and Behavior* 2, no. 6 (2012): 806–13.

Villarica, Hans, "Maslow 2.0: A New and Improved Recipe for Happiness," *The Atlantic*, August 17, 2011, https://www.theatlantic.com/health/archive/2011/08/maslow-20-a-new-and-improved-recipe-for-happiness/243486/#. TkvKIRv8USE.facebook.

Vogt, Hans-Ueli, and Michael Bänziger, Das Bundesgericht anerkennt die Business Judgment Rule als Grundsatz des schweizerischen Aktienrechts, GesKR, 2016.

"W. L. Gore & Associates, Inc.," Great Place to Work, https://www.greatplacetowork.com/certified-company/1000289.

Wade, Michael R., Andrew Tarling, and Remy Assir, "Agile Leadership in an Age of Digital Disruption," IMD: Research & Knowledge, https://www.imd.org/research-knowledge/articles/agile-leadership-in-an-age-of-digital-disruption/ (last visited July 31, 2019).

Walker, C. Eugene, *Clinical Psychology: Historical and Research Foundations* (New York: Springer, 2013).

Walters, Kath, "How My Cancer Changed My View of Leadership: McKinsey & Co's Michael Rennie," SmartCompany, October 19, 2012, http://www.smartcompany.com.au/people-human-resources/leadership/how-my-cancer-changed-my-view-of-leadership-mckinsey-a-cos-michael-rennie/.

WebFinance Inc.: BusinessDictionary, "corporate scandal," http://www.businessdictionary.com/definition/corporate-scandal.html (last visited November 6, 2019).

"What Are Psychometric Tests?" Institute of Psychometric Coaching, https://www.psychometricinstitute.com.au/psychometric-guide/introduction_to_psychometric_tests.html.

"What Is Corruption?" Transparency International, http://www.transparency.org/what-is-corruption/#define (last visited March 18, 2017).

Wilkinson, David, "Kelly's Typology of Followership," Ambiguity Advantage, June 23, 2008, http://ambiguityadvantage.blogspot.ch/2008/06/kellys-typology-of-followership.html (last visited March 9 2018).

Williams, Ray, Psychology Today, Why Every CEO Needs a Coach, https://www.psychologytoday.com/blog/wired-success/201208/why-every-ceo-needs-coach (last visited July 14 2017).

Williamson, Oliver E., "Calculativeness, Trust, and Economic Organization," *Journal of Law and Economics of the University of Chicago*, vol. 36 (1993).

Wilson, Sarah, "The Ego, The Superego and the Id," How to Understand People, *The Guardian*, March 6, 2009, https://www.theguardian.com/lifeandstyle/2009/mar/07/ego-superego-id-sigmund-freud.

Wittwer, Jürg, I Am the Monkey: *How to Successfully Manage and Live in Foreign Cultures*, Charleston, SC, 2016.

Xiaodong, Yue, Jiang Feng, Su Lu, and Hiranandani Neelam, "To Be or Not to Be Humorous? Cross Cultural Perspectives on Humor," *Frontiers in Psychology*, vol. 7 (2016).

Your Finance Book, "World's 8 Biggest Corporate Scandals of All Time," http://yourfinancebook.com/biggest-corporate-scandals/ (last visited July 25, 2017).

Zak, Paul J., "The Neuroscience of Trust," Harvard Business Review, vol. 95, no. 1 (2017), 84–90.

Zenger, Jack, and Joseph Folkman, "What Inspiring Leaders Do," *Harvard Business Review* (2013).

Zürcher, Fabian, digitaltag.swiss, Künstliche Intelligenz: Wer hat Angst vor ihr?, https://mag.digitaltag.swiss/2017/11/10/kuenstliche-intelligenz-angst-und-neugierde/ (last visited December 30, 2017).

Zweifel, Thomas D., "The Rise of Robots and the Future of Work: Will We All Lose Our Jobs?," LinkedIn, February 26, 2016, https://www.linkedin.com/pulse/rise-robots-future-work-we-all-lose-our-jobs-dr-thomas-d-zweifel/.

Lightning Source UK Ltd.
Milton Keynes UK
UKHW010053301120
374345UK00001B/6